In the Process of Becoming

OXFORD STUDIES IN MUSIC THEORY

Series Editor Richard Cohn

In the Process of Becoming

*Analytic and Philosophical Perspectives on Form
in Early Nineteenth-Century Music*

JANET SCHMALFELDT

OXFORD

UNIVERSITY PRESS

Oxford University Press, Inc., publishes works that further
Oxford University's objective of excellence
in research, scholarship, and education.

Oxford   New York
Auckland   Cape Town   Dar es Salaam   Hong Kong   Karachi
Kuala Lumpur   Madrid   Melbourne   Mexico City   Nairobi
New Delhi   Shanghai   Taipei   Toronto

With offices in
Argentina   Austria   Brazil   Chile   Czech Republic   France   Greece
Guatemala   Hungary   Italy   Japan   Poland   Portugal   Singapore
South Korea   Switzerland   Thailand   Turkey   Ukraine   Vietnam

Published by Oxford University Press, Inc.
198 Madison Avenue, New York, New York 10016

www.oup.com

Oxford is a registered trademark of Oxford University Press.

Library of Congress Cataloging-in-Publication Data
Schmalfeldt, Janet, 1945-
In the process of becoming : analytic and philosophical perspectives on form in early nineteenth-century music/
Janet Schmalfeldt.
    p. cm.—(Oxford studies in music theory)
Includes bibliographical references and index.
ISBN 978-0-19-509366-7
1. Music—19th century—History and criticism.   2. Music—19th century—Analysis, appreciation.   3. Musical
form—History—19th century.   I. STitle.
ML196.S35 2010
781.809'033—dc22   2010012668

For Charles and Bonnie,
with gratitude.

CONTENTS

PREFACE

Let me anticipate a pun that the title of this study will invite among the many colleagues and friends who know something about my work: this project has been in the process of becoming a book for a very long time. Perhaps its "origins" can be traced all the way back to my childhood. It was then that, as my mother's piano student, I first encountered often simplified versions of pieces by the composers with whose music this work centrally engages—for example, the Adagio from Beethoven's "Pathétique" Sonata; Schubert's "Serenade" ("Ständchen," from *Schwanengesang*); one of Mendelssohn's *Songs without Words* (Op. 67, No. 5); a "Prelude in C Minor" by Chopin (it was, of course, Op. 28, No. 20; and Schumann's "Melody" (the first piece in his *Album for the Young*). I knew hardly anything at the time about these composers, but I knew that I would be devoted to their music for the rest of my life.

Readers who, on the basis of my first two chapters, may be led to imagine weightier origins for this study in the writings of Theodor W. Adorno and Carl Dahlhaus might ultimately feel deceived. Allow me to explain. In the aftermath of my work on the music of Alban Berg, I returned to the early nineteenth-century European repertoire most especially with a desire to examine processes of *form* in this music that my American training in Schenkerian theory had seemed to neglect. As I clarify in my first chapter, it was only after I had arrived at new analytic terms for attempting to capture the dynamic potential of formal processes that I discovered a philosophical source for the amplification of those terms—a critical and interpretive dialectical tradition within which the Hegelian concept of *becoming* was brought into contact with ideas about form in the music of Beethoven. This is a tradition whose origins coincided with the historical moment in which "form" began to emerge as a self-standing music-theoretical concept. In that Adorno and Dahlhaus have been the leading proponents of the "Beethoven-Hegelian" tradition within the last century, they both take center stage in my first two chapters, and the mottos I have borrowed from them—*becoming*, "form as process"—pervade every chapter to follow. Scholars of both Adorno and Dahlhaus have tended either to neglect or to disparage the capacities of these two for genuine music-analytical insight—a position to which I take strong exception; in particular, Adorno's unfinished *Beethoven* fragments reveal a philosopher-musician grappling over the course of his maturity with highly sophisticated aspects of Beethoven's music. But this study employs analytic techniques developed beyond the lifetimes, and maybe even the interests, of both Adorno and Dahlhaus; and so the presence of both recedes as the book proceeds. My debt to their ideas nevertheless remains profound.

I owe an even greater debt to the work of William E. Caplin. It was my privilege to serve as Caplin's colleague at McGill University during the years in which he was striving toward the completion of his now celebrated *Classical Form*. In the preface to that study, he generously acknowledges my encouragement of that project, but I owe him so much more. As readers will ascertain soon enough, Caplin's theory of classical *formal functions* rests at the basis of decisions I take as to when local and large-scale thematic processes in early nineteenth-century music "overturn themselves," to become something other than what they had promised to be. As one of just three colleagues, William Caplin has read all the drafts of my chapters for this book; I cannot thank him enough for his help.

I am equally indebted to Charles Fisk, who has submitted to the reading of each of my chapters, from one stage to the next, and who has endured frequent phone calls for advice. Charles and I are fond of remembering the occasion on which, as new graduate piano students in the Yale School of Music, we walked into one another's lives; the preface to Charles's own wonderful book about Schubert preserves the memory—of our encounter in a practice room over Schubert's B-flat Major Piano Sonata. Since then, we have shared countless enthusiasms, aspirations, preconcert rehearsals, discussions about piano fingerings, and ideas in general about the repertoire that my study addresses. It was Charles who introduced me to Bonnell Robinson—photographer, art historian, and critic par excellence of my writing. I dedicate my book to these two loyal friends, with gratitude for their enduring support.

I could not have been more fortunate when Patrick McCreless agreed to serve as the developmental reader of my complete manuscript for Oxford University Press. His thoughtful and favorable responses to my work bolstered the confidence I greatly needed in that penultimate stage of my project; his suggestions were superb.

Within the context of an informal seminar, several of my colleagues in the music department at Tufts University offered helpful and sympathetic comments about my chapter 1. In particular, department chair and musicologist Joseph Auner raised fabulous questions, thus pointing to ideas that wanted greater clarification. I extend a huge thanks to him, for his ongoing support of my efforts, and for the outstanding leadership role he has played in helping all of us within our department to achieve new goals in the shaping of a vibrant music program.

My inclusion within endnotes of original German texts for key pronouncements by Adorno, Schlegel, Hegel, and Dahlhaus came about at the gentle insistence of my long-standing colleague and friend Eva Linfield, another reader of chapter 1. Eva's suggestion was invaluable, not least because it put me back in touch with sources in the language I only wish I had begun to study earlier in my career.

Philip Acimovic, M.A. graduate in composition at Tufts, undertook the first stage of translating my annotated music examples into computer notation. When he left for a months-long trek on the Appalachian Trail, Jean Foo, also a Tufts graduate in composition, completed this arduous task. The three of us struggled mightily to attain accuracy and clarity; I shall be forever grateful to these two former students, then colleagues—for their expertise, their camaraderie, and their abiding patience. My heartfelt thanks extends as well to my good friend Tufts Professor Emeritus Mark DeVoto, who prepared reductions for Schumann's "Widmung" and for excerpts from Mendelssohn's Octet. If notational errors remain, the oversights are all mine.

Invitations to present papers at numerous conferences in recent years have served as perhaps the greatest stimulus toward completion of this study, even though preparations for those appearances sometimes led me off the direct path to a finished manuscript. For example, the materials of my chapters 1, 2, 6, and 9 originated as the bases of presentations I made at meetings of the Society for Music Theory. I first aired my views, now in chapter 4, about Beethoven's "Bridgetower" Sonata, Op. 47, at the 2005 International Orpheus Academy for Music Theory, in Ghent. It was my great honor in 2002 to deliver one of the early versions of chapter 5—on performance, analysis, and Schubert's Sonata, Op. 42—in seminars on performance and analysis that I held in Porto Alegre, Rio de Janeiro, and Salvador, Brazil. A second version of what is now chapter 6, on "music that turns inward," became a keynote address, in Utrecht, 2004, at the Sixth Conference of the Dutch-Flemish Society for Music Theory. To the organizers in Tallinn, Estonia, of a 2006 conference on the music of Mozart, I am thankful for their willingness to accept a paper on "Mendelssohn the 'Mozartean'"; in greatly revised and expanded form, that lecture has been incorporated within chapter 7. Finally, two different papers on the music of Chopin, at conferences in Freiburg and Warsaw in 2007, have been interwoven and expanded to yield chapter 8.

In several cases, conference participation was contingent upon the agreement to publish papers within conference proceedings. For this and other reasons, portions of my book have appeared earlier in article form. I express deepest appreciation to the publishers of the following articles for permission to incorporate materials in this study:

"Form as the Process of Becoming: The Beethoven-Hegelian Tradition and the 'Tempest' Sonata." *Beethoven Forum* 4 (1995): 37–71.

"On Performance, Analysis, and Schubert." *Per Musi: Revista Acadêmica de Música* 5–6 (2002): 38–54.

"Music That Turns Inward: New Roles for Interior Movements and Secondary Themes in the Early Nineteenth Century." *Tijdschrift voor Muziektheorie* 9/3 (2004): 171–95.

"Coming Home." In *Interdisciplinary Studies in Musicology* 5, edited by Maciej Jabłoński and Michael L. Klein, 139–84. Poznań, Poland: Rhytmos, 2005. Colloquial version published in *Music Theory Online* 10.1 (2004).

"Chopin's Dialogue: The Cello Sonata, Op. 65." In *Chopin's Musical Worlds: The 1840's (Warszawa 2007)*, 265–91. Warsaw: Narodowy Instytut Fryderyka Chopina, 2008.

"Beethoven's 'Bridgetower' Sonata, Op. 47." *New Paths: Aspects of Music Theory and Aesthetics in the Age of Romanticism*. Collected Writings of the Orpheus Institute 7, 37–67. Leuven: Leuven University Press, 2009.

In the Process of Becoming

CHAPTER One

Introduction

The Idea of Musical Form
as Process

> We do not understand music—it understands us. This is as true for the musician as for the layman. When we think ourselves closest to it, it speaks to us and waits sad-eyed for us to answer.[1]
>
> —Theodor W. Adorno, *Beethoven: The Philosophy of Music*

Theodor Adorno's lifelong commitment to the study of a wide range of musical styles urges us to believe that he speaks here of music in general—Music, the allegorical muse that has held its sway over humanity from the beginning of time. But there can hardly be any doubt that, with this statement, destined for a book about Beethoven, Adorno especially had the music of one composer in mind. From probably as early as 1933 until not long before his death in 1969, Adorno's greatest passion might well have been his desire to complete his *Beethoven* study; today we have only the 370 preparatory notes that he accumulated during those years. As a reason for why the book remained unwritten, the editor of those notes speculates that the appalling period in which Adorno survived while expelled by the Nazi regime had become so utterly remote from the " 'better worlds' of which Florestan sang" that Adorno's fragments "could only mournfully reflect the mourning with which Beethoven's music mystically 'speaks' to humanity, in vain awaiting its answer."[2]

We can be certain, however, that, had Adorno completed his monograph, its overarching thesis would have underscored the critical starting points for my own essays in this volume. From Adorno, we have the following: "Beethoven's music is Hegelian philosophy: but at the same time, it is truer than that philosophy." And leading to that claim:

> [T]he Beethovenian unity is one which moves by means of antitheses; that is to say, its moments, taken individually, seem to contradict each other. But therein lies the meaning of Beethovenian *form as process*, so that through the incessant "mediation" between individual moments, and finally through the consummation of the form as a whole, the seemingly antithetical motifs are grasped in their identity.[3]

3

What is Hegelian about Beethoven's process itself for Adorno is its aspect of *becoming* (*Werden*), hence the Adornian title of my work.

I open with the poignant epigraph from Adorno for personal as well as substantive reasons, and I shall draw upon his philosophy of music while departing from him in ways that will be quickly recognized by scholars of his work. The two compositions by Beethoven that I explore in depth—the first movements of his "Tempest" Sonata (below and in chapter 2) and his Violin Sonata, Op. 47 (in chapter 4)—happen to be among those pieces to which Adorno returned many times within his Beethoven fragments; but the core repertoire in my study—works by Schubert, Mendelssohn, Chopin, and the Schumanns—is representative of music toward which Adorno, with devotion but regret, directed a fundamentally negative critique.[4] For Adorno, the greatest music understands us because, in Stephen Hinton's words, this music, "as nonconceptual insight, can inform our consciousness where words and concepts may fail."[5] From Adorno himself, we have it that Beethoven's greatest music understands the inability of philosophies and societal realities to right the world, yet it nonetheless expresses *hope* that this could somehow still be accomplished; the "humanity" in Beethoven's work "shows how to lead a life which is active, outwardly productive without being narrow—a life of solidarity."[6] Adorno did not deny, however, that, in the shadow of Beethoven's achievement, post-Beethovenian composers of the early nineteenth century struggled, in different ways and by different means, to reflect upon the new self-awareness and inwardness that a failed revolution had engendered. I address the music of the Romantic generation in search of how such new reflections may have found their expression through formal innovation, and because this is the music that, over many years as pianist and theorist, I have especially longed to understand.

Adorno (1903–69) remains the single most vibrant, difficult, and prolific writer about music among twentieth-century philosophers; for no other philosopher or social theorist have musical and philosophical concepts assumed such a mutually inseparable relation, nor has the aspect of *form* in music played such a crucial role. Thus, as both a post-Hegelian dialectician and a critic of Hegel's philosophy, Adorno emerges as the leading twentieth-century exponent of what I call the "Beethoven-Hegelian tradition." That tradition, which I characterize and trace in chapter 2, bears upon relationships between philosophical and musical thought from around the beginning of the nineteenth century, when form in music began to occupy a central place in critical writings about music. As a step toward restoring to the term "form" some of its philosophical and aesthetic associations in the early 1800s, let me rehearse some of the circumstances within which this new concern for form arose.

∞

Certainly the notion of form in music would not have emerged as central to theoretical discourse outside the context of profound cultural shifts over the course of the eighteenth century, reflected especially in the political, philosophical, literary, and artistic endeavors of a society that would soon look beyond Enlightenment perspectives. For late eighteenth-century European musicians, that society had begun to witness the breakdown of church-and-court patronage, the increase (especially in Paris, London, and Vienna) of public concerts, and the emergence of a professional middle-class audience that would not only expand the market for household fortepianos and printed scores but also provide readership for the new enterprise of the music journal.[7] Composers now faced the prospect of greater independence, with all the individual freedoms and risks that commissions, reviews, new performance venues, renown or notoriety, and an active public of *Kenner* and *Liebhaber* might bring.[8]

With the inauguration in the mid-eighteenth century of a new philosophical subdiscipline to which Alexander Baumgarten gave the name *Aesthetica* (from the Greek *aistheta*, "things perceived"), music found itself steadily rising within philosophical rankings of the fine arts. By the end of the century, Immanuel Kant devoted the first part of his third, last, and culminative critique—*The Critique of Judgment* (*Kritik der Urteilskraft*, 1790)—to the subject of aesthetics. Beauty for Kant "should surely be a question only of form," as opposed to charm or emotion.[9] Kant's uncertainty as to whether music can be fully defined as a fine art—that is, whether the perception of music as "beautiful" is a reflective judgment—elicits critical responses to his epistemology that would soon lead German Romantics to rank music above all the other arts. Around the same time, the term "form" begins to appear, without definition and all but equated with "rhetoric," in the writings of the music theorist Heinrich Christoph Koch.[10] Without claiming even the remotest connection between Koch and Kant, one can note that the earliest references to "form" as an abstract concept, a category in its own right, make their appearance when cultural changes were yielding an altogether new relationship between composers and their listeners, and when music itself—in particular, instrumental music—was becoming a topic for renewed philosophical investigation.

Faced with the gradual dissolution of the patronage network, late eighteenth- and early nineteenth-century composers would depend more overtly upon a market-based culture and a musically educated *public* audience, while also cultivating the support of music academies, societies, and friends in high places.[11] Indeed, we speak of "public" genres—for example, the symphony, the comic opera, and the concerto, all of which achieved international prominence in the 1700s. And, while the transmission of musical conventions has undoubtedly played a necessary role in the formation of *all* musical styles, there may be something distinctly "public" about the exchange of techniques that resulted in the firm establishment of specifically *formal* conventions in late eighteenth-century music. We need not be surprised, then, that, as late as 1807, Koch perpetuates the public-oriented *rhetorical* concept of form—the "metaphor of the oration"—that had prevailed in theoretic descriptions of large-scale movements throughout the eighteenth century.[12] Mark Evan Bonds clarifies that "rhetoric" is to be understood here in Aristotle's sense: "the faculty of discovering the possible means of persuasion in reference to any subject." "In this sense, form is the manner in which a work's content is made intelligible to its audience. Conventional patterns, by providing listeners with points of reference and predictability, facilitate the presentation of a content that necessarily varies from work to work."[13]

At the same time that composers were growing more dependent upon their public, increased opportunities for operas and public concerts as well as sales of scores for household performances offered successful composers the hope that an ever larger public was becoming well acquainted with their works. This would mean that familiarity with musical conventions would become much less the privileged domain of composers and performers; a well-informed lay audience could also be expected to recognize conventions as well as departures therefrom. The ramifications of this social phenomenon are wide-ranging, and they provide the chief premise for my study. Many have noted that late eighteenth-century composers developed numerous strategies—irregularities in harmonic syntax, "off-tonic" openings, evaded cadences, "false recapitulations," to name just a few—for manipulating conventions to foil the listener's expectations. I argue that techniques of this kind, as applied ever more self-consciously to the dimension of form, acquire increased significance as a means of communication from composer to performer and listener in early nineteenth-century music.

Four factors, all inextricably connected, must be emphasized as critical to the development of compositional and theoretical views about form at the turn of the century. The first of these is the idea of *absolute music*, or "pure" instrumental music—an idea that is distinct from but closely associated with the notion of the autonomy of music, or what John Neubauer has called the "emancipation of music from language."[14] Although it was actually Wagner who coined the term "absolute music," Carl Dahlhaus has argued that the concept "originated in German romanticism" and that "it owed its pathos—the association of music 'detached' from text, program, or function with the expression or notion of the *absolute*—to German poetry and philosophy around 1800."[15] Here, for example, are the well-known words of Friedrich Schlegel in 1797–98:

> All *pure* music must be philosophical and instrumental (music for thought)...a certain element of philosophical speculation is not at all foreign to the spirit of pure instrumental music. Must not purely instrumental music create its own text? And is not its theme developed, confirmed, varied and contrasted, just as is the object of a sequence of philosophical speculation?[16]

Perhaps no single aesthetic idea surpasses the notion of absolute music in justifying an examination of nineteenth-century concepts of form from a philosophical perspective. Whether one privileges the "mysticism" of absoluteness over its "formalism,"[17] it cannot be denied that absolute music raised new questions as to how the "contents" and "forms" of music could potentially enable music to embody, or emulate, an autonomous totality, that is, without apparent recourse to extramusical ideas. The idea of absolute music—and of course its legitimization of instrumental music—undoubtedly motivated the nineteenth-century advance toward a pedagogy of form.

Entangled with the inception of this idea, indeed, hardly separable from it as a second factor inspiring concerns about form, is the corresponding emergence of the concept of the *musical work*—an early nineteenth-century development given considerable philosophical attention in recent decades and whose origin, as well as enduring influence, has been critically assessed by Lydia Goehr. In her view, the idea of music as an emancipated fine art—"an independent, autonomous practice, depending on nothing ultimately but itself"—required for its sustenance "the fusion of two traditional concepts: music and productive art." "Originally the term 'art' (*ars* or *technē*)...designated a skill in making products, a skill in practical performance.... The idea of producing works was not usually considered an end in itself."[18]

> As music began to be understood first and foremost as one of the fine arts, it began clearly to articulate its need for enduring products—artefacts comparable to other works of fine art. Hence the emergence of a work-concept in the field of music in the mid- to late-eighteenth century.... But it was only with the romanticization of fine art around 1800 that theorists found a really successful way to give substance to the idea of a musical product. At this moment, the work-concept became the focal point, serving as the motivation and goal of musical theory and practice. All references to occasion, activity, function, or effect were subordinated to references to the product—the musical work itself.[19]

In Goehr's account, signs that the idea of the musical work became a regulative force can be uncovered in respect to all aspects of music notation, performance, and reception, in and after 1800. For example, if music must now, like the plastic arts, produce a commodity, must now "find an object that could be divorced from everyday contexts, form part of a collection of works of art, and be contemplated purely aesthetically," then "transitory performances"—the hallmark, for example, of the Mozartean composer-performer—and "incomplete scores" would no longer do. The greater the functional separation between composer and performer, and the more an established "work" would be performed and repeated by musicians who had no personal contact with the composer, the more urgent became the need for increasingly precise notation and the publication of full scores, so that "music could now be preserved in a manner suitable for a fine art."[20] When "composers began to individuate works as embodied expressions and products of their activities, they were quickly persuaded that that fact generated a right of ownership of those works to themselves." Thus, by as early as 1793 in France and shortly thereafter in Germany and England, copyright laws transferred ownership of musical works from publishers to composers and gave them control over dedications as well as titles; the demand for an *original* work led to policies ruling against the borrowing of musical materials, under the new concept of musical plagiarism.[21] Finally, and now to Goehr's main philosophical concern, the work-concept engenders *Werktreue*—the current term for "being true or faithful to the work" and thus to its text (*Texttreue*). In reverence for the "classical" *work*, audiences to this day, in concert halls that became a vogue in the nineteenth century, are admonished to keep silent and not even "tap [their] many feet—not without a certain discomfort at least."[22] And performers, including me, seek scores that claim to be *Urtexts*.

It should be self-evident that, with "musical works" as finished masterpieces, to be recognized and accessible as such, the early nineteenth century would see the emergence of "a new form of music criticism, and what came at this time to be called analysis." "It became just as familiar, under the influence of the new aesthetic, to talk about musical forms—the sonata, symphony, and concerto—as unique to music itself. Musical form was no longer to be thought of as following the text or the shape of some 'extra-musical' occasion, but as independently designed and independently coherent."[23] Music-technical terms still in currency today—rhetoric-derived form-functional terms such as *idée*, *périodes*, *parties*, *reposes* (*cadences*), *antécédent*, *conséquent*—thus enter into the early nineteenth-century composition treatises of Antoine Reicha, a friend of Beethoven, and J. J. de Momigny.[24] But it was the 1810 analysis of Beethoven's Fifth Symphony by E. T. A. Hoffmann—arch-Romantic and proto-Hegelian—that confirms the powerful influence of philosophical ideas on notions of form in music. Hoffmann's essay (discussed in chapter 2) brings me to the third and fourth factors of critical importance to the development of a nineteenth-century *Formenlehre*—Beethoven, and his music.

Few would dispute Goehr's position that it was Beethoven the person, more than any other composer, who, through his actions and his demands, showed future composers how they "could take artistic advantage of the autonomous art of music" and how they could *choose* the source of their livelihood while doing so. "Ultimately, [Beethoven] changed and was believed to have changed so many things having to do with how musicians thought about composition, performance, and reception, that the subsequent Beethoven mania, or the Beethoven Myth as it has come to be called, is justified, if such a thing is ever justified, on much more than aesthetical grounds alone."[25] Yes, indeed. But what about the aesthetic grounds? What about Beethoven's *music*?

The narrative of that music's impact upon, for example, Schubert, Berlioz, Mendelssohn, Schumann, Liszt, Wagner, Brahms, Mahler, and even Chopin will probably continue to be written and revised, with new angles, in generations to come. Within my substantiation of a Beethoven-Hegelian tradition in chapter 2, all of the leading figures in my own narrative—Hoffmann, Adolph Bernhard Marx, Arnold Schoenberg, Adorno, and Dahlhaus—regard Beethoven's music as their inspirational paradigm. One can safely say that self-proclaimed theories of form in tonal music begin, and proceed, with efforts to account, both philosophically and analytically, for Beethoven's music. It can be added that no other composer's works receive commensurate attention in the writings of Heinrich Schenker.

∞

I arrived at the central metaphor of this study—the concept of *becoming*—long before I came to recognize its role within German Romanticist and idealist thought. During my earliest years as a teacher at McGill University, I greatly benefited from the opportunity to follow the progress of my colleague William E. Caplin's study on formal functions in classical music—the treatise well known today as

Classical Form (1998).[26] During our time together at McGill, Caplin and I spent hours debating issues of form; now at long distance, our debates continue. If I can claim any one contribution to Caplin's work, it would concern the topic I pursue in this volume—*the special case whereby the formal function initially suggested by a musical idea, phrase, or section invites retrospective reinterpretation within the larger formal context.* For such cases, the term "becomes" seemed right to me, and the double-lined right arrow ($\Rightarrow$), borrowed from symbolic logic, provided a means of representation.[27] If one were thus to perceive that, say, the opening passage of a movement initially projects the characteristics of an introduction but retroactively functions as a main theme, one could represent that analytic perception as "Introduction $\Rightarrow$ MT."

For what kinds of listeners might the idea of retrospective formal reinterpretation be of interest? Discussions about modes of listening to "classical" music run rampant with adjectives for the listeners they describe—for example, "attentive," "informed," "responsive," "experienced," "close listeners," "stylistically knowledgeable." I do not deny that listeners to whom my idea of processual formal reinterpretation might appeal will be those especially atuned to stylistic formal tendencies in late eighteenth- and early nineteenth-century European music. But I believe that listeners and performers devoted to the music I address do not need to share the technical vocabulary and expertise of musicologists and theorists in order to sense, for example, the promise of a formal outcome that is not fulfilled; performers in particular tend to be sensitive to such transformations, whether or not they describe these in words. In short, my study unabashedly promotes a type of "structural listening" that has been both disparaged and defended in recent literature;[28] it invites both first-time and "first-time" listeners to listen "both forward and backward," as Adorno has recommended.[29] I hold as well that repeated hearings can only enrich the memory of expectations and surprises that a first-time hearing may have aroused.

Only much later did I discover that this decidedly experiential and process-oriented approach to the perception of musical form encroaches upon a long-standing tradition in which Hegelian concepts have been brought to bear on the question of form in the music of Beethoven. In the last century, the guardians of the Beethoven-Hegelian tradition have been Adorno and Dahlhaus. The following passage from Dahlhaus's collection of essays on Beethoven should give readers a preliminary understanding of both his and my concerns:

> Traditional formal schemata were like a "subject" for composition to Beethoven: they were neither adopted [nor] rejected, but were used as material which changed its function according to the context in which it found itself. Elements of a slow introduction…change their purpose, without the memory of their original function being extinguished.…The ambiguity requires the listener "implied" by Beethoven to possess both an awareness of tradition and the ability to see beyond the customary.[30]

Dahlhaus's favorite example of the idea of form as process—an illustration much inspired by August Halm—can be found in his recurring discussions of the first movement of Beethoven's "Tempest" Sonata, the Piano Sonata No. 17 in D Minor, Op. 31, No. 2.[31] Dahlhaus contends that this movement will continue to be the topic of controversy "as long as the disputants go on suppressing the contradictions between motivicism, syntax, and harmony…by stressing one element at the expense of another. They would do better to understand these 'antitheses' as the vehicle of a *dialectics*, by means of which the *form of the movement comes into being* as a musically perceived transformational process."[32]

The crux of the matter for Dahlhaus is the argument about whether the beginning of the "Tempest" should be regarded as an introduction or as the exposition of a theme, given that the subsequent passage (mm. 21–41) provides the "more substantial manifestation" of the initial idea but also serves the modulatory function of a transition. In Dahlhaus's view, the argument is itself "a waste of time; it requires a decision when the whole point is that decision is impossible, and ambiguity should be understood as an aesthetic quality." A dialectical conclusion inevitably follows: "The beginning of the movement is *not yet* a subject, the evolutionary episode is one *no longer*"; because Beethoven "goes straight from a protoform to developmental elaboration, the form *is* process."[33]

The metaphor that emerges so emphatically here is the image of form coming into being, the notion of *becoming*. For its inception as a keynote of German Romantic thought, we can turn to what Arthur Lovejoy has called the "first official definition" of the term "romantisch"—Friedrich Schlegel's 1798 pronouncement that Romantic poetry is "a progressive universal poetry": it is a kind of poetry that "is still in becoming (*im Werden*); indeed, this is its very essence, that it forever can only become, and never be completed."[34] With the publication in 1817 of Hegel's *Encyclopaedia Logic*, becoming achieves the status of "unity *in* the diversity" of the antithesis Being and Nothing. In other words, becoming unites the imagining of a concept and of its opposite—its negation, what it is *not*—in such a way that they "overturn into one another," thus losing their "one-sidedness"; the mental synthesis that results at once *cancels* but also *preserves* the distinction between the two. To demonstrate this, Hegel invokes the everyday notion of a "*beginning*": "the matter [itself] is *not yet* in its beginning, but the beginning is not merely its *nothing*: on the contrary, its *being* is already there, too. The beginning itself is also becoming, but it expresses already the reference to the further progression."[35]

The verb *aufheben* is Hegel's term, as influenced by F. W. von Schelling, for describing the *result* of the process of becoming. At the moment when one grasps that becoming has united a concept and its opposite, or negative, then all three elements—the one-sided concept, its opposite, and becoming itself—vanish. And *what has become* is a new moment—a stage, a synthesis—in which the original concept and its opposite are no longer fixed and separate, but rather identical, determinations, in the sense that the one cannot be thought, or posited, outside the context of the other. The original concept has thus been *aufgehoben*.[36]

In its nontechnical sense, the notion of becoming has itself become a pervasive, albeit vague, metaphor for the effect of all music perceived phenomenologically as a temporal art.[37] But outside the Beethoven-Hegelian tradition, the implications of becoming for what Bonds has called "the paradox of musical form" have only begun to be considered. For Bonds, the paradox lies in whether form should be regarded as "conformational"—a fixed pattern, an ideal type against which the individual work can be gauged, or whether form refers to the "generative"—the unique shape of the specific work.[38] Beethoven's music urges Dahlhaus toward a third, and most extreme, possibility: since "form *is* process," the musical process, the becoming of music, "is itself—paradoxically—the result."[39]

Bonds and Dahlhaus would agree, however, that there can simply be no perception of "form" whatsoever—form as conventional type, form as unique shape, or form as process—outside the context of a received tradition. For without the latter, to distinguish the unique from the conventional would be a purely arbitrary act. And only if Beethoven's listeners can be expected to recognize some of the conventions associated with the formal function of "introduction," as opposed to, say, "main theme," or "transition," will they entertain the notion that the opening of the "Tempest" might enact a dialectical formal process.

My assessment of Dahlhaus's views about the first movement of the "Tempest" Sonata begins in chapter 2 with an effort to determine some of the meanings that accrue to such terms as "formal function," "introduction," and "[main] theme" as understood by Dahlhaus and others who, like him, have expanded upon Schoenberg's theories of form. If, as I have argued elsewhere,[40] we can acknowledge a correspondence between Schoenberg's idea of a nonmodulatory "theme" and the Schenkerian concept of a complete middleground harmonic-contrapuntal structure, then the formally ambiguous passage at mm. 1–21 of the "Tempest" might theoretically qualify as a "main theme" (to be shown by means of voice-leading graphs coordinated with formal terms). As we shall see, a Schenkerian analysis of this passage further uncovers an all-encompassing "enlargement" (*Vergrösserung*) of the ascending-arpeggiation idea marked largo at mm. 1–2. That detail could be said to give to the complete passage what Schenker would call an "organic" coherence; as such, it works against Dahlhaus's view of the passage as unstable and loosely constructed.

On the other hand, neither the formal nor the Schenkerian observations made thus far address those immediately perceptible features of the passage that might evoke the character of an introduction—for example, the recitative-like opening on the inverted dominant, the eccentric, improvisatory alternation of largo and allegro tempi, the extremely irregular sequential relationship of the opening "antecedent" (mm. 1–6) to its "consequent" (mm. 7–21), and the tremendous, cadenza-like expansion of the cadential six-four chord at mm. 13–20. To perceive this extraordinary passage as "not yet" a main theme, we need to recreate the experience of hearing it *in time*, for the first time, for only when a perfect authentic cadence is achieved with the elision at m. 21 (Koch's *Tacterstickung*, to be represented by the symbol ↔ in my music examples) can we suspect that a "theme" in either the formal or the Schenkerian sense has been presented and completed. And only when we begin to perceive the function of a modulatory transition at mm. 21–41 can we imagine that our assumption is being confirmed. Even then we will wait much longer, but in vain, for a final confirmation at the beginning of the sonata-form recapitulation: yes, the recitative-like opening returns at the point where we should expect to hear that beginning, but now a true recitative emerges.

If, after all this, we might retrospectively be justified in regarding the passage at mm. 1–21 as "an introduction that *becomes* a main theme"—that is, Introduction ⇒ MT—we should want to make the following crucial qualification. The expression "Introduction ⇒ MT" does not mean that a final analytic verdict favors the notion of a main theme; on the contrary, the expression *in its entirety* serves to represent the formal function, and its central element—the "becoming" sign—stands for the central idea to be conveyed.

∾

Details about the "Tempest" within this preliminary account will be familiar to any reader who knows the movement. What I regard as a chief contribution is my renewal of an effort to imbue both formal and Schenkerian concepts, *taken together*, with a capacity to capture, if tenuously, the dynamic, processual nature of the musical experience. One can argue that ideas of temporal process are intrinsic to the theories of *both* Schenker and Schoenberg, the progenitor of recent formal theories. For example, consider what might be Schenker's most frequently cited avowal in his final publication:

> In the art of music, as in life, motion toward the goal encounters obstacles, reverses, disappointments, and involves great distances, detours, expansions, interpolations, and, in short, retardations of all kinds. Therein lies the source of all artistic delaying, from which the creative mind can derive content that is ever new. Thus we hear in the middleground and foreground an almost dramatic course of events.[41]

Much less known but representative is the following statement by Schoenberg, from an unpublished manuscript:

> Theorists see in existent forms something given, whereas in reality something so resistant as a given…which one can grasp complete in itself, never has been or will be given [in music]. Rather, musical form is something coming-into-being [*Entstehendes*] (to say something come-into-being [*Entstandenes*] may already be incorrect), at every time newly coming into being, and never except in the finished artwork itself something at hand, that can be transmitted and further utilized.[42]

But until not so long ago, divergent outlooks on the concept and especially the origin of form in tonal music prevented theorists of form and Schenkerian scholars from acknowledging such ideas as mutual concerns.[43]

As Schenkerians know well, Schenker's "new theory of form," the full exposition of which he promised in the final chapter of his *Free Composition* (*Der freie Satz*), never saw the light of day; had it appeared, its objective, as announced in that chapter, would most certainly have been to eradicate all earlier formal theories, once and for all. To be sure, the leading introductory textbooks on Schenkerian techniques by subsequent authors have from the beginning faithfully included chapters dealing with large-scale formal paradigms—"one-part" (undivided) form, "two-" and "three-part" forms, sonata, rondo, and, in the case of Allen Forte and Steven E. Gilbert's *Introduction to Schenkerian Analysis*, variation form;[44] these are the precise formal categories, in the same order, that Schenker classified in his chapter on form (he also offered a section on fugue). In all of those studies, including Schenker's, one recognizes the concession that "forms," in the sense of broad conventional plans, or conformative types, have played a nontrivial role for composers across the eighteenth and nineteenth centuries. To put it another way, "the perspectives embodied in conventional views of form are practical and reflect the kinds of issues that composers often consider in practice."[45] For Schenkerians, a distinction must be made, however, between tonal "forms" and tonal "structures"— or between "outer" and "inner" forms. There would seem to be no alternative as a means of countering Schenker's final position—that form originates in the background and derives from this through the technique of *Auskomponierung*, such that the uniqueness of a work and its form emerge as strictly middleground-to-foreground phenomena. If the origin of form resides in the background, then Schenker must vehemently reject all notions of form that take foreground elements as their first principles.[46] Thus the following from Schenker:

> [M]usic finds no coherence in a "motive" in the usual sense. Thus, I reject those defi-
> nitions of song form [for example] which take the motive as their starting point and
> emphasize manipulation of the motive by means of repetition, variation, extension,
> fragmentation, or dissolution. I also reject those explanations which are based upon
> phrases, phrase-groups, periods, double periods, themes, antecedents, and conse-
> quents. My theory replaces all of these with specific concepts of form which, from
> the outset, are based upon the content of the whole and of the individual parts; that
> is, the differences in prolongations lead to differences in form.[47]

We could hardly formulate a stronger condemnation of what were to become Schoenberg's central ideas—his "starting points": the notion of the *Grundgestalt* ("basic shape," "basic idea") as a concrete musical representation of the composer's vision; the realization of a *Grundgestalt* through the technique of "developing vari-ation" as a temporal process; and the concept of formal function of parts within the whole. Nor could a sharper ideological line have been drawn to separate Schenker's fundamental principles from both past and current theories of form in general.

Those who, like me, have advocated the integration of formal and Schenkerian theories can note that, despite residual signs of conflict, the topic of form in Schenkerian scholarship has, in recent years, regained something of the status it long held for theorists and aestheticians of the nineteenth and early twentieth cen-turies.[48] And yet, for example, the one exhaustive effort to evaluate and reformulate Schenker's *Formenlehre*—Charles J. Smith's 1996 study—focuses almost exclusively upon large-scale (complete-movement) *Ursatz*-driven "conformational stereotypes" that Schenker himself explicitly identified in reference to specific pieces within *Free Composition*. Smith's goal is to revise Schenker's middleground formal categories by creating new voice-leading archetypes, displayed with new, alternative graphs, that reflect the foreground "sections," "harmonic relations between sections," and thematic designs that define discrete formal types. The result—a new "formal theory of structure"—demonstrates (tautologically, as Smith more or less concedes) that "*form and fundamental structure are essentially the same thing*," that taxonomic and unique forms are "*reconciled*: they turn out to be relatives, extracted from different places within one large formal/structural family tree."[49]

Although Smith's article won a publication award from the Society for Music Theory in 1999, it was largely greeted with silence from within the Schenkerian community.[50] Since then, Nicholas Cook has taken issue with Smith's resketching of a graph by Schenker, to suggest in general that "the attempt to integrate the different elements of the music within a single summative representation may not necessarily be the most productive way in which to deploy Schenkerian techniques."[51] Referring to my "Reconciliation" article of 1991 (see note 40), Gianmario Borio argues, on the one hand, that

> [t]he question regarding the possibility—and perhaps also the necessity—of a reconciliation of [Schenkerian and Schoenbergian] methods finds its legitimization, retrospectively, in the fact that they share basic concepts or 'ideal types' and, potentially, in the conviction that an approach to tonality might benefit from the fusion of the two horizons which for decades were separated by an insurmountable barrier.[52]

By contrast, Cook is not so sure that a reconciliation can or should be made. His reasons: having examined the development of Schenker's thought from within the contexts of conservative political and cultural traditions that were "widespread in the German-speaking countries at the turn of the twentieth century," Cook laments the ultimate loss of Schenker's willingness in his early writings to embrace a mode of dialectical thinking—an analytic practice that entertained "interaction" as well as potential "contradiction."[53] For Cook, contradictions between, say, formal design and tonal structure, of the kind that Smith tries to eliminate (and that I discuss in 1991), or between, say, "phrase" or "formal function" and the unfolding of an *Ursatz*-replica, simply cannot be mediated without our acknowledgment that, in its final manifestation, Schenker's monistic (rather than pluralistic) idealism, "of a Platonist or Leibnizian type,"[54] leaves no room for such negotiations. At best:

> A Schenkerian—or post-Schenkerian—analytical practice predicated on the interaction of different parameters or structural principles needs ways of representing such interaction more explicitly than the traditional Schenkerian graph, whether through the incorporation of different elements within a single representation or through the use of complementary representations….Rethinking the *Ursatz*-dominated synthesis of *Der freie Satz*, in short, has opened up possibilities within a broadly Schenkerian practice, and in its relationship to other analytical approaches, that were progressively foreclosed during the final decade of Schenker's life.[55]

I take this statement from Cook as a recommendation that expresses his hope for the future of the Schenkerian enterprise, his sobering critique notwithstanding. The practice of incorporating "different elements" within single or complementary representations has been my analytic modus operandi for many years, as it has occasionally been for other Schenkerian analysts; such a practice will be much in evidence within the music examples in this book. Cook may well have had highly complex representations in mind; mine can be described quite simply. Within my Schenkerian graphs, formal terms have been aligned with passages that project specific formal functions or that call for retrospective formal reinterpretation; alternatively, scores in which formal annotations, supported by harmonic readings, serve to clarify my formal views will for the most part include Schenkerian-oriented "analytic overlays" (Forte and Gilbert's term).[56] By these means I reaffirm my commitment to the thesis that a consideration of the "interactions" and the often fascinating "contradictions" between tonal structures and formal designs should want to be paramount for analysts who seek to distinguish what is conformational from what is unique about the individual musical process.

On the other side of Schenker's ideological divide, and especially on this side of the Atlantic, there has been a resurgence of interest in tonal form over the last decade, as inspired first by the appearance of Caplin's *Classical Form* and then by the publication in 2006 of James Hepokoski and Warren Darcy's *Elements of Sonata Theory*. In neither of these texts are Schenkerian analytic techniques employed, but the authors of both respectfully refer to Schenkerian concepts by way of comparisons with their own theories.[57] A third publication—the 2009 essay collection *Musical Form, Forms & Formenlehre*—brings Caplin and Hepokoski into dialogue with one another and with James Webster, whose work has reflected a "skeptical" but sympathetic attitude toward Schenkerian theory over many years. Webster's essay in the volume refers to Kurt Westphal's 1935 distinction between *Form* and *Formung*—"form-as-shape" versus "form-as-process"—and endorses the latter within the context of his own "multivalent" analytic method.[58] The tone of the debates among Caplin, Hepokoski, and Webster (in the form of comments on each author's essay and then responses to the comments), though tactful, is obliquely blunt and tendentious; like the best of tennis pros, each author strives to serve an ace and then defends the net against a passing shot (with Caplin, the ace is for formal function; with Hepokoski, for Sonata Theory and dialogic form; with Webster, for multivalent analysis). But we can trust that this provocative exchange will thoroughly invigorate discussions about classical form and encourage diverse approaches to its analysis. More as well: *Musical Form, Forms & Formenlehre* arrives just in time for a clarification on my part as to where my work can be situated in relation to the contributions of three leading experts on form.

First, Webster's "self-consciously Toveyan" multivalent analytic method, with its concern for the interactions of "different 'domains': tonality, musical ideas, rhythm, dynamics, instrumentation, register, rhetoric, 'narrative' design, and so forth," "erects no typologies or grand categorizations, makes no attempt to account for the entirety of any class of works or structures."[59] The same must be said of my study. In the chapters that follow, my concerns will be "multivalent" in respect to the many musical dimensions I address, but my approach will be composer- and piece-specific, rather than typological or taxonomic. If indeed a "theory of early nineteenth-century form" can one day be produced, I only argue here that one of its principal tenets must be the idea of processual approaches to form; this is the idea that threads its way through my pages, serving as the central focal point, but sometimes ceding its centrality to characterizations of other early nineteenth-century formal tendencies.

Second, I see Hepokoski and Darcy's "dialogic form"—"form in dialogue with historically conditioned compositional options"[60]—as an attractive new expansion of an old idea, one that Adorno in particular developed dialectically through his notion of mediation (*Vermittlung*; see chapter 2), and one that, as stressed above, rests at the basis of this study. There can be no such thing as the perception of formal transformation, no becoming, if we cannot posit the notion of culturally available norms—"guidelines shared by composers and a community of listeners at a given historical time and place," "common options or generic defaults"[61] to which nineteenth-century composers reacted, trusting that digressions from those options would be recognized as such. In short, the basic premise of the Hepokoski/Darcy project is also mine.

Third, it should already be evident that the central concept of Caplin's *Formenlehre*—his theory of formal functions and their associations with specific moments in musical time—plays the leading role in my interpretation of formal processes and transformations within this volume. As Caplin clarifies, this concept was "inspired by Schoenberg and his students, especially Erwin Ratz."[62] Less well known is that Caplin's sharply defined form-functional categories, and his amplifications of those introduced by Schoenberg, fulfill a long-unmet need expressed by Adorno. Consider Adorno's note to himself in 1944:

> Certain expressive configurations in Beethoven have attached to them certain musical symbols.... But where do these symbols find the almost incomprehensible power to convey such expression in practice? This is one of the most central questions. For the present, the only answer I can imagine is that the origin of meaning in Beethoven lies in *purely musical functions*, which are then sedimented in the scattered technical means available at the time, to which they accrue as expression. All the same—cannot these functions themselves be traced back to expression?[63]

These questions remained with Adorno, and so, at the end of his life, he again seeks answers, now by proposing a "material theory of form in music" [*materiale Formenlehre der Musik*],

> that is, the concrete definition of categories like statement [*Setzung*], continuation [*Fortsetzung*], contrast [*Kontrast*], dissolution [*Auflösung*], succession [*Reihung*], development [*Entwicklung*], recurrence [*Wiederkehr*], modified recurrence [*modifizierter Wiederkehr*], and however such categories may otherwise be labeled. And so far not even the beginnings of an approach have been made regarding such a "material theory of form" (as opposed to the architectonic-schematic type of theory). These...categories are more important than knowledge of the traditional forms as such, even though they have naturally developed out of the traditional forms and can always be found in them...such a "material theory of musical form"...would not be a theory of form for once and always, but would define itself within itself historically, according to the state of the compositional material, and equally according to the state of the compositional forces of production.[64]

Caplin's form-functional theory does not embrace a material post-Hegelian philosophy, but one cannot help imagining that Adorno would have been interested in Caplin's achievement. The more authoritatively such functions as, say, "introduction," or "continuation," can be defined in reference to a broad survey of models, the stronger the basis we have for proposing that they can be "overturned" and yet retrospectively "preserved" within the formal process. On the other hand, I shall submit (in the final section of chapter 2) that the more rigidly such categories are established on the sole grounds of historical precedent, the less likely we will be willing to acknowledge genuine formal innovations, even when, to paraphrase Adorno, they so emphatically "speak to us" and wait for us to answer.

Finally, my analyses in the chapters to follow pointedly underscore the position that classical formal functions and theme types continue to thrive in music of the Romantic generation. This will come as no surprise to those who take for granted the "classicism" of Mendelssohn's music (discussed in chapter 7) or to analysts of, say, Chopin's mazurkas and waltzes, in which an utterly individual harmonic language transforms, but does not "deform," regular sentential and periodic themes within postclassical small-binary and -ternary dance forms (see chapter 8). It is, however, the very manifestations and vestiges of classical formal procedures in the music of the composers represented in this study that permit them critically to draw upon but then subvert their listeners' "classical" expectations, to invoke but then revoke classical cadences (a Schubertian tendency, discussed in chapters 5 and 6), to stretch the normal classical boundaries and dimensions of themes and sections beyond what could possibly have been imagined in Haydn's and Mozart's generation—in short, to adopt new, distinctive approaches to form, with new, attendant demands upon performers and listeners. Friedrich Blume's once influential theory of a unified, continuous, unbroken "Classic-Romantic style" leans heavily upon the argument that Classic and Romantic "genres and forms are common to both and subject only to amplification, specialization, modification, and the like"; for Blume, "Romanticism is no definable style but a spiritual attitude."[65] His survey of genres is impressive for its comprehensiveness, but, like Charles Smith, he limits his discussion of forms to established full-scale types rather than *Formungen*—to products rather than to processes, as Scott Burnham might say.[66] This study argues that the evidence of new, processual approaches to form will be uncovered through an intensive consideration of form-functional reinterpretations *within* thematic materials themselves—that is, within the paths that movements take on their way to becoming products, in the sense of completed "musical works." And it should be clear at this point that, in the new "spiritual attitude" of the Romantic generation, an outlook imbued with post-Enlightenment philosophical ideas about form that encouraged listeners to perceive music as *musical thought*, I see the emergence of a distinctive Romantic style.

Precedents for my work in the area of experiential and phenomenologically oriented studies on music as process have been many.[67] I shall single out just two of these, because of their powerful influence upon me many years ago and because they remain the seminal essays of their kind.

With an enchanting title that borrows a phrase from Yeats, Anthony Newcomb's 1983 essay "Those Images That Yet Fresh Images Beget" opens by lamenting the long-standing "division of form from meaning, of structure from expression" provoked by the camps that took sides either for or against Eduard Hanslick's assertion, in his 1854 *Vom musikalischen Schönen* (*On the Musically Beautiful*), that "forms moving in sound are the content of music" (*Der Inhalt der Musik sind tönend bewegte Formen*). Newcomb purports to attempt "a reconciliation—to assert that musical form is the seat of musical expression." He proposes that "*formal processes* themselves create expressive meaning"; by formal process he does "not mean the schemas of traditional *Formenlehre*, but rather form as the sense we make out of the individual phrase, the individual section, finally even the individual piece—the formal interpretation we place upon the music *as it unfolds in time*."[68]

The subject of Newcomb's study is Wagner's music, with reference to Wagner's own stated goals (Wagner "consistently viewed form as process instead of as static schema"), to literary criticism of the nineteenth- and twentieth-century novel, to Frank Kermode's tension between "paradigm" and "fiction or text," or between "convention and vicissitude," to the Russian formalist critics' characterization of "plot" versus "fable or archetypal story," and to Edward T. Cone's distinction between "synoptic and diachronic ways of experiencing an art work." For Newcomb:

> Whatever the words chosen, the opposition is fundamentally the same: between form as static schema—as visual, atemporal image—and form as temporal procedure....On the other hand, Wagner does not simply disregard formal schemata. He could not, even if he would. E. H. Gombrich in *Art and Illusion* has made clear that neither the musician nor the visual artist can do without formal conventions, schemes, images, paradigms—call them what you will. Without them music, like all arts, would lapse into incomprehensibility.[69]

In his analyses of excerpts from Wagner's *Die Walküre* (1870) and *Siegfried* (1876), including the entire Act I, scene 2 of the latter, Newcomb applies Kermode's idea of "disconfirmations of endings" to two of Wagner's "general kinds of constructional devices: shifts of formal implication as we move through the form, and refusal to allow the implied forms to achieve closure." I should well have cited the following from Newcomb in my 1995 article about the Beethoven-Hegelian tradition and Beethoven's "Tempest" Sonata;[70] Newcomb's premises about Wagner's formal strategies are specifically of the kind I addressed then and return to now:

> [Wagner] is intent on frustrating the fulfillment of the fixed, conventional, closed schemata and on *forcing us to relocate ourselves, to find our center anew, in a procedure whose formal meaning we are constantly asked to reassess....*The forms or procedures of many [Wagnerian] units change as the units proceed. A unit may imply one form at one point, then not allow that form to complete itself, *forcing the listener to reinterpret the initial passage as part of a different process, with new boundaries.*[71]

However, with my emphasis on Hegelian dialectics as one source for the interpretation of such processes, with my references to classical formal functions that had not yet been rigorously categorized in 1983, and most especially with my choice of repertoire—music that sharply predates Wagner's mature operas—I depart from Newcomb in obvious ways. In this volume I argue that composers long before Wagner, in music he knew so well, had already explored processual formal techniques comparable to those that Newcomb brilliantly describes. As a highly influential article on narrativity in nineteenth-century music, Newcomb's essay suggests the relevance of my study to the outpouring of subsequent work in that field.[72]

In his "Music Theory, Phenomenology, and Modes of Perception," from 1986, David Lewin's points of departure are Edmund Husserl's study of internal time consciousness and Izchak Miller's commentary on Husserl's work.[73] In Miller's words, as cited by Lewin, "our conscious experiences, or—as Husserl calls them—our *acts* of consciousness, are themselves processes, albeit mental processes. How do we, then, succeed in being reflectively aware at any given moment of the continuity, or the passage, of our mental acts?"[74] In response to this question with regard to musical perception, and using 1980s symbolic computer language that sustains its appeal today, Lewin develops a system for examining the idiosyncratically *recursive* aspects of Husserl's perception-structures. These structures "characteristically involve themselves in loops with other perception-structures" that are "typically in characteristic *relationships* to the given structure (e.g. of retention, protension, implication, realization, denial)."[75] As a first example, Lewin presents in music notation what I shall describe as a cadential progression (I^6–ii^6–V^7 . . .) that, as "Perception (a)," will be perceived by musicians at "now-time X" to promise but not complete the motion to the cadential tonic. The example of "Perception (b)" at now-time Y provides the expected tonic resolution; "Perception (c)," at now-time Z, leads to a deceptive cadence. Lewin argues that Perceptions (c) and (b) change nothing about Perception (a). In Perception (c), Perception (b) "continues to 'exist,' and it retains in retrospect at time Y all the functions it had at time X. Indeed it acquires a new function as well, in connection with Perception (c); one characteristic thing that (c) 'perceives' is precisely *that (b) is not being confirmed* by the event of time Y. . . . One must not think of (b) as 'disappearing' and of (c) as 'replacing' (b)."[76] Although Lewin invokes Hegel's phenomenology only to consider whether Hegel does or does not deny the subject-object distinction of classical European philosophy, he would surely have been aware that his own phenomenology explicitly captures in new detail both the idea and the language of Hegel's *aufheben*, or, for that matter, Dahlhaus's application thereof. If, for Lewin's "Perception (c)," we substitute Dahlhaus's perception that a modulatory transition, rather than a main theme, begins at m. 21 in Beethoven's "Tempest," this perception *does not replace* Dahlhaus's initial perception—that the movement begins as if it would be an introduction. The original perception still exists; it has not disappeared; it has been overturned but at the same time preserved. And therein lies the process of becoming.

Of greater relevance to my work is Lewin's concluding view that the subject-object paradigm, pervasive in studies of musical perception, "fits very poorly with the present-tense activities of composers and performers." For Lewin, " 'the music' that a composer is composing right now" cannot be regarded as an "object" to the composer; rather, it is "something 'of the composer.'" Likewise, for the performer in the act of performing, "'the music' as what-is-being-played-right-now is far from prior to the performer's activity." In short, "since 'music' is something you *do*, and not just something you *perceive* (or understand), a theory of music can not be developed fully from a theory of musical perception (with or without an ancillary dialectic)."[77]

I cannot claim that Lewin's position will be reflected on every page of what follows in this volume, but I ask that it be understood as a given. The composers whose music I address will be implicitly portrayed by me as *doers*—as individuals who once composed "right now," and who, moreover, have made compositional *decisions*, whether with method or with madness.[78] I also suggest throughout the study that creative compositional procedures of the kind I address could not have been made outside the context of personal aspirations and cultural milieux. For example, it can be argued that the first movement of Beethoven's "Tempest" Sonata—often regarded as an emblem of his reported "new path"[79]—stands in a class of its own, from the formal and every other viewpoint. But signs pointing toward the "new path" can be identified both in Beethoven's earlier compositions and in the music of the generation that preceded him. Beethoven the person *learned* from his predecessors about the possibilities of new, processual treatments of form. There can simply be no doubt about this, and new evidence, extending beyond the work of leading Haydn and Mozart scholars, is explored in chapter 3.

The performer as *doer* steps onstage in chapters 4 and 5. In chapter 4, I hypothesize that the short-lived but deeply personal camaraderie between Beethoven the composer-pianist and George Bridgetower the virtuoso violinist results in what verges on a collaborative enterprise between performer and composer—Beethoven's op. 47. In chapter 5, I reassess the manner in which I once portrayed relationships that performers and music analysts might hold, and I then propose that the overt but unique response of one composer to the oeuvre of another—Schubert's response to Beethoven's music—yields an even more extreme case in which the inseparable bond between composer and performer comes to the fore: with Schubert in his Piano Sonata, Op. 42, it is often what the *performer chooses to do*, at moments of genuine formal ambiguity, that will shape our perception of the formal process.

Adorno's idea that formal processes in music have the capacity to embody the most profound social tendencies of their time takes center stage in chapter 6. In manifestation of the early nineteenth-century preoccupation with interiority, and with Beethoven as the model, Schubert's music moves inward—in the first instance, toward an interior theme; in the second, toward an interior movement. These internal moments serve as centers of gravity, focal points of the greatest intimacy, toward which everything that precedes would seem to be drawn, and from which all that follows radiates outward.

With Mendelssohn in chapter 7, I turn again to a composer's personal, biographical circumstances—Mendelssohn's early associations with Goethe, with the Beethoven-Hegelian A. B. Marx, and with Hegel himself; the Mendelssohn who from childhood onward was proclaimed "a second Mozart"; the teenage Mendelssohn who would already dare to imitate Beethoven's late quartets in his earliest ones; the ultimate Mendelssohn, destined to become the conservative "classicist" in the annals of textbook music histories. Here Mendelssohn's D-minor Piano Trio, Op. 49, and his formally cyclic Octet, Op. 20, elevate to its zenith the idea that enormously expanded thematic processes might invite *multiple* retrospective reinterpretations. But the long-range goal of this chapter is to identify at least one aspect of what makes Mendelssohn's compositional voice uniquely Mendelssohnian, and I find that voice within the effortlessly "Mozartean" motivic/ thematic transformations that tend to emerge in his codas.

Chapter 8 addresses another, much discussed tendency of nineteenth-century music—its shift toward harmonic *mediant* (third) relationships that undermine the classical tonic-dominant axis. In this chapter, I propose that Chopin's harmonic idiom highlights that tendency: his "signature progression," ubiquitous within all his genres and on multiple levels of structure, is the ascending thirds motion I–III–V. Processual formal reinterpretations play a role in my survey of excerpts from Chopin's earliest mazurka to his final completed composition, the Cello Sonata, Op. 65. In reference to this last work, and as in chapters 4 and 5, I focus upon the collaborative relation between composer and performer, over many centuries a source of creativity for both; here the example is the dialogue between Chopin as pianist and his closest non-Polish friend, cellist Auguste Franchomme, as enacted in the Largo from Chopin's Cello Sonata, Op. 65.

Finally, chapter 9 moves from "becoming" to a "homecoming" of sorts. This is a meditation on what "home" might mean especially to those from whom it has been taken away, and a reflection on how certain final moments in the early music of Robert Schumann—music often composed as a private communication to Clara Wieck—would seem to express the idea of a longing to "come home." In this last chapter, as throughout the book, may it be understood that "perceivers" of formal processes—in this case, myself as music analyst—are, like Lewin's composers and performers, also "doers." The analysis and interpretation of music are, for better or worse, also performances, subject to (self-)criticism and to revisions the next time around. Performers inevitably hope that they have reached, moved, and inspired their listeners. Music analysts can only hope for the same.

CHAPTER Two

The Beethoven-Hegelian Tradition and the "Tempest" Sonata

I am not the first, nor will I be the last, to associate Beethoven with Hegel, for reasons more profound than the coincidence of their births in 1770. No two figures loomed larger over the European cultural landscape of the early nineteenth century. Hegel's ontology has been described as "quite dead,"[1] and Beethoven's music has elicited strong criticism from feminist perspectives.[2] But these factors themselves suggest that the last moments within the historical processes initiated by Hegel and Beethoven have hardly come and gone. Just as, for example, leftist intellectuals in the early 1990s urgently reassessed post-Hegelian Marxism in light of the failure of state socialism in Eastern and Central Europe,[3] so have Anglo-American musicologists and theorists given intense scrutiny to the writings of Theodor W. Adorno and Carl Dahlhaus—both post-Hegelian dialecticians, and both ones for whom Beethoven plays a pivotal role.[4]

Much may be gained from approaching the works of Adorno and Dahlhaus as manifestations of a long-standing tradition in which Beethoven's music serves as an agent within the kind of historical process that Hegel's philosophy predicates. Central to this distinct mode of thought within the larger domain of Beethoven reception is the development in Germany of concepts about *form* that are chiefly inspired by Beethoven's music, but also imbued with the spirit of Romanticism and influenced by an idealist epistemology that found its last system builder in Hegel. Dahlhaus's most provocative statements about form are those in which he most overtly identifies his role as the guardian of what I shall call the Beethoven-Hegelian tradition. For Dahlhaus, like Adorno, it is first and foremost Beethoven's music that invites our perception of form as a dialectical process in the precise Hegelian sense.

Formation of the Tradition

Traces of the origins of the Beethoven-Hegelian tradition emerge in the monumental review of Beethoven's Fifth Symphony by E. T. A. Hoffmann in 1810, an essay whose introduction has long been recognized as "one of the charters of romantic music esthetics."[5] With his familiar progression from Haydn (who "grasps romantically the human element of the human life") through Mozart (who "takes up more the superhuman, the wondrous element that abides in inner spirit"), to Beethoven (whose music "sets in motion the lever of horror, fear, revulsion, pain, and…awakens that infinite longing which is the essence of Romanticism"),[6] Hoffmann generally constructs the platform on which Robert Schumann and his contemporaries would later elevate Beethoven as the true founder of Romantic music. And Hoffmann provides what Dahlhaus himself has identified as the hermeneutic model that, drawing on the precedents of Wilhelm Heinrich Wackenroder and Ludwig Tieck, "gained fundamental meaning for the theory of [absolute] instrumental music."[7]

Dahlhaus finds Hoffmann's implicit "system of categories," or pairs of "antitheses"—plastic/musical, ancient/modern, heathen/Christian, natural/supernatural, rhythm/harmony, vocal/instrumental—to be prefigured in the works of A. W. Schlegel and Jean Paul Richter, but also explicitly present in F. W. J. von Schelling's *Philosophy of Art* of 1802.[8] A link between Hoffmann and Hegel arises here: Schelling is the precocious young colleague who arranged in 1806 for Hegel's first academic appointment, and Schelling's philosophical writings during the years 1795–1802 are said to have "anticipated almost all of Hegel's main themes."[9] It should not be surprising, then, that Hoffmann's review also reflects earlier and contemporaneous discussions of the Spirit (*Geist*); the infinite, or Absolute (represented for Hoffmann in the form of "pure" instrumental music); the "system of categories" (Hegel's post-Kantian critique of which leads to his own "antitheses"); and, of course, Romanticism, an abiding influence upon Hegel, his criticisms notwithstanding. Within the realm of Hoffmann's music criticism, such proto-Hegelian concepts converge on the music of Beethoven.

Certainly the most decisive contributions to the formation of a Beethoven-Hegelian tradition are the theoretical writings about Beethoven and musical form by Adolph Bernhard Marx (1799–1866). The extent to which Hegel's philosophy influenced Marx's theory of form remains a question for consideration below, but a direct line of influence from Hoffmann to Marx has been well established.[10] Both lived in Berlin at a time when the University of Berlin, founded by Wilhelm von Humboldt in 1809 and advanced by the presence of J. G. Fichte and Friedrich Schleiermacher, had become the site of Hegel's renowned lectures, following his appointment in 1818. Whereas Hoffmann's years in Berlin (1814–22) overlapped with Hegel's only toward the end of Hoffmann's life, Marx's seven-year tenure (1824–30) as editor of the *Berliner allgemeine musikalische Zeitung* coincided precisely with that period during which, according to one witness, "in the eyes of the Prussian educational and cultural ministry, it was almost a crime not to be a Hegelian."[11]

Like Hoffmann, and like an ever-widening circle of German literary and music enthusiasts, Marx both revered and idealized Beethoven. Also like Hoffmann, albeit with a reversal of Mozart and Haydn in Hoffmann's three-stage Mozart-Haydn-Beethoven progression, Marx viewed the history of music as the progress toward one synthesizing and culminative goal. In Marx's teleology Beethoven's music serves as the end-point, but it also heralds a "new era" of criticism and theory, one whose task would be the development of a capacity for discerning how musical form—as a dynamic, organic, and dramatic process—guarantees the "wholeness" of the composition through the realization of its spiritual content, its fundamental *Idee*.[12]

Marx's new era recalls Hegel's burst of optimism in the preface of his first full-scale work, the *Phenomenology of Spirit* (1807): "[I]t is not difficult to see that ours is a birth-time and a period of transition to a new era.... the Spirit in its formation matures slowly and quietly into its new shape."[13] Yet Scott Burnham has stressed that "Marx started from what he perceived to be the end-point of musical history [Beethoven] and interpreted the rest of that history as a process of development up to that point."[14] Such a maneuver seems all too one-dimensional in comparison with Hegel's vision, and Burnham has underscored it as evidence in favor of dissociating A. B. Marx from Hegel. Meanwhile, Hegel's own apparent end-point—his concept of the Absolute—undergoes continued debate among Hegelian scholars. Whereas J. N. Findlay calls Hegel's philosophy a "relative Absolutism," Robert C. Solomon proposes an "*absolute relativism*." But Solomon stresses that "[Hegel] felt compelled to deny [this] with his unproven appeal to the Absolute, that ideal conceptual harmony that was so visibly absent in finite human affairs."[15] Following Solomon, one might say that Hegel's "unproven appeal to the Absolute" is A. B. Marx's appeal to Beethoven. So would it also be for Adorno, who idealized Beethoven's "second-period style" but found "implicit in Beethoven's late style ... the eventual dissolution of all the values that made bourgeois humanism the hope of a human civilization."[16]

But it is not my point here to prove, or disprove, A. B. Marx's debt to Hegel. No scholar of Marx would deny that Marx's *Formenlehre* reflects many of the philosophical and aesthetic concerns—both Romantic and idealistic—that were also the preoccupations of his contemporaries, including Hegel; moreover, to develop the notion of an *ongoing* Beethoven-Hegelian tradition, I need only propose below certain good reasons why it has long been a commonplace to regard Hegel's influence on A. B. Marx as indisputable. I argue, simply, that, while the influence of the Beethoven-Hegelian tradition remains very much a part of our musicological heritage, the value its philosophical content might have for music analysis has been all too much discounted.

The fate of Marx's *Formenlehre* is a case in point. To be sure, Marx has been deemed the principal founder of the theory of musical form; he has also taken much of the credit, or blame, for having inaugurated the tradition of courses and textbooks on form. His formal categories—for example, his three *Grundformen* (the *Satz*, the *Gang*, and the *Periode*) and his progressively larger-scale types, the *Liedformen*, the scherzo, the variation form, the rondo forms, the *Sonatinenform*, and the culminative *Sonatenform*—inspired the codifications of high-classical forms by later nineteenth-century theorists; and, with modifications, many of the same categories have remained staples of our present-day formal vocabulary. But with the standardizing of classical forms, and thus the establishment of form itself as an abstract concept, there arose Mark Evan Bonds's "paradox"—the question of whether form is "conformational" or "generative." Within the twentieth century, the conformational came to be negatively associated with the conventional; the generative continues to be privileged in association with innovation, or, to invoke the Romantic ideal, genius.

Burnham and Bonds have independently suggested that Marx recognized the validity—indeed, the *necessity*—of both perspectives on form. Bonds in particular has stressed Marx's distinction between *Kunstform* and *Form*: whereas *Kunstformen* is Marx's term for the conformational, that is, the basic formal patterns shared by a large number of individual works, *Form* is the manner in which "the content of the spirit has been determined . . . [and] made comprehensible to the understanding."[17] Thus, in Burnham's terms: "Form [for Marx] is not a constraint, but a condition, of content."[18] Put this way, Marx's view finds a dialectical counterpart in Hegel, for whom "the only genuine works of art are precisely the ones whose content and form show themselves to be completely identical."[19]

If Marx indeed thought of form and content as inseparable, then the general historical verdict on him needs to be appealed, for that verdict has long held that Marx was a rigid systematizer of textbook forms whose "basic principle of composition" amounts to nothing more than "construction from a supply of ready-made building blocks."[20] Such a verdict would have to be understood as a condemnation of Marxian *Formenlehre* by proponents of Heinrich Schenker's "new theory of form." In the final stages of Schenker's theory, form finds its origin within the *Ursatz* of the background rather than in such foreground entities as Marx's *Satz*; far from evolving as expansions of initial building blocks, individual forms derive from the totality of the *Ursatz* through the unlimited techniques of *Auskomponierung*.[21]

In his defense of Marx's ahistorical progression from simple forms to more complex ones, Burnham sees Marx as the inspired composition teacher who urges his students to think of form as a dynamic process at each stage in their development. Accordingly, Marx's elemental *Grundform*, the *Satz*, is hardly a building block, nor does it provide the source of form; rather, his fundamental formal principle, and thus the dynamic basis of the *Satz* itself, is the dialectic of a "primary opposition between the state of rest and that of motion."[22] When a particular four-bar *Satz* is followed by a complementary four-bar *Gegensatz*, this is because the pattern of "rest-motion-rest" (*Ruhe-Bewegung-Ruhe*) expressed by the *Satz* creates only a "one-sided satisfaction": the content of the *Satz* itself determines that a *Gegensatz* must follow in order that a rising, an intensification, a highpoint, a return, and an ultimately stronger state of rest be achieved. One might say, then, that the original *Satz* "becomes" a *Vordersatz* relative to the *Gegensatz*, now composed to function as a *Nachsatz* within the larger *Grundform*-type, the eight-bar *Periode*. But then each component of the period—*Vordersatz* and *Nachsatz*—might "will its own expansion," might want "*to become* a larger whole";[23] thus might the eight-bar period become a two-part, sixteen-bar *Liedform*, with smaller *Vorder*- and *Nachsätze* embedded in each half of the sixteen-bar structure. The notion of such processes—sometimes additive, sometimes more evocative of cellular division, but always "organically" motivated—informs the rationale with which Marx guides his composition students through increasingly complex *Kunstformen* toward the goal of greatest coherence in the sonata form, the crowning formal achievement of his era, and the form that reaches its fullest maturity in the hands of Beethoven.

Taking to task German critics who have labeled Marx's derivation of forms as historical/teleological (Hegelian), genetic/biological (as in Goethe's plant metamorphosis), or a flawed mixture of the two, Burnham insists that these writers have either underemphasized or overlooked the role of pedagogy in Marx's theory. However, at the highpoint of his argument, Burnham implicitly places Marx within the epistemological tradition of the young Hegel and his predecessors: Marx's derivation and ordering of existing musical forms were done

> in such a way as to expedite the assimilation of these forms in the developing mind of the composition student. It is not musical form, or the *Satz*, which necessitates its own metamorphoses through each stage; it is rather the artistic capability of the student which grows and requires new formal possibilities. The artistic spirit posited by Marx as the motivation behind the various stages in the *Formenlehre* is the burgeoning artistic consciousness of the developing student. Each new level implies the use of material which will not fit into the older stage; at each level a new formal strategy is internalized by the student. Preserved at every stage of this progression is the emphasis on artistic and structural wholeness, the central aspect of Marx's aesthetic view of the musical artwork.[24]

It would be easy enough to read Burnham's summary as the mere description of a pedagogical method to which any gifted teacher of music theory might ascribe. In addition, the method itself invokes the metaphor of the *Bildungsweg*—the educational journey—so prevalent in German literature and philosophy from Herder, Lessing, Kant, Goethe, Schiller, Hölderlin, Fichte, and Schelling to Hegel himself. Like Goethe's Wilhelm Meister, or like the multifaceted spirit, the protagonist of Hegel's *Phenomenology*, Marx's composition students follow an arduous educational path through stages, or *Stationen des Weges* (stations of the way), toward greater (in Marx's case, artistic) self-consciousness.[25] Although they ostensibly do not experience alienation followed by redemption, a persistent theme of the *Bildungsgeschichte* genre, at least some degree of suffering might attend the novice's task of composing a sonata form. Beyond these observations, the most striking feature of Burnham's account is its allusion to the dialectical relation between subject and object that characterizes idealist philosophies of Hegel's time. Burnham's summary can be reinterpreted in the following manner.

As subjective individuals, Marx's students presumably begin by taking musical form to be an objective phenomenon; but by *internalizing* formal strategies at each new stage within their musical development, they grow ever more conscious that *form is composed* and that they themselves are the composers. Each of Marx's stages calls for a movement of the mind outward, toward the object as Marx's concept, followed by a return inward, at which point the student finds the materials of the preceding stage to be at one and the same time annulled, preserved, and raised to a higher level, in Schelling's and Hegel's multiple, equivocal sense of *aufgehoben*. In the final stage, Marx's students become aware that all the mysteries of musical form are intrinsic to themselves, as moments in their own educational development.[26]

∾

I have discussed Marx, and Burnham's interpretation of his work, at length because the Beethoven-Hegelian tradition overtly begins with Marx and because his theory of form anticipates the dialectical outlook developed by Adorno and Dahlhaus throughout their writings about Beethoven. I now posit that a foremost intermediary between Marx and Dahlhaus, and perhaps the single most influential preserver of Marx's dynamic formal premises, is Arnold Schoenberg.

As a pedagogue, Schoenberg made no apologies for his teaching of conventional tonal forms in the sense of Marx's *Kunstformen*. As a composer, he shared with Marx the position that *Form* in the generative sense is the process that gives articulation, external shape, and comprehensibility to the composer's *Idee*. Indeed, Schoenberg's concept of the *Grundgestalt* finds an early precedent in Marx's theory: like Schoenberg's "basic shape," Marx's "formation of the *Hauptsatz*"—the composer's initial theme—plays the determinative role in the formal and motivic process that follows.[27] This rigorous approach to composition must of course be viewed as organicist, but it also bears comparison with what is known as the movement of thought in Hegelian logic: both theorists honored the notion that "*musical* thoughts" within a composition should arise as if impelled by a logical necessity. And, finally, both found the clearest compositional demonstration of such a principle in the music of Beethoven—in what Adorno called "*das Beethovensche Muss*."[28]

On the other hand, the well-documented influence of Arthur Schopenhauer and Eduard Hanslick on Schoenberg, not to mention the vast compositional and historical changes that separate Schoenberg from Marx, can help to account for Schoenberg's very different attitude toward "idea." Given that form for Marx is "the revelation of the *Idee*, the incarnation of thought" in the musical work, Marx's *Idee* must be understood as thought (*Gedanke*).[29] But since the composer's thought can be temporally realized only as a continuous process, it can be conceptualized by Marx the critic only in explicit association with an extramusical program—one that at best expresses the narrative of a dramatic confrontation; as examined in detail by Burnham, Marx's *Idee* "must have a palpable connection with sensuous reality in order to be suitable for musical representation."[30] By contrast, most of Schoenberg's writings about idea, or *Gedanke*, make an emphatic distinction between thought as an extramusical concept couched in language and a "musical thought" (*musikalische Gedanke*)—an idea that is strictly musical. Patricia Carpenter finds the immediate precedent for Schoenberg's distinction in the work of Hanslick. Taking Immanuel Kant's *Critique of Judgment* to be the "modern locus for the tension between aesthetic form and aesthetic idea," she contends that Schopenhauer's solution to the Kantian problem of form versus content in music was satisfactory to neither Hanslick nor Schoenberg. For Schopenhauer, music expresses "the will itself" for the very reason that it is "the language of the feelings" and of the passions rather than of verbal concepts.[31] For Hanslick and Schoenberg, "the ultimate content of music is not feeling, but musical ideas"; and, given that "the musical idea is sheerly musical, there is no separation of form and content."[32]

Certainly not an avowed Hegelian, but ever determined to demonstrate the historical validity of his own music, Schoenberg prepares the way for Adorno's post-Hegelian historiography by tracing the origins of his developing-variation technique to the music of J. S. Bach, that is, to "the art of producing every audible figure from one single one," which "had reached such a pitch that in it the transition to a different kind of art is already beginning. Henceforth, the art would be to subject these figures themselves to variation, it no longer being enough to juxtapose them, but rather to show how one gives rise to another."[33] The new art would be "the style of 'developing variation,'" which Schoenberg specifically equated with the "homophonic style" of "the classic composers—Haydn, Mozart, Beethoven, Schubert, Mendelssohn, Schumann, Brahms, and even Wagner."[34] The course progressively charted by those composers would constitute the "path to the new music" of Schoenberg himself. Although he acknowledged Bach and Mozart as his primary teachers, it was Beethoven from whom Schoenberg claimed to have learned not only "the art of developing themes and movements" but also "the art of variation and of varying."[35] Moreover, in the work in which Schoenberg most fully presents himself as a teacher of tonal form—his *Fundamentals of Musical Composition*—Beethoven is the primary source of his examples.

Beethoven's techniques of development and variation are precisely those aspects of his treatment of form that so preoccupied Adorno in his critique of European music from late Beethoven to Schoenberg and beyond. On the issue of development, Adorno perpetuates a tradition already begun with A. B. Marx; as the grand *Bewegung* within a large-scale *Ruhe-Bewegung-Ruhe* dynamic, the development section of the sonata form had furnished Marx with the dialectical justification for elevating that *Kunstform* above all others. Adorno found that in Beethoven "the development...becomes the focal point of the entire form." At the same time, development recalls the older procedure of variation—the technique whereby a *theme* or idea undergoes change while nevertheless retaining its original identity. Expressly invoking Hegel's subject-object dialectic, Adorno never hesitates in referring to the composer's original theme—the product of inspiration (*Einfall*)—as the "musical subject": "'*Einfall*' is not just a psychological category, a matter of 'inspiration,' but a moment in *the dialectical process manifest in musical form*. This moment marks the irreducibly subjective element in this process and, by means of its inexplicability, further designates this aspect of music as its essence." Conversely, the technique of developing variation—the "working out" of the theme—"represents the process of objectivity and *the process of becoming*." To achieve a synthesis of these moments is to reconcile the dialectical opposites of subjective freedom and objective reality; in Adorno's view the semblance of such a reconciliation arises in the music of Beethoven's second period, but it was never to be achieved again. Although Schoenberg emerges as the heir apparent to Beethoven, he carried the developing-variation procedure to such an extreme in his twelve-tone music that the distinction between model and variant, theme and its development, the subjective and the objective, is destroyed. "Everything, yet nothing, is variation."[36]

To appreciate Adorno's reverence for Beethoven and his sympathetic but despairing assessment of Schoenberg's twelve-tone music, we must confront Adorno's claim that the arts in general, and their forms in particular, have the capacity to reflect or embody the most profound social tendencies of their time. From the inference in A. B. Marx's writings of a dialectical relation between content and form, Adorno moves toward an explicitly Hegelian antithesis in which the assumption of an "interdependency of form and content in all music,"[37] now reinterpreted in response to the materialist philosophy of Karl Marx and informed by the work of Adorno's colleague Max Horkheimer, acquires sociological significance. No composer begins with a *tabula rasa*. To the extent that the artistic materials, forms, and techniques of the age into which a composer is born serve as starting points, contemporaneous conventions of form constitute the social parameter of the composer's art, and form itself is thus as much an objective principle as it is the realization of the composer's subjective content.[38]

From the tragic perspective of the German-Jewish intellectual expelled by the Nazis, Adorno saw the bourgeois humanism of the late eighteenth century—Beethoven's starting point—as that last historical moment wherein the possibility of a reconciliation between the individual as subject and society as Other "was at least enough of a reality to suggest its own conceptual categories of form to the artist's imagination."[39] This is the period in which Beethoven assimilated the sonata form and enabled it to express the semblance of an autonomous totality. In his sonata forms Beethoven's "musical subject" would not only advance with new freedom into the generalizing, objective realm of the development, but also return to itself in the recapitulation with a vigor and individuality that evoke the overcoming of social destiny. The purpose of Beethoven's recapitulations would be

> *to confirm the process as its own result*, as occurs unconsciously in social practice. Not by chance are some of Beethoven's most pregnant conceptions designed for the instant of the reprise as the recurrence of the same. They justify, as the result of a process, what has been once before. It is exceedingly illuminating that Hegelian philosophy—whose categories can be applied without violence to every detail of a music that cannot possibly have been exposed to any Hegelian "influence" in terms of the history of ideas—that this philosophy knows the reprise as does Beethoven's music: the last chapter of Hegel's *Phenomenology*, the absolute knowledge, has no other content than to summarize the total work which claims to have already gained the identity of subject and object, in religion.[40]

In the end, however, Adorno could regard neither Hegel's philosophy nor Beethoven's music as having captured anything more than the illusion of a synthesis. To be sure, nineteenth-century composers probed the conflict between the subjective and the objective with ever-increasing self-consciousness. But it seemed to Adorno that these two categories "resist unification just as strongly as the bourgeois concept of the individual stands in perennial contrast to the totality of the social process. The inconsistency between the theme and what happens to it reflects such social irreconcilability."[41]

In the words of Rose Rosengard Subotnik (whose "landmark studies on Adorno, beginning in the 1970s, literally brought Adorno to the attention of American musicology"),[42] Adorno did not pretend to understand, nor did he adequately elucidate, the complex process of mediation (*Vermittlung*) through which "the essential tendencies of a given historical moment become translated into the formal aspects of great art."[43] It can nonetheless be emphasized that *conventions* of form play a crucial role within the process. With Adorno, A. B. Marx's distinction between *Form* and *Kunstform* itself acquires the status of a subject-object antithesis: the individual composer's unique, subjective form can neither be recognized as such nor embody a social reality unless it has been placed by the critic in dialectical opposition to the received *Kunstformen*—the objective formal traditions—upon which the composer inevitably draws. Whereas feminist and other cultural theorists have joined Subotnik in applauding Adorno's disdain for any kind of analytic "formalism" that excludes social critique, they cannot in good conscience discount his lifelong preoccupation with both the concept and the analysis of form. In what appears to have been his last public lecture about music analysis, the interdependency of the "formal schema" and the "formal deviation" remains as central as ever to Adorno's impassioned plea for what he called "structural listening"—a topic that has provoked a poststructuralist critique from Subotnik and others.[44]

Likewise, musical "coherence" (*Zusammenhang*) holds a dialectical relationship with music's "aspect of 'Becoming'" (*Aspekt des Werdens*), its unceasing "development from out of itself" (*aus sich Herauswerdendes*). On the one hand, all Becoming in music is illusory, since "the music, as *text*, is really fixed and thus is not actually 'becoming' anything as it is already all there." On the other hand, "music is actually only a coherence [it only becomes fixed] when regarded as a Becoming," by which Adorno presumably means that we perceive coherence in music only when we hear individual musical events as arising one from another. Herein lies Adorno's "paradox for musical analysis" (and Bonds's "paradox of musical form"). Adorno concludes that the "real weakness of analysis up to now" is its neglect of the moment of Becoming. His exhortation to analysts provides the challenge of the present study: "May 'Becoming' continue always to have its problematic existence!"[45]

By implication, not all music requires a consideration of becoming for Adorno, since the basic assumptions of some music—especially the "radical serial and aleatory music" of the postwar generation—preclude such concepts as "dynamic coherence."[46] Adorno associates becoming chiefly with what he calls "motivic-thematic" composition; more specifically, from the roster of composers to whom he turns in his lecture for concrete examples—Webern, Schoenberg, Mahler, Berg, and of course Beethoven, but not Wagner—he betrays his bias toward motivic-thematic music produced in Vienna. As for precisely how the becoming of music might be captured in analysis, Adorno's comparisons of Beethoven with Hegel characteristically yield the sharpest clues. Of particular relevance are his observations about "music of Beethoven's type" in the third of his three studies on Hegel.

Titled "Skoteinos, or How to Read Hegel," this study tacitly underscores the premises of Adorno's own "negative dialectics" by attempting to elucidate the concept of the nonidentical within Hegel's work. Adorno argues that readers of Hegel (whom he may have underestimated) all too often regard the three-part movement of the concept—from identity through its negation (nonidentity) to synthesis—as strictly an advance forward: "In that the reflection of each concept, which is linked with the reflection of reflection, breaks the concept open by demonstrating its inconsistency, the movement of the concept always also affects the stage from which it breaks away." Thus: "The advance is a permanent critique of what has come before, and this kind of movement supplements the movement of advance by synthesis."[47] In short, the third member of the three-part schema—the so-called synthesis—also reveals itself as a *return* to the first member, or starting point, now "modified and under different illumination." It is as an analogue for Hegel's modified return that Adorno introduces "music of Beethoven's type," namely, music in which the recapitulation—"the return in reminiscence of complexes expounded earlier"—"should be the result of development, that is, of dialectic."[48]

Hegelian-like perspectives on the sonata form as a three-part dialectical movement have abounded in the literature from A. B. Marx's time onward.[49] Surely, however, Adorno's post-Hegelian interpretation is at once the most rigorous and the most extreme. His analogue of the Beethovenian recapitulation "transcends mere analogy": "the conception of totality as an identity immanently mediated by nonidentity is a law of artistic form transposed into the philosophical domain. The transposition is itself philosophically motivated."[50] Thus, the process of learning how to read Hegel will be enhanced by learning how to listen to (and analyze) the "highly organized music" of Beethoven's type. Just as in Hegel the presentation of a concept often "makes a backward leap," just as "one must read Hegel by describing along with him the curves of his intellectual movement, by playing his ideas with the speculative ear as though they were musical notes,"[51] so must Beethoven "be heard multidimensionally, *forward and backward at the same time*:

> Its temporal organizing principle requires this: time can be articulated only through distinctions between what is familiar and what is not yet familiar, between what already exists and what is new; the condition of moving forward is a retrogressive consciousness. One has to know a whole movement and be aware retrospectively at every moment of what has come before. The individual passages have to be grasped as consequences of what has come before, the meaning of a divergent repetition has to be evaluated, and reappearance has to be perceived not merely as architectonic correspondence but as something that has evolved with necessity.[52]

At the risk of oversimplification, table 2.1 juxtaposes the interdependent pairs of concepts that have emerged above as antitheses for Adorno. If the ever-reflective

Table 2.1 Adorno's Antitheses

Subjective freedom	Objective reality
Theme	Development; variation
Content	Form
Deviations	Schemata
Essence; coherence	Becoming
Identity	Nonidentity

correlatives, antitheses, and "on the other hand" juxtapositions of Dahlhaus's dialectic fundamentally embrace similar categories, they do this more subtly, as from the dispassionate outlook of one for whom Adorno's pessimistic historiographical biases can no longer be sustained. In Stephen Hinton's view, Dahlhaus

> knew all too well that history is construction. In selecting the facts on the basis of explicit or implicit criteria, the historian imposes a perspective and narrative framework. Dahlhaus's creeping dissatisfaction with nineteenth-century German historiography from Hegel to Adorno became particularly apparent in recent years. By way of undermining the notion of historical necessity inherent in Hegel's "objective spirit" and Adorno's "tendency of musical material," he began to replace the monolithic singular *Geschichte* with its plural *Geschichten* ("histories" and "affairs").[53]

Dahlhaus clearly distances himself from Adorno in, for instance, his 1979 essay "Zu Adornos Beethoven-Kritik." Here August Halm's "third musical culture" (whose prophet was Bruckner) and Ernst Bloch's vision of a "concrete utopia" (to be attained through new music) appear as forerunners of Adorno's views within a "little noticed tradition in the shadows of Beethoven-hagiography": their ideologies prefigure Adorno's sociology of music by focusing upon the *Systemcharakter* of Beethovenian music—"the perfection and the seamless, functional self-containedness of [Beethoven's] musical forms"—as pivotal within their dialectical but strictly aesthetic claims.[54] And yet, Dahlhaus's own ideas about musical form, content, theme, formal function, and processuality in his writings about Beethoven emphatically reflect upon Schoenberg's and Adorno's contributions to the Beethoven-Hegelian tradition. About this there can be no mistake.

The antitheses of object and subject, the exoteric and the esoteric, formal conventions and the individualization of these become established as central themes of Dahlhaus's *Ludwig van Beethoven* in his very first chapter, whose conventional biographical title—"Life and Work"—serves the ironic purpose of announcing not what the chapter covers, but what it questions. As one solution to the myriad problems and misconstrued assumptions that attend the biographer's efforts to link a life and an oeuvre, Dahlhaus proposes the need to distinguish between what he calls the "biographical subject"—the composer as an individual—and the "aesthetic subject," imagined as "one who sustains the musical process," and unique within each individual work. The tendency to blur this distinction in the case of Beethoven has been especially strong because his work has been "perceived as 'subjective' to a degree that was unknown to earlier generations." At the same time, the audience for whom Beethoven's works were destined "was the anonymous general public, not the intimate circle of friends that C. P. E. Bach had in mind when he said that a composer must be moved himself if he is to move others. And as the intimate circle grew into a 'public,' so the aesthetic subject parted company with the biographical subject ever more decisively."[55]

What Dahlhaus describes here is the undeniable "historical reality" of increased "formalization," wherein "the biographical 'source' becomes…merely the 'starting-point'"; the determinative factor is "the outcome of the process that works itself out in the form," that is, "the progressive 'assumption' of the content into the form."[56] Like Adorno, Dahlhaus singles out Beethoven's second period as the crucial historical moment. For Dahlhaus, this is the period in which Beethoven discovered a concept of form that paradoxically *mediates* between extreme exotericism (outwardly directed expression) and extreme esotericism (expression turned inward), between the apparently concrete and the motivically abstract. From Schoenberg, Dahlhaus draws upon developing variation as the formal process by which "what the motivic material means is decided by the course the music takes…and that course is unmistakably determined by formal considerations, not programmatic ones." In this view, the individualization, or "rupturing," of formal conventions—for instance, the insertion of a recitative in the recapitulation of the "Tempest" Sonata's first movement—"is a structural principle that need not necessarily be motivated by non-musical considerations."[57]

But the withdrawal of the biographical subject into the aesthetic subject also finds its correlative for Dahlhaus in the dialectics of subject and object, which "the historian cannot simply forget," "as if Hegel or Wilhelm von Humboldt had never formulated it, even though it was still unknown to eighteenth-century thought." Dahlhaus likens the aesthetic subject to the Hegelian "self,"

> which is unable to know itself until it sees itself reflected—refracted—by the object.…Since the dialectics of subject and object is, in terms of the history of ideas, a discovery of the period around 1800, it is not surprising that the subject that is forever active in musical formal process (and not merely temporarily during the genesis of the piece) does not seem to have found itself until Beethoven. The aesthetic subject is to some extent the subject who composes and continues to exist in the piece, having been written into it as *energeia*.[58]

It follows for Dahlhaus, as for Adorno, that the processuality of Beethoven's music requires a uniquely active response on the part of the listener:

> In turn, the sophistication of the process of composition creates the need for an analogous sophistication in the act of listening to music; the process of composition itself cannot be reconstructed, only a reception that reflects it, recognizing the relationship between the musical object and its perception. The aesthetic subject is thus the empirical person of neither the composer nor the listener, but an imaginary subject that combines the creative activity of the former and the re-creative activity of the latter.[59]

The listening process, or what Dahlhaus called the "structure of musical hearing," is his foremost concern in the section of *Ludwig van Beethoven* titled

"Form as Transformation"—originally published in 1977 and probably the earliest essay in the book. It is worth noting that Dahlhaus's 1977 readers were presumably ones to whom he could say: "No one denies the commonplace that musical form represents a process." Be this as it may, analysts and listeners continue to think of music as fundamentally proceeding toward an *outcome*—a "deep structure," "a box containing a ready-made meaning," "a kind of imaginary simultaneity, in which music as form comes into its own."[60] For Dahlhaus, the distinction between outcome and process is questionable: "To regard musical perception exclusively as a path toward a goal is to mistake how it works." And then, echoing Adorno as cited above: "Rather, the process is itself—paradoxically—the result." Or, in paraphrase of Hegel: "[M]usical form is not subsumed in the lucidity that it finally reaches, or appears to reach. Rather, the 'real' meaning that emerges at the end is—to express it in a paradox—only part of an overall sense which exceeds that and includes the provisional meanings that the consciousness has left behind but not forgotten. *The path, not its end, is the goal.*"[61]

Both in "Form as Transformation" and in his chapter on "The New Path" of Beethoven's middle period, Dahlhaus all but equates that path with the new, radically processual character of Beethoven's forms in works written in and after 1802. Thus middle-period compositions—for example, the "Tempest" Sonata; the variation cycles opp. 34 and 35; the "Waldstein" Sonata, Op. 53; the "Eroica" Symphony, Op. 55; and the String Quartet, Op. 59, No. 3—serve as Dahlhaus's models of processuality and transformation throughout his book. A more broadly based "phenomenological outline" is, however, the goal of the 1977 "Form as Transformation" essay. There Dahlhaus attempts to set forth "fundamental structures [of hearing] which can be agreed as established within the bounds of certain historical, ethnic and regional, and social traditions." He argues that, once the dialectical process of musical perception has been grasped, insight into this mode of listening need not be limited in its range of operation to Beethoven's works: even with apparently simple forms, a phrase or period whose meaning—by which Dahlhaus means *formal function*—is certain from the outset is "a merely borderline case of transformation."[62]

By 1984, Dahlhaus had found reason to undertake the historicist's circumscriptive review of processuality in general, and perhaps even of his own earlier phenomenological outline in particular. From the shortened version of his 1984 "Eine wenig beachtete Formidee" translated and reprinted in *Ludwig van Beethoven*, we now learn that the idea of musical form as process is a matter of interpretation rather than a self-evident state, and that it has come to be taken too easily for granted: "Undoubtedly music—as an event in time, or one in which time is implicit—proceeds, but not everything that 'proceeds' (or 'goes forwards') is a 'process.'" Dahlhaus now directly associates the concept of musical process with two categories of thought: (1) the notion of " 'musical logic,' a category filled ever fuller over the years by theorists from Johann Nicolaus Forkel to Arnold Schoenberg" (recall the references above to "logical necessity" in connection with Hegel, A. B. Marx, Schoenberg, and Adorno); and (2) "the 'organic' model, one of the characteristic models of nineteenth-century ways of thinking." The organicist metaphor itself rests on the principle that "from an original, given substance—a theme, a 'motivic cell,' a '*Grundgestalt*'—there 'grows' a form, which 'develops' over a period of time; the 'growth' is determined by what Aristotle called 'entelechy': potential that sets its realization as its goal." "Process" in music thus implies both a generative "source subject" and "goal-directed lawfulness," or " 'lawfulness without laws,' to borrow a Kantian paradox."[63]

With reference to the motivic content of short passages from two of Beethoven's early piano sonatas—the first movements of op. 2, no. 3 and op. 14, no. 2—Dahlhaus now proposes an alternative metaphor, to supplement but not replace the notion of musical process. Borrowed from the theory of historiography, his new model is the "history of events," whereby a historical event is regarded not as the result of a goal-directed development but rather as the outcome of an action in which a number of mutually independent subjects, or agents, "work with and against each other—without, as a rule, any of the actors foreseeing that outcome." By analogy, a musical configuration might better be regarded as an "event" rather than a developmental "result" when, by unexpectedly conjoining earlier motives or elements of disparate origins, it enables those earlier events to be understood as constituents of a "history."[64] One senses that Dahlhaus's supplementary interpretative model has been motivated by issues far more profound than those raised by the two passages from Beethoven that he discusses. If the determinist philosophical doctrine of historical necessity had long ago reached a dead end for Dahlhaus, then perhaps all the more reason why applications of logical necessity to music must also be given historical as well as technical boundaries.

On the other hand, Dahlhaus's analytic observations about op. 2, no. 3 and op. 14, no. 2 strictly concern motivic combinations rather than form. Conversely, his demonstrations of processuality in Beethoven's music always involve form, or, more precisely, the interaction of motivic relationships and *formal functions*. That this latter concept is inextricably associated with the issue of late eighteenth-century *formal conventions* should perhaps be self-evident; for example, the names for formal components that have become standard in theories of sonata forms— *main theme* (*Hauptsatz, Hauptgedanke*; often called a first, or principal, subject), *transition, secondary theme* (or second subject, or subordinate group), *exposition, development, recapitulation*—generally describe formal functions, to the extent that they identify the place and purpose, or formal role, such components fill within the overall plan. But form-functional categories have been disparaged by Schenkerians and often adopted uncritically in discussions of form. Indeed, Dahlhaus's preoccupation with formal function might well be missed by readers unfamiliar with the Schoenbergian tradition that he shares with Adorno, Erwin Ratz, and William E. Caplin. Among these writers, Adorno and Dahlhaus stand apart in their efforts to shed a post-Hegelian dialectical light upon the idea of formal function in reference to processuality.

As the key passage that expresses Schoenberg's own claims on the concept of formal function in relation to motive, Dahlhaus cites the following, from Schoenberg's "Brahms the Progressive":

> I wish to join ideas with ideas. No matter what the purpose or meaning of an idea in the aggregate may be, no matter whether its function be introductory, establish-

ing, varying, preparing, elaborating, deviating, developing, concluding, subdividing, subordinate, or basic, it must be an idea which had to take this place even if it were not to serve for this purpose or meaning or function.[65]

Although Schoenberg's statement is impressive for the compendium of formal functions it provides, Dahlhaus concedes that Schoenberg postulates the primacy of developing variation over formal functions, and he notes that Schoenberg's outlook "has more to do with his own practice as a composer than with the classic-romantic tradition to which he refers": "If 'logic' is understood as the principle that allows it to be said why a particular variation comes in one place and not in any other," then where formal conventions remain operative, "the decisive factor is not an abstract 'logic' of motivic development (a logic detached from the formal groundplan) but the blending [*Vermittlung*: mediation] of that logic with the functions and stations of a formal process."[66] Such individual "blendings" have everything to do with what makes a work unique; thus, conventions become characteristics that define the singularity of the particular work.

Finally, it is through what Dahlhaus, following Ludwig Finscher, calls the "reflecting nature of Beethoven's treatment of sonata form" that formal functions take on a dialectical role for the listener who is thoroughly acquainted with that form as a heuristic model. For their similarity to his observations about the "Tempest" Sonata, Dahlhaus's remarks about another movement from the same opus—the opening of the E-flat Piano Sonata Op. 31, No. 3—provide an appropriate demonstration of this point:

> Firstly, the opening of the movement starts by seeming to be an introduction, and only later reveals itself as the main theme. Secondly, the continuation (bar 18), which seems to be a transition (and indeed is such in the recapitulation), loses that role to an evolutionary section (bar 33) which must be regarded as the "real" transition. By this means Beethoven shows that musical form is something created by the subject. "Introduction," "main theme," and "transition" prove to be categories that are not "given" as part and parcel of the musical object but are "brought to" the structure. When the understanding of form is unreflecting, the subject is not conscious of its creative activity; it thinks of itself as the organ for the reception of a clearly defined "thing" with certain "characteristics." It is only on being encouraged *to exchange categories for others*, that the listener becomes aware of himself as subject, and of his creative role in the formal process.[67]

Dahlhaus and the "Tempest" Sonata

As the foremost preserver of the Beethoven-Hegelian tradition, Dahlhaus was also the readiest to substantiate his views by offering concrete analytic observations. His analyses are, however, like epigrams; they aim to stimulate rather than to have the last word. Such is surely the case with his few specific remarks about the Sonata Op. 31, No. 3 cited above. And the same must be said about the terse statement that serves now as the starting point for my reconsideration of the exposition of Beethoven's "Tempest" Sonata—Dahlhaus's proposition that "the beginning of the sonata is loosely constructed, and both harmonically and syntactically open-ended, so that at first it seems to be an introduction, not the exposition of a theme."[68]

Each of the primary terms of this claim assumes a collective understanding. But even Dahlhaus's first term—beginning—cannot be taken for granted: he sometimes refers only to mm. 1–2, at other times to the passage at mm. 1–20, as the apparent introduction. It must also be noted that Dahlhaus treats the terms *introduction* and *theme* dialectically, in the sense that an introduction *is* what a theme *is not*—"loosely constructed," "harmonically and syntactically open-ended," and thus *not* "thematic in character."[69] Conversely, we might infer that a theme for Dahlhaus is tightly constructed and tonally closed. But he has been known to provide full historiographical validation for *multiple* notions of "theme"—as Hugo Riemann's generative fundamental idea (recalling Marx and Schoenberg), as substance dialectically inseparable from form (recalling Adorno), as affect or character, as fully rounded melodic shape, and finally, as recurrent rhythmic and harmonic elements. Given that none of these characterizations rules out the notion of theme as a short, two-bar idea, we need not be surprised to learn from Dahlhaus that the "abstract" arpeggiated triad at the beginning of the "Tempest" links the "preliminary form of the theme (bar 1) with its more substantial manifestation (bar 21)."[70]

By contrast, Dahlhaus freely interchanges the terms "theme" and "subject" (the latter with both its rhetorical and idealistic philosophical overtones) when he refers to what I shall mean by "theme" below: such larger-scale entities traditionally known as main theme or second subject. In fact, he defends Riemann's seemingly "bizarre" but ultimately "useful" idea that the tonally closed sections in a sonata exposition are thematic, whereas sections that modulate—transitions and developments—are nonthematic, even though they tend to feature what Riemann himself called "thematic-motivic working[-out]." Dahlhaus maintains that these correlations are "deeply rooted in the tradition of independent instrumental music; and it is no exaggeration to say that they are among the fundamental preconditions of formal thinking in the instrumental music of the eighteenth century."[71] As well, they provide the basis for his assertion that the passage at mm. 21–41 of the "Tempest" is no longer a theme. Rather than remaining tonally closed, this "evolutionary episode" effects the modulation; in other words, it *becomes* the transition. As clarified in chapter 1 and shown in example 2.1, above graph A at m. 21, my symbol for the expression "becomes" is the double-lined right arrow ($\Rightarrow$).

This discursus on what "theme" might mean for Dahlhaus has yet to clarify why he holds that the beginning of the movement is *not yet* a theme, and it has not accounted for his vagueness about the length of the apparent introduction. Dahlhaus describes introductions as unstable and intrinsically provisional (*vorläufig*), by which he means that "what may be expected to issue from [them] remains indeterminate." Unlike developments, which have as their goal the recapitulation of the main-theme materials that have often served as their starting point, introductions lack both a thematic starting point and a thematic goal, in the sense that their goal is the thematic starting point itself.[72] All of the introductions Dahlhaus discusses here—the openings of Beethoven's Cello Sonatas, Op. 5, Nos. 1 and 2,

Example 2.1. Beethoven, Piano Sonata No. 17 in D Minor, Op. 31, No. 2, first movement, annotated voice-leading graphs for the exposition, mm. 1–63

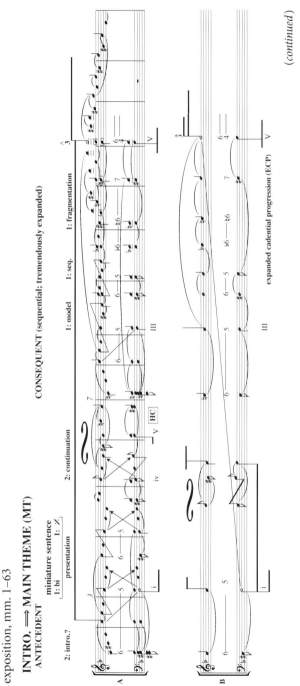

(*continued*)

Example 2.1. cont.

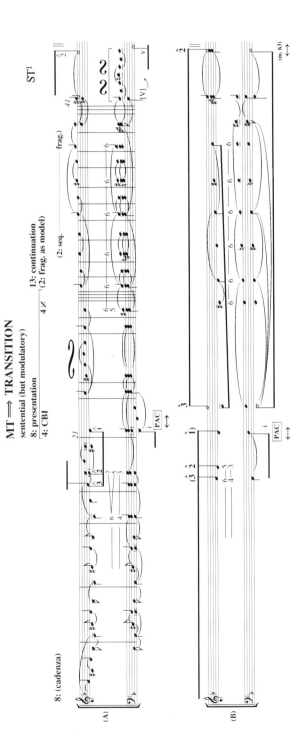

his Seventh Symphony, and Florestan's aria in Act II of *Fidelio*—are slow and of the large-scale rather than the two-bar type; in other words, they serve as *slow introductions*, rather than as *thematic introductions*, Caplin's term for short intro-ductions to a theme.[73] However, to the extent that the terms "unstable" and "provi-sional" can be applied to both the opening largo of the "Tempest" and the broader passage at mm. 1–20, Dahlhaus's vagueness might well be deliberate.

Is it possible for us to recapture the experience of hearing the "Tempest" for the very first time—without a score, no less? Perhaps not; but if we could, then we would remember that first-time listeners cannot initially be certain about either the key or the mode of the movement as the pianist lingers on the fermata of m. 2. To say that what they can expect remains indeterminate would be an under-statement. The largo tempo immediately suggests the tradition of the slow intro-duction, well established by 1802; but on the basis of what precedents is one to interpret an introduction that begins with the rolling of a sixth-chord? Only the harpsichordist's *ad libitum* prelude to an accompanied recitative comes to mind.[74] If Beethoven is now evoking that operatic idiom, would not the expected recitative—with Shakespeare's Prospero, or Miranda, possibly in mind[75]—follow the tradition of serving as *introductory* to an Allegro movement proper, perhaps along the lines suggested at the hypothetical example 2.2? Or is it too much to expect that the movement proper will have the usual allegro tempo? Maybe this will be a slow first movement, like, for example, Mozart's Adagio movement at the beginning of his first String Quartet, K. 80 (1770), or like the first-movement Adagio of his Piano Sonata, K. 282 (1774). Then again, perhaps Beethoven is about to revisit the *quasi una fantasia* tradition that he explored in his two Piano Sonatas Op. 27, even though he has *not* attached that subtitle to this work. Finally, is there a chance that an Allegro movement proper will begin immediately after the fer-mata at m. 2? If this were to happen, then without a doubt the largo idea would retrospectively become the kind of short but slow introduction that Beethoven, in a much different mood, later explored at the beginning of his Piano Sonata, Op. 78; or the largo could be regarded as comparable to the two-bar thematic introduc-tion, marked *Grave*, that Chopin made memorable as the opening gesture for his Sonata in B-flat Minor, Op. 35.[76]

Example 2.2. Beethoven, op. 31, no. 2, first movement, hypothetical opening

Especially with such later music in mind, one might expect Beethoven to lead directly from the unstable largo idea to something like the fully stable, tonic-defining version of the same that ultimately appears at mm. 21–22. Had the composition unfolded thus, an immediate registral connection from the low C♯ in the bass of m. 1 to the low D♮ of m. 21 would have been achieved. But it is precisely this unmediated clarification of his materials, this direct connection from the preludial protoform of an idea to the idea itself, that Beethoven avoids. And the allegro gesture that he chooses instead could only have been predicted through the gift of prescience. Described as "diametrically opposed" to the largo idea (Leon Plantinga), with its descending scalar motion from $\hat{5}$ to $\hat{1}$ creating an antithesis to the largo's triadic ascent (Dahlhaus),[77] the passage at mm. 3–6 would seem at first to relate to the largo only by dint of its violent contrast. But its tonal and phrase-structural design suggests otherwise.

After all, the harmonic content of the first bar of the allegro—the D-minor triad prolonged by a voice exchange (example 2.1, graph A)—now strives to clarify the key and the mode. A two-bar tonic-prolonging unit results from the immediate repetition of the new basic idea (abbreviated "bi" in example 2.1), and the repetition itself signals the beginning in miniature form of the type of theme that Schoenberg identified as the sentence (*Satz*).[78] To the initiating phase of the sentence, where, within the context of a tonic-prolongational progression, an idea is stated and then directly repeated, Caplin has given the name *presentation*. What follows—the *continuation*—tends to destabilize the presentation, mobilize the theme, and direct it toward a cadential goal.[79] Within Beethoven's miniature four-bar sentence (as a compression of the model eight-bar type), the continuation, beginning at m. 5, destabilizes the tonic harmony by reiterating the basic idea within a subdominant context; that harmony in turn prepares the half cadence (HC) at the downbeat of m. 6, marked "Adagio" and ending with a fermata. Thus, in retrospect, and strictly within the context of mm. 1–6, the two-bar largo idea might, indeed, be said to function as a thematic introduction: it leads toward a "thematic starting point" at m. 3—a short, possibly itself provisional, but tightly constructed "theme-type," at least in Schoenberg's sense of that term.[80] Dahlhaus himself had published an influential essay on the sentence, and yet he holds that the allegro passage is not "thematic in character"; moreover, he regards the tonic harmony at mm. 3–4 as only "provisional and not fixed."[81] We must assume for the moment that the bases for these views will be found by relating the events of mm. 1–6 to what follows at mm. 7–20, a passage about which Dahlhaus has little to say.

Like the fermata at m. 2, the adagio with its fermata at m. 6 seems to insist that we *participate* in the formal process by again allowing us time to wonder what might happen next. Might the by now predictable Allegro movement proper begin, in which case the entire passage at mm. 1–6 would retroactively become a dominant-oriented introduction? Once again, the next event could not have been predicted, if only because the chromatic third-related C-major sixth-chord at m. 7 bears no syntactic relationship to the dominant, with its C♯, at m. 6. But now, as the largo idea at mm. 7–8 again gives way to the allegro at m. 9, a recurring pattern can be noted: a varied sequential repetition of the opening materials has begun, and the choice of scale step for the sequence—the mediant (F major = III)—is a conventional one within the minor mode. Beethoven then extends the sequential 6-5 pattern to gain the subdominant through chromatic ascent, now stalling on that scale step while reducing the pattern to further chromatic ascent in sixths (example 2.1); thus approached, the goal of the sequence—the cadential six-four on the dominant at m. 13—becomes the first inevitability of the movement. The familiar middleground harmonic scheme i–III–V has emerged, and the cadential six-four strongly suggests that an authentic cadence in the tonic is at hand. But the cadential six-four has been achieved only after three starts-and-stops and an arduous ascent to the highest register and loudest dynamic thus far. If form in music, as in the other arts, involves the concepts of proportion and balance, then the improvisatory, cadenza-like flourish that extends the cadential six-four all the way from m. 13 to its resolution within the perfect authentic cadence (PAC) at mm. 20–21 seems logical if not necessary. The authentic cadence in the home tonic—the typical conclusion of a late eighteenth-century main theme—serves as the much delayed goal of the entire process at m. 21, and this throws into question Dahlhaus's unqualified proposition that the beginning of the sonata is "open-ended."

It is safe to say that Schoenberg himself would have regarded the authentic cadence at m. 21 as the closure of what has become a *main theme* (MT). Post-Schoenbergian formal theorists would undoubtedly invoke Schoenberg's concept of the *period* (antecedent-consequent) in order to substantiate that view. But given that the "consequent" is a much-varied and tremendously expanded *sequential* repetition of the antecedent, this improvisatory-like "consequent" can barely be perceived as such, so that even the most adamant of Schoenberg-oriented analysts would want to stress that only the vestiges of a periodic plan remain discernible in Beethoven's main theme.

At the basis of Schoenberg's notion of a theme one senses Riemann's simple correlation between "thematic" and "tonally closed," but Schoenberg's concept is at once more complex and more specific. As Caplin has put it, a theme for Schoenberg is "a complete musical complex that includes a soprano and bass counterpoint, a definite harmonic plan, a phrase-structural design, and cadential closure."[82] We can note that, instead of Riemann's "tonal closure," Schoenberg emphasizes the less restrictive "cadential closure" as the requisite ending for a theme; thus, for Schoenberg a theme might be modulatory, or it might end with a half cadence. When, however, the complete musical complex is nonmodulatory, and tonally closed, in the sense that it concludes with a perfect authentic cadence in the key that has served as its point of departure, then this type of theme often projects a complete middleground harmonic-contrapuntal structure of the kind that Schenkerians would describe as the replica of an *Ursatz*-form. My voice-leading graphs at example 2.1 demonstrate that Schenkerian analysts would have grounds for asserting the completion of a middleground *Ursatz*-replica at m. 21.[83]

With its alignment of formal terms at the appropriate places above the treble staff, graph A shows that the Schoenbergian antecedent and consequent each begin by establishing a perceptible resting point along the path of a large-scale ascending arpeggiation that leads to the primary tone $\hat{3}$—the F♮ at the melodic apex in m. 13. The conventional initial ascent (*Anstieg*) by arpeggiation tends to feature the tones of the tonic triad. As shown at graph B, and more simply in the background summary at example 2.3, Beethoven's <A–C–F> motion ruptures that convention, and only the contrapuntal 6-5 pattern of his sequence breaks the more fundamental parallel fifths evident within the middleground plan. There are

two characteristically Schenkerian but controversial features of the graphs: (1) the
3̂–2̂–1̂ descent of the fundamental line (the *Urlinie*-replica) is delayed until the last
minute, at the cadence in mm. 20–21, and it is more than somewhat concealed, for
motivic reasons discussed below; (2) only the unstable, nontonic six-four supports
the arrival of the primary tone. With the diagonal line in graph B that relates the
primary tone at m. 13 back to the tonic harmony at m. 3, I assert the primacy of
that tonic as the fundamental harmonic point of departure, and thus I challenge
Dahlhaus's view that it is "provisional and not fixed." Without acknowledging that
the contrapuntal 6-5 pattern at mm. 1–3 expresses the dependency of an unstable,
inverted dominant upon a stable tonic, we would have no grounds for claiming
that a varied, sequential repetition of that same pattern occurs at mm. 7–9 and
again at mm. 10–11; moreover, the miniature sentential design of the allegro
gesture that begins at m. 3 presupposes a genuine tonic-prolongational presentation. And yet, these features do not eradicate the impression that the fleeting
tonic of mm. 3–4 has been overpowered by the dominant harmony with which the
passage at mm. 1–6 begins and ends. The notion of a genuine tonic as scale step
(*Stufe*) at m. 3 becomes fully plausible only after the chromatically intensified stepwise ascent in the bass through the fifth-span from D♯ to A♮ at mm. 3–6 has been
retrospectively perceived as nested within a slower-moving ascent over the same
path from the D♯ of m. 3 to the dominant of m. 13 (see graph B). In short, although
the completed Schenkerian graph would seem to represent a single, final view, its
production itself entails the process of hearing the music *in time* and interpreting
it multidimensionally.

Example 2.3. Beethoven, op. 31, no. 2, first movement, background summary

It is, of course, the short-range arpeggiation of the largo idea at mm. 1–2 whose
goal—the a¹—is the first tone of the long-range arpeggiated ascent; Schenkerians
would not miss the opportunity to suggest that the latter is a transposed, organically inspired enlargement (*Vergrösserung*) of the initial arpeggiation idea. Put
simply, this particular Schenkerian reading proposes that an organic coherence
informs the underlying structure of the complete passage; as such, and like the
Schoenbergian formal view, this reading rubs against Dahlhaus's assertion that
the passage is unstable and loosely constructed. But to the extent that the graphing procedures at example 2.1 reveal *motivic* processes set in motion within the
passage, they reinforce Dahlhaus's processual outlook.

For analysts concerned with the more palpable implications of the opening
materials, it has become a commonplace to note that the initial allegro gesture looks

forward to the basic idea of the secondary theme at mm. 42–45. I shall argue that the manner in which the a¹ is prolonged within the allegro has an even more determinate series of consequences for the movement as a whole. As shown in example 2.1, graph A, the move to the subdominant at m. 5 permits the upper neighbor B♭ to initiate a partially concealed, chromatically inflected *turn* around the A♮, within which the lower neighbor G♯ itself takes the improvised turn at m. 6. Within the cadenza-like descent of the "consequent," the neighbor relationship B♭–A♮ recurs in sharp relief, thanks to the *sforzandos* at mm. 16–18, and it is this specific neighbor motive that covers up the fundamental $\hat{3}$–$\hat{2}$–$\hat{1}$ descent at mm. 20–21. If Dahlhaus is correct in perceiving at first that only with the elision (↔) of the cadence at m. 21 does the movement proper get under way, it is especially because with the new, tonic-grounded compound basic idea (CBI) at mm. 21–24, the arpeggiation figure in the bass now leads immediately to the treble's turn around A♮ in its simplest, most complete form. A process has led to a revelation, and thus to the effect of a "thematic starting point": the turn, no longer concealed, or provisional, enters directly into dialogue with the stabilized arpeggiation, assuming what promises to be a substantive motivic role within the movement.

To demonstrate that both the turn figure and the ascending arpeggiation infiltrate later materials of the exposition, I might simply point to the representations of these elements in the graphs at examples 2.1 and 2.4. But if "the path, not its end, is the goal," as Dahlhaus believed, then to treat recurring motives as finished products misses the path.[84] Adorno and Dahlhaus would say that what creates the semblance of motivic logic in tonal music has to do with our perception that old motives take on new *formal functions* as the movement unfolds. Beethoven would seem to have encouraged that perception by self-consciously treating form itself as if it were the manifestation of growth processes by which motivic ideas fulfill their destinies; as a result, motivic content simply cannot be separated from the formal process his music undergoes. At the least, then, the inclusion of formal terminology in a voice-leading graph can serve as an effort to capture something of that process. But formal annotations may be regarded only as a first step in that direction, since decisions about form, themselves a matter of interpretation, are dependent upon content, and since there remains the task of interpreting the motivic and formal interaction.

For instance, the graphs of the passage at mm. 21–41 in example 2.1 summarize a recurrence of the middleground arpeggiation idea, now made prominent in the foreground through the continued dialogue between the treble and the bass. The annotations in the graph propose that this arpeggiation begins within the context of what promises to be a stable, expanded sixteen-bar sentence in the home key. In other words, the formal design of the material, in coordination with the intensifying effect of the new continuous triplet motion, fully substantiates our initial impression that a main theme has finally begun. Of enormous significance here is that the bass line begins by once again traversing the stepwise ascent from D♮ to A♮ completed at mm. 3–6 and writ large over the middleground span of mm. 3–13; the resumption of that ascent at mm. 21–33 retrospectively validates the idea of a genuine tonic at m. 3. Meanwhile, the arpeggiation in question— the motion <A–D–F–A>—precisely outlines the home-tonic triad, as we might have expected the earlier long-range arpeggiation to have done. But by the point at which the arpeggiation is completed, its tonal meaning has changed, for the modulation into the secondary key, the dominant minor, has already begun. Technically speaking, the arpeggiation has in the end accomplished the simpler task of transferring the tone of its point of departure—the a^1—to the higher register, where it now resolves to the G♯ within the dominant of the new key. From the motivic viewpoint, the arpeggiation has conspired with all other elements of the formal plan to suggest the beginning of a main theme while instead fulfilling the function of a transition.

By tracing the path of the turn motive over the course of the secondary theme-group, as shown at example 2.4, we can assess Dahlhaus's view that the uniqueness of a work arises from the composer's blending of motivic logic with the functions and stations of a formal process. The turn had withdrawn from the transition process at m. 29, where the fragmentation technique (Heinrich Christoph Koch's *Zergliederung*) resulted in its elimination; it reenters with a vengeance at m. 41 to emphasize the point of arrival of the new dominant (see the last measure of example 2.1, graph A). Assuming the expanded form of two interlocking turns, this motive now becomes the propulsive, continuous accompanimental figure within the presentation and continuation of what I shall call the first secondary theme (ST^1: mm. 42–63).

The theme itself begins at m. 42 by prolonging the dominant of the new key achieved at the end of the transition—a technique that Beethoven had explored in his very first piano sonata, op. 2, no. 1, and one that destabilizes the theme while also obscuring the formal boundaries. Within the continuation-like fragmentation at m. 52, the dominant pedal and the turn figure break off just in time to allow for an impassioned descent from the highest to the lowest register explored thus far. Now at mm. 55–56, a new, imperious, harmonically reinterpreted form of the turn around A♮ brings a halt to the continuous eighth-note motion and specifically recalls the turn foreshadowed at mm. 3–6, then realized at mm. 22–24. The forcefulness of the recollection has led some analysts to regard m. 55 as the beginning of a new theme.[85] In Schoenberg's sense of that term, this would not be the case, since the preceding theme has not yet achieved cadential closure. Rather, the turn *prevents* closure through its insistence upon the noncadential i^6-chord within the new key; moving as it does to and from the Neapolitan as neighbor, the A-minor sixth-chord casts a dark shadow back to the opening chord of the movement, with which it holds register, voicing, and all but the C♮ in common. The immediate repetition of the two-bar turn (mm. 57–58) completes a presentation prolonging the i^6, and the continuation (mm. 59–63), with its characteristic fragmentation, regains the high f^3 of m. 49, as if compressing the motion to that same goal-tone in mm. 1–13 (compare examples 2.1 and 2.4), but then driving through the subdominant to the elided authentic cadence at the downbeat of m. 63. The passage at mm. 55–63 thus features a sentential design, but within the broader context its function is cadential: it provides an expanded cadential progression—i^6–iv–V–i—without which the theme would not have completed the process of beginning, middle, and end. Finally, if motivic "logic" can be taken simply to mean the perception that events are *motivated* by earlier events, then certainly the development of the turn motive follows a

Example 2.4. Beethoven, op. 31, no. 2, first movement, annotated graph for the exposition, mm. 42–87

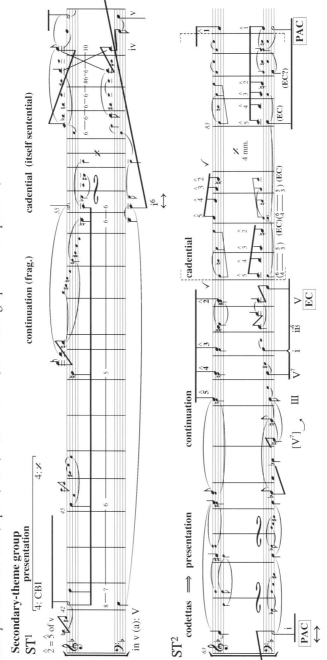

logical path—from accompanimental figure to the bolder, allusive initiator of the cadential phase of the theme. In both cases, the turn has been uniquely modified to accommodate the formal function, but the function has itself been qualified by the turn.

The elided cadence at m. 63 simultaneously marks a retrieval of the turn around A♮ and its repetition, such that one might imagine this new beginning to be a varied repetition of the preceding cadential function. But as a result of the inverted counterpoint relative to mm. 55–58, the turn now assumes the role of the bass; once we grasp the harmonic significance of this newest metamorphosis, the notion of a varied repetition must be abandoned. After all, an authentic cadence has just been achieved; within a soft (albeit *sforzando*-accentuated) dynamic, the turn embellishes a tonic pedal in support of the Picardie tonic major. Each of these characteristics points to the possibility that a postcadential codetta and its repetition have begun. Indeed, it is not inconceivable that the A-major tonic chord is about to resume its function as the home dominant within the repeat of the exposition. However, when the bass slips downward to the G♮ at m. 69, the idea of codettas must also be abandoned, if not forgotten. The new texture and the sequential repetition destabilize the passage in the manner of a continuation, and then a perfect authentic cadence is unequivocally promised at the downbeat of m. 75. If a continuation function has thus emerged, then what had promised to be first a varied repetition and then codettas at mm. 63–68 has now *become* a presentation (codettas ⇒ presentation) in the precise formal and phenomenological sense that I presently propose.

We are being asked by the music to exchange categories for others (Dahlhaus); the music, like Hegel's texts, needs to "be heard forward and backward at the same time" (Adorno). Moving backward, we might now sense that a *second* secondary theme (ST²) surreptitiously began at m. 63, and that its presentational beginning proceeded to a continuational middle. But what about its ending? An evaded cadence prevents the expected authentic closure at m. 75. That event motivates the exchange in double counterpoint at mm. 75–87, where, invoking the tradition that I have colloquially called the "one-more-time" technique, the repeated $\hat{5}$–$\hat{4}$–$\hat{3}$–$\hat{2}$ descents are again prevented by evaded cadences from closing to $\hat{1}$.[86] Perhaps harmonic closure finally occurs when the dominant pedal gives way to the tonic at m. 85, but we wait for the melodic closure until $\hat{1}$ is finally reached at m. 87. And at this point we may recognize that the entire passage at mm. 75–87 has served a *cadential* role. As the Adorno-Dahlhaus motto puts it, the process is—paradoxically—the result.

The performer who takes the repeat of the exposition forces us now to *revise* our impression that the opening of the movement might have been an introduction: genuine large-scale introductions are *not* included within the repeat of an exposition. But in the absence of an expositional repeat, our views about the opening might be ever more influenced by outstanding features of the development and recapitulation, among which the following must be recalled. First, for the listener who may have expected Beethoven's initial largo idea to lead directly to something like the allegro idea at mm. 21–22, it should come as reassuring that the development begins with precisely that order of events (at mm. 93–99). Here, admittedly, not one but three statements of the largo idea prepare the entry of the allegro, which begins in the unlikely region of F♯ minor (♯iii). Second, from that point forward, the development focuses exclusively upon the sentential but modulatory materials of mm. 21–41—the passage from the exposition that becomes the transition. Even the sentence-like design is maintained here, with the chromatically ascending 5-6 sequence now intensifying the original ascent by sixths. However, the climactic goal of the developmental core is the traditional one, the home dominant at m. 121, after which the *tremolando* effected by the double-neighbor simplification of the turn from m. 41 maintains the intensity within a "standing-on-the-dominant" (*das Stehen auf der Dominante*).[87] An expansion of the B♭–A neighbor motion over the span of mm. 139–43 completes the diminuendo and the descent into the low register, and the resolution to A♮ at m. 143 coincides with the return of the largo idea from mm. 1–2 (example 2.5). Finally, both the largo idea and its sequential repetition from mm. 7–8 now yield the well-known recitatives that they originally seemed to promise in the exposition. Although the allegro from mm. 3–6 follows upon the first recitative, the second recitative leads to an altogether new allegro (mm. 159–71), within which the chromatically ascending 5-6 sequence from the development again achieves the home dominant (at m. 171), this time for the

Example 2.5. Beethoven, op. 31, no. 2, first movement, mm. 137–62

purpose of preparing the recapitulation of the complete secondary theme-group in the home key.[88]

Decisions about the large-scale formal divisions of sonata-form movements often depend on the uncomplicated task of comparing the exposition with the recapitulation. Suffice it to say that in this case the beginning of the recapitulation has the effect of obfuscating rather than clarifying the design at the beginning of the exposition. It is not uncommon for composers to condense their main-theme materials and introduce new transitions in the recapitulation; nor is it unusual for a main theme to avoid closure in the recapitulation, merging instead with the beginning of the transition function. But recapitulations in late eighteenth-century sonata forms tend to be marked by a return of the main-theme materials in the home key. With this, we come to perhaps the most obvious reason why Dahlhaus implies that the passage at mm. 21–41 in the exposition is no longer a *main* theme: it does not return in the recapitulation. In fact, what does return is Dahlhaus's apparent introduction, now condensed and transformed to such a degree as to exaggerate those qualities that had originally made it seem to be not yet a theme. Enveloped as they are within the blur of a sustained pedal, the recitatives sound "disembodied": they would seem to come from outside the movement itself— "from a fathomless, locationless depth of subjectivity whose mark on the work is not a trace but a disfigurement," as Lawrence Kramer proposes.[89] And yet, does the return of the opening material confirm that it really was the main theme in the first place? Has Dahlhaus overstated his case?

With the expression "introduction *becomes* main theme," that is, Introduction ⇒ MT, I propose that a reconciliation is in order. Neither the periodic view of the opening passage nor the *Ursatz*-form of the graph at example 2.1 manages to capture the formal ambiguity that Dahlhaus astutely addresses. But we cannot ignore the authentic cadential closure at m. 21, or deny the return of the opening materials at the only moment later that can thus be perceived as the beginning of a recapitulation. To overlook these events is tantamount to proposing that Beethoven did not compose the movement against the background of the sonata-form model; and yet, without taking that model into account, Dahlhaus would have no basis whatsoever for his claims.

Understood as an express reference to Hegelian thought, the term "becoming" strives to accentuate the process, rather than the result, of Beethoven's opening passage. Becoming unites a concept and its apparent opposite—in this case, introduction and main theme. Once the moment of becoming has been grasped, neither the concept nor its opposite can remain one-sided, in the sense of fixed and separate; rather, main theme can no longer be imagined outside the context of introduction. This, then, is how I wish to use the expression "introduction becomes main theme": rather than favoring the notion of a main theme as the final verdict, the expression suggests that *what has become* preserves our memory of the original conflict.

Had Schoenberg and Dahlhaus been willing simply to endorse Wilhelm Furtwängler's notion of *Fernhören*—"distance-hearing"—as a valuable premise of Schenker's theory,[90] then perhaps they might have perceived the long-distance arpeggiations shown in my graphs and the gradual emergence of the turn figure as manifestations of the developing variation of a *Grundgestalt* at mm. 1–6. Conversely, had Schenker not disdained the notion that foreground ideas might serve as generative source subjects, he might have encouraged greater attention in general to the perception of music as process. The background idea of an *Ursatz*-form at mm. 1–21 need not be regarded as incompatible with the foreground observation that the passage *raises the question* of an introduction. If there were only one value to be gained from the Beethoven-Hegelian tradition, it would be the directive that in Beethoven's music questions of this kind must be pursued.

Post-Dahlhausian Critiques

Since the publication in 1995 of the article that has served as the basis for this chapter thus far,[91] it has been my great fortune that both William Caplin and James Hepokoski (see chapter 1) have addressed Dahlhaus's views on the "Tempest" Sonata and my interpretation of these. Their critiques offer fresh perspectives on the first movement of the "Tempest," while driving home the likelihood that there will never be a last word about this endlessly provocative work. The essays by Caplin and Hepokoski afford me the opportunity to offer new observations in response to theirs.[92]

The question of a secondary theme

Whereas Caplin credits me with having "accurately" identified "the component formal functions within the overall sonata form"(87), Hepokoski posits a vastly different outlook on the movement's exposition. As scholars of Hepokoski and Warren Darcy's Sonata Theory understand, a sonata exposition will have *no secondary theme* if its transition is not punctuated by a *medial caesura* (MC)—"a brief, rhetorically reinforced break or gap that serves to divide an exposition into two parts, tonic and dominant."[93] The absence of such a break at or after m. 41, where the dominant of the new key is achieved, and the persistence of the dominant pedal in the following measures press Hepokoski to argue against the idea of a secondary theme and in favor of a "continuous," rather than two-part, exposition. But it is the "generic strain," the "tension" between two readings—continuous exposition (with no secondary theme), or perhaps a secondary theme beginning at m. 42 (but with a "problematically articulated" MC at m. 41)—that is the "central expressive point" of this passage for Hepokoski (194).[94] And here, despite their opposing views, Caplin and Hepokoski verge on reinforcing each other's overall formal interpretation, as well as mine.

For Caplin, the Hepokoski/Darcy MC as defined above is not a requirement for the ending of a transition as followed by the beginning of a secondary theme. But like Hepokoski, Caplin focuses upon Beethoven's persistent dominant pedal (my example 2.4 shows that it remains in effect all the way from m. 41 to m. 54) as a source of considerable formal ambiguity. Granted, many of Beethoven's secondary themes begin with dominant harmony, often via extended dominant pedal. Like me, Hepokoski mentions Beethoven's first piano sonata, op. 2, no. 1, as an example; Caplin's table 4.1 (102) classifies all twenty instances of this technique within the composer's piano sonatas. Moreover, the tradition of extending the half-cadential goal of a transition by means of a postcadential standing-on-the-dominant—the Hepokoski/Darcy "dominant-lock"—had become established well before Beethoven's time. Thus in Caplin's view, "first-time" listeners would "probably assume" that the dominant pedal at mm. 41–54 "functions post-cadentially as the last part of the transition." Only by working backward, from the decisive PAC in m. 63 to what Caplin and I regard as an exclusively cadential unit at mm. 55–63, will it be confirmed that the dominant-prolonging passage at mm. 42–54 can be heard as a "loosened" presentation (mm. 42–49: tonic and dominant versions of the compound basic idea reversed), followed by a continuation (mm. 50–53: fragmentation) that leads to the cadential function, as shown in my example 2.4. In short, Caplin endorses my view that a genuine ST¹ emerges at mm. 42–63; he holds, however, that we will not understand this to be the case until the moment when the dominant prolongation "leads so logically into the cadential unit." Whereas Hepokoski acknowledges ambiguity with regard to the formal function of the passage at hand, Caplin goes further: he concludes that "the end of the transition 'becomes' the beginning of the subordinate theme" (103). In effect, Caplin has shrewdly amplified my claim in 1995 (and on p. 46 above) that the dominant prolongation at the beginning of ST¹ "destabilizes the theme while obscuring the formal boundaries."

That I apparently missed this golden opportunity for a processual reinterpretation can most likely be attributed to my early experiences as a performer of the sonata, which occurred prior to my efforts to write about it as an analyst. Although Beethoven calls for a *subito piano* at m. 41, the undisguised turbulence at the onset there of the interlocking turn figure has never quite made it possible for me to pretend for a moment that I am simply riding the quiet wave of a postcadential standing-on-the-dominant. A "recessive dynamic" would have been useful for creating this effect, but Caplin admits that, with the crescendo leading to *forte* at mm. 49–52, "Beethoven makes it difficult to project a recessive character" (119). Perhaps the pianist could choose the crescendo as the very moment for imagining an end-of-transition to "have become" the middle of a secondary theme; but already by m. 45 the growing intensity and the gradual registral ascent of the *agitato* idea drawn from the initial allegro gesture suggest, both pianistically and psychologically, an anxious struggle toward a goal, rather than the complacency of having already achieved one.

Introduction or main theme

Caplin advances a retrospective formal reinterpretation where I do not, but he takes issue with all three moments in which this is precisely what I do advocate. In reference to the first of these, the opening of the movement, Caplin and Hepokoski again adopt positions of surprising similarity, differences in their respective theories notwithstanding. The tone of Caplin's argument can be gently caricatured as follows: how could *any* listener who understands the nature of classical introductions, main themes, and transitions *possibly even consider* hearing an introduction at the beginning of the "Tempest"? Hepokoski notes that "Beethoven provided bars 1–21 with strikingly nontraditional music" (184), but he regards Dahlhaus's "new-path" proclamation about processual form in the "Tempest" to be "overdrawn"—"a declaration of cultural solidarity with a long line of Austro-Germanic writers and high-modernist twentieth-century composers" (186). In the end, the main-theme function of the opening of the "Tempest" is just as "generically unambiguous" for Hepokoski (193) as it is for Caplin.[95]

It can be mentioned here that "new-path" reactions to the opening of the "Tempest" have become legion, and that many of these have emanated from writers who associate themselves neither with Dahlhaus's idea of processual form nor with Austro-Germanic solidarity. A case in point is Richard Kramer's critique of Barry Cooper's speculations about Beethoven's single extant sketch for the first movement—in Kramer's words, "an entry so stunning as to suggest that we are witness to some vaulting conceptual leap."[96] For Kramer, "the opening figure signifies the spontaneous process of improvisation"; there is a new "turning inward" here, "toward a newly subjective figuring of the composer's voice—of the composer as protagonist." "If Emanuel Bach's fantasies, and Mozart's, begin on tonics and play within the ground rules of genre, Beethoven's sonata begins a step earlier in the process. Genre is reinvented. That is its point." Here Kramer refers to the fact that in *no* piano sonata by Haydn, Mozart, or Beethoven prior to the "Tempest" did these composers begin on an inverted dominant.[97]

To Dahlhaus and to me Caplin would seem to ascribe the view that mm. 1–21 of the "Tempest" might at first be heard as a *slow* introduction—a claim that neither Dahlhaus nor I have made, and one that would seem preposterous: only five of the opening 21 measures take a slow tempo. Caplin's straw-man argument against a slow introduction proceeds as follows (89–90): (1) slow introductions do not include passages in the fast tempo of the exposition proper; (2) as contrasted with the underlying "periodic hybrid" of the opening of the "Tempest," slow introductions rarely exhibit the conventional forms typical of main themes; (3) they tend to end with a half cadence, followed by a postcadential standing-on-the-dominant (but in *Classical Form* Caplin acknowledges exceptions to this rule, for example, the elided PAC at the end of the slow introduction of Beethoven's Piano Sonata Op. 13);[98] and (4) slow introductions are not included within the repeat of the exposition. (Nor, it might be added, do they tend to return before or at the beginning of the development or recapitulation; the return of fragments of the introduction before the beginning of both these sections in op. 13 again serves as an exception.) With this last point, the possibility of a long-range retrospective reinterpretation seems to have been dismissed by Caplin: we cannot know that mm. 1–21 will be repeated until the pianist repeats the exposition.

The first point above is the crucial one—how to interpret Beethoven's alternating largo and allegro tempi. Hepokoski compares the opening largo idea with what he regards as initiatory, or preparatory, modules heard most especially at the beginning of main themes in minor-mode symphonies (and "often sounded in stern octaves"; two examples from Haydn as well as the opening "'fate' motto" of Beethoven's Fifth Symphony are cited); but Hepokoski concedes that such opening gestures appear in the allegro tempo of the movement proper (187–90). (The anomaly of Beethoven's initial largo tempo and his mysterious, rolled sixth-chord serves as Hepokoski's point of departure for an intriguing "predator-prey" narrative as extended over the complete movement.) For Caplin, the opening largo idea— much too short to constitute a slow introduction—can plausibly be understood to serve as a *thematic* introduction to the antecedent phrase of the main theme, one of the options I myself raised in 1995 (see "2: intro?" in my example 2.1). But especially given that the largo idea returns to introduce the consequent phrase at mm. 7–8, "the notion that an 'introduction becomes main theme' would not apply, since a thematic introduction is already embraced within the structural expanse of the theme it is introducing" (90).

Let us pause here to note that Caplin's and Hepokoski's arguments in support of an unambiguous main theme at the beginning of the "Tempest" systematically draw upon precedents and later manifestations of what can unequivocally be regarded as introductions and main themes. Caplin stresses that the opening of the "Tempest" cannot be heard as a slow introduction because he knows of no slow introductions that include the fast tempo of the exposition proper. *But neither Caplin nor Hepokoski offers a single precedent for a compound-tempo main theme.* The "stop-and-go fermatas" within the thematic introduction to the main theme of the Fifth Symphony, completed six years after the "Tempest," come the closest for Hepokoski to Beethoven's strategy in the "Tempest." In the absence of precedents, both authors place the "Tempest" within the context of broader, generic features of classical main themes—their sometimes "hesitant" nature (Caplin, 95), their "expanded-upbeat quality" (Hepokoski, 193), relative to the more ongoing, directional nature of transitions. For Caplin, only a lack of understanding about these characteristics can account for why "so many critics" hear an introduction at the start of the "Tempest" sonata (91).[99]

Caplin invokes Leonard B. Meyer's distinction between primary ("syntactical") and secondary ("statistical") parameters to compare the fundamental harmonic, tonal, and phrase-structural stability of main themes with their tendency toward instability through such secondary details as rhythmic discontinuities, textural contrasts, and dynamic changes; these secondary qualities "work together to project an indecisiveness and lack of clear momentum, and so they give the impression that the music is not yet entirely launched, in short, 'introductory' in nature" (91).[100] Along similar lines, the opening of the "Tempest" serves as a "large-scale anacrusis" for Hepokoski, and "all such anacrusis-passages suggest a process of 'becoming,' followed by 'arrival'" (193). By contrast, transitions are harmonically, tonally, and formally less stable but "more secure"—more uniform in respect to texture, durational patterning, and dynamics (Caplin, 91–92).[101] "The forward-driving gears of a sonata movement often clench in earnest only with a *forte*-[transition] acceptance" of an "idea proposed more modestly" by, say, a "quieter, closed, more static" main theme (Hepokoski, 193). Put simply, both authors reject my view that m. 21 of the "Tempest" marks the beginning of "MT ⇒ Transition."

Perhaps it is no coincidence that both authors choose the opening of Beethoven's Piano Sonata Op. 2, No. 3 to exemplify their views (Caplin also discusses the openings of op. 10, no. 1, op. 13, and the other two sonatas of op. 31).[102] Surely no one would deny that the transition in op. 2, no. 3—with its "*fortissimo* outburst of steady sixteenth-note activity" at m. 13, and its textural homophony (Caplin, 92)—provides the forward-driving gears of this movement. But now for a response. I counter that a comparison of the opening of the "Tempest" with the main theme of op. 2, no. 3—in fact, a comparison with *any* of Beethoven's main themes in his piano sonatas prior to this piece—thoroughly undercuts, rather than strengthens, the idea of an unambiguous main theme here, while at the same time underscoring the exceptional novelty of this extraordinary passage. Whereas, for instance, the initial rests, the *sforzandos*, and the syncopations within the main theme of op. 2, no. 3 arguably create the effect of hesitation, these "destabilizing forces" (Caplin, 92) hardly disrupt the *rock-solid stability* of this theme's purely tonic orientation and its single, steady allegro tempo. By comparison, the unstable *sequential* design of the opening of the "Tempest" and its alternating tempi continue to strike this analyst, like others, as without precedent and thus eminently worthy of a new formal category. In point of fact, one could propose a continuum over the span of Beethoven's first-movement sonata forms up to and well beyond 1802, in which his main themes become ever more "introduction-like"; within such a continuum, the opening of the "Tempest" would emphatically mark a processual highpoint.[103]

ST² and the final cadence of the exposition

I have proposed that, subsequent to the elided close of ST¹ at m. 63, the passage at mm. 63–68 might at first be heard as postcadential codettas, retrospectively to become ST²'s presentation phrase (thus codettas ⇒ presentation). Caplin contests that view, on the basis that the upper voice of this passage, rather than stably focusing upon the tonic scale degree, actively ascends from $\hat{3}$ to $\hat{5}$ and also creates "an enormous registral expansion" (109). Had the ascent continued upward at mm. 68–69, to the tonic pitch an octave higher, hence fulfilling the promise of a $\hat{1}$–$\hat{3}$–$\hat{5}$–$\hat{8}$ arpeggiation, it would have looked forward to the *forte* codetta (closing section) of the exposition of Beethoven's Overture to *Coriolanus*, Op. 62 (1807), as shown at example 8.4 in Caplin's *Classical Form*;[104] thus, the question here of potential codettas or immediate presentation does not seem critical to me. Conversely, the question as to just where we reach the close of ST²—that is, the final cadence of the exposition—should be of interest, if not of serious concern, to analysts, performers, and listeners alike. With his answer to this question, Caplin stands alone. Hepokoski flatly proclaims that the "essential expositional closure"(EEC) occurs at m. 87 (200). I equivocate (m. 87 or m. 85?). Of the many writers about the "Tempest," Caplin is to my knowledge the first to choose m. 75.

The debate hinges upon whether or not Beethoven effects an *evaded* cadence at m. 75, as I have proposed. Caplin disputes this view, despite the absence of a "literal tonic bass" on the downbeat of this measure—and despite, I shall add, the composer's request there for a *subito piano*, a telltale sign of cadential evasion. Looking beyond mm. 75–76, Caplin infers a i–V$^{4/3}$–i^6–V progression within the inverted counterpoint of mm. 77–78; he proposes this as the "basic contrapuntal model" for mm. 75–76 and then argues that the entire passage at mm. 75–87 is *tonic*-prolonging (112–13), in contradistinction to the dominant prolongation I show at example 2.4. With this reading in place, Caplin must now conclude that "there remains just one candidate for cadential closure—the downbeat of bar 75": here, and only here for Caplin, "a genuine cadential dominant (b. 74) resolves to tonic" (113). But given that "the expected authentic cadence never materializes," Caplin posits a new moment for retrospective reinterpretation: beginning at m. 75, "evaded cadences becoming codettas" (115). With this conclusion, Caplin apparently acknowledges the *effect* of the repeated cadential evasions I show at example 2.4, even though his idea of tonic prolongation at mm. 75–87 eliminates these.[105]

Caplin opposes the view that the essential expositional closure occurs at m. 87 (or at m. 85) because "this moment is not marked by an independent cadential progression from dominant to tonic" (113). His objection to my reading would seem to betray a misunderstanding of the technique I have defined as the "one-more-time" repetition. Preceding a series of such repetitions, "the dominant whose resolution to a cadential tonic is evaded is a penultimate event within a disruptive process that locally breaks the linear descent."[106] As shown at example 2.4, the cadential progression that Caplin has not found in my reading consists of the indisputably cadential dominant at m. 74, where a fundamental linear descent achieves 2̂, and its eventual resolution to the tonic at m. 87, where the soprano voice finally reaches the tonic scale degree. I have attempted to portray the events between these two cadential pillars as incursive "one-more-time" repetitions that delay the cadence by prolonging the cadential dominant on its way to the tonic. In light of the possibility that this interpretation escaped Caplin and others in their reading of my 1995 article, large vertical brackets now circumscribe the "one-more-time" passage at example 2.4, and a clearer effort has been made, via a broken beam, to connect the bass tone of the cadential dominant at m. 74 with its last manifestation at m. 83.[107]

As with the question of where the ST^1 of the "Tempest" might begin, a performer's instinct underlies my reluctance to relinquish the idea of genuine evaded cadences in mm. 74–85. Performances of this passage to which I have aspired—for example, Richard Goode's 1983 recording,[108] or the brilliant 2002 recording by Malcolm Bilson[109]—are ones in which Beethoven's crescendo at m. 72–74 is given full force so that the *subito piano* at m. 75 can be truly *subito*, creating the effect of an involuntary catching of the breath, as if the chance to reach safety and closure has just been snatched away. In what follows, Goode and Bilson allow for no letup in tempo, and they highlight the contrapuntal exchange between right and left hands by giving a crescendo to the *ascending* line within each two-bar unit, rather than focusing on the descent. At the end of the passage, especially Goode's crescendo within the composer's hairpin dynamic is huge; he saves his diminuendo for the very last second. In short, to my ears these pianists do not play this passage as a series of codettas; instead, they press on, in search of a cadential goal that they find only at m. 87. Within the overall context of the movement, this approach seems right to me.

But as Caplin suggests, alternative pianistic treatments of this passage, as well as of the others he addresses, may be chosen to elicit alternative intuitions about their form-functional roles (116–22). Elsewhere, and especially in chapter 5 of this study, I argue that Beethoven's music initiates new stylistic directions whereby, as conventional classical formal processes become gradually transformed or "deformed," new cases of genuine formal ambiguity increasingly arise; in such cases, it is as if the composer invites the *performer* to be "in charge"—to play a determinative role in our understanding of the formal process. Thus, the alliance between composer and performer—with both of these understood as *listeners par excellence,* to say the least—grows all the stronger as composers of the early nineteenth century in Europe react to the impact of Beethoven's music. If the debate among Caplin, Hepokoski, and myself about formal processes in Beethoven's "Tempest" has been warranted, then perhaps Beethoven might occasionally invite the *performer* to help us settle our differences.[110]

CHAPTER Three

The Processual Legacy of the Late Eighteenth Century

James Webster's *bête noire* in his seminal 1991 work on Haydn's instrumental music is the notion of "Classical style" as it came to be promulgated in the early twentieth century. Then and in numerous publications ever since, Webster has argued that this concept remains "anachronistic, inherently ambiguous, and shot through with conservative aesthetic-ideological baggage." For Webster, who rightly holds that Haydn's music "was masterful in every period of his life, including the earliest," an insidious aspect of the concept is that its valuative component "banishes Haydn's early and middle music, indeed all pre-1780 music, to a pre-Classical ghetto."[1] Along lines distinct from but similar to my account of the Beethoven-Hegelian tradition, Webster portrays the development of the notion of Classical style as one in which ideas both organicist and evolutionist (in the "teleological/reductive sense") found their godsend in Adolf Sandberger's mediating principle of *thematische Arbeit* (translated as "thematic development"). For subsequent historians, it was primarily upon the discovery of this principle—and only after trial, error, and the inevitable crisis (clearly of the *Bildungsweg* type)—that Haydn and Mozart achieved the mature, classical perfection of "absolute" music through the grand synthesis "of homophony and counterpoint, traditional and galant, strict and free, *Kenner* and *Liebhaber*."[2] Webster's critique of this "fairy-tale" narrative avoids references to post-Hegelian dialectics, but surely a Hegelian influence upon the narrative can be sensed. For Haydn scholars who share Webster's dissatisfaction with such standard ideas of "Classical style," disdain might not be too strong a word for the privileging of Beethoven's music that has characterized the Beethoven-Hegelian tradition.[3]

Webster's foremost aim in the 1991 text is to show that Haydn's numerous "through-composed" and "cyclically integrated" works, as represented by his "Farewell" Symphony No. 45 (1772), "call into question the notion that coherent multimovement instrumental cycles were unknown before Beethoven."[4] Toward that goal, Webster devotes a chapter to the topics of "progressive, nonsymmetrical form" and "the rhetoric of instability" in Haydn's symphonies. There he laments the tendency within Haydn literature to favor "form-as-shape" (in German, *Form*) over "form-as-process" (*Formung*); noting that studies by Donald Francis Tovey, Edward T. Cone, Charles Rosen, and Leonard B. Meyer offer exceptions to this rule, he adds that, characteristically, not a single movement by Haydn had yet been considered in narrative theories about music.[5] As Webster proceeds, one begins to discover the subtext; or, rather, one starts to experience the full weight of the anonymous summary statement on his book's jacket cover: "[Professor Webster] stresses the need for a greater appreciation of Haydn's early music and of his stature as Beethoven's equal."

To the many who, like me, hold Haydn's achievement in the highest regard, the need for this stress might seem superfluous. And those who cannot imagine Haydn as Beethoven's "equal" may have been stunned by Webster's claim. Equal in what respects? Webster strategically saves his definitive answers for his final chapter, and he presents them in the form of responses to his close readings of selected statements about Beethoven's Third and Fifth Symphonies by, respectively, Joseph Kerman and Lawrence Kramer. Summarizing those technical and rhetorical features that Kerman claims Beethoven "perfected at a stroke" in the Third, Webster concludes: "The verdict is obvious. The Farewell Symphony incorporates every one of these features, and it integrates them in a through-composed, end-oriented work, as radical as any from Beethoven's middle period." Moreover, by allowing the D-major interlude of his first movement to "remain mysterious and unresolved" until the end of the double finale, the "*ancien-régime*, 'pre-Classical' [Haydn]... achieved greater coherence in his symphony as a whole than the 'revolutionary' [Beethoven] of 1803."[6] Webster's selections from Kramer's essay emphasize, in turn, that Kramer sees Beethoven's Fifth as a "re-thinking, a detailed problematizing, of the formal impulses that support the Classical symphony," wherein, for example, "ruthless expressivity is aimed at producing a crisis," and "a dialectical antagonism springs up between [tonic] minor and [tonic] major"; finally, "procession gives way to process." Webster concludes that "every word of [Kramer's] description applies with equal justice to the Farewell."[7]

It seems safe to say that, while no two listeners can be expected to hear the same music in precisely the same way, listeners past and present who have heard both Haydn's "Farewell" Symphony and Beethoven's Fifth have experienced these two works in very different ways—and this despite the two composers' shared compositional techniques. Webster's tribute to Haydn's unequaled achievements came none too soon; but in resting his case primarily on a catalogue of Haydn's technical innovations, and in particular on the standard of "coherence" as a substitute for the "organicist shibboleth of 'unity,'" he has fruitfully encouraged historians and analysts since then to ask ever more intently how and why Haydn's and Beethoven's music would seem to inhabit different aesthetic, dramatic, and psychological realms. As this chapter unfolds, I too pursue that question, by redirecting it toward Webster's and Kramer's focus upon form-as-process.

Among Kramer's many observations about Beethoven's Fifth not discussed by Webster in 1991, one in particular stands out as inapplicable to Haydn's "Farewell," its popularity notwithstanding: Kramer ascribes to the Fifth "an excessive fame that subliminally obscures and even degrades the music." The question as to just why this happened has motivated ardent full-length inquiries into the circumstances of Beethoven reception by such authors as Elisabeth E. Bauer, Scott Burnham, Tia DeNora, David B. Dennis, Leon Botstein, Stephen Rumpf, Michael Spitzer, and Mark Evan Bonds, among others.[8] Also focusing on Beethoven, but upon the legacy that he inherited, rather than on his reception, scholars too numerous to count here have, over many decades, addressed the topic of Beethoven's indebtedness to Mozart and Haydn. In this domain, the overviews and contributions of Lewis Lockwood and Elaine Sisman have, like those of Webster, been invaluable.

Lockwood's subject in his 1994 article, as clarified by its title, is Beethoven's Mozart legacy, from the outset due in part to the "Mozart vogue" that Maximilian Franz, a Mozart enthusiast, initiated when he succeeded Maximilian Friedrich in Bonn as Elector in 1784. With Mozart performances in town, including the teenage Beethoven's own renditions of Mozart concertos, and with Mozart's works well represented in the Bonn library, Beethoven in the 1780s "was learning deep lessons from his study of Mozart, in chamber music above all but possibly also in other genres."[9] "Of course, his central influence in the 1780s was not solely Mozart, in view of Haydn's importance and the availability of Haydn's works in Bonn, but it was primarily Mozart at this time."[10] For Lockwood, Mozart's influence remained powerful throughout Beethoven's career, from his "imitation" phase (the formative Bonn period), through a phase of "appropriation" (during his first Vienna decade, from 1792 to around 1802–3), and onward toward an "assimilation" of all he had learned from both Haydn and Mozart (within his "unmistakably Beethovenian" middle period), to be followed by a distancing from the world of those two composers but also by stylistic manifestations of "his personal allegiance to their roles as fathers and masters."[11]

The material evidence for this narrative (another *Bildungsweg*) is abundant, as marshaled by Lockwood and others. Not only do we have the young Beethoven, evidently in 1790, acknowledging a passage "aus Mozart gestohlen" in one of his sketches, and then revising it ("Beethowen ipse"),[12] or Beethoven, in his first years in Vienna, composing variation sets on arias from Mozart operas as well as copying out parts of Mozart's String Quartets K. 387 and K. 464 in preparation for composing his quartets op. 18. More telltale for Haydn, Mozart, and Beethoven scholars are examples of "Beethoven's modeling procedures, in which he based some of his pieces on works by Haydn and Mozart, choosing the ordering of movements, their keys and formal types, and details of texture, harmonic planning, and even melodic contour, as templates."[13] But Elaine Sisman warns readers that they "will find one essay declaring a piece to be based clearly on Mozartean procedures, while another will assert the same piece to be based on Haydn. How does one tell?"[14] Signs of appropriation in Beethoven's First Symphony, Op. 21 (1800)—his "homage," "laced with one-upmanship," to the "C major symphony tradition"— prompt Sisman to present an even-handed analysis of his debts, to *both* Mozart's "Jupiter" and Haydn's Symphony No. 97; in the end, however, "it is from [Haydn's] 97th that Beethoven derives the most striking effects of his first movement."[15]

Sisman's opening account of Beethoven's musical inheritance takes a broad, synoptic approach. Her review of "some of the dominant elements in European music in the last few decades of the eighteenth century" underscores the mutability of distinctions between, on the one hand, genres, styles, and rhetorical "topics" that had become conventions by then, and, on the other, "oppositions" such as public versus private performance venues, *Kenner* versus *Liebhaber*, "difficult vs. accessible, gallant vs. learned, elevated vs. plain, serious vs. popular, and tragic vs. comic." In the light of these often overlapping categories, she concludes that "genre-types and movement-types were complex, multifarious, and sophisticated entities at the end of the eighteenth century, offering an extraordinary range of expressive and formal possibilities."[16]

Rather than proposing specific one-to-one correspondences between works by Beethoven and their "models," I look back from the turn of the nineteenth century for broad indications of Beethoven's lineage in respect to form, and thus I follow the synoptic model that Sisman offers within the first part of her essay. But I turn here to a distinctive aspect of his inheritance that neither she nor Lockwood discusses, nor one that has played a central role in studies of Beethoven reception, yet one that returns to Webster's concern for *Formung*—form-as-process. To put it simply, let me propose that the breadth and sophistication of formal and expressive options Sisman observes in late eighteenth-century music can be attributed in no small measure to an ever-growing interest in processual approaches to form.

What do I mean by this, in the case of three of Beethoven's predecessors—Haydn, Clementi, and Mozart? And how, in the long run, might a consideration of late eighteenth-century formal processes contribute to the idea that both stylistic continuity and an undeniable change of direction mark the music of Beethoven's first maturity? For answers to these questions, I begin by revisiting the oft-discussed opening of a sonata-form movement by Haydn—the first movement of his String Quartet in C Major, Op. 33, No. 3.[17]

Haydn—String Quartet in C Major, Op. 33, No. 3 (Hob. III:39), First Movement

Like others, I am drawn here to a movement from the op. 33 quartets partly because of their sociological significance. As historians know well, in 1779 a new contract between Haydn and his patron, Prince Nikolaus Esterházy, "removed the restrictive clause in the original agreement that forbade him to compose for anyone else without prior permission,"[18] thus freeing him to accept commissions, make new dedications, and sell his music to publishers on his own. In 1781 Haydn took it upon himself to solicit subscribers for manuscript copies of the op. 33 quartets in advance of their publication. Whether as a smart sales pitch, or for other good reasons as well, Haydn, like Beethoven around 1802, promised that these works would be "of an entirely new and special kind" ("auf eine gantz neue besondere art"). By the early 1800s, Haydn, now in failing health, may have regretted that he could not himself continue to forge his way into the new expressive realms opened by Beethoven's "new path,"[19] but Beethoven clearly would not have found that path without the precedent of both Haydn's music and his enterprising approach to marketing. Many have noted that the op. 33 quartets mark a turning point in communicative strategies among composers, performers, and listeners. With these works Haydn invited a new, anonymous class of performers and listeners into the private, aristocratic realm of chamber music. In doing so, and having all but created the genre of the string quartet (his opp. 9, 17, and 20 quartets had already enjoyed wide distribution throughout the continent), he would now not only further establish and affirm quartet and sonata conventions but also initiate new listeners into the delight of recognizing that conventions can be jestfully broken down.[20]

As with all the other five sonata-form first movements within the op. 33 quartets, Haydn opens this movement with a main theme (MT); his exposition begins with an ultimately unified harmonic-contrapuntal process that closes, at m. 18, with a cadence in the home key (example 3.1). But the opening chord of the theme already breaks from a tradition well established in countless earlier movements by Haydn himself and others: rather than beginning with the conventional root-position tonic, the initial three bars of the theme withhold the root, suggesting instead the less stable I^6-chord. Or, as Webster has put it, these opening bars are "baseless": the opening sonority is "off-tonic," because the true bass voice—the cello—does not enter until the second beat of m. 4.[21] To make sure that we do not miss this unsettling detail, Haydn also withholds the "chirping" entrance of his initial melodic idea (bi) until the second bar; thus, we hear only the undefined interval of the sixth in the introductory m. 1, as if we are supposed to be eaves-dropping on a movement that is already in midstream. For Richard Kramer: "To begin this way, in the provocation of such ambiguity, is to set a plot in motion."[22]

The five-bar compound basic idea (CBI) that burgeons from *piano* to *forte* in mm. 2–6 now unequivocally proposes C major as the tonic, by reference to its dominant-seventh harmony. But then two beats of silence mark the end of the idea, giving us a split second to think about what might happen next. Listeners today who know the Allegro main theme of Beethoven's First Symphony, premiered in 1800, might recognize that Haydn's next event—the sequential repetition of his CBI in and on what would be the supertonic (ii) in C major—sets a precedent for Beethoven: but the completely unpredictable onset of that sequence might well be just as surprising for present-day first-time listeners as it must have been for audiences in 1781. To say the least, Haydn's sequence has the effect of destabilizing the key that his opening had so firmly proposed.[23]

And yet, the emphatic confirmation of C major within the CBI in mm. 2–6, as followed by the sequential repetition of that idea in mm. 7–12, suggests the formal function of a *presentation*—the first part of the Schoenbergian theme-type known as the sentence, as discussed in chapter 2. Although Schoenberg's remarkable analyses of eighteenth-century formal conventions have received attention only within the last few decades, what he defined as a sentence had already become a standard theme-type by 1781, to the extent that, during the silence of m. 12, Haydn's most astute listeners might themselves have expected a completion of the theme by means of what we today call a *continuation*. In other words, they may have predicted that Haydn would now put this theme back on its initial tonal track, perhaps granting to the supertonic its usual role as a dominant preparation leading to, say, V6/5, and possibly reducing the length of any new repeated gesture in order to fragment and mobilize the theme, thus intensifying its approach to a cadence. Haydn first thwarts and then fulfills such expectations. His *compressed*

Example 3.1. Haydn, String Quartet in C Major, Op. 33, No. 3, first movement, mm. 1–18

continuation—only half as long as his presentation—begins at m. 13 with, once again, the introductory gesture, but here that gesture has moved further afield from C major than at any earlier point. Does the dyad <B♭–D> at m. 13 stand for the submediant of ii? For minor v? With the viola now genuinely assuming the role of bass voice, the first violin interprets that dyad as a component of iv⁶ moving to V within the region of the supertonic, and then the descending sequential fragment at m. 16 provides a last-minute preparation for the cadential progression in C.

The *subito forte* dynamic at the elided cadence on the downbeat of m. 18 reinforces a new beginning on root tonic, mobilized by the cellist's eighth-note diminution of its quarter-note ascent in m. 4; the fuller, four-part texture here is of the kind that one might expect at the beginning of a main theme.[24] But the ensuing nine-bar phrase (example 3.2) leads to a clearly defined home-key half cadence, after which the original introductory gesture—now presenting the dyad <B♮–D> at m. 27—introduces the beginning of a first secondary theme (ST¹). This new theme simply *asserts* the key of the dominant, G major, and it begins in the second violin with the MT's opening idea, thus exemplifying Haydn's so-called "monothematic" technique, better described here and in general as "mono-idea." In short, the nine-bar phrase has served as a nonmodulatory transition;[25] and it is worth noting that Haydn's secondary theme, like his main theme, begins on the now-motivic I⁶-chord.

Are there details about the opening of Haydn's C-major Quartet that might be compared with aspects of the opening of Beethoven's "Tempest," Carl Dahlhaus's quintessential form-as-process movement (see example 2.1)? Like Dahlhaus with the "Tempest," at least one author has attributed to the opening of Haydn's movement the character of a "quasi-introduction, an opening that is not quite a beginning."[26] Objections to this observation would be of the precise kind discussed in the closing section of my chapter 2, but the observation itself should not be taken lightly, and it invites further comparison of the two movements.

Haydn's buoyant I⁶-chord creates an initial moment of instability; Beethoven's first gesture—the slow, deep, recitative-like arpeggiation of the A-major sixth-chord—remains tonally ambiguous until the fleeting D-minor tonic defines the opening chord as the dominant in first inversion. Haydn's supertonic sequential repetition and his genuinely ambiguous dyad at m. 13 most certainly destabilize his theme; the beginning of Beethoven's sequential consequent—on V⁶ of III—also seems deliberately to lead us off the harmonic track, though perhaps less so by 1802. Haydn's brief silences are not as portentous as Beethoven's fermata at m. 6, made potent by the impulsive alternation of his largo and allegro tempi. On the other hand, without a program announcing the fundamental key of op. 33, no. 3 (and Webster informs us that "no names of keys appeared in the sources"),[27] the tentative nature of Haydn's opening might tempt post-"Tempest" listeners to imagine that the initial three-bar prolongation of the sixth-chord will serve as a thematic (short) introduction, on the inverted dominant, to a movement in F major or minor! But this point is both anachronistic and moot. What quickly contradicts such a perception is Haydn's emphatic *forte* confirmation of his home key in mm. 3–6; indeed, this gesture, far from provisional, might even have sounded extraordinarily conclusive, were it not

Example 3.2. Haydn, op. 33, no. 3, first movement, mm. 18–32

for the first violinist's flourish on the downbeat of m. 6, a repetition of the same gesture in m. 5, now pausing on the active $\hat{5}$.

Haydn knows just how to capitalize not only upon the potential finality of his opening compound idea but also upon its initial rootlessness. As shown in example 3.3, an elided authentic cadence in E minor (iii) at m. 108 retroactively marks the end of the last core of his development section and what could be the beginning of a retransition. The E♮ in the viola here is the violist's E♮ from m. 1—the source of the original harmonic instability; but the initial interval, the sixth, has been replaced by a fifth. As if entering too soon, the first violin now introduces the return of the head idea from mm. 2–3, even though the lower strings have not yet relinquished E minor. The progression iii–($V^{[2][4/3]}$)–I^6—follows, with the cello providing the root tonic only on the second beat of m. 111—that is, only at the point where the original root-position tonic had emerged in m. 4. As a result, only at m. 111 might it occur to listeners that the *process* of recapitulation has already begun at m. 108. I do not hesitate to suggest, then, that Haydn's retransition "*becomes*" the beginning of his recapitulation (retransition ⇒ recapitulation).[28]

Finally, as shown at example 3.4, the ultimate moment of Haydn's coda at last reinterprets the main theme's CBI to give it the conclusive role it had almost possessed from the outset. Here the cello sustains its rightful role as the bass, substituting a second-inversion triad for the original I^6-chord and treating it as a cadential six-four.

Example 3.3. Haydn, op. 33, no. 3, first movement, mm. 106–13

Example 3.4. Haydn, op. 33, no. 3, first movement, m. 158 to end

Haydn—Piano Trio in C Major (Hob. XV:27), Finale

The central preoccupation of the Beethoven-Hegelians has always been sonata form, and processual interpretations have tended to focus upon the boundaries, or the absence thereof, between the more or less large-scale moments within that formal plan. Dahlhaus may have avoided writing about Haydn's processual techniques because he knew that, despite the extraordinary range and diversity of Haydn's works over a very long career, it is partly due to the popularity, the dissemination, and the imitations of his music during the 1780s and 90s that notions of such boundaries and large-scale formal functions became established as conventions in the first place.[29] One cannot claim that a formal tradition is being transformed, or "deformed," unless one can assert with some confidence that a received convention has been invoked. Let us take, for example, the case of transitions as paths to a secondary theme.

Thanks especially to familiar sonata-form movements by Mozart, Beethoven, and a host of later composers, it has become a commonplace to expect (and teach) that the beginning of a transition will often be relatively pronounced, and that the end of a transition tends to be clarified as *distinct* from the beginning of the secondary theme it prepares.[30] Exceptions to these "rules" might then be marked as unconventional, or deserving of their own category, or perhaps highly processual in music around the turn of the nineteenth century. As noted above, the transition within Haydn's C-major Quartet features a pronounced beginning and a distinct ending; in this movement Haydn helps to establish later theoretical norms. But in so many of his sonata-form movements—from his symphonies, his keyboard works, and especially his quartets throughout his career—Haydn prefers to obscure, or downright deny, such boundaries. In other words, it is not uncommon for Haydn's secondary-theme region to emerge without a break from a modulatory passage that has begun imperceptibly. And, as is even the case in the C-major Quartet, only with the appearance of a closing section, or final secondary theme, will Haydn often provide the relatively tight-knit and tuneful passage characteristic of, say, Mozart's first secondary themes. For an extreme example of Haydn's tendencies in these respects, I turn to one of his late works— the finale of his Piano Trio in C Major (Hob. XV:27), possibly completed by 1795, but definitely by 1797 (example 3.5).

To listeners knowledgeable about rondo and sonata-rondo forms, the character and structure of the opening materials within this exuberantly eccentric movement might promise one or the other of those large-scale designs. Why? Because at the basis of Haydn's sparkling, quirky opening theme we have a symmetrical, tightly knit eight-bar period (of the interruption type),[31] typical of rondo refrains; the period and its repetition then become the first part, or *a*-section, of a main theme that takes the form of a *small ternary* (*a–b–a′*), so that at the beginning of the movement, we hear the "rondo refrain" twice, as represented by *a* and *a′*. We must wait until the end of the exposition to learn that a sonata form, rather than sonata-rondo, has been fully under way: a retransition to the return of the "rondo refrain" fails to materialize, and the exposition takes a repeat.[32] Even confronted with Haydn's dazzling presto tempo, listeners will likely have no problem in recognizing the repeated periodic form of the main theme's opening *a*-section. The *b*-section of this small ternary—with its characteristic emphasis upon the dominant—should also be very discernible as such. Troubles for analysts of form begin only at the downbeat of m. 43, the point where the main theme closes. Or does it?

The pianist's new tremolo figure at m. 43 seems for a second to suggest a new beginning here, but that impression is canceled when we perceive that mm. 44–45 repeat the cadential idea of mm. 42–43, with the violin imitating the piano over the tonic pedal. A second, varied repetition spins off from the first, and then yet another, at mm. 46–49. As a dramatic character, the pianist now gets "stuck," or "distracted," to use Gretchen Wheelock's term,[33] and what had seemed to be expressing the function of a codetta series has apparently become "*dys*functional." On the other hand, perhaps the pianist has simply been winding up for the change of direction that is finally released at mm. 49–50. Still rushing along in two-bar units, the pianist relinquishes the tonic pedal and moves to the submediant, quickly reinterpreting this as a ii-chord within the key of the dominant. Voice exchanges project the progression ii–V in the new key, and now a modulation has been completed for good. But given, on first hearing, that we cannot know this for sure, we may not yet realize that the codettas of mm. 44–49 *have become* the beginning of the transition (codettas ⇒ transition).[34]

The next question is, Where does the transition end? Only when, at mm. 54–56, we note the stability of the tonic-prolongational progression I–(V4/3)–I in the

Example 3.5. Haydn, Piano Trio in C Major (Hob. XV:27), finale, mm. 36–83

Example 3.5. cont.

new key, might we suspect that the preceding new dominant has prepared the beginning of a secondary theme. By now, however, the pianist's part has become a challenging *moto perpetuo*—Haydn's tribute to the virtuoso woman pianist for whom he composed the work.[35] If that new dominant—the usual goal of a transition—has indeed served as its end-point, it has hardly been emphasized as such. Here, then, is what William E. Caplin classifies as the transition that omits its "ending function": there has been no cadential articulation, no standing-on-the-dominant, and really no emphasis whatsoever beyond the purely metric within the strong-weak two-bar groups.[36]

But just when we might sense that a secondary theme has begun, it falls apart: the new two-bar idea at mm. 54–55 does nothing more than scamper upward, generating the first irregular three-bar unit since the *b*-section of the main theme (at mm. 21–23). I hear the effect of recklessness evoked by this irregularity as the signal that a potential secondary theme has made a "false start." It wants a higher register. When it gains this, the theme begins again at m. 59, and this time an immediate (varied) repetition of its two-bar idea produces a genuine presentation. Now we are being led to expect a sentential continuation; instead, a mere two-bar cadential idea (mm. 63–64), made flamboyantly sassy with its chromatic incomplete neighbor tones, takes an evaded cadence and a "one more time" repetition.

Nothing has prepared us for what follows. An elided deceptive cadence (DC) at the downbeat of m. 67 prevents the "one more time" statement from reaching its expected full close. As the bass now climbs upward from the local $\hat{5}$ (D♮) through $\hat{6}$ to $\hat{7}$, the descant undertakes a stepwise descent from $\hat{8}$ (G♮) through $\hat{7}$ to $\hat{6}$; together these two voices converge at m. 70 to project, of all things, the dominant seventh of B minor. In short, a detour pretends to take us into the mediant of the dominant (iii of V), only then to clarify itself as an ingenious way of composing out the motion from V to I. When the basic idea of the secondary theme returns at mm. 75–76, the detour begun at m. 67—having become an eight-bar interpolation—endows the return with the quality of a specific narrative turn: having twice lost its way, or willfully wandered off, this secondary theme is now in a hurry to close. It starts all over again, with its presentation as heard at mm. 59–64; but when its cadential idea then achieves the elided authentic cadence at m. 81, we might begin to realize, after twenty-eight full measures, that the theme itself never fundamentally promised to be anything more than a six-bar phrase! As if to make amends, the composer concludes the exposition with a new, tightly knit, eight-bar sentence as closing section (or ST², mm. 81–89), and he rounds this off with a series of codettas.[37]

Whimsical as it may seem, the idea that a skeletal six-bar plan rests at the basis of Haydn's secondary-theme process gains complete confirmation in his recapitulation (example 3.6). With compression clearly at a premium, Haydn now forgoes every one of his original expansion techniques; what returns as the *only* trace of the exposition's secondary theme is none other than the six-bar plan, extended to eight bars by the "one more time."[38] Haydn soon demonstrates why he has *not* recapitulated his magnificent eight-bar interpolation, but with an intuition of his genius for formal integration, one might sense even during his recapitulation that his reasons will be profound. As the dramatic capstone of his coda, a full eight-bar

Example 3.6. Haydn, Piano Trio in C Major, finale, mm. 185–96

prolongation of that remarkable dominant-seventh chord in B minor once again delays the bass motion from F♯ to G♮; but now the G♮ supports the home V⁷, which in turn, and with a climactic sixteenth-note tremolo in all three parts, prepares the final appearance of the "rondo refrain" (example 3.7).[39]

Clementi—Piano Sonata in F Minor, Op. 13, No. 6, First Movement

Let us now consider movements by the two young composers—one only four years older than the other—who, on Christmas Eve in 1781, found themselves pitted against one another in a virtuoso piano competition staged by the Emperor Joseph II. Without wishing to accentuate the historical rivalry between Clementi and the younger Mozart, I shall nonetheless present certain aspects of a sonata-form movement by Clementi as *foils* to sonata procedures in an operatic trio by Mozart.

Now notorious is the fact that when Muzio Clementi (1752–1832) was a mere fourteen years old, his father sold him to a wealthy Englishman—one who had no greater ambition than to transport this teenager's budding musical talents from Rome to a country estate in Dorset. Although there is little to be known about Clementi's

Example 3.7. Haydn, Piano Trio in C Major, finale, mm. 210–26

seven years as an indentured servant of Peter Beckford, it seems that his move from the Italian metropolis to the rustic countryside of England nearly nipped Clementi's compositional aspirations in the bud. Rather than compose, the young Clementi was obliged to spend lonely, unguided hours each day practicing and studying the music of such composers as Corelli, Paradies, Handel, and Domenico Scarlatti.[40] It is especially Scarlatti's influence that can be sensed at the beginning of a work that Clementi wrote long after he had left Dorset for London, with trips to Paris and Vienna—his Piano Sonata in F Minor, Op. 13, No. 6, from 1785. The Scarlatti-like brevity of Clementi's six-bar main theme, shown at example 3.8, is all the more striking in that, as with many of Scarlatti's openings, repetitions of an initial one-bar idea generate only a four-bar phrase, whose closing gesture then takes two cadential repetitions. As the exposition of this movement unfolds, vestiges of Scarlatti's style recede in the light of formal features much more characteristic of continental late eighteenth-century sonata forms. Moreover, we can all but presume that this dark, impetuous, brooding music, with its expansive keyboard range, would have been taken very seriously by the young Beethoven.

Example 3.8. Clementi, Piano Sonata in F Minor, Op. 13, No. 6, first movement, mm. 1–19

Clementi's transition affirms a technique already explored by, among others, Haydn and Mozart but exaggerated here: at m. 7, his transition begins as if it will be a complete repetition of his main theme, sometimes called a "counterstatement," but also eligible for representation as "repetition of MT ⇒ transition." In fact, this passage precisely repeats all but the last bar of the main theme in the lower register. Only at the end of m. 11 does the abrupt motion to the mediant (III = A♭ major) begin to propel a modulation onto the tonicized dominant of that secondary key. Rather than obscuring the boundary between the end of his transition and the beginning of his secondary theme, Clementi goes out of his way to emphasize it: in what would become the high-classical tradition, he insistently *stands on the new dominant* for a full four bars (mm. 16–19), and he further frames that phrase with his expectant fermatas at mm. 15 and 19.

Now come two secondary themes (example 3.9). The first (ST¹) begins with a registrally expansive four-bar idea (CBI) and leads through a continuation to the elided cadence at the downbeat of m. 29, at which point the second secondary theme (ST²) begins. We are given two chances to reflect upon the harmonic and motivic content of ST², since this theme takes an expanded repetition beginning at m. 38. As for ST¹, Clementi's initial idea is generated by the head soprano motive of his MT—a reminder that Haydn's "monomotivic" technique was not exclusively Haydn's. Concerning ST², here is a theme that dares to exploit only an *expanded cadential progression* (ECP) as its harmonic basis: its initial six bars simply prolong the harmony that so often traditionally initiates a cadential progression—the I⁶; the single voice doubled at the octave at mm. 36–38 then provides the concluding V—I.

Those octave-doubled figures may also have the function of drawing our attention to both the most processual and the most "progressive" (in the sense of innovative) feature of Clementi's work—its intense proto-Schoenbergian *motivic* integration. At m. 1 in example 3.8, I label the initial left-hand motive—<E–F–D♭–C>—as motive *x*, characterized by the semitone incomplete neighbors to 1̂ and 5̂. I also suggest that the *shape* of motive *x* is immediately reflected within the soprano's head motive at mm. 1–2. At m. 4 the interaction of the two parts produces but reorders the original pitch-class content of motive *x*. Surely the bizarre *sforzandos* at mm. 16–18 have been "motivated" by motive *x*; the turn figure here highlights the juxtaposition of semitones both above and below the new 5̂ within the mediant (the minor mode's lowered 6̂, as echoed by raised 4̂). If but retrospectively, this moment would seem to signal that semitone incomplete neighbors will motivically pervade the work, as indeed they do even in Clementi's forthcoming slow movement and in his Presto finale. But the idea that motive *x* is genuinely "generative" becomes inescapable when that motive returns at m. 29—now transposed and rhythmically augmented—to create the basic idea of ST². The expanded closing gesture in octaves at mm. 45–49 clinches the argument: this outburst begins with an *x*-variant, inverted and reordered, and ends, as at mm. 36–37, with a reference to both the original and the transposed form of the motive.

Two outstanding details about the development and "recapitulation" in this movement have particular relevance to the question of sonata-form conventions and unique approaches in the 1780s. First, and perhaps as a result of Clementi's sojourn in

Example 3.9. Clementi, op. 13, no. 6, first movement, mm. 20–49

Vienna, his development section explores what some would regard as a *false recapitulation*, comparable to those so strongly associated with Haydn: a return of the main theme that has been prepared as if it will be the real thing, but that retrospectively becomes "premature," either within the tonic or in the "wrong" key (example 3.10).[41] Clementi's realization of this technique is, however, uniquely his own. His unusually grim choice of key for the "false-recapitulation effect" anticipates the key of his forthcoming slow movement—C minor, the dominant minor; a modulation to that key is confirmed by m. 64, where a four-bar standing-on-*its*-dominant pretends to signal the end of the development. A fifth bar, at m. 68, introduces a variant of motive *x*. But only at the hypermetrically weak sixth measure do the first four bars of Clementi's main theme emerge as precisely transposed into the new key. It is the elaborate ("wrong") dominant prolongation at mm. 64–68 that creates the effect of a "true" recapitulation at m. 69, but the sense of a new beginning here is obfuscated by that "extra" preceding measure. Clementi now also exploits a striking feature of his main theme: since this theme itself begins on a dominant pedal, the retransitional dominant prolongation and the false recapitulation can merge seamlessly with one another.

As the second detail of concern, Clementi's false-recapitulation effect turns out to be his *only* main-theme recapitulation; in other words, it retrospectively stands in the place of the real thing. When the key of the minor dominant is abandoned at m. 73, Clementi presses onward through the Neapolitan to achieve the conventional goal of a development—the home dominant—by moving directly to a transposed statement of the memorable *sfzorzando* phrase that had marked the end of the exposition's transition. An abbreviated home-key return of the main theme might have followed at m. 84, despite its recent appearance in the "wrong" key; *or* Clementi's reference to the end of the transition might now lead us to expect a home-key version of ST[1]. In fact, his earlier keyboard sonatas explored both techniques. And this suggests that, even as late as 1785, a recapitulation concept had not become conventionalized for him: the return of *either* the main theme *or*, as in most of Scarlatti's sonatas (Hepokoski and Darcy's Type 2 sonata), simply the secondary theme in the home key might occur within the second part of a sonata, in which cases the term "recapitulation" in its modern sense seems inappropriate.[42]

Example 3.10 confirms that, much to our potential surprise, Clementi's apparent point of recapitulation at m. 84 begins *not* in the home key, but rather with his ST[1] in its *original* key of the mediant (A♭ major). But an ascending-step sequence then quickly transforms that theme and leads to the dramatic climax of the movement—an expanded cadenza that closes in the home key at m. 101. As a result, the subsequent ST[2] and its expanded repetition now assume the role of providing the only stable affirmation of the home key within this recapitulation.[43]

In 1807 or 1808, Clementi revised this sonata along with others. As shown at example 3.11, his only radical revision in this movement suggests that, by then, he had become self-consciously concerned about the nature and impact of a recapitulation. Does Clementi's substitution of the progression V–VI for V–III at the revised mm. 84–86 have greater or lesser shock value? Or might there have been a *motivic* reason for Clementi's change? Without providing an answer to the first question, my annotations in example 3.11 propose an affirmative response to the second.

Example 3.10. Clementi, op. 13, no. 6, first movement, mm. 63–85

Example 3.11. Clementi, revised version of op. 13, no. 6 (published as op. 14, no. 2), mm. 83–86

Mozart—*Le Nozze di Figaro*, Act I, No. 7, Trio in B-flat

What most especially distinguishes Clementi's op. 13, no. 6, at least on the surface, from piano sonatas by Mozart, and endows it instead with premonitions of Beethoven, is what Dahlhaus called the "blending of a [motivic] logic with the functions and stations of a formal process" (see chapter 2); to the very dark and bitter end, multifarious forms of Clementi's motive *x* seem to drive this movement and obsessively influence its form. As legend has it, Clementi himself may have been driven at the time by the searing upset of a failed attempt to kidnap the woman he loved; such real-life drama has been known to release unforeseen creative energy. But, as many have noted, the fictitious drama of *opera* may also have been one of the strongest catalysts for the transformation of formal conventions in the late eighteenth century. I offer a celebrated case in point—from Mozart's *Le Nozze di Figaro*, premiered in 1786. Whereas Clementi's motive *x* might motivate the interaction of form and content in his movement, we can look to the interactions of the Count, Basilio, and Susanna in the B-flat Trio of Act I, "Cosa sento!," to find Mozart's motivation for a false-recapitulation effect within the vestiges of a sonata form. In what follows, I travel over a well-worn analytic path but bring recent formal concepts into play; my processual approach to Mozart's formal strategies engages with several of the many commentaries about this set piece.[44]

As *Figaro* lovers know, it is the wedding day of Figaro and Susanna, and we are in the ill-chosen room that is to become their bedroom. First Cherubino, the Count's page, and then the Count himself have come to the room secretly to confess their love for Susanna. Upon hearing the Count approach, Cherubino has hidden behind an armchair. When the Count hears the voice of Don Basilio, his music master and court gossip, he too moves to hide behind the chair, while Cherubino miraculously slips around to sit in it, concealing himself beneath a lady's robe. In comes Basilio, maliciously eager to rub it in that Cherubino is infatuated with both Susanna and the Countess. Infuriated by this news, but also terribly caught off guard, the Count now discloses himself. The MT of the Trio's sonata exposition thus begins, as shown in example 3.12, with the orchestra's introductory *fortissimo* dominant-seventh outburst—a "cue" to the Count, prompting him to pull himself together and display his authority over Basilio ("Tosto andate," "go at once").[45] A nonmodulating transition serves as Basilio's hypocritically subservient reply; like the sly Basilio, this appar-

Example 3.12. Mozart, *Le Nozze di Figaro*, Act I, No. 7, Trio in B-flat Major, mm. 1–27

ently inoffensive "transition theme" (TR-theme) will insinuate itself into the formal design with the intent of *deforming* it.[46] Two secondary themes then arise—Susanna's tremulous flare-up in the dominant minor (the beginning of ST[1] is shown in example 3.12 at m. 24), during which she pretends to faint,[47] and the duet in the dominant major (ST[2]), wherein Basilio and the Count, faking solicitude, try to calm her down (mm. 43–57, not shown). Worth noting here is that the duet opens canonically, with Basilio—not the Count—serving as leader.

With reference to my outline of Mozart's formal and dramatic design (table 3.1), I draw attention to the events of the "development" section. Standing in for a typical sonata-form development, the "core" of this development eschews the typical model-sequence design of cores and begins instead with a complete restatement of ST[2] in the gentle subdominant (E♭)—an exceptional tonal region for development sections, but one that underscores Basilio's and the Count's continued efforts to placate Susanna. Starting in that key but modulating to a home-key half cadence (at m. 92), Basilio's TR-theme then returns to provide a reassuring disclaimer: "What I said about the page was only my suspicion" (mm. 85–92; a standing-on-the-home-dominant ensues at mm. 92–100, characteristic of the end of developments). As Basilio the catalyst cleverly predicts, these words have the effect of inciting the Count all over again, and thus arises the dramatic motivation for a varied return, in the home key, of the Count's imperious MT (mm. 101–9).

We learn soon enough, however, that a only a "false recapitulation" has begun, and for good reason. The Count now interrupts the formal process because he needs to digress into a recitative; he cannot wait to tell that just yesterday he discovered the naughty Cherubino with yet another woman, Susanna's young cousin Barbarina. Having utterly fallen under the influence of Basilio's gossip, the Count then appropriates Basilio's TR-theme as he begins to act out yesterday's discovery. When he lifts the robe on the armchair as if it were yesterday's tablecloth, he of course again discovers Cherubino in the living flesh.[48] His shock, Basilio's glee, Cherubino's embarrassment, and Susanna's mortification now give some cause for the beginning of a true recapitulation, but, relative to the exposition in this scene, the dramatic situation has entirely changed.[49] What had been motivated only by Basilio's alleged "suspicion" about Cherubino has apparently become a reality.

As many have noted, the application of sonata-form procedures to dramatic situations calls for an imaginative treatment of the recapitulation if the musical return to a reexposition in the home key is not justified by the ongoing plot; and in operatic drama, as in real life, processual change is usually inevitable. How does Mozart manage to pull off a genuine recapitulation? As Siegmund Levarie has suggested in his study of *Figaro*, the very employment of a recapitulation here is the "supreme joke" of the Trio.[50] In my own words, Mozart takes his cue from the manipulative Basilio, who, after all, is the music master: by forcing his characters sheepishly to revisit the materials of their exposition, Mozart exposes and punishes all of them for their essential *fraud*. After all, no one has stolen into Susanna's bedroom with noble intentions, and Susanna herself has tried to pretend that Cherubino is not present. Better yet, there would seem to be no little coincidence that Mozart has assigned the formal function of a nonmodulating *transition* to the first appearance of Basilio's theme: because the TR-theme stays in the home

Table 3.1 Mozart, *Le Nozze di Figaro*, Act I, No. 7, Trio in B-flat Major

Outline of the formal design and dramatic action (with text translations)

Exposition (mm. 1–65)

Introduction (mm. 1–4): Prolongs V^7 as an expanded upbeat. (No "cadence" at m. 5.)	Angered by Basilio's gossip about Cherubino, the Count emerges from his hiding place behind the chair. Basilio is thrilled, Susanna horrified. Note the Count's initial descending third –$\hat{5}$ to $\hat{3}$.
The Count's **MT** (mm. 5–15): An eight-bar ascent from $\hat{3}$ to $\hat{8}$, overlapping with a three-bar cadential idea (I–(vi)–ii65–V^7–I): descending thirds in bass.	Anger mounts; dotted rhythms; lordly rhetoric. **C.**: "What do I hear? Go at once and expel the seducer."
Basilio, **Transition (TR-) Theme** (mm. 16–23), nonmodulating: An eight-bar descent via the descending-thirds sequence, closing with half cadence (HC). The motion from I to vi moves twice as slowly as the Count's at m. 13.	False servility descends; Basilio appropriates the Count's rhythm but placates by eschewing the dotted figure. **B.**: "I've come at a bad time. Forgive me, my lord."
ST^1 (mm. 24–43): Susanna transforms the dominant of **B.**'s HC into a tonic in v (f); her four-bar CBI leads to a repeated four-bar idea over dominant pedal (mm. 28–36); a cadential phrase follows, first to deceptive cadence (DC), then to the elided PAC in V (F) at m. 43.	Agitation; Susanna joins in but pretends to faint (while adopting the manner and the later F-minor cavatina opening of her cousin Barbara). **S.**: "What ruin! [Che ruina = Cherubino]. I'm overcome with terror."
ST^2 (mm. 43–57), as a duet in V: A sentence with two presentations and a "one-more-time" repetition of the continuation, leading to PAC (m. 57).	Basilio and the Count begin in canon, with **B.** leading: "Ah, the poor girl has fainted! Oh god, how her heart is beating!"
codettas (mm. 58–66): A repeated four-bar phrase reviving **S.**'s agitated **ST^1** motive.	**B.** to **S.** (knowing that **S.** knows that Cherubino is in the chair): "Gently, on to this chair." **S.** (now forced to pretend to revive): "Where am I? What do I see?" (adopting the Count's initial descending third).

(continued)

Table 3.1 *cont.*

"Development" (mm. 66–146).

Pre-core (mm. 66–69): An abrupt shift into a four-bar standing-on-V/vi.	**S.** adopts the Count's outraged dotted figure: "What insolence! Go away!"
"Core" (mm. 70–146): **ST²** complete, in the soothing subdominant (IV = E♭; mm. 70–84).	**B.** and **C.** to **S.**, with **B.** again leading the canon: "We're only here to help you." (**C.**): "Don't be disturbed, my dear. (**B.**): "Your honor is secure."
Basilio's **TR-theme** ⇒ **false retransition**: Begins in IV but modulates to the home-key HC (mm. 85–92).	**B.**: "What I said about the page was only my suspicion."
Standing-on-the-home-dominant (mm. 93–100). The "new" rhythm (from the codettas) will now pervade the false recapitulation.	**S.** (to **C.** about **B.**): "It's a plot, a lie. Don't believe the impostor."
False recapitulation: The Count (mm. 101–46). The basic idea (BI) of the Count's MT, followed by closure in the home key (mm. 101–5); this four-bar phrase is then repeated. Model-sequence to HC (m. 115) and standing-on-the-dominant (mm. 115–21).	Triggered again by **B.**'s reference to Cherubino, the Count returns to his state of anger. **C.**: "That fop must go." **S.** and **B.**: "Poor boy!" **C.**: "Poor boy?! But I've found him out again." **S.** and **B.**: "What?"
Recitative: The Count (mm. 112–28)—an interpolated quasi-cadenza prolonging V.	**C.**: "Yesterday I found your cousin's door locked: I knocked, and Barbarina opened it, more flustered than usual. My suspicions aroused by her appearance, I look and search in every corner." (**C.** begins to illustrate his actions.)
TR-theme ⇒ **true retransition** (mm. 129–46), now appropriated by the Count and extended, but again arriving at the home-key HC. The TR-theme's descending contour is then reversed.	**C.**: "And very, very softly lifting the tablecloth [**C.** now lifts up the robe concealing Cherubino in the chair], I see the page [**C.** discovers Cherubino]!" **C.**: "Ah, what do I see?" **S.**: "Cruel heavens!" **B.** (with glee): "Ah, better and better!"

True Recapitulation (mm. 147–201)

The BI of the Count's **MT**, leading to closure and then repeated (mm. 147–55), as in the false recapitulation. Merging with:

C. (ironically): "Most esteemed lady! Now I understand how it is!" **S.**: "Nothing worse could happen. Righteous gods! What next?" **B.**: "So it goes with all beautiful women. There's nothing new about it."

New transition (mm. 155–67): Ascending-step sequence to the home-key HC (m. 159) and standing-on-the-dominant (mm. 159–67), which introduces **B.**'s new "laughing" motive. Cadence "of limited scope" at m. 167.

Text repetition; same as above.

ST² in the home key (mm. 168–75), with its first presentation now omitted.

Text repetition; same as above.

Basilio's **TR-theme** (mm. 175–82), delayed until now because it was heard just before the true recapitulation, and because it now exposes Basilio's character—deceitful, ironic, and manipulative.

B.: "What I said about the page was only my suspicion."

Return of the new transition materials (mm. 182–90), to "correct" the previously reversed ("inverted") recapitulation of ST² and **B.**'s TR-theme.

Text repetition: same as above for the three characters.

ST² again in the home key (mm. 191–201), again with its first presentation omitted.

Text repetition: again the same as above.

Coda (mm. 201–21): "One-more-time" repetitions of three-bar and then two-bar cadential gestures (mm. 201–12), followed by final codettas, the last ending with the Count's initial descending third—$\hat{5}$ to $\hat{3}$.

Text repetition; again the same as above.

key and concludes with Basilio's noncommittal half cadence, this theme is flexible; it can recur in unexpected places—that is, whenever Basilio decides to take control of both the form and the drama with his intrusive but seemingly innocuous remarks. As we have noted, it is Basilio's TR-theme that engenders both the false-recapitulation effect and the opening of the true recapitulation; in both instances a transition retrospectively "becomes" a retransition—false in the first case, true in the second.[51] Moreover, only after ST² has returned in the home key does Basilio again sing his TR-theme (now marked by the composer as *con malignità*, "with malice"), and the delay of this gesture—with its toxic text—emerges as the most powerful agent of the joke: with Cherubino now in full view, who but the unctuously ironic Basilio would dare to repeat his claim that what he had said about the page was only his "suspicion"?!

I close this chapter with the irony of Mozart's recapitulation because I think that it demonstrates with verve where the opportunities for processual approaches to form stood at the point where the young Beethoven entered the scene.[52] Mozart's music seems to sparkle with the confidence that, thanks to his own music and that of his predecessors, his listeners were prepared to take pleasure in recognizing specific formal conventions associated with his style. On the other hand, the *Figaro* Trio finds Mozart just as confidently *disrupting* established conventions in response to the dramatic process, and the facility with which he does this suggests that he is sure his listeners will get the point. Without such assurance, Beethoven and post-Beethovenians could not possibly have invited us to go even further—to become full-fledged participants in the formal process as we actively attempt to interpret *un*conventional formal plans and their dramatic import. It is no accident that the Beethoven-Hegelians chose Beethoven, rather than Haydn, Clementi, or Mozart, as their hero; but the makings of this hero fully reside in the processual legacy that he inherited.

Where does this leave us on the question of how and why the music of Beethoven, and of those who would follow him in the early nineteenth century, would seem to move beyond Haydn and Mozart into different realms? As Scott Burnham puts it, directly taking on Webster, "how can we explain the fact that Beethoven, and not Haydn, became the canonic composer, the embodiment of music?" For Burnham, "One feels that there is more at stake" in Beethoven's use of compositional techniques he shared with Haydn.

> The precedence of some of the material features of Beethoven's heroic style in the works of Haydn permits us to give a more defined shape to what is truly unprecedented in Beethoven: the sense of an earnest and fundamental presence burdened with some great weight yet coursing forth ineluctably, moving the listener along as does the earth itself.... So compelling is the ethical thrust of the Beethovenian process that it carries the stamp and authority of necessity in mainstream musical thought.[53]

In the chapters that follow here, I continue to pursue the *technical* means by which Beethoven, Schubert, Mendelssohn, Chopin, and Schumann explored the "Beethovenian process," in the hope that I can lend fresh support to Burnham's eloquent account.

CHAPTER Four

Beethoven's "Bridgetower"
Sonata, Op. 47

Excitement has long been palpable in accounts of the première of Beethoven's Sonata for Piano and Violin in A, Op. 47. We have it directly from Beethoven's pupil Ferdinand Ries that, in the early morning hours of May 24, 1803, Beethoven summoned him to copy the violin part of the first movement as fast as possible; Beethoven's performance, with the renowned virtuoso violinist George Augustus Polgreen Bridgetower, was to occur at 8 o'clock that morning in the Vienna Augartensaal. Ries reports that the piano score was "noted down only here and there" and that Bridgetower had to perform the second movement from the manuscript—presumably by reading it from over Beethoven's shoulder—because "there was no time to copy it."[1] Best of all, Beethoven and Bridgetower must surely have given their audience an astounding display of spontaneity and camaraderie. Bridgetower recounts that, within the repeat of the first movement's exposition, at the fermata in m. 27, he imitated, thus anticipating, the pianist's cadenza—the C-major arpeggio—in m. 36 (see example 4.4). Beethoven was so pleased that he jumped up, embraced Bridgetower, and said, "Noch einmal, mein lieber Bursch!" ("Once again, my dear boy!"). He then held the *sostenuto* pedal as Bridgetower repeated the cadenza.[2]

Ries, Bridgetower himself, Carl Czerny, and Anton Schindler have all asserted unequivocally that Beethoven composed his op. 47 sonata *for Bridgetower*.[3] Elliot Forbes has disagreed. In his 1967 revised edition of Alexander Thayer's Beethoven biography, Forbes argues that the sketches for the first and second movements, to be found in the last pages of the Wielhorsky sketchbook, date from "early 1803," thus prior to Bridgetower's arrival in Vienna later that spring. Forbes concludes that "at the start of its composition Beethoven did not have Bridgetower in mind."[4] As a sample of the op. 47 sketches from the Wielhorsky sketchbook, excerpts from the first page of these have been reproduced in example 4.1. Note that many of the essential elements of the first movement, including those treacherous broken thirds for the pianist in the development section, are already much in evidence.

In 1980, Sieghard Brandenburg challenged Forbes's view. Brandenburg's complex reassessment of the Wielhorsky sketchbook need not be rehearsed here, but

Example 4.1. From the Wielhorsky sketchbook, *Kniga eskizov Beethoven za 1802–1803 gody* [*Ein Skizzenbuch Beethovens von 1802–1803*], ed. Natan Fischmann (Moscow, 1962). Annotations added his argument warrants our consideration; namely, given that Beethoven's sketches for Op. 47 can be assigned a later date and Bridgetower's arrival in Vienna an earlier one, the likelihood that they had already met before Beethoven began composing op. 47 is strong. As Brandenburg says: "It is difficult to accept that a violin sonata constructed in such a completely concertante manner would have come into being uninfluenced by the violinistic qualities of that very violinist by whom it was performed for the first time."[5] Brandenburg's conclusions about the genesis of op. 47 have not, to my knowledge, been refuted; nor, however, have their ramifications been fully explored.

Readers will recall Carl Dahlhaus's claim that the processual character of form in the first movement of the "Tempest" Sonata defines the "new path," or "a wholly new style," that Beethoven determined to explore around the year 1802. Within the year that followed, no works after the op. 31 sonatas save for the "Eroica" Variations, Op. 35 and the Violin Sonata, Op. 47 more fully substantiate the idea that Beethoven had found his new path. Nor would Beethoven ever again compose an accompanied sonata "scritta in uno stile molto concertante, quasi come d'un concerto" ("written in a very concertante style, almost like that of a concerto"), as he put it—a work of unparalleled virtuosity and fire for both players. Indeed, even the first reviewer of op. 47 in the *Allgemeine musikalische Zeitung* saw subsequent performances as dependent upon the coming together of "two virtuosi to whom nothing remains difficult, who possess so much spirit and understanding that, with practice, they could write similar works themselves."[6] Like Brandenburg, I would like to believe that we can attribute this remarkable composition most especially to the coming together of Beethoven and Bridgetower.

What can we know about George Augustus Polgreen Bridgetower? A mere seven-page biographical sketch by one F. G. Edwards, published in the *Musical Times* in 1909, served as Thayer's sole source of information; for Josephine R. B. Wright in 1980, Edwards's account remained "the most comprehensive study of Bridgetower."[7] From Edwards we learn that Bridgetower may have been born in Biala, Poland, to a Polish mother, and that his father, like him, was known as "the African prince."[8] Edwards proposes 1779 as the approximate year of Bridgetower's birth. In his 2005 monograph, Clifford D. Panton supplies the birth year as 1778, making Bridgetower eight years younger than Beethoven.[9] Panton is right to stress that this person of color, whose father is said to have been Abyssinian (Ethiopian) from the West Indies, came into the world "during the famous slave trade triangle that existed…between Europe, the African continent and the Americas," and at a time when negative images of black people had begun to abound in Europe.[10] Reviews from Paris and then England (Bath, then London) permit Edwards to establish beyond question that, already by the late 1780s, Bridgetower's elegant, accomplished father had succeeded in displaying his son as an astonishingly brilliant child prodigy. For example, in the *Bath Chronicle* of December 3, 1789, it is reported of "Master Bridgtower" [sic] that his "taste and execution on the violin [are] equal, perhaps superior, to the best professor of the present or any former day."[11] From the very outset, however, it would seem that race would be an issue for Bridgetower. The 1789 review in *Le Mercure de France* of his début in Paris, as a "jeune Nègre des Colonies," includes the following observation: "His talent, as

genuine as it is precocious, is one of the best replies one can give to the philosophers who wish to deprive those of his nation and his color the faculty of distin-
guishing themselves in the arts."[12]

By the time the twenty-five-year-old George Bridgetower met up with
Beethoven, he had long before taken London by storm and performed concertos
with Haydn (in 1791,[13] 1792, and 1794), with whom he may have studied when
his father was serving as Prince Nicolas Esterházy's personal page at the Esterházy
estate in Eisenstadt.[14] He had won the patronage of the Prince of Wales (later to
become George IV); he had gained the esteem and friendship of leading musicians
in London, including the violinist-composer Giovanni Battista Viotti; with letters
of introduction from the English court and from Dresden, he was about to achieve
a "most brilliant reception among the highest musical circles" in Vienna.[15] In fact,

Figure 4.1. Beethoven, 1801. Engraving by Johann Joseph Neidl after a drawing by
Gandolph Ernst Stainhauser von Treuberg. By permission of the Beethoven-Haus,
Bonn.

on May 18, 1803, shortly before his concert with Bridgetower, Beethoven himself sent an introductory letter on Bridgetower's behalf to Baron Alexander Wetzlar.[16] It is tempting to wonder whether, when Beethoven and Bridgetower met for the first time, they might have seen themselves in one another. Consider the portraits juxtaposed in figures 4.1 and 4.2—of Beethoven around 1801, roughly thirty-one years old, and Bridgetower looking close to the same age. Beethoven was often described as dark-eyed and dark-complexioned: at home in Bonn as a young boy he was called *der Spagnol* (the Spaniard); Thayer, recalling the anecdote that Prince Esterházy referred to Haydn as "a Moor," speculates that Beethoven "had even more of the Moor in his looks" than Haydn.[17] But whether or not a shared sense of "otherness," of being marked as "different," or "foreign," might have drawn these two men together, most pertinent here is the possibility that in Bridgetower Beethoven met his match as a performer—a virtuoso of the magnitude for which he himself had won his earliest renown, and one who, like himself, could not only dazzle but move his listeners to tears.[18] Here was someone for whom Beethoven could compose the most brilliant, technically demanding, and passionate violin sonata of his career.

That Beethoven's "new path" involved an intensive, maybe even obsessive, attention to molecular, often pitch-specific motives as generative forces surely finds

Figure 4.2. A miniature of Bridgetower, attributed to Chinnery. BL PP 1931 1 pcx (vol. 182), 296. By permission of the British Library.

confirmation in most writings about op. 47; for example, the analyses of Rudolph Réti and Owen Jander hinge almost exclusively on this facet of the first movement, although the generative elements they identify are not the same.[19] Little effort, on the other hand, has been made to consider just how the composer's taut motivic network interacts with his phrase-structural, tonal, and midlevel formal processes to create such an enormous expansion of his first movement's sonata form—one that seems especially conceived to enhance the effect of a fabulous dialogue between two musical soul mates in the heat of an exchange. Réti appears unaware that the finale of op. 47 was composed first, but both he and Jander propose connections among all three movements. For Suhnne Ahn, "the finale generates most of the ideas for the entire work," and yet the evidence she provides for this view is meager.[20] In short, a new consideration of the op. 47 sonata is warranted. I focus in particular upon some of the technical, motivic, and formal challenges that the violinist and pianist share on an utterly equal footing in the first movement—details that all but suggest a compositional collaboration between the two.

As a magnanimous first tribute to his violinist, Beethoven gives the opening four-bar phrase of his Adagio introduction solely to the violin (example 4.2). Never in his accompanied sonatas had he done this before, nor would he ever do it again within an Adagio opening. As the violinist negotiates the initial A-major chord, with two double stops in quick succession, sonatas of an older kind might momentarily come to mind; Bridgetower eventually became well known for his exquisite performances *from memory* of Sebastian Bach's sonatas for unaccompanied violin (recall the double-stopped openings in the Adagios of Bach's sonatas in G minor and A minor).[21] The violinist's serene, but exceedingly difficult, opening phrase,[22] all in the tonic major, is about to establish a pattern: as the movement unfolds, it will be the violinist who consistently introduces new materials, and then the pianist who follows suit. But both in the introduction and within the slow-moving opening part of the first secondary theme (ST[1]; see example 4.6), the pianist's varied repetition seems to serve as a gentle warning; at both of these moments, the pianist introduces modal mixture, inflecting the minor mode as if to say, "Mein lieber Bursch, there's a more somber side to the musical world we've begun to explore together." Moreover, within both the slow introduction and ST[1], the music hesitates, it takes time to reflect, it gives the impression of groping toward an outcome; in both cases, the outcome is a release of energy more ferocious than anything in Beethoven's earlier works.

As the pianist's inverted minor-subdominant chord in m. 5 moves to the dominant at m. 6, and then on to the submediant in m. 7, a second warning begins to emerge. As within so many vocal and instrumental works from the turn of the nineteenth century onward, Beethoven will treat the semitone relationship $\hat{5}$–$\hat{6}$—in this case E–F—as his pervasive resource for local and long-range motivic continuity, on multiple levels of structure and in ever-changing formal contexts. A second pitch-specific semitone—the dyad G♯–A, or $\hat{7}$–$\hat{8}$—will join forces with the E–F motive, or its reverse, F–E, sometimes underscoring the instability of a neighbor relationship, sometimes counteracting this by providing closure. Most important, Beethoven assigns a specific rhythmic character to the two dyads: again and again each of these will appear in the context of upbeat/downbeat, and

Example 4.2. Beethoven, Sonata in A for Piano and Violin, Op. 47, first movement, mm. 1–18

short–long, short–long. In fact, the violinist's very first gesture—the opening double-stopped chord, which must be broken—anticipates this rhythmic detail. Put simply, Beethoven will make it impossible for his listeners to miss the generative role of his two dyads; he *insists* that we follow the developmental path they will take. The first appearance of the F–E motive occurs in both the treble and the bass at mm. 5–6. (Here and elsewhere in my examples, I have literally "flagged" these motions, borrowing from Schenkerian analysis the practice of flagging metric neighbor tones and slurring these to their stemmed tones of resolution.) The violinist has already introduced the G♯–A motion at mm. 2–3; when the pianist harmonically reinterprets the violinist's melody at mm. 6–7, we now hear the two semitones *simultaneously*—G♯-to-A and E-to-F, moving together in parallel tenths.

What then engenders an imitative dialogue between the two instruments (at mm. 8–11) should begin to reveal itself. The violinist's entries within this exchange allow for crescendos—first to the *sfp* on F, resolving to E, then to the *sfp* on A, resolving to G♯—at which point the pianist, now doubling the violin with another crescendo, again presents both dyads in tenths. As within the pianist's first phrase, the bass at mm. 11–13 again moves upward via semitones to the dominant (the G-major chord) of the mediant, C major. This time the violinist, having reached the peak of the crescendo in m. 12, takes a surprising plunge downward, to the descending semitone C-to-B. First-time listeners, and maybe even later ones, cannot be expected to know that the violinist has just anticipated the *contour*, but only one of the two pitch-specific semitones, of the head motive in the forthcoming Presto (mm. 19–20). As Réti has suggested, the rest of this Adagio can be interpreted as a search for the other semitone—E–F. When the pianist's E–F♯ (mm. 13–14) becomes E–F♮ in m. 15, a voice exchange transfers that interval to the violinist; seven successive iterations of the E–F dyad, as supported by the pianist's tonicized subdominant, confirm that this *must* be the sought-after semitone. Now everything is in place; it is as if a spring has been coiled, and the fermatas at m. 18 caution us that it is about to be released. When that happens at m. 19, both players might experience a split second of relief; but, to paraphrase Réti, now the real work begins.

As shown at example 4.3a, Réti subdivides the first phrase of the Presto into three seminal segments, which he identifies as I, prime shape; II, step-ladder; and III, 4 + 3 (ascending fourth, followed by falling third). My alternative view, at example 4.3b, betrays the influence of my Schenkerian training and takes a critical stand against Réti's apparent indifference both to harmonic progression and to scale degree; a consideration of these dimensions can substantiate long-range motivic voice-leading connections that Réti does not address. For example, my reading proposes that a stepwise ascent through the interval of a seventh—<F–G♯–A–B–C–D–E> (a reinterpretation of Réti's step-ladder)—fundamentally carries the violinist's line to the primary tone of the movement, the mediant-supported E♮ as 5̂ at the fermata.[23] An audacious extension of this ascent will especially emerge within the movement's coda. The arrival on E♮ completes a long-range "composing out" of the Presto's opening E–F motive over the span of the complete phrase: as a broad neighbor tone, the F♮ at m. 19 resolves both registrally and harmonically to the E at the fermata.

Example 4.3. (a) From Rudolph Réti, *Thematic Patterns in Sonatas of Beethoven*, ed. Deryck Cooke (New York: Da Capo, 1992; orig. publ., 1967), 145. (b) Alternative view (levels 1, 2, and 3)

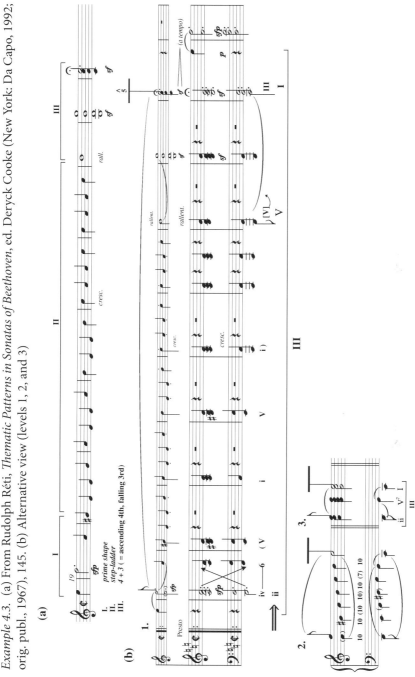

Let me acknowledge my respect for Rudolph Réti's *Grundgestalt*-oriented analysis of op. 47. But I believe that so much more can be gained if we consider the development of Beethoven's motivic ideas in light of his formal processes, and so I proceed accordingly. I examine how motives and phrases combine to create huge thematic structures within the exposition—ones that represent a considerable break from classical conventions.

William Caplin has noted that the violinist's opening Adagio phrase participates as a compound basic idea (CBI) within a phrase structure that resembles a modulating sixteen-bar sentence, compressed over the span of mm. 1–13.[24] In fact, the introduction's opening sentential design looks forward not only to the Presto's main theme (MT) but also to the transition and the first of the two secondary themes within the Presto movement proper. As Caplin puts it, "of all the large-scale units of classical form, slow introductions are the least predictable in their organization."[25] In this case, however, the introduction, though characteristically hesitant and ultimately unstable, opens with the clearest, most conventional formal design of the movement as a whole. The enormous, highly individualized sentences that follow will expand upon the general pattern and dynamic of a sentence in completely unprecedented ways.

For example, in virtually every one of Beethoven's earlier violin and cello sonatas, one can find an opening theme, sometimes in more than one movement, that gives each instrument a chance to present the initial phrase or phrase-group. Mozart's violin sonatas establish this duo-sonata convention, beginning with the rondo finale of his C-major Violin Sonata, K. 296 (1778). These "equal opportunity" openings tend to take the form of simple main-theme repetitions, or antecedent-consequents, or written-out varied repetitions within small binaries, or repetitions that retrospectively become the beginning of a transition. To my knowledge, the main theme of op. 47 strikes upon an entirely new path, comparable in part only to the opening of the "Tempest." The violinist takes the lead at the beginning of the Presto (example 4.4), but what seems at first like an imperfect authentic cadence in the "wrong" key—the mediant—concludes the phrase at the fermata in m. 27. Now it is the pianist's turn, but the same "wrong" goal is achieved at the cadenza in m. 36. The fermatas have the effect of bringing the thematic process to highly unusual halts—moments of reflection and then showing-off that seem to prevent a genuine "main theme" from taking shape. Given that main themes by definition close in the home key, neither of the two closures in the mediant can serve to bring this theme to completion; something else will be needed. Beethoven's solution is to create a heightened continuation phrase—one that invites us retrospectively to interpret the two preceding phrases as compound basic ideas within a massive presentation. In coordination with the pianist's new, driving, continuous eighth-note motion, the compression of the continuation creates the effect of urgency. A most striking feature of the continuation, moreover, is its motivic content. Having opened with the seminal <E–F–A–G♯> idea, the violinist begins again at mm. 37–38 with the E–F semitone; here, and for the first of several times to come, the motive appears in a new harmonic guise. Now an ascending-step sequence allows the motive to strive upward chromatically, until, at the apex of the phrase, the counterpart semitone G♯–A provides the climax and then brings closure into the first and only genuine authentic cadence thus far, as elided (↔) at m. 45.

Example 4.4. Beethoven, op. 47, first movement, mm. 19–45

It would be hard to imagine a more purely violinistic figure in 1803 than the one with which the transition begins (example 4.5). Beethoven seems determined to put Bridgetower physically to work in the most strenuous, and most visually exciting, way—via repeated, continuous string crossing. From his first piano sonata onward, Beethoven had certainly written hundreds of bars

Example 4.5. Beethoven, op. 47, first movement, mm. 45–78

of broken octaves for the piano—"murky bass," as this and variants of it are called. The specific octave gestures that the violinist and pianist exchange at the beginning of the transition are new to the piano; they have been so clearly inspired by the violin. As another lengthy sentential structure now gets under way, we can note that these gestures are also the product of motivic thought: the violinist's two-bar tonic-oriented pattern, imitated by the pianist to create a four-bar unit, provides a new submetric neighbor-tone setting for the G♯–A semitone; the dominant-oriented response at mm. 49–51 gives the pianist a lightning opportunity to highlight the neighbor-motion E–F–E over the bar line. The eight-bar unit heard thus far could well have served as a simple presentation within a sixteen-bar sentence, but the "equal opportunity" tradition yields a repetition of the entire eight bars, with the two performers exchanging roles. As within the main theme—and especially in light of this devilish Presto tempo, which clearly suggests that two notated bars stand for only one "real" bar (I discuss this notational technique in chapter 7)—the eight-bar repetition sounds more like a repeated CBI than like a repeated presentation. What follows confirms that impression: this time the continuation will nearly balance the sixteen-bar presentation; it will be a thrilling twelve-bar unit in which an ascending-step sequence and *sforzandos* on the offbeats lead to a climactic half cadence in the new key, E minor (= v), at m. 73. At the beginning of the over-powering eighteen-bar standing-on-the-dominant that ensues, Réti hears a reference in the violin part to his *prime shape*, the head motive of the main theme, now transposed and with the two dyads reversed. Whether or not Réti's view is persuasive, we can surely agree that this passage offers a striking anticipation of the transition Beethoven was to compose for his "Waldstein" Sonata just six or seven months later.

As the goal of the transition, the beginning of Beethoven's ST¹ could not possibly provide greater contrast (example 4.6). This is no ordinary "lyrical second theme"; the texture and register suggest a chorale, maybe even an inward-turning

Example 4.6. Beethoven, op. 47, first movement, mm. 87–116

prayer. The melody of the new basic idea is nothing more than a very broad turn, repeated—on two structural levels, no less—and then ever so beautifully extended via diminution to a half cadence. It transforms the G♯–A motive into something ineffably tender and contemplative, while also recalling the character and tempo of the Adagio introduction. In the recapitulation this recollection will be all the more overt: here within the exposition the key is the proto-Schubertian *major dominant* (see Schubert's Piano Sonata in A Minor, D. 784); in the recapitulation it will become the home-tonic major, thus reminding us that Beethoven's violinist opened the introduction in that major mode but then yielded immediately to the pianist for a "landmark" major-to-minor move that would determine the mode of the Presto.[26] When the pianist returns to the minor dominant at m. 107, a plaintive, rueful dialogue begins—an interplay that seems profoundly intimate. Perhaps it should come as no surprise that, at the Adagio in mm. 115–16, both players appear to have become lost in mutual thought, so much so that no cadence emerges to close this theme.

What follows at the Tempo I (example 4.7) is so clearly a return to the aggressive momentum of the transition materials that some writers hear that

Example 4.7. Beethoven, op. 47, first movement, mm. 117–32

passage as having been *interrupted* at m. 90.[27] For example, Lawrence Kramer at first describes the chorale-like passage as "merely a parenthesis"; then he listens again and recognizes that "a parenthesis, too, can make a difference."[28] If we take seriously the observation by theorists of form that secondary themes within classical sonata-form movements close with authentic cadences, then a "new theme" does not begin at m. 117, because the preceding theme has not yet closed. I dare to propose that the explosive passage beginning at m. 117 might be heard as yet another huge continuation, one that balances an equally huge presentation—the violinist's tender sixteen-bar chorale as a CBI, and the pianist's soulful response as its varied repetition. In other words, like the MT and like the transition, this ST[1] takes on the structure, if not the character, of a sentence, to be concluded only with the tumultuous cadence at m. 144. But perhaps the sheer length of this process, not to mention the extreme contrast of its two parts, rules against such a view. At the least, it can be said that the octave leaps in both instruments within the continuation have been prepared by the violinist within the presentation, thus creating one motivic link—one small element of continuity. However one might choose to characterize the formal function of this passage, we can note that it drives to its cadence as if hell-bent upon reaching the fundamental, culminating theme of the exposition—the second secondary theme (ST[2]).

Here, for the first and only time, the pianist takes the lead (example 4.8). Epitomizing their role as carriers of the short–long rhythm, semitones, both as neighbor and then passing tones, now give the pianist the means by which to make an exultant ascent through an entire octave span; then turns, borrowed from ST[1], allow for a slower descent from scale degree $\hat{8}$ to $\hat{5}$, at which point this exceptionally concise theme reaches its cadence and is snatched by up the violin. A canonic imitation between the violin and the piano's bass line intensifies the repetition, and then evaded cadences twice extend the theme by motivating "one more time" repetitions of its cadential idea. The cadence finally achieved at m. 176 hardly seems like a goal, because the codettas that follow are unrelenting in the intensity with which they revive the transition's basic idea. The pianist's crashing chords urge the violinist to *slow down*; but when the violinist finally relinquishes eighth notes for whole notes and a fermata, one has the impression that this has happened purely out of exhaustion—from those extremely difficult bowings persisting right up until the end.

To summarize, I portray the exposition of this movement as one in which two comrades, both virtuosi, collaborate but also challenge one another, within a dialogue that may be one of the most stunning demonstrations in the classical repertoire of what can happen when composers and performers "perform" their fundamental interdependency. Like these two protagonists, but not in any way as if "assigned" to one or the other, two pitch-specific dyads collaborate to create a remarkable motivic network—one that spans across enormously contrasting themes of unprecedented length. Let me now draw attention to details within Beethoven's development section and his coda that surface as further manifestations of the motivic, formal, and technical ideas proposed thus far as fundamental to this movement.

Example 4.8. Beethoven, op. 47, first movement, mm. 140–79

The development begins by underscoring the preeminent role of the semitone E–F; like the exposition, it opens with that specific motive in its original register. Here, however, the F♮ itself becomes the local tonic: the pianist introduces a quiet, major-mode version of ST² in that key. Apparently, neither instrument finds comfort in this gentler version of the theme; already by m. 200 the pianist is ready to abandon F major and hand the eight-bar phrase over to the violinist, who repeats it sequentially in G minor. A second sequence of the phrase begins in E♭ at m. 210, becomes fragmented, and results in some of the most brutally dissonant imitative counterpoint one can find in Beethoven's oeuvre. As can be ascertained by examining the violin part from m. 214 onward, the pretense here is a straightforward descending-fifths sequence, but the pianist's strident octaves all but annihilate the logic of that progression. The best one can do is note that the goal of this fracas is the dominant of the key with which the development began—F, but now F minor.

Within the terrifying passage in broken thirds and sixths that the pianist now faces, F minor again serves as an anchor (at m. 246), and then, after one last statement of ST² in D♭ (at mm. 258–69), as the point of departure (at m. 270) for the retransition, which reaches the home dominant at m. 300. Within the ensuing dominant prolongation, the neighbor-motion E–F–E again takes center stage in both parts; the pianist's cadenza even absorbs the F♮ within the dominant-ninth chord, beginning at m. 308 (example 4.9, m. 310). But now the G♯–A dyad must have its turn! And Beethoven can grant this to the pianist's part (see mm. 313–15) by giving the violinist a sequential repetition of the pianist's cadenza, here prolonging the dominant of the subdominant (iv)—that is, the dominant of the very harmony with which the exposition eccentrically began. The violinist's sequence in turn motivates a "false recapitulation," a full-fledged statement (at mm. 326–35) of the main theme's first phrase, but now in D minor; this is of course the "wrong" key for a conventional recapitulation, but the *right* key, the subdominant, for a false recapitulation in this movement. A great advantage of this maneuver is that it lands the phrase on an F-major chord at m. 334—one more opportunity to reinforce the role of F♮ as a pivotal tone in this movement. The semitone with which the false recapitulation began—A–B♭—then serves (at mm. 336–40) as the impetus for the move toward the true home-key recapitulation; but note that the chord on F (at mm. 340–43) plays the penultimate role in this modulation.

Now to Beethoven's coda, with excerpts shown at examples 4.10 and 4.11. The bridge into this section, with its move (at mm. 513–16) into the key of the Neapolitan (♭II = B♭), seems to have been motivated by the point just before the true recapitulation, in which the semitone A–B♭ played the pivotal role. This is the calm before the final storm. As the neighbor motion F–E insinuates itself in the pianist's bass (at mm. 527–32), we approach the beginning of the main theme for its last appearance. This time the theme does what it has perhaps been longing to do for some time now: here the original stepwise ascent through the seventh will be expanded over the range of an entire octave plus seventh (example 4.10). The double-neighbor motion <E–F–D–E> (at mm. 545–46) brings the ascent to a halt, and then the climax of the entire movement begins.

Example 4.9. Beethoven, op. 47, first movement, mm. 310–44

Example 4.10. Beethoven, op. 47, first movement, mm. 532–66

Beethoven tends to simplify his essential ideas in his codas, and this movement provides a case in point. Here the coda's climactic statement, beginning at m. 547, and given a "one-more-time" repetition at m. 553, features a segment of the original ascent in retrograde, now providing the fundamental *Urlinie* descent for the movement as a whole. There then follows a simplification of both the ascent and the *Urlinie* descent: each is reduced to a mere tonic

arpeggiation, first up, then down. Finally, for a movement whose Adagio introduction has inspired not only an Adagio moment with fermata in ST[1] (in both
the exposition and the recapitulation) but also nine additional fermatas, the two
last Adagios with fermatas might seem inevitable (example 4.11). The violinist's Adagio, at mm. 575–78, gives the E–F motive one final major-mode setting;
this statement seems to be hopeful—wistful for a positive outcome. The pianist's
Adagio dashes the violinist's hope. Here the minor-mode plagal progression (iv-
i)—so rich with the memory of the opening of the Presto, and so redolent of the
lament tradition with which it is associated—would seem to express something
beyond sorrow, something so deeply personal that it cannot be put into words.
From this perspective, the gruff, *furioso* conclusion at the Tempo I becomes a
heroic effort to put away such dark thoughts. The movement cannot, however,

Example 4.11. Beethoven, op. 47, first movement, m. 575 to end

escape its two motivic semitones: they pervade the music all the way into the
pianist's final G♯–A.

One certainly cannot claim that the technique of creating intermovement
motivic connections was new for Beethoven in 1803.[29] But from the first to the second movement of op. 47, his increasing concern for a motivically cyclic approach
to composition could not be more evident. As shown in example 4.12a, Beethoven's

second movement, in F major, features a theme for variations in which the first phrase begins with F–E and the second with G♯–A; relative to the Presto, the direction of each of the two semitones has been reversed. Especially salient are the materials of the B-section within this theme as rounded binary (example 4.12b): the cadential progression in the dominant at mm. 21–22 highlights the E–F motion, with F♮ now as an incomplete neighbor; then, twice within the standing-on-the-dominant phrase, the pianist labors upward by step to the E and embellishes it again with the F. In case we have missed the point—hardly a chance by now—the phrase concludes with a fragmentation that yields two more *sforzando*-accented F♮s (in m. 26).

It is now well known that the finale of op. 47 was originally meant to serve as the last movement of Beethoven's earlier A-major violin sonata, op. 30, no. 1 (1802). Scholars and performers alike agree that Beethoven's decision to transfer

Example 4.12. Beethoven, op. 47, second movement: (a) mm. 1–8; (b) mm. 17–28

this finale to op. 47 was wise, as was his last-minute addition of a big, loud A-major chord in the piano at the beginning of the movement, clearly a reference to the pianist's initial harmony within the first movement's introduction (example 4.13a). After that chord, the pianist's very first interval is G♯–A. But the pianist's voice is only a counterpoint to the violinist's soprano here; given that this movement is in A *major*, analysts will search in vain for the counterpart semitone, E–F♮.

On the other hand, the *idea* of the semitone within a short-long rhythm—materializing wherever it can be realized—unquestionably rests at the basis of this marvelous movement. Just as notable as the pervasiveness of semitones is the undeniable connection, observed by Réti, between the ST[1] of the finale (example 4.13b) and ST[2] of the first movement (at mm. 144–56).[30] If in the first movement that theme stormed its way upward through the octave, in the finale the octave ascent, followed again by the slower descent from $\hat{8}$ to $\hat{5}$, embraces the jaunty,

Example 4.13. Beethoven, op. 47, finale: (a) mm. 1–8; (b) mm. 60–70

tarantella character of the movement as a whole, as if to brush away the memory of the earlier turmoil.

∞

Leo Tolstoy may have contributed the single most provocative moment in the reception history of Beethoven's op. 47. I refer to his famous novella, *The Kreutzer Sonata*, from 1889, and to recent musicological efforts to interpret this work in respect of the role that music has played in the construction of gender relations. Tolstoy probably knew nothing about George Bridgetower's role in the première of the sonata, but it seems clear that he recognized in this piece what Lawrence Kramer has described as "its explosive incongruity," its "importation of formal monumentality and emotional ferocity" into a medium that hitherto, and even long thereafter, was associated with the salon.[31] Thus when the protagonist of the story, in the thick of a disastrous marriage, introduces his wife to a violinist, arranges for her as amateur pianist to rehearse privately with him, and finally witnesses their semipublic performance of op. 47, he senses that a social boundary has been mightily crossed; the performance itself serves as the catalyst for the husband's jealousy and his brutal murder of the wife.

About the first movement of op. 47, Tolstoy's protagonist asks:

> Do you know the first movement, its presto? You do?... Ah! It is a fearful thing, that sonata. Especially that movement. And in general music's a fearful thing! What is it? I don't know.... What does it do? And why does it do to us what it does? They say music exalts the soul. Nonsense, it is not true!... It has neither an exalting nor a debasing effect but an agitating one.... Music makes me forget myself, my real position; it transports me to some other position not my own.

And, a little later, he says: "Take that Kreutzer Sonata for instance, how can that first presto be played in a drawing-room among ladies in low-necked dresses? To hear that played, to clap a little, and then to eat ices and talk of the latest scandal?"[32]

For me as pianist, a most amazing detail about Tolstoy's novella is that he portrays the wife as having been able to work up a performance of Beethoven's "Kreutzer" over the span of roughly one week! But it goes without saying that the character of the "Kreutzer" plays the greater role in the story than its technical difficulties. For Kramer, what the husband hears in the first movement, "what he has turned procurer in order to hear it, is a movement of transcendence, a breaking-through into a spirituality quite inconsistent with the lust, décolletage, and triviality of the drawing room."[33] Both Kramer and, before him, Richard Leppert stress that not only is Beethoven's first movement "not salon music: it is not music of and for women. It is fundamentally masculine, even phallic, in character as Beethoven's music can be.... The feminine is erased from the score. [The] wife and her partner both take on the sonoric roles of men, a violation scripted by Beethoven that [the husband] cannot tolerate."[34] Finally, Kramer reminds us that "for many years it was considered indecent for women to play [the violin]";[35] this was certainly the case in 1803. And yet, neither Kramer nor Leppert considers the specific male violinist who premièred op. 47. Nor, by the way, does Bridgetower make an appearance in Jander's or Réti's analysis; for that matter, he becomes a mere footnote or one-liner, if not utterly disappears, in the commentary about op. 47 by such preeminent Beethoven historians as Maynard Solomon, William Kinderman, and Lewis Lockwood.

Since Beethoven most surely did not compose op. 47 with a female violinist in mind, and if his writing in the first movement—especially the continuous string-crossing idea at the beginning of his transition, which pervades the movement—was inspired by violinistic technique, then perhaps it should not be at all surprising that the Presto of op. 47 has been interpreted as "masculine." This outlook does not, of course, explain the many differences in character between op. 47 and the other nine sonatas for violin that Beethoven produced—none of them presumably with women violinists in mind. In short, perhaps Beethoven really did write the first movement of this piece "with Bridgetower in mind."

Reports have it that Beethoven and Bridgetower were constant companions during the month of May 1803, when Bridgetower was in Vienna; two short letters from Beethoven to Bridgetower during that month—whether before or after their performance together (the dates do not clarify)—attest to their intimacy.[36] More pertinent, a manuscript of the exposition of the first movement discovered in 1965 confirms that Beethoven originally dedicated his op. 47 to Bridgetower, as follows: "Sonata mulattica Composta per il Mulatto Brischdauer/ gran passo e compositore mulattico" ("mulatto sonata composed for the mulatto Bridgetower, great loon and mulatto composer").[37] However it might be translated, I take "gran passo" as jocular and deeply affectionate.

The story also goes that their friendship broke up "over a girl"[38]—possibly because Bridgetower made a snide remark about a woman of whom Beethoven was fond. We will undoubtedly never know what really happened; but a letter from Ries to publisher Nikolaus Simrock on October 22, 1803, indicates that already by then Beethoven had decided to dedicate the op. 47 sonata to the renowned Parisian violinist Rodolphe Kreutzer and to Louis Adam, the foremost pianist in Paris at the time. Why? Here we have an explanation, and it smacks of unabashed opportunism. Beethoven's dissatisfaction with his freelance life in Vienna had led him to threaten a move to Paris; his *Eroica* Symphony, carrying the dedication to Napoleon until May 1804, his op. 47, and probably even his newly begun opera *Léonore* (based on J. N. Bouilly's French libretto) were all to have paved the way for a smooth entrée into Parisian musical life.[39] The great irony here is that Kreutzer detested Beethoven's works and refused ever to perform op. 47. As for Bridgetower, after around 1848 he seems to have slipped into obscurity. He died in a back street of London in 1860; his death certificate is signed with an X by an illiterate woman.

On a brighter note, let us applaud the fact that stereotypes of the past about music as gendered "masculine" or "feminine" are now being critically examined and contextualized, and that they are for the most part avoided today. Now, one can hear recorded performances of op. 47 by, for example, Martha Argerich and

Gidon Kremer, Clara Haskil and Arthur Grumiaux, Lambert Orkis and Anne-Sophie Mutter, and, especially touching, Claude Frank and his daughter, Pamela. Whatever the gender combination, performers of op. 47 would, I think, all agree that this piece cries out for an extraordinary synergy—a genuine coming together of soul mates in music. Bridgetower himself felt that the "Kreutzer" Sonata should have been the "Bridgetower" Sonata. Let us take this opportunity to bestow upon him what should most probably have been his fortune.[40]

CHAPTER Five

On Performance, Analysis, and Schubert

In his "Analysis in Context," from 1999, Jim Samson proposed that "it is tempting to see the history of [music-]analytical thought as an almost classical Hegelian cycle, where analysis had first to achieve independence before it could achieve self-awareness, and with that an acknowledgement of its dependencies."[1] Compared with the history of music analysis, the history of thought among writers in English about the relation of analysis to performance covers a drastically shorter time span, but Samson's statement has relevance to this newer domain. When, in 1983, I began to prepare a paper about two of Beethoven's Bagatelles, Op. 126, in the form of a dialogue between an allegorical music Analyst and her colleague the Pianist/Performer, I encountered resistance from both mentors and colleagues. Within that very structuralist-dominated decade—at the heyday of Schenkerian and atonal theory in American academia—the idea of "analysis for performers," or "analysis of performance," had not even begun to gain currency, much less independence, as a field of inquiry; I would be stepping aside from my work at that time on the music of Alban Berg and trying to break new ground. I have no regrets today, because it seems that the publication of that paper in 1985,[2] along with studies by many others since then, contributed in the long run to the emergence of an independent, and also *interdependent*, line of investigation, addressed below.

But I paid quite a price for my efforts. Not all of my readers were happy with the relationship I posited for my Performer and my Analyst. The problem: I seem to have given the Analyst the upper hand. From the perspectives of, first, Lawrence Rosenwald (1993), and then Joel Lester (1995) and Nicholas Cook (1999), I had created a "Puritan conversion narrative": the exchange between Analyst and Pianist was one in which the Analyst seems to have had all the answers and the Pianist, grateful for some analytic advice, "was blind, but now can see."[3] Since then, I think I can claim considerable growth toward a self-awareness of the kind that Samson mentions. It has been clear to me for a long time both how and why I opened my work to the kind of criticism Rosenwald, Lester, Cook, and others have raised.

In 1983 I had trusted, of course, that my two characters would be recognizable to many as representative of my own concerns at the time—for example, my efforts to prepare my first complete performance of the Bagatelles[4] and to grapple with how my analytic training could serve my performance aspirations. In the broadest sense, I was trying to come to grips with how, or whether, the kinds of analysis I teach as a music theorist might be useful to the many young performers who take my courses. But more than anything else, my article was an effort to bring two facets of myself into dialogue with one another.[5] In short, I had assumed readers would notice that my Performer analyzes and my Analyst performs.

In my effort to characterize what is unique about performance, and thus to create two distinct personae, with their separate tasks and goals, I seem to have exaggerated their differences. My Performer does indeed get the credit for the Analyst's effort to interpret structural details in *dramatic* terms, but the Analyst clearly takes charge of the analysis, leaving the Performer mainly to perform the bagatelles (she did this within the 1983 presentation but lost her chance in the 1985 article). Given that not all music analysts perform, and that performers tend not to regard themselves as analysts, the kind of dialogue I created might be said to have some basis in reality. But for many analysts who are also performers, the reality of the performance–analysis relationship is usually a great deal more complex.

Readers must surely have noticed that the Performer in my article is just as "verbal"—maybe even as "analytical"—as the Analyst. The two of them most certainly cannot be construed as representing, or invoking, vestiges of the Cartesian mind–body antithesis—in this case, Analyst as mind, Performer as body—that occasionally arise in discussions of analysis versus performance.[6] Indeed, the processes of thinking, feeling, and using the body to perform interact inseparably for performers who also analyze.[7] Most important, I had intended to give both characters equal authority within their exchange. But the Analyst fails to clarify that many of her analytic views had in fact been inspired by the Performer. Nor does the Performer grasp the opportunity to demonstrate that performances can, and usually do, influence and even determine analytic interpretations, just as much as analyses can, and often do, inform performances. In this chapter, I invite the *Performer* to make that case with reference to Schubert.

Studies about the performance/analysis relationship have come a long way since 1985. We have managed to recover from several even more severe cases of the Analyst as Authoritarian.[8] Many have responded to Lester's complaint, in 1995, that until around then, something was strikingly absent from much of the performance/analysis literature—"namely, the performers and their performances."[9] Writers have since acted upon Cook's plea, in 1999, that "performance should be seen as a source of signification in its own right," and that analytic theory is itself performative.[10] But for general readers, the separate challenges and goals of performers and analysts may nevertheless remain more obvious than the attributes, interests, and skills that these two types of musicians hold in common.

For example, I cannot be the only pianist for whom initial studies in music theory and analysis led to a burst of enthusiasm for considering one's performance repertoire in analytic terms. I can no longer remember what it must have been like to play a piece without being consciously aware of melodic scale degrees, harmonic progressions, cadences, formal divisions, and voice leading on a fairly detailed local level. I dare say that when other musicians began, like me, to study Schenkerian theory, the very tangible ideas of, say, middleground neighbor motions, registral connections, voice exchanges, and unfoldings made sense to them because these relationships were in some completely uncomplicated way already part of their experience in performing and listening to tonal music. I shall admit that, for many years now, I have rarely chosen a fingering, made a decision about pedaling or articulation, or even considered how I will enter and exit the keys without having arrived at some kind of analytically based sound image, if only a vague one. Conversely, I would not have entered the field of music theory and analysis had I not, much earlier, gained a profound love of music through my efforts to perform it. The discipline of preparing for performances, and the energy, imagination, courage, and focus that performing requires may well be the theorist's best possible preparation for classroom teaching and the presenting of papers about music. In short, for many theorists and performers, the Analyst and the Performer may never have been as distinct one from another as I originally portrayed them to be.[11]

Whether primarily as performers or analysts, musicians are, after all, strange creatures, in ways that might never be fully understood. Just as beginners in music and scholars in other disciplines sometimes express amazement—even disbelief— that the deaf Beethoven could have composed his Ninth Symphony without actually having been able to "hear" the sonic results, they can be mystified by the idea that strong musicians and musical literates, and not just Beethoven, can *hear* the music in scores they silently read. Though such a skill is undoubtedly shared by most of the readers of this book, at least one distinguished musicologist would presumably need to discount that ability as a means of experiencing a genuine, perhaps even "drastic" and thrilling, "performance" on grounds that the labor of the performer(s) is not visible, the sound of the music is not materially present, and the performance is not live.[12] Cognitive scientists and psychologists of music continue to run experiments on the phenomenon of absolute and relative pitch, musical memory, and other skills that many musicians enjoy but cannot explain.[13] Theodor Adorno held that, like Hegel's texts, "music of Beethoven's type" must be heard "multidimensionally, forward and backward at the same time" (see chapter 2). Even though live performances demand that players be fully "in the moment," pianists who perform, say, Schubert's Sonata in A Major, D. 959, will most likely "hear backward" to the opening of its first movement when they reach Schubert's extraordinary reminiscence of the opening theme in its final bars. Let us not forget that many performers, and especially pianists, render complete concerts *from memory*; analysts who do not perform regularly cannot claim this mental skill, but when they have studied a piece thoroughly, written about it, or discussed it repeatedly with colleagues or students, their recall of the full score, backward and forward, is often complete. As debatable as this may seem, why should we not imagine that it is possible for performers and analysts alike to experience the present and the past simultaneously within a musical work, even while thinking about its future goals? For performers, this skill is enhanced by their very corporeal involvement in making the music: like analysts who can turn the pages of a score backward and forward, singers and instrumentalists cannot help but remember where they have been musically and where they will be going, because their vocal cords, their fingers, their breathing will remind them. Like Proust's celebrated *madeleine*, or like the returns of Vinteuil's *petite phrase*, such sensual, tactile, and sonic reminders sometimes allow for the past (in Proust's case, the distant past) and the present to intermingle in the moment not only for musicians but for most human beings.

I have been led to the central topic of this book—musical form as process—by the performer in me as much as by my analytic and theoretic concerns. The distinctive feature of this study has been its effort to capture something of the *processual nature* of the musical experience. As a temporal art, music in performance insists that we hear it diachronically; thus, we perceive all performances—of *any* kind of music—as processual, if only in the ordinary sense that they must begin at some point in time and end sometime later. Less ordinary, I claim, is that, toward the end of the eighteenth century and into the next, new compositional approaches to certain, by then well-established conventions of musical form seemed intent upon shifting our focus away from the perception of forms as the product of successive, functionally discrete sections within a whole. Instead, these new approaches encouraged the idea that the formal process itself becomes "the form." Listeners of this kind of music are being asked to *participate* within that process, by listening backward as well as in the moment—by *remembering* what they have heard, while retrospectively reinterpreting formal functions in the light of an awareness of the interplay between conventions and transformations. As perhaps the most active of all listeners, performers themselves are being urged to play a far more authoritative role in articulating such form-defining moments as beginnings, middles, and endings, while projecting the overall shapes that these might define. It is the idea of *form coming into being* that I persist in exploring here, as I consider some of the challenges of performing the first movement of Schubert's Piano Sonata in A Minor, Op. 42 (D. 845).

I begin by offering some historical background about this piece of the kind that I think both performers and analysts would want to consider. Of Franz Schubert's three piano sonatas in A minor, the one whose opening is shown at example 5.1 was the last to be written—before the end of May in 1825—and the first of *any* of his piano sonatas to be published. When the firm of Pennauer put forth this work as Schubert's op. 42 in 1826, favorable reviews in Leipzig and Frankfurt helped to establish his status as a composer for the piano.[14] But Schubert was hardly a newcomer to solo piano music at that time. Already by the end of his teenage years, during 1815–18, he had experimented with perhaps more than eleven piano sonatas—leaving some movements incomplete, or some sonatas with but one or two movements, creating sonata fragments, as it were; many of these pieces are audaciously original.[15] Yet, by 1823 Schubert's only published work for the piano was his highly innovative *Wandererfantasie*, Op. 15. Quite possibly his op. 42 was the first of his piano sonatas that Schubert deemed worthy of publication.

Needless to say, Schubert's artistic standards were of the very highest order. Probably as late as 1823, and thus after his completion of the "Unfinished" Symphony, Schubert was invited to choose and present one of his orchestral works for a performance. He declined the offer, because he claimed to have nothing that he could "send out into the world with a clear conscience," when "there are so many pieces by great masters, as for instance, Beethoven's Overture to *Prometheus, Egmont, Coriolanus*, etc., etc., etc."[16] That the name of *just one* composer—Beethoven, the overpowering musical figure in Vienna throughout Schubert's lifetime—should flow automatically here from Schubert's pen comes as no surprise; Schubert could not help but be continually inspired and challenged by Beethoven. As proposed by the Schubert scholar John Gingerich: "[I]t is difficult to think of another composer on the absolutely highest level in the Western tradition who had more powerful, more immediate, more intimidating models of achievement before him than Schubert had with Mozart, Haydn, and Beethoven."[17] The very idea, then, that Schubert was willing to send his op. 42 sonata out into the world may well have some relevance in efforts to interpret its character and its design.

Like others, I would like to believe that Schubert never genuinely doubted his capacity to attain *on his own terms* a level of achievement entirely worthy of comparison with Beethoven's. But possibly by the end of 1822, when he may already have fallen prey to syphilis, Schubert must also have realized that his time was running out, and he may have assigned to himself a measure of the responsibility for actions that would inevitably shorten his life.[18] According to two of his friends, in 1823 Schubert produced some of the songs for his great cycle *Die schöne Müllerin* while hospitalized and dangerously ill. By March 31, 1824, Schubert's mood, as suggested in his now well-known letter to Leopold Kupelwieser, embraced an astounding admixture of hopelessness and professional resolve. Quoting Gretchen's (Goethe's) "Meine Ruh' ist hin," from one of his earliest, most famous songs, Schubert says: "I feel myself to be the most unhappy and wretched creature in the world. Imagine a man whose health will never be right again, and who, in sheer despair over this, ever makes things worse and worse, instead of better.... I seem once again to have composed two operas for nothing." But then Schubert announces that he has just completed two string quartets and an octet, and that he has plans for a third quartet, as the next step toward the genre of the "great symphony." Finally, he tells his friend the news in Vienna that there will soon be a concert of Beethoven's latest works, and he concludes: "God willing, I too am thinking of giving a similar concert next year."[19]

Unfortunately, the "concert next year" did not occur until four years later, in March of 1828—on the anniversary of Beethoven's death; eight months after that, Schubert was dead, at the age of 31. But apparently by 1825 he had indeed worked out most of his "Great" Symphony in C Major, while also completing the op. 42 sonata and then the Piano Sonata in D Major, D. 850. These works, along with the chamber pieces from 1824 and the instrumental works that followed in such an astonishing spate of creativity until his death, constitute what Gingerich has called Schubert's "Beethoven Project"[20]—that is, Schubert's forthright commitment to meeting Beethoven on his own turf, by not only composing but also now publicly presenting works in Beethoven's favored instrumental genres. Following Charles Fisk, I see Schubert's "Beethoven project" as his preeminently self-affirming "Schubert project," and as an act of the greatest courage.[21] Moreover, I am particularly attracted to the A-minor Sonata, Op. 42, because of its place within the initial stages of that project, shortly after the beginning of the end of Schubert's life. But Gingerich's idea of a "Beethoven project" could not be more appropriate as a basis for this discussion. There is only one composer to whom one might directly turn in search of precedents for Schubert's remarkable formal and motivic strategies in his op. 42 first movement, and that composer is, of course, Beethoven.

Readers will recall that, concerning the first movement of Beethoven's "Tempest" Sonata, Carl Dahlhaus has said: "The beginning of the movement is *not yet* a subject, the evolutionary episode is one *no longer*."[22] I now apply Dahlhaus's observation to Schubert's sonata. The annotated score at example 5.1 shows a broad, brooding beginning whose obsessive orientation on dominant rather than tonic harmony suggests that an introduction to the sonata-form proper is gradually building to a climax. Not a single root-position tonic harmony will fall on a downbeat until the cataclysmic *fortissimo* at m. 26—a "structural downbeat" if there ever was one. At that moment, the much-awaited resolution of the pent-up dominant is provided by a bold new idea that sounds for all the world like the beginning of the sonata's main theme (MT). But a sequential repetition of the new idea initiates a modulation into the secondary key of this sonata exposition—the mediant, C major. And then a prolongation of the dominant of that new key prepares the beginning, at m. 40 (see example 5.2), of what must ultimately be regarded as a first secondary theme (ST[1]). The the apparent MT begun at m. 26 has thus unquestionably "become" (⇒) the transition. And from this it follows that what seemed like an introduction at the beginning must have been the MT after all. Or, better put, this is what it has become.

Dahlhaus's statement about Beethoven's "Tempest" conjoins his caveat that it is useless to try settling once and for all the question of whether Beethoven's beginning is an introduction or a main theme. I am proposing precisely the same about Schubert's opening. The beginning of this movement is not yet the MT when we hear it *in time*, for the "first" time; it becomes the MT only in retrospect, that is, only after we realize that the subsequent modulatory passage can no longer be regarded as the MT. The process itself of "Introduction becoming MT" would seem to be what Schubert is highlighting. And, to invoke his contemporary, Hegel, we might say that the *becoming* itself is what dialectically unites our opposing perceptions—introduction versus MT.

What does this processual interpretation of Schubert's opening mean to me as a performer of the movement, and to what extent has it been influenced by the performer in me? This latter question is particularly hard to answer, because I began analytically to conceive of the idea of dual, progressively changing formal functions around the same time that I began preparing for my first performance of this piece. The following can, however, be stressed: the formal ambiguity of Schubert's opening convinces me that performers of this movement are very much in charge of how listeners will perceive the unfolding design. To explain, I propose multiple ways in which the performer might be free to project the materials of mm. 1–26.[23]

Whether or not the pianist thinks of the opening four bars as an antecedent phrase, the convention of a two-bar basic idea followed by a two-bar contrasting idea that leads to a half cadence would undoubtedly suggest this type of phrase to analysts of form. (Such a view necessarily rests, however, upon the implication of tonic harmony in mm. 1–2, discussed below.) The idea of an antecedent as an opener is further confirmed when what promises to be a consequent phrase unequivocally begins at m. 5. But consequents by current definition end with an authentic cadence; here no such cadence is achieved. Instead, let us say that the

Example 5.1. Schubert, Piano Sonata in A Minor, Op. 42, D.845, first movement, mm. 1–39

potential consequent "becomes" an expanded "second antecedent," in that, like the first, it ends with a half cadence (at m. 10). Now we might be prepared to regard the two half cadences as ones "of limited scope,"[24] while reinterpreting the two antecedent phrases as the expansive presentation of a large, compound basic idea (CBI, mm. 1–4) and its expanded repetition (mm. 5–10). If this is what we perceive, we will then be expecting a continuation of comparable length, such that a single, somewhat expanded theme, based upon the sixteen-bar sentence, may be completed. Here the pianist might either confirm or negate such expectations; if ambiguity, rather than clarification, is already at the basis of the compositional plan, the pianist is free to choose.

Admittedly, on every recording of this movement that I have studied, the pianist responds to the new texture and rhythm at m. 10 by directly initiating a somewhat faster tempo, or by gradually achieving this over the next two to four bars. That said, I propose that when pianists make an effort to camouflage their acceleration, or to treat Schubert's *a tempo* marking at m. 10 literally, as a request to resume the initial moderato tempo, then the perception that a single thematic process is continuing onward will most likely be reinforced. I roughly describe Andreas Staier's strategy here, on a richly resonant fortepiano. Maurizio Pollini's approach is similar, but his moderato tempo itself seems a bit plodding; the opening tempo he resumes is already on the slow side, and he gives the impression of maintaining that tempo throughout the exposition.[25] If, on the other hand, pianists indeed observe both of Schubert's *poco ritardandos*, including the one at m. 3, and even if they have lingered for only a split second on either the accented E♮ in m. 1 or its neighbor tone, the F♮ in m. 5, then at what moment has there been the establishment of a stable tempo to resume?! I cannot claim, strictly speaking, that a classical *slow introduction* might be at hand, but Schubert's markings encourage a marvelously reflective, maybe even hesitant, certainly introduction-like performance of mm. 1–10. Perhaps because they sense that the forthcoming new idea at m. 26 calls for a faster tempo than the basic idea of mm. 1–2, various performers respond to the *a tempo* at m. 10 with a faster tempo than at any earlier moment so far. The faster the tempo chosen, and the more immediately it is established, the more likely it is that we will hear the downbeat of m. 10 as the beginning of a distinctly *new* thematic process, or as the discrete second part of a small-binary theme. This is what the recordings of pianists Richard Goode and András Schiff suggest, at least to me. In fact, their almost *subito* faster tempos at m. 10 (Goode) or m. 11 (Schiff) already establish the pace that they will generally hold all the way to the end of the first secondary theme.[26]

Finally, the manner in which the pianist approaches the tonic downbeat at m. 26 will have everything to do with how listeners retrospectively interpret Schubert's formidable opening. Even the slightest pause on, or *ritardando* into, the dominant of m. 25 can suggest, I think, that this is the goal harmony, already achieved back at m. 10 and simply prolonged ever since. By contrast, a strong sense of direction onto the tonic at m. 26, even if with a broadening over the bar line, will emphatically convey the effect of an elided authentic cadence here. And this in turn could help to suggest that an apparent dominant-prolonging introduction has, at the very last minute, closed in the characteristic manner of a main theme.

Granted, I know of no recorded performance in which the dominant of m. 25 seems to be the pianist's goal. Despite the vast registral and textural discontinuities created at m. 26, and perhaps because of the nearly unbearable suspense that the dominant prolongation creates, performers seem consistently to project the idea of an authentic cadence at m. 26. The split second that Andreas Staier steals before the downbeat of m. 26 is perhaps just great enough to raise a question, but even here I sense that the tonic is Staier's goal.

In short, when held to the light of *classical* formal principles, Schubert's opening conforms neither with a slow introduction nor with any conventional type of classical theme (main or secondary); the conception is uniquely postclassical. Although a performer's faster tempo at m. 12 might convey that either a continuation or the second part of a small-binary theme is under way, analysts would need to concede that this second part fundamentally prolongs dominant harmony until m. 26—not at all characteristic of continuations or small binaries. As for the latter, if a genuine half cadence marks the end, at m. 10–11, of a small binary's first part, and if that goal— the dominant—is then postcadentially prolonged until m. 26, where do we locate the *cadential progression*, with its requisite cadential dominant as penultimate harmony, in order to corroborate the idea of an authentic cadence at m. 26, and thus the close of the theme?[27] If the tonic is Staier's goal at m. 26, then it is as if he asks us to hear that a potential "ending" dominant at m. 10 has perforce "become" a penultimate dominant at m. 25. I hold that to create this effect, or not, is in the hands of the pianist.

Staier especially lingers on the chord that serves as the upbeat to the dominant at m. 4. Whether he had a conscious reason for doing so is not our business; we can thank him in any case for inviting us to hear the subtle first appearance of a motive whose powerful, insidious presence can be sensed throughout this movement and into those that follow. I refer to the bass motion F-to-E, from scale-degree $\hat{6}$ to $\hat{5}$—one of the two pervasive, pitch-specific semitone motives in Beethoven's op. 47 (discussed in chapter 4), with antecedents as old as plainchant and, from one century to the next, often associated with lament. For another minor-mode example, recall the turn figure that emphasizes the neighbor $\hat{6}$ in relation to $\hat{5}$ at mm. 21–24 and mm. 55–59 in the first movement of Beethoven's "Tempest." Neighbor-tone gestures of this kind, in both the major and the minor mode, function as motives in so many of Schubert's songs that they can be regarded as one of his trademarks; the openings of his "Gretchen am Spinnrade" (1814), "Erlkönig" (1815), and "Du bist die Ruh" (1822) offer cases in point.[28] In his op. 42 sonata, Schubert's processual, "organicist" treatment of the F-E motive might suggest that he had become well acquainted with Beethoven's last piano sonatas, and especially op. 111, published in 1823 (see Beethoven's focus upon the neighbor motion A♭-to-G at the beginning of the Allegro con brio ed appassionato in his first movement). On the other hand, Schubert's interest in complex motivic networks, often involving the $\hat{6}$–$\hat{5}$ relation, already becomes evident early in his career, and the later his works, the more they seem to be concerned with motivically cyclic connections from one movement and even one opus to the next—an observation that challenges Adorno's "Schubert" and the Schubert of Adorno's interpreters, to whom I return below.

Within this opus, Schubert gives us *five* initial opportunities to sense that the F–E motion is progressively emerging as a chief protagonist within the music drama. First we have the bass motion that Staier highlights at mm. 3–4, where already the E♮ as internal pedal sounds as a simultaneity against the F. Next comes the highpoint F♮ at m. 5: might it even be a ninth over an implied dominant pedal? Whether yes or no, this F♮ clearly behaves as a neighbor to the E♮ in m. 1, and it returns to the E♮ in m. 6. Then we have the unforgettably striking chromatic bass motion F♯–F♮–E at m. 8–10, arising when the bass line fills in the span from tonic to dominant. Schubert will return with a vengeance to this chromatic bass descent in his coda (see example 5.6). At m. 12, he finds another, ever bolder means of sounding the F♯ and the E♮ simultaneously.[29] Finally, having introduced the F♯ of m. 9 as the bass tone of an augmented-sixth chord, Schubert reinterprets that harmony in a manner well explored by 1825, especially by Schubert himself: he returns to his augmented sixth at m. 20 but now treats it as the dominant seventh of the Neapolitan. At the same time, he brings his syncopated rhythm to its climax and forces the F♯ into the role of pedal point, thus delaying and heightening its return as a neighbor to the E.

William Rothstein has written about the some of the pitfalls performers can face when told or motivated to "bring out" structural details. As Rothstein says: "Most listeners . . . do not go to concerts or listen to recordings to hear an analytical demonstration."[30] For analyst-performers, these are words to live by: here we can heed them as a preventive from needlessly banging out Schubert's bass line within this extraordinary first climax. On the other hand, our approach to the passage might well be enhanced by a sensitivity to its dramatic implications: with each of its successive appearances, the motivic F♯ seems to be striving all the more arduously for some kind of autonomy, even though we sense that it must always in the end descend to the E. In our quest for a narrative, or for a psychological process that we might be enacting when we perform this music, it might also be worth considering the extramusical topics of two earlier works in which Schubert saliently explored the same harmonic reinterpretation of an augmented-sixth chord—his *Wandererfantasie* and his "Death and the Maiden" Quartet.

The insistence with which the new idea at mm. 26–27 enters and proceeds suggests that, like the F♯ relative to the E, the new idea proposes itself as a *rival* to the opening gesture of the movement. Gaining momentum over the course of the transition, this "hammering" idea overflows into the first secondary theme at m. 40 (example 5.2). Now it becomes gentler, more dance-like and playful in its major-mode environment; but beneath the surface of the theme's model–sequence–continuation design over the span of mm. 40–48, one might just be able to hear vestiges of Schubert's *omnibus* progression in the transition at mm. 36–37.[31] Performers would be hard put to "bring out" these omnibus underpinnings, and I concur with Rothstein that this is usually the case with such concealed repetitions. But the performer is fully in charge of how listeners will perceive the cadential progression at m. 50, or its expanded version at mm. 59–61. In both cases these progressions come "too soon": after the presentation of a four-bar idea (mm. 40–43) and its sequential repetition, we have good reason to expect at least an eight-bar continuation; only three bars follow. By introducing a pronounced *ritardando* in m. 50, the pianist could easily convince us that a relatively stable half cadence has been achieved here, despite the presence of the seventh within the dominant, uncharacteristic of classical half cadences. Conversely, by avoiding a *ritardando*, but instead by catching one's breath, so to speak, just before the *subito piano* beginning of the repetition at m. 51, the pianist could create the effect of an evaded cadence. Perhaps this is the better choice here, given that the repetition of the secondary theme seems to be a "one-more-time" effort, motivated by a failure to close, and again refusing closure at m. 61—this time through absolute silence.[32]

Despite the lack of closure, what follows—an utterly unexpected return of the opening idea—would appear to initiate another secondary theme (ST²), followed

Example 5.2. Schubert, op. 42, D.845, first movement, mm. 40–63

by a series of codettas (example 5.3). Now we might begin to understand that the elusive formal and motivic behavior of Schubert's opening will have enormous repercussions as the movement continues to unfold. It would seem that Schubert very deliberately set forth multiple formal possibilities so that he could explore and exploit several of them in due time. Recall the potential antecedent-consequent plan that the very opening of the movement promised. The first two phrases of ST^2 now reawaken that original expectation: here variants of the initial basic and contrasting ideas return in the mediant minor, at first pausing, as before, on the dominant, but then closing on the tonic to create the effect of a consequent. As if, however, to sug-

Example 5.3. Schubert, op. 42, D.845, first movement, mm. 64–94

gest that these main-theme materials are not willing to be conventionalized, a third phrase—another consequent?—enters to disturb the classical symmetry. Do the deep, somber whole-note chords representing dominant harmony at mm. 75–76 stand for a half cadence, or do they lead, *finally*, to authentic cadential closure at m. 77? The pianist is again in charge here. Both the physical and the visual effect of relaxation at m. 76 will suggest the half cadence ; but given that codettas appear to follow, direction into the tonic at m. 77, as if elided, might be the best plan.

The codettas seem at first to propose a reconciliation: the transition idea has become subdued. But then a new version of the MT idea intrudes, at mm. 82–83, to insist on its priority in this piece. Just how are we to understand the harmonic meaning of this purely melodic gesture? Or, for that matter, what are the harmonic implications of the idea to which it alludes: the opening idea of the movement? Peter H. Smith, in his analysis of Schubert's opening, argues for a dominant under-pinning.[33] Perhaps especially as a performer, I hear *tonic* harmony, both at the beginning of the movement and at m. 82. This may be because I am strongly influenced by the first of only two harmonized appearances of the idea—within the development section (at m. 106), where the idea is given tonic support in D minor. But if, at m. 82, the descent of the idea through the scale-degrees $\hat{3}$–$\hat{2}$–$\hat{1}$ in A minor suggests an A-minor harmony, then let us note how strongly this idea seems to want to pull the music away from the key of C major and back into the home tonic. In mm. 87–89, a fragment of the transition idea persists in sustaining the key of C major. But at the very end of the exposition, we have nothing but a single offbeat chord, and it happens to be the home dominant.

The first stage of Schubert's development section—his *pre-core*, to use William Caplin's term[34]—begins by prolonging that same home-dominant harmony, through yet another variant of the MT idea, now alternating with its codetta version in the higher register (see example 5.3). This unharmonized registral dialogue has posed as yet unsolved mysteries, at least for me, even after I found fingerings and physical motions to accommodate the registral shifts. Here Schubert's music establishes, once and for all, the compositional—and perhaps now psychological—priority of his initial basic idea. His development section will be obsessively concerned with variants, expansions, and fragmentations of that idea, to the complete exclusion of transition or secondary-theme materials.

The pre-core effects a modulation into the key of the subdominant, D minor, and sets the stage for the song-like first *core* (mm. 105–120), which proceeds, via a chromatic ascending-step sequence (5-6 series), to none other than the key of F minor (vi)—a now tonicized reference to the motivic F♮ (recall the beginning of Beethoven's development in his op. 47, as discussed in chapter 4). Core II (mm. 121–46), with its increasingly urgent sixteenth-note tremolo figure, continues the ascending-step sequence (5/3–6/4) but breaks from this at m. 134, settling on the dominant of the subdominant. The V-of-iv is now reinterpreted as the beginning of yet another omnibus-related progression (mm. 137–42), and this one becomes climactic; but then, as Richard Kramer has said, "the music seems to vanish altogether in a breathtaking, and nearly inaudible, dominant in F♯ minor."[35] Pianists, I think, have the liberty here to treat the ensuing silence as unmeasured and immeasurable; an impasse has been reached, and we are a long way from home.

Example 5.4. Schubert, op. 42, D.845, first movement, mm. 151–87

When the silence has been overcome, a direct but hesitant reference, in F♯ minor, to the MT's antecedent phrase serves as the point of departure for core III and hints, but only hints, at a false-recapitulation effect. The new imitative exchange and the modulation to the home dominant within this "wrong-key" return might now, for a mere moment, seem to be promising the "real" recapitulatory return at m. 152 (example 5.4), where a sequential repetition begins in the home key. But again a modulation, now to the dominant of C minor, cancels the allusion to A minor and makes it merely illusory. On the other hand, this second sequence propels the music along a determinate, purposeful path—one already chosen earlier: the model-sequence plan initiated in F♯ minor will now proceed via ascending minor thirds, to create a *symmetric division of the octave*, as partially shown at example 5.4. (See the circled bass dominants at mm. 156–78—G–B♭–C♯–E; the ascent by minor thirds begins with the C♯ in m. 147 and the E in m. 150.) Incorporated within this process is a return, at m. 166, of the idea from the formally ambiguous m. 10. That idea proposes to initiate a final core (IV), but starting at m. 178, the materials from m. 18 return to recreate a "standing-on the-home-dominant"; thus, what was once the problematic, ambiguous part of Schubert's opening has now been placed in the service of a retransition. From the viewpoint of a *structural-tonic* return (rather than a "double return," combining home-tonic harmony with the opening materials of the exposition), the recapitulation then begins precisely where a MT had appeared to begin in the first place—with the transition materials, at m. 186! In short, it is as if Schubert had created the ambiguous, multivalent, dominant-prolonging passage within his opening measures for the express, long-range purpose of reinterpreting this as the stunning, culminating approach to his unorthodox recapitulation.[36]

When ST² returns at m. 224, the pianist, physically engaged, will be predisposed to discover the processual, long-range motivic rationale for that *extra* third phrase, here beginning at m. 232 (example 5.5): the fifth finger of the pianist's left hand will find itself once again wanting to linger on the very same F♮ that Andreas Staier highlighted in m. 3. Now we can appreciate just why Schubert could not possibly have begun his recapitulation with his opening materials. His exclusive focus upon his MT's basic idea within the development section looms as a crucial motivation for omitting a conventional main-theme recapitulation; even more decisive, in the recapitulation ST² comes into such a close rapport with the MT materials that it is tempting to think of this theme as the stable, definitive MT form toward which that theme had been striving over the course of the complete movement.

Then, however, the F♮ initiates a remarkable series of attempts to break free from the E. The first of these arises with the V–VI progression into m. 237 (example 5.5), complete with parallel fifths and octaves (rather than an elided deceptive cadence, these deliberate parallels suggest *evasion*, in the sense that the VI-chord does not serve as a goal, because the dominant at m. 236 fails to resolve); the progression is repeated at mm. 241–42. There follows a terrifying three-stage coda, with each stage closing in silence, each stage longer and more intense than the preceding; here the rival ideas—the hovering MT-variant and the hammering transition gesture—join forces anew, in a manner that suggests both futility and defiance (example 5.6). It is as if the composed-out return of the bass line's

Example 5.5. Schubert, op. 42, D.845, first movement, mm. 232–39

Example 5.6. Schubert, op. 42, D.845, first movement, m. 275 to end

chromatic descent F♯–F♮–E from the opening of the movement (mm. 8–10)—now *twice* transforming a dominant-seventh into an augmented-sixth—knows that it is taking a circuitous path to delay the inevitable but determines to assert its authority as the agent that will achieve an overwhelmingly goal-oriented conclusion.

∞

A new translation, published in 2005, of Adorno's hitherto neglected 1928 "Schubert" essay elicits an admirable summary by Scott Burnham:

> Adorno's essay on Schubert opens by invoking a fraught move across the threshold that separates the death of Beethoven from the death of Schubert. He goes on to read Schubert's music through a series of dichotomies whose opposite terms are distinctly Beethovenian: Schubert's themes are self-possessed apparitions of truth rather than inchoate ideas that require temporal evolution; his repetitive, fragmentary forms are inorganic rather than organic, crystalline rather than plantlike. Above all, Adorno develops the idea that Schubert's music offers the repeatable truth of a landscape rather than the processive trajectory of a teleological history. Schubert's themes, like landscapes, are forms of permanence that cannot be fundamentally altered but can only be revisited.[37]

In the essay itself, Adorno, referring to Schubert's "first A-Minor Sonata," observes that "there are two ideas constituting a movement, not in contrast as first and second theme, but contained within both the first and the second thematic groups—this is not something to ascribe to a motivic economy that is sparing with material for the sake of unity, but rather to the return of the same in diversity."[38] The translators of the essay identify this A-minor Sonata as the early D. 537 (published as op. 164 around 1852).[39] Adorno's comments suggest more strongly that he is talking about Schubert's first *published* A-minor Sonata—the one I have discussed above: I submit that Adorno's "two ideas" are the "rival ideas" that have played such a pervasive role in my analysis.[40]

Do those ideas remain "self-possessed"—nonevolving, ever present, and repeatable because what is repeatable "is only what is in itself unique, and never what has been created subjectively and thus over the course of time"?[41] In comparing what happens to Schubert's two ideas over the span of the movement with, say, what happens to the opening largo and allegro ideas of Beethoven's "Tempest," we might want to agree emphatically with Adorno. And yet, what about the "atmosphere" enveloping the two ideas—that which "changes around things that remain timelessly the same"?[42] If the atmosphere in this movement changes over time, one can only imagine sunshine shedding but the briefest of light on the landscape of the first secondary theme, with clouds growing ever darker, and maybe even the threat of thunder, toward the end. Paradoxically, my first experience of "landscape" in what I take to be Adorno's sense came upon hearing the development section in the opening movement of Beethoven's *Pastoral* Symphony: there the changing "atmospheric" conditions are the changes of harmony and pedal point that cast a new radiance upon each sequence of the huge idea that remains "timelessly the same," itself consisting of nothing but a one-bar gesture given twelve-fold repetition (mm. 151–62). On a brilliant summer afternoon's stroll across the meadow, we gaze around us, turning to the left, then to the right, and we discover ever more breathtaking vistas in each direction. But as a rare prototype for the massive nondevelopmental model-sequence plans of many of Schubert's later secondary themes and development sections, the idyllic atmosphere of Beethoven's pastorale landscape hardly compares with Schubert's characteristically more troubled settings. Richard Leppert puts it well: "Schubert looks to the horizon while gazing inward.... Whatever [landscape *is* for Schubert], it's out *there*: it's an other, but it's also partly the otherness of the self.... In Schubert, Adorno hears the reciprocity that emerges when the subject recognizes in the object not difference but, however disconcertingly, sameness."[43]

A landscape with "forms of permanence" does not emerge for me in this A-minor Sonata. Rather, Schubert's processual treatment of form, the dialectic tensions he effects between two diametrically contrasting ideas, their efforts toward reconciliation, and their ultimate struggle together to achieve an ending all suggest one of the most striking cases in his oeuvre of a Beethovenian trajectory toward teleological closure at all costs. Unlike the famous omnibus progressions in the twentieth song of Schubert's *Winterreise* (mm. 57–65, 69–75), which pretend, as the Latin word suggests, to go everywhere, but in the end go nowhere, the simpler omnibus variants in this sonata prolong a dominant while determining its goal. Schubert's overt and concealed transformations of his F–E ($\hat{6}$–$\hat{5}$) motive attest to the influence of organicist treatments of this scale-degree relationship well before and long after his time. In short, Adorno's "Schubert" may identify a Schubert for whom this sonata makes an exception. But nothing could be more appropriate about Schubert from Adorno than his sense that Schubert's music is "so deeply steeped in death that death held no fears for it."[44] Within this sonata, one might imagine that Schubert's instrumental persona is saying (and I don't use this expression facetiously), "Reports of my death have been greatly exaggerated."

I shall not be so reckless as to insist on some one overriding narrative that performers should try to convey in this movement. Whatever Schubert's message might be, example 5.7 suggests that it has not been completed at the end of his violent coda. The excerpts shown there—(a) from the opening of Schubert's second movement; (b) from his third-movement Scherzo, where the Trio resides in the motivically significant key of F major; and (c) from the beginning of his finale—all reveal that the F–E relationship persists as a subcutaneous *idée fixe*, to be probed in new guises throughout the complete work. I suggest, however, that Schubert's first movement embraces a haunting obsessiveness, of the kind, for example, that thoughts of death might bring; I also hear a fierce determination not to give in to the obsession—a commitment sustained all the way to the end of the sonata's finale, where the composer explicitly cycles back (at mm. 524–27) to the beginning of the first movement's ferocious codettas, shown at example 5.6 (mm. 295–301).

Example 5.7. Schubert, op. 42, D.845: (a) second movement, opening; (b) Scherzo, mm. 139–50 (from the Trio); (c) finale, opening

(a)

(b)

(c)

This interpretation has found its inspiration in the combining of analytic and performance preoccupations with insights from other kinds of scholars—biographers, musicologists, and cultural historians. The knowledge gained from them about Schubert's illness and about his "Beethoven project" should remind performers and analysts that music can not be construed as an autonomous activity, separate from cultural, sociological, psychological, and deeply personal concerns. Gingerich has said: "If anyone could be assumed eligible to suffer a crippling case of 'anxiety of influence' it was Schubert. But Schubert neither ignored Beethoven, nor fought him, nor was he silenced by Beethoven's imposing precedent."[45] The three portentous silences in Schubert's coda will each be overcome more powerfully. Here, then, Schubert urges us as performers to reach with him for the greatest heights, against all odds.

CHAPTER Six

Music That Turns Inward

New Roles for Interior Movements and Secondary Themes

Beethoven once claimed: "There is hardly any treatise which could be too learned *for me*."[1] Scholars have nevertheless been reluctant to give him credit for anything more than a superficial understanding of the treatises of Immanual Kant. After all, Beethoven refused to attend lectures on Kantian epistemology at the University of Bonn in the 1790s, even though certainly by then Kant's philosophy had become the talk of all Germany. When, in 1820, Beethoven copied from a newspaper article a paraphrase from Kant's *Critique of Practical Reason* (1788), he gave birth to the persistent view that his enthusiasm for Kant rested simply on a shared moral outlook: "The moral law within us, and the starry heavens above us—Kant!!!"[2] And yet, of all the Kantian slogans Beethoven might have chosen, few could better have encapsulated the definitive, revolutionary, and undeniably *moral* principle upon which all of Kant's thought rests: in what has been called a "root and branch rejection of all ancient moralities," Kant insisted that neither nature, nor God, nor the starry heavens, nor any other external order defines the moral law for us; the sources of the good are *within us*, and our potential for freedom, self-determination, and dignity as rational beings depends on our obligation to act accordingly.[3]

It is the expression "within us" that I draw upon here. The slogan that inspired Beethoven is a virtual signpost on the path of Western philosophy all the way from Plato to the present. The path is *inward*, and toward the end of the eighteenth century, the outcome was a tremendous expansion of what it can mean to be a "subject with inner depths," as separate from the objects of this world. The path I describe leads to nothing less than the modern Western notion of selfhood—the one that prevails today, even if we now call ourselves "postmodern." As "selves," we regard our thoughts, our feelings, our capacity to reason, our unconscious as residing inside us—in our mind or our "heart," rather than somewhere out there. And this "inside/outside" opposition seems so utterly natural that we can hardly imagine it as Western rather than universal, formed rather than given, and relatively recent rather than timeless.[4]

The philosopher Charles Taylor portrays the path toward modern inwardness as stretching over more than two millennia, but he sees the Kantian late eighteenth century as a particularly critical moment in the journey. Like Jean-Jacques Rousseau before him, Kant rebels against that rosy Deist notion of a providential cosmic order, in which everything is adaptable to human needs. Also like Rousseau, Kant essays to recover the distinction between good and bad, moral and immoral, which had been done away with by the most radical proponents of Enlightenment naturalism—those utilitarian secularists who had argued that only our self-preserving, disengaged reason as a neutral faculty within a neutral world can free us from the errors of religion and the injustices of society. Well before 1804, when Beethoven scratched the title "Bonaparte" from the first page of his Third Symphony, the failures, injustices, betrayals, and atrocities of the French Revolution had given the lie to the notion that Enlightenment progress—toward freedom, equality, fraternity, and benevolence—could be achieved within a moral vacuum. And yet, pre-Napoleonic utopian aspirations, now nourished by the new autonomy and morality that Kant locates within the individual, survive and remain vivid, for example, in Hegel's notion of the dawning of a "new age," or in Beethoven's *Fidelio* and his Ninth Symphony. Moreover, such aspirations run concurrent with what Taylor, following M. H. Abrams,[5] sees as another turn inward—an "expressivist turn" especially associated with German and English Romantics, for many of whom the *voice of nature within us* becomes the source of goodness and truth.

Kant himself was aware that to internalize moral responsibility is to risk the implication of a polar opposition—a real breach—between nature, on the one hand, and the individual, on the other. The idea of nature within us, or nature as "a great current of sympathy, running through all things"[6]—this was the world picture that, for writers such as Wordsworth and Shelley in England, for Herder, Novalis, and Schelling in Germany, could bridge the gap and heal the divisions between the self and others, the individual and the world outside. But, as Taylor puts it: "If our access to nature is through an inner voice or impulse, then we can only fully know this nature through articulating what we find within us." In other words, we can realize our nature only by *expressing* it, in some medium; when we do this, we realize our own unique potential, and we give our lives a definitive shape.[7]

It should take only a moment of reflection to note that we have slipped here from the realm of morality into what seems like the realm of art. If we consider the extent to which artistic creation has come to be associated with self-realization, then the distinction between realizing the goodness of one's inner nature and expressing oneself through art—in short, the distinction between the moral and the aesthetic—begins to dissolve. Already with Kant, the idea of aesthetic contemplation had shifted from the object itself to the quality of the experience in us that it evokes. Now the attention moves directly to the artist, whose activity in turn shifts away from mimesis—the imitation of nature outside us—and toward the expression of *nature within*. Taylor regards this development as a distinctly modern "revolution of moral ideas": "[Expression] is now what realizes and completes us as human beings, what rescues us from the deadening grip of disengaged reason."[8] Thus does the philosophy of nature he describes become a religion of nature; finally, art itself, as an expression of our spiritual selves, threatens to replace religion. So many of the ideas about art, and especially about music, that we have come to associate with the early nineteenth century—organicism, originality and imagination as artistic requirements, the emergence of the concept of a *musical work* (see chapter 1), instrumental music's claim to autonomy, the power of Beethoven's music to transport us into the "spirit-realm of the infinite"[9]—such ideas gain new meaning when one considers them as inextricably linked to the moral bases of expressivist philosophy. To attempt causal explanations for this intersection of philosophical and aesthetic ideas would, I think, be reckless, but I shall risk the general observation that the cultural milieu in which all of the above-mentioned ideas mingle and flourish is one in which inwardness had become a preoccupation. With this premise in place, let me turn to the idea of inwardness in early nineteenth-century music, and especially in the music of Schubert.

The notion that music can speak "From the heart—may it go to the heart!," as Beethoven once put it,[10] is probably quite ancient; but it takes on new depths during his lifetime and beyond. For example, Friedrich Schiller (1759–1805) proposed that "the entire effect of music…consists of accompanying and producing in *sensuous form* the *inner movements of the emotions* through analogous external motions.…If the composer and the landscape painter penetrate into the secret of those laws that govern the *inner movements of the human heart*,…then they will develop…into true portraitists of the soul."[11] Johann Gottfried Herder (1744–1803) came to believe that music, as spirit (*Geist*) itself, surpasses all the other arts because it is "related to motion, great nature's *innermost* power."[12] August Wilhelm Schlegel (1767–1845) held that *sound* is the "innermost" of the five senses; because of its incorporeality, music presents passions "to our *inner sense* entirely according to their form, without any reference to objects," thus allowing them "to breathe in a purer ether."[13] Pronouncements of this kind abound at the turn of the nineteenth century, and they are emphatically relevant to past and recent claims that, with Mozart as predecessor, Beethoven and Schubert explored new kinds of subjectivity and new levels of interiority through musical means.

To be sure, Susan McClary traces the representation in music of interior feelings all the way back to Josquin and the sixteenth-century madrigalists, and she sees the development of tonality itself as a primary vehicle for the "narratives of centered subjectivity" portrayed in late seventeenth-century *opera seria* under the regulation of Enlightenment codes of affect.[14] In fact, it is thanks to tonality, for McClary, that instrumental music gradually becomes capable of expressing subjectivities without the aid of text and stage. In the late eighteenth-century sonata form, with the first movement of Mozart's "Prague" Symphony (1786) as her focal point, McClary hears not just the emergence of a "subject" but also the process of its construction: "as in the contemporaneous Bildungsroman—the narrative formation of an autonomous musical self as it ventures into other terrains, strengthens its innate resources through motivic development, and finally consolidates the secure identity that confirms the viability of the centered subject."[15] But with reference both to Mozart's secondary theme and to his slow second movement, McClary also notes "a demonstration that the persona thus fashioning itself also harbors deep *inner feelings*…the darker sides of subjectivity: longings and painful vulnerabilities locked away from the public view, scarcely even acknowledged by the individual who bears and nurtures them."[16] And in Beethoven's late String Quartet in A Minor, Op. 132 (1825), McClary diagnoses a loss of belief in Enlightenment as well as musical conventions—"a shattered subjectivity," "a level of interiority that refuses to marshall its impulses into the tidy wrappers of eighteenth-century form."[17] Along similar lines, Lawrence Kramer characterizes the exemplary early nineteenth-century "subject" as broken and disenchanted—the product of a change of location of the "self," from "the nexus of social relations to a private interiority."[18] This "modern, bourgeois, post-Kantian, post-Enlightenment" subject has "learned to speak familiarly of cleavages between head and heart, classic and romantic, reason and imagination, nature and freedom, public and private, depth and surface."[19] Emerging from within that kind of intellectual environment in Vienna, Franz Schubert utilizes the Lied "as a vehicle for exploring the great transformations of subjectivity characteristic of his era." In Kramer's view, Schubert knew how to resist, escape from, subvert, and sometimes even transgress the order of the rationalized Austrian world, with its "taint of compromise, not to mention corruption and hypocrisy" on such matters as marriage and sexuality, and its political repressiveness in the aftermath of the Congress of Vienna.[20]

Few writers on the topic of interiority in music have been as persistent as McClary and Kramer in challenging us to consider music as a force that can both reflect and shape its own and subsequent cultures. I attempt to rise to that challenge here, and I strive to do so with genuine analytic concern for "the music itself," to use what remains a provocative expression. Although notions of inwardness in nineteenth-century music have become commonplace, the idea that *formal processes* in music substantiate such notions has not been widely explored. Let me explain.

I concentrate upon the tendency within early nineteenth-century instrumental works toward cyclic and processual formal techniques that draw new kinds of attention to deeply felt, song-inspired interior movements and secondary (as opposed to main) themes. In such pieces, the music itself would indeed seem to "turn inward": an interior moment, or movement, becomes the focal point of the complete work—the center of gravity toward which what comes before seems to pull, and from which all that follows seems to radiate. I see processes of this kind as a key to Schubert's music in general, certainly as a cultural and aesthetic sign of his times, and—by the way—as perhaps the most profound source of Schubert's influence on Robert Schumann. For an exquisite first example, let us turn to a single-movement work from the very last year of Schubert's life—his Allegro in A Minor for Four Hands (D. 947), completed in May of 1828.

This sonata-form movement, whose opening is shown at example 6.1, carries the nickname "*Lebensstürme*"—"Storms of Life." Schubert was not the culprit here; by the time the publisher Anton Diabelli gave the work that title when he printed it in 1840, Schubert had been dead for twelve years. Maurice Brown thinks the title "absurd" and "catchpenny"; Alfred Einstein regards it as "trivial," "hardly consistent with the direction 'Allegro ma non troppo'—'not too fast.'"[21] I would like to think that Diabelli's title reflects a touch of insight: what seems extraordinary to me about this piece is that Schubert leads us into his unforgettably hushed, hymn-like secondary theme as if for all the world to evoke a blessed lull—a source of inward calm, a safe haven, somehow protected from psychological storms all around.

Schubert's stormy opening embraces two main themes—the ferocious, *sforzando*-laden blast of energy that drives to the dominant and then gives way to silence (example 6.1)[22] and the quieter but still agitated sentential theme whose

Example 6.1. Schubert, Allegro in A Minor for Four Hands, *Lebensstürme*, Op. 144 (D.947), mm. 1–11

repeated continuation subsides with a perfect authentic cadence in the home key at m. 23 (example 6.2). Note that the second main theme (MT²) begins by drawing upon, but tempering, MT¹'s thrice-heard *sforzando* gesture—the suspension figure and its upbeat at mm. 3, 4, and 6 (brackets within examples 6.1–6.4 signal recurrences and variants of this rhythmic motive). The resultant two-bar idea basic idea (mm. 12–13) will now become pervasive; to trace its successive transformations is to follow Schubert's circuitous but determinate path toward the relief and safety of his secondary theme. At mm. 23–24 the basic idea, now in imitation, would seem to initiate a transition, but the modulation promised by an ascending-thirds sequence peters out, and the suspension figure becomes augmented, from the value of quarter note to half (at m. 32, and at the half cadence in m. 35). This little promise of respite is brutally retracted when MT¹ returns with a vengeance at m. 37, thus perhaps inviting us retrospectively to reinterpret the preceding passage

Example 6.2. Schubert, op. 144 (D.947), mm. 12–23

as a contrasting middle, or B-section, within a potential *small-ternary* (A–B–A′) design. But now the storm unleashes all its fury: what was once a cadential idea (at mm. 7–10; see example 6.1) becomes the model (at mm. 43–46) for an extreme chromatic intensification of the descending-step sequence, and then some rather treacherous triplets for both players lead to a half cadence on the *home* dominant at m. 59. In short, what might have been a small-ternary reprise (A′) seems to "have become" (⇒) the transition that had failed to materialize earlier; but, once again, no true modulation occurs.[23]

As shown in example 6.3, our basic idea now rises, impassioned, into the primo player's high register and becomes embroiled in an imitative exchange with the secondo's middle voices in thirds, all over a home-dominant pedal qua tremolo ("murky bass"). As numbered in the score at m. 59, four contrapuntal strands emerge here; seven bars later (at m. 66), these are treated to a rare instance, for Schubert, of "quadruple counterpoint," albeit without a change of harmony.[24] As if this were not enough turmoil, musically speaking, m. 73 introduces the first really radical mutation of the basic idea's rhythmic motive: this now becomes syncopated and *sforzando*-accented, giving tremendous thrust into one more heightened standing-on-the-dominant phrase (mm. 73–76) and its elided repetition (mm. 77–80). Finally, the wind shifts, the clouds begin to part, and there is nothing left but the syncopated rhythm in the bass, which sinks as if beneath the surface of a roiling sea, downward into quieter waters (example 6.4).

Example 6.3. Schubert, op. 144 (D.947), mm. 59–61, 66–68

Example 6.4. Schubert, op. 144 (D.947), mm. 81–103

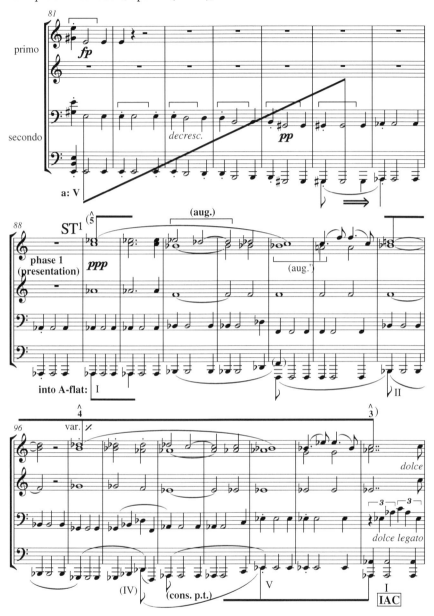

But to what depths does this descent in the bass really go? My unfolding sign at mm. 81–86 in example 6.4 signifies that the bass merely works its way through an arpeggiation of the home dominant-seventh chord and then pauses on its third, otherwise known as the home-key leading tone, G♯. An enharmonic sleight-of-hand transforms G♯ into A♭. And then, emerging from above, as if moored by the most tenuous of anchors—only an instant earlier, an unstable leading tone!—the hymn-like first secondary theme (ST¹, example 6.4) begins stably in A♭ major. From within the canonic instrumental repertoire, I can think of only two earlier secondary, or internal, themes that begin in the key of the leading tone, and, as disclosed below, one of them is not by Schubert.[25] The relationship of home key to leading-tone key has traditionally been regarded as exceedingly remote; here, by contrast, the descent through the home dominant seventh in the bass and the rhythmic motive that propels this conspire to create the effect of moving into a deeply private region *within* the home key's domain (not to mention, of course, that A minor shares one common pitch with A♭ major, the C♮). As the ST¹, marked *ppp*, now begins to unfold, the continued repetition of the rhythmic motive in the bass suggests that that motive, first introduced all the way back in m. 3, has been pointing toward, or anticipating, its role within the ST all along. The theme's melody reinforces this suggestion: at m. 91, as at mm. 32 and 35, the motive regains its suspension feature and becomes rhythmically augmented.

My analytic overlay for this first part of the ST in example 6.4 proposes that, on the middleground, a chromatic descent from $\hat{5}$ to $\hat{3}$ in the descant binds together an eight-bar phrase and its varied repetition; the chromatic tone D♮ allows for the transformation of an ordinary minor ii-chord into a veritable beacon of light—the radiant major II-chord as goal of the first phrase. The end of the second phrase relinquishes what would have been its eighth bar (not shown) to a new *dolce* beginning, generated by "linkage" at m. 104 to the dotted figure at m. 102. A second stage within a *three-phase* (not "*phrase*") ST thus gets seamlessly under way, and its more active character—note the new quarter-note triplet motion in the secondo's right hand—would seem to be responding to the first phase in the manner of a continuation relative to a presentation. A repetition (at mm. 113–16) of the continuation's cadential idea (mm. 109–12) leads to the perfect authentic cadence at m. 116; then the codetta-like third phase resumes both the register and the hushed, heavenly, reassuring mood of the presentation. What especially invites us to hear all three of these phases as parts of just one thematic process (ST¹) in A♭ major is the presence throughout of the crucial rhythmic motive, augmented.

From this point forward, Schubert's inward theme begins to radiate outward, as if to shed its blessing over the entire rest of the exposition. At the *ppp* cadence in m. 132, the solo bass line once again takes up its descent through a dominant-seventh chord—this time one whose root would be the A♭. Again, the bass pauses on the third of the chord, the C♮ here; and now—as if by pure luck!—we make a secure landing on the leeward shore that we had been expecting to reach in the first place, the conventional secondary key of the mediant (III), C major (example 6.5). Now that C major has been gained, we will rest here for the remainder of the exposition. What follows over the span of the next 45 bars is a complete, varied repetition of the three-phase ST in the new key. Here the secondo's quarter-note triplets shift into the primo's highest register, creating an ethereal glow above the theme's melody, now folded into the primo's middle register. The resultant texture, so characteristic of Schubert's duets, sounds marvelously diaphanous,[26] but only if the primo's left-hand thumb can manage quietly to project the melody, while her right hand maintains the *ppp* in the triplets. When, at m. 179, the ST reaches its final cadence, the triplets break away from the upper register and now march into the bass, while a much-welcomed *crescendo* leads into a jubilant *forte* fanfare that promises to provide the closing of this exposition. But no! An evaded cadence at m. 190 motivates a "one-more-time" repetition of the fanfare (at mm. 191–98); this sets the stage for a jubilant overflow into two more highly active secondary themes and a closing section, which, upon repetition, becomes a retransition to the exposition's repeat. In short, the blessing that the inward ST[1] bestows now becomes cause for expansive celebration, in what is one of Schubert's longest expositions ever. But, truth be told, the storms of life do not subside for good until the return of the ST complex within Schubert's wonderful recapitulation. For instance, note the beginning of the development section (example 6.6)!

One last word about the "*Lebensstürme*." Like nineteenth-century four-hand pieces in general, including transcriptions, this music "moves inward" in another, very basic social way. For Thomas Christensen: "The physical spaces of nineteenth-century bourgeois Victorian life were rigorously divided into public and private spheres. As a refuge from the noise and anonymity of urban life in the street, market,

Example 6.5. Schubert, op. 144 (D.947), mm. 132–41

into III (C):

Example 6.6. Schubert, op. 144 (D.947), mm. 257–63

and workplace, the bourgeois home offered warmth, privacy, and domestic security"; it became "the incubator of bourgeois sensibility," "the insular space looking out upon—but protected from—the dangers and estrangement of the outside." Within this safe haven, the upright pianoforte served as "a sonic hearth…associated with the most intimate musical genres—the lyrical piano piece, the Lied, the sonata," and, of course, the piano duet.[27] Of the many functions that four-hand music filled, its role in the domestication of art—in bringing all kinds of music inward into the home, where it can be privately studied and actively performed (rather than just passively heard)—surely this function was the paramount one. As Kramer sees it, the "nonmaterial counterpart" to the interior of the home is the "interior of the subject": "Mirroring each other, these form the basic locales of an unrationalized inner world to pose against the rationalized one."[28] In this sense, then, the "*Lebensstürme*" inhabits both locales.

As a culminating example of Schubert's inward-turning music, I address his Piano Trio in E-flat Major, Op. 100 (D. 929); here an interior *movement*—the second movement, Andante con moto—serves as the inward source. Robert Schumann could not have known that the haunting main theme of this Andante draws inspiration from a Swedish song. But the unexpected returns of that theme—at first troubling, then exalted—within the Trio's finale must surely have figured in Schumann's recollection that, when, in 1828, the Trio first appeared in print, it "went across the ordinary musical life of the day like an angry thunderstorm."[29]

In order to approach this work from the viewpoint of "music that turns inward," we shall first need to turn back for a moment to precedents in Beethoven—and not so much to Scott Burnham's "Beethoven hero" as to Karol Berger's "Beethoven the dreamer."[30] It is not difficult, on the one hand, to think of certain interior slow movements by Beethoven that would seem to provide the center of gravity for the complete multimovement work; the slow movements of his Fourth Piano Concerto (in G Major, Op. 58; 1805–6) and his "Ghost" Piano Trio (in D Major, Op. 70/1; 1808) come to mind. On the other hand, Schubert's E-flat Trio explores a more integrative process—the type that I shall call "*formal cyclicism*"; this is the case whereby a passage from one movement within a multimovement work overtly recurs in a later movement, thus affecting its large-scale form. At table 6.1, I list Beethoven's instrumental experiments in this direction. With two exceptions (marked by asterisks), these works involve recollections within finales of materials from earlier *slow* movements or *slow* introductions—thus passages that by tradition tend to be lyrical, pensive, "inward," and private. Four cases in table 6.1 involve one of Beethoven's favorite processual strategies—the composing of a seemingly self-contained slow movement that, in refusing to close, retrospectively "becomes" (⇒) an introduction to the finale proper.[31] For Berger, the returns of such introspective materials within finales can represent intrusions of an "other

Table 6.1 Instrumental Works by Beethoven That Feature or Tend toward "Formal Cyclicism"

String Quartet No. 6 in B-flat Major, Op. 18, No. 6 (1800):
  Adagio, *La Malinconia*, ⇒ introduction to finale; finale recalls *La Malinconia*.
Piano Sonata No. 13 in E-flat Major, Op. 27, No. 1, *Sonata quasi una Fantasia* (1800–1):
  Finale (movement 5) recalls self-contained Adagio movement (movement 4).
*Symphony No. 5 in C Minor, Op. 67 (1807–8):
  Finale (movement 4) recalls Scherzo (movement 3).
Sonata for Cello and Piano No. 4 in C Major, Op. 102, No. 1 (1815):
  Adagio ⇒ introduction to finale; the opening of the first movement (Andante) recurs as an interpolation and bridge into the finale proper.
*Piano Sonata No. 28 in A Major, Op. 101 (1816):
  Adagio ⇒ Introduction to finale; the opening of the first movement (Allegro ma non troppo) recurs as an interpolation and bridge into the finale proper.
Piano Sonata No. 31 in A-flat Major, Op. 110 (1821–22):
  Adagio (with recitative and Arioso dolente) ⇒ introduction to fugal finale; the Arioso recurs to interrupt the fugue and thus delay its conclusion.
Symphony No. 9 in D Minor, Op. 125 (1822–24):
  Finale recalls all three earlier movements.

Asterisks mark two works that do not involve recollections within finales of materials from earlier *slow* movements or *slow* introductions.

world" upon "a mind torn between two distinct ontological regions." Sometimes the "other world" is the world *beyond*—Kant's "unknowable realm of *noumena*" with which Beethoven and his contemporaries were preoccupied. Just as often the "other world" is Beethoven's own world *within*—the one into which his deafness drives him, but where his art comforts him.[32]

Not emphasized by Berger is that Beethoven's "world within" can hold immense personal grief. Take, for example, the Arioso dolente passage within his Piano Sonata in A-flat Major, Op. 110 (1821–22). Early within his finale, this passage first appears in the tonic minor, as shown at example 6.7b; when an intensified variant of the Arioso returns to interrupt the finale's fugue, no words can describe the degree of anguish that the passage now seems to express (example 6.7c); here, by the way, is that one precedent not by Schubert—in the minor mode, no less—for the *Lebensstürme*'s ST in the leading-tone key (in this case, G minor relative to A♭ major). In the light of such an intense expression of interiority, perhaps it is no coincidence that, of all Beethoven's formally cyclic works, op. 110 most strongly invites comparison with Schubert's inward-turning Trio, their fundamental differences notwithstanding.

The most obvious similarity between the two works, and one that few listeners would miss, is that in both cases a slow, interior, song-like passage is chosen for return in the finale (three returns in Schubert's original, uncut version). Less

Example 6.7. Beethoven, Piano Sonata No. 31 in A-flat Major, Op. 110: (a) Scherzo (second movement), opening; (b) finale, mm. 8–10; (c) finale, mm. 106–19

(a)

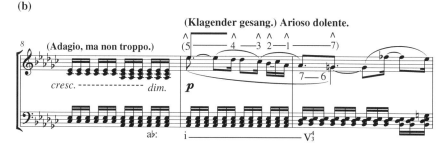

(b)

(Continued)

Example 6.7. cont.

(c)

obvious is that in both pieces materials from an earlier movement motivically foreshadow, and thus subtly point toward, that central slow passage.[33] I am not the first to note that the initial idea of Beethoven's brusque second-movement scherzo, itself drawn from a popular song, becomes the basis of the Arioso's opening melody, drastically transformed (see example 6.7, a and b).[34] By contrast, only one writer about Schubert's Trio (to be identified soon) has to my knowledge noted that, already deep within the modulating ST[1] of his first movement, a fleeting four-bar phrase, sequentially repeated (and heard again twice in the recapitulation), cunningly anticipates a central gesture within Schubert's second movement, the Andante.

We turn first to the interior source itself—the main theme of the Andante (example 6.8), and its inspiration, the Swedish song (example 6.9). The poem and a translation follow.

"Se solen sjunker ner"

Se solen sjunker ner	See the sun is going down
back höga bergens topp	behind the peak of the high mountain,
förnattens dystra skuggor	before night's gloomy shadows
Du flyr o sköna hopp.	you flee, O beautiful hope.
Farväl, Farväl	Farewell, farewell,
ack vännen glömdebort	ah, the friend forgot about
Sin trogna väna brud	his true dear bride,
Sin trogna väna brud	his true dear bride,
Sin trogna väna brud.	his true dear bride.
La, la, la, la.	

—*Translation by Benta Bob*[35]

Readers who know Schubert's theme (example 6.8) will surely agree that it is haunting in all respects; it certainly seems to have haunted the many writers, including this one, who have struggled to characterize it. Both Kramer and Leo Treitler hear the theme as a threnody; for Treitler the pervasive "trudging figure" in the piano "registers the tattoo of a funeral march."[36] But Kramer, who (like Treitler) does not observe that this theme is inspired by the Swedish song (example 6.9), notes that its funereal aspect does not quite "tally" with the solo melody sung by the cello: this melody is "Lied-like," "folkloric or balladic," "with its tessitura of a baritone voice"—"more melancholy than mournful, more sensuous than somber."[37] Like the song, Schubert's Andante theme takes the form of a small binary; we shall soon want to give special attention to the melodic/harmonic content of the idea at the beginning of its second part—that is, at mm. 11–12.

It is worth noting here that the overall form of the Andante movement replicates a type identified as special at the time to Schubert and probably significant for him in the most personal sense. In the years following his death, a story written by Schubert himself was discovered among his papers; its title is "Mein Traum" ("My Dream"), and it carries the date of July 3, 1822. As interpreted by Maynard Solomon and then Charles Fisk, Schubert's story unfolds in five scenes, producing the simple pattern A–B–A'–B'–A". Scene A stands here for the comfort of home and family happiness, the setting in which the story begins. B stands for banishment from that home—in both cases, the protagonist's exile, inflicted upon him by his father for not being able to enjoy the pleasures of a feast and a garden. After the anguished second exile, in which the wandering protagonist sings of love and pain, he experiences a blissful, symbolic homecoming in which he is reunited with a now loving father.[38] Fisk has been the first to note that the A–B–A'–B'–A" pattern of the story finds a musical and narrative correspondence in the large-scale forms of several of Schubert's slow movements composed after the writing of "Mein Traum"—most notably, the Andante second movement of the "Unfinished" Symphony (D. 759; October 1822), the Adagio of the C-minor Piano Sonata (D. 958; 1828), and the second *Moment musical*, in A-flat Major, Op. 94 (D. 780; 1828?).[39] Fisk does not observe that the Andante of the E-flat Trio features this same formal type, but this may be because here the musical characters of A and B have been reversed: here the B-theme, appearing first in the mediant, E♭ major, and then in the tonic major, clearly evokes the brighter light; by contrast,

Example 6.8. Schubert, Piano Trio in E-flat Major, Op. 100, D.929, second movement, mm. 1–22

Example 6.9. The Swedish song "Se solen sjunker ner"

a transformation of the melancholy A-theme—the movement's MT—provides the central emotional crisis (at mm. 104–28), and the movement ends in gloom rather than bliss.[40] This obvious reversal of a formal pattern to which Schubert elsewhere subscribes gives him the opportunity to *delay* the joyous homecoming—the apotheosis return of the A-theme in the tonic major—until the very last minute, the last page of his finale. But his stretching of the narrative's time span does not just begin with the Andante; the story, whatever it might be, already gets under way in the first movement, if almost imperceptibly.

Example 6.10 begins at m. 42 of that movement, just a few measures after the transition into the ST[1] has begun. Let us consider this passage within the context of the very opening of the movement, where the MT's initial four-bar compound basic idea—a bright, robust, unison, E♭-tonic-declaiming gesture—immediately gives way to a fragment of that idea in the submediant, thus already looking toward the Andante's key of C minor. Note the truly drastic manner in which a transposed repetition at m. 44 of the pianist's lightning chromatic ascent from m. 38 hurls us, completely unprepared, into the strangely remote realm of ♭vi, C♭ minor (gratefully

Example 6.10. Schubert, Piano Trio in E-flat Major, first movement, mm. 42–77

*(B minor is the key in which the Andante's MT twice returns in the original finale.)

Example 6.10. cont.

notated in B minor). As the ST[1] then begins in that key, perhaps one can sense within the rhythm and texture of its repeated chords a premonition of the "trudging figure" in the Andante's MT. My annotations in example 6.10 propose that a long-range descending-thirds sequence—B to G to E♭—guides the sequential repetition of the ST[1]'s expansive nine-bar model momentarily back into the home key at m. 66. But then a new model slips gently into C minor, and here (see the asterisks at m. 72) is where Schubert seems already to have begun dreaming about a singular moment to come within his Andante.

To hear where the asterisked passage at m. 72 moves inward, we now turn back to the Andante's MT, at example 6.8: what was just the hint of an idea in the first movement reemerges—stabilized, simplified, and now very memorable—at the beginning of the Andante MT's second part, mm. 11–12. Two striking details make this association unmistakable, at least for me: within the domain of C minor, the first of these is the unusual leap from $\hat{2}$ to $\hat{5}$, especially vocalized by the appoggiatura in the cello; the second is the distinctive modal progression, tonic-to-minor-v^6 on its way to III, wherein the leading tone is avoided in the bass. This modal detail is significant: the idea at mm. 11–12 is one of three gestures that Schubert directly derived from the modal-inflected Swedish song, shown at example 6.9; we find the idea at the beginning of the song's coda, at m. 20–21, and it recurs at mm. 24–25.

I was reluctant to recognize a foreshadowing of the Andante's "trudging figure" within the chordal rhythm of the first movement's ST^1 until I noted that the first part of that theme, the nine-bar model with which it opens (mm. 50–58), returns to make another descending-thirds journey within this sonata- movement's coda; there the theme reverses its original journey, now approaching B minor from the stability of the home tonic, rather than leading *from* B minor to that key. B minor is the key in which the Andante's MT will return twice within Schubert's original, uncut version of his finale. In fact, the very last gesture we hear in the coda of the first movement, just before the Andante begins, carries the chordal rhythm. If this rhythm, the signature feature of the first movement's ST^1, really does play the subtle role of pointing toward, and leading us into, the Andante, then surely one purpose of the return of that rhythm in Schubert's *third* movement—namely, within the trio of his scherzo-trio form—must be to reconfirm the importance of that role within the overall cyclic design (see mm. 39ff. of the trio).

The one writer who has identified the connection between Schubert's first and second movements is Brian Newbould. He made the discovery before I did; I stumbled upon it independently. To clinch his argument (and mine), Newbould reports that the passage beginning at m. 72 in the first movement was *not present* in Schubert's first draft. In Newbould's words: "It seems likely that Schubert added it after completing his slow movement, and perhaps the finale."[41] In other words, it is quite possible that Schubert, having permitted his Andante theme cyclically to radiate outward and forward into his finale, decided as well to create one ephemeral moment in his first movement that would point inward to the Andante.

Now for just a few observations about the finale itself. Like a number of Schubert's last movements (and a few of Beethoven's), this one has been denigrated. Treitler describes it as "one of those endless rondos...going on in an endless pattern of mindless energy" (the movement is in sonata form, not rondo or even sonata-rondo). Kramer hears the finale as "little more than written-out vamping, entertainment music on a bad night."[42] Even Schubert must have had a few doubts about this finale: for reasons we will never know, he cut some 100 bars prior to publication. Both Treitler and Kramer recognize, in so many words, that the overflow of "patter" in the movement's exposition serves as a fabulous *foil* to the exquisite, etherealized returns, in the development section and in the coda, of the cello's melody from the Andante's MT. But neither of these writers finds any kind of relationship between that earlier theme and the other materials of the finale. In particular, Kramer seems disturbed by the "nervous, repercussive texture" of the finale's pervasive ST^1, the beginning of which is shown at my example 6.11.[43] (Not shown is the abrupt manner in which this theme is approached.)

Example 6.11. Schubert, Piano Trio in E-flat Major, finale, mm. 73–82

Readers will recognize that the melody I superimpose above the violin line at example 6.11 is the cadential idea from the MT of the Andante—that soulful gesture which seems in turn to be remembering the first song of Schubert's *Winterreise* cycle. As shown in example 6.9 (mm. 15–19), this is one of the three ideas that Schubert borrowed from the Swedish song. The descending leaps of this gesture and its focus upon scale-degrees 3̂–2̂–(4̂–3̂)–1̂ surely bear comparison with the opening of the finale's ST¹, but these similarities are likely to be dismissed as purely subliminal. And that's just the point I want to make! Already at this moment, the Andante's MT has begun to radiate its message outward toward a final transformation, but recollections of the Andante are meant to be insidious, only gradually recognizable, and yes, haunting.[44] When, still within the finale's exposition, the ST¹ itself comes back, its return is initiated by an evaded cadence that interrupts a second ST as if slapping it in the face, to snap it out of its ebullience (see example 6.12, m. 163). The wake-up call takes the form of a fully-diminished seventh chord, marked *ffz*; its recurrence at m. 178 (not shown) would seem to be for the sake of saying, "Listen here! Listen carefully to the hidden content of my all-pervasive ST¹!"

Example 6.12. Schubert, Piano Trio in E-flat Major, finale, mm. 162–70

Finally, but *only* within his original version for the end of the development section, Schubert begins to bring his Andante theme and his ST[1] into immediate rapport with one another: now the pianist's triplets in hemiola alternate with statements of the ST[1]'s basic idea, providing the accompaniment, along with the violin's pizzicato chords, for the cello's Andante theme. When, as shown at example 6.13, the cadential idea from the Andante at last returns in direct counterpoint with the ST[1]'s opening gesture, the kinship of the two ideas becomes as if epiphanically confirmed.

Formally and dynamically contextualized, this passage, like the others I have addressed, lends support to the view that Schubert's E-flat Trio "turns inward" more sharply than any of his earlier works of this kind, some of which I list at table 6.2. In each of the Trio's outer movements, an abrupt transition into a striking secondary theme marks that theme's role in pointing toward, or pulling back, to the centrality of the Andante movement—the expressive core of the work as a whole. Finally, the observation I make at example 6.13 lends solid support to Newbould's as well as John Gingerich's view that Schubert did not do his finale a service when he chose to make his cuts (in doing this, Schubert shortens his movement by only about one and one-half minutes). Like Gingerich, I strenuously argue in favor of

Example 6.13. Schubert, Piano Trio in E-flat Major, finale, mm. 505–13 (original version, from Franz Schubert, *Neue Ausgabe sämtlicher Werke*, Series VI, vol. 7, ed. Arnold Feil, as published by Bärenreiter, 1975)

performances of Schubert's original, uncut finale, and I am pleased to note that performers on several recordings of the Trio apparently agree with me.[45]

Lawrence Kramer compares the returns in the finale of the Andante theme to the calling up of revenants—ghosts from dark places in the mind, "phantoms of anxiety and denial" in Freud's sense, but also enactments of desire, uncanny "Doppelgängers" that come to fill a void. What Schubert's revenants bring to his finale is "the expressivity—rich, nostalgic, evocative—of a lost melody, an absent voice." For Kramer, the end of the finale's coda "sounds patently trumped up"; here, where the Andante theme returns one last time, now as if radiantly redeemed and redeeming, that it *fails* for Kramer to "integrate the music of the revenant into the putative normality" of the finale is "perhaps the only good thing one can say for it."[46] Some readers will surely take exception to this radical view, but whatever narrative one brings to this

Table 6.2 Some Examples of "Inward-turning" Instrumental Works by Schubert

Individual movements or works with secondary or interior themes that serve as focal points:

Fantasy in C Major for Piano, "Wandererfantasie," D. 760 (1822; publ. as op. 15, 1823): the central slow "movement"—a set of variations on Schubert's song "Der Wanderer" (1816)—serves as the motivic matrix for all the other "movements."

Piano Sonata in A Minor, D. 784 (1823; publ. as op. 143, 1839): the hushed, hymn-like ST (in E major) adapts but tempers the effect of the MT's and the transition's insistently repeated rhythmic motive; this ST is the inward calm in the face of outer turmoil.

Fantasy in C Major for Violin and Piano, D. 934 (1827; publ. as op. 159, 1850): its center, and motivic source, is a set of variations on Schubert's song "Sei mir gegrüsst" (1821–22).

Impromptu in F Minor, D. 935 (1827; publ. as op. 142, 1839): the wistful, duet-like central episode (in iii, then III), itself a complete rounded binary, takes a full recapitulation in the home tonic, thus anticipating Schumann's "parallel forms" (see Daverio 2001 and Fisk 2001).

String Quintet in C Major, D. 956 (1828; publ. as op. 163 in 1853): ST[1], beginning in E♭ major, has generally been regarded as the signature theme of the movement; the MT's opening neighbor-chord progression immediately points toward the forthcoming role of E♭.

Multimovement works in which the *slow* movement serves as the expressive core:

Symphony in B Minor, "Unfinished," D. 759 (1822; publ. 1867): some have speculated that Schubert never "completed" this symphony because he became satisfied that the slow second movement serves as a conclusive cyclic response to the first (see Solomon 1997 and Fisk 2001).

Octet in F Major, D. 803 (1824; publ. as op. 166, 1853 and 1889): materials from the Adagio introduction to the first movement return within the Andante molto "*ombra* scene" as introduction to the finale; the Andante molto itself returns just before the coda (see Gingerich 1996).

String Quartet in D Minor, "Der Tod und das Mädchen," D. 810 (1824; publ. 1831): its slow second movement, and subtle motivic source, is a set of variations on Schubert's song by the same name (1817).

String Quintet in C Major, D. 956 (1828; publ. as op. 163 in 1853): the slow second movement is generally regarded as the expressive core of the work.

Cyclic elements have been noted in all three of Schubert's last piano sonatas—in C Minor, D. 958, in A Major, D. 959, and in B-flat Major, D. 960 (all from 1828; all publ. 1839), and each sonata features a profoundly moving slow movement that could be regarded as the work's expressive core. In each case, motives and specific tonal regions anticipate materials of the slow movement, and subtle references back to that movement can be found in the scherzo and/or finale. It is generally agreed that the A-major Sonata, whose finale closes with a direct return to the opening of the first movement, is Schubert's most overtly cyclic work next to the E-flat Trio (see especially Fisk 2001).

Trio, I argue that it must be radically different from that of any earlier cyclic work, including Mendelssohn's Octet, Op. 20, to be addressed in chapter 7. A mere recollection of the conclusion of Beethoven's op. 110 sonata, where the finale's fugal subject rises to ecstatic, transcendental heights, might be enough to establish how utterly new and different Schubert's cyclic conclusion sounds. Whereas Beethoven's fugal transformation seems like a genuine triumph, an overcoming of the despair of his Arioso dolente, Schubert's ending simply allows the profound inwardness of his melancholy solo Andante song to open outward, to be released from its privacy and celebrated for the private treasures it has held. But perhaps the release comes too late. I invite the listener to be the judge.

CHAPTER Seven

Mendelssohn the "Mozartean"

It was around the year 1840 that Felix Mendelssohn seems officially to have become the all-time quintessential "Mozartean." That was the year in which Robert Schumann, in his review of Mendelssohn's newly published Piano Trio in D Minor, Op. 49 (1839), described him as "the Mozart of the nineteenth century; the most brilliant among musicians; the one who has most clearly recognized the contradictions of the time, and the first to reconcile them."[1] Schumann's publicized opinion had, however, been privately proclaimed a full nineteen years earlier, by none other than Goethe. In 1821, the eleven-year-old Mendelssohn stayed in Weimar as a guest in the Goethehaus for two weeks, during which time Goethe hosted two gatherings for the implicit purpose of pitting Felix the child prodigy against Goethe's childhood memory of the young Mozart. On these occasions, Felix performed a breath-taking improvisation on a song, played a Bach fugue and the Overture to Mozart's *Le Nozze di Figaro* from memory, sight-read difficult manuscripts from Mozart and Beethoven in the possession of Goethe, and, along with three Weimar court musicians, gave a performance of one of his own youthful piano quartets. Asking Mendelssohn to leave the room, Goethe consulted with his guests and then congratulated his friend, the child's elderly teacher Carl Friedrich Zelter: "[W]hat your pupil already accomplishes bears the same relation to the Mozart [of age seven] that the cultivated talk of a grown-up person does to the prattle of a child."[2] A year later, Heinrich Heine reported in a letter to Berlin that "according to the judgment of all musicians, [Felix] is a musical miracle, and can become a second Mozart."[3]

Although few have held that Heine's prediction became true, comparisons of Mendelssohn and Mozart as *Wunderkindern* have continued to hold their place to the present day, and Mendelssohn consistently outranks Mozart. For example, in 1995 Charles Rosen minces no words: "Mendelssohn was the greatest child prodigy the history of Western music has ever known. Not even Mozart or Chopin before the age of nineteen could equal the mastery that Mendelssohn already possessed when he was only sixteen";[4] this was the age at which he composed his first enduring masterpiece, the Octet in E-flat, Op. 20. In 2005 Richard Taruskin echoes precisely Rosen's opinion, as does Robert Levin, the highly acclaimed pianist on period and modern instruments and a distinguished Mozart scholar.[5] The expression "Mozartean grace" becomes predictable in descriptions most especially of Mendelssohn's early music. Biographical comparisons of the two also frequently arise: they both had precociously talented older sisters; both had phenomenal musical memories, and both were virtuoso pianists as well as improvisers (Mendelssohn composed highly "Mozartean" cadenzas for Mozart concertos and performed them as if he were Mozart himself); both were organists and occasionally played chamber music publicly as violinists (Mendelssohn was regarded as the greatest organist of his day); and, for those who take stock in astrology, both were born, along with Schubert, under the sign of Aquarius.

On the other hand, Mozart became a hard-working musician at the scandalous age of seven, when his father launched him and his sister on a grueling continental tour that would last for three years; although his sole composition teacher seems to have been his ambitious father, his early travels allowed him to absorb a "variety of musical influences," so that, in the words of R. Larry Todd, he "developed a cosmopolitan style."[6] By contrast, Mendelssohn's instruction in composition did not begin in earnest until his tenth year, when Zelter was hired to replace Ludwig Berger as a tutor. Even then, no one was pushing Felix to become a musician; rather, he would also be tutored in Latin, math, history, and geography, with some spare time for poetry and drawing, toward the goal of entrance into the University of Berlin. Zelter was known as a highly conservative teacher: he instilled in Felix a lifelong devotion to the music of Bach and Handel, based his teaching of counterpoint and figured bass on the treatises of Kirnberger and Marpurg, and required his student to model his compositions after Mozart and Haydn, rather than on the contemporary styles of, say, the "heroic" Beethoven or the "romantic" Weber.[7]

There is good reason, then, why references to Mendelssohn's "Mozartean grace" tend to arise most often in discussions of his early compositional endeavors. But Zelter notwithstanding, Felix's music already began to betray the influence of Beethoven by around 1823. Most astonishing, as noted by Rosen and others, is that when Mendelssohn, still only a teenager, began blatantly to imitate Beethoven's music, he had the audacity to choose as his models not so much the familiar works from Beethoven's middle period but, instead, scores on which the ink had hardly dried—Beethoven's last quartets. Mendelssohn's String Quartet in A Minor, Op. 13, from 1827, opens and closes with Adagios, in A *major*, based upon a love song titled "Frage" (op. 9, no. 1), which he had composed earlier that year; the head motive of the song, for the question "Ist es wahr?", gently invokes Beethoven's much darker "Muss es sein?" from the slow introduction to the finale of his op. 135 quartet (1826). Laying stress on the profound extent to which Beethoven's late quartets (as well as his Fifth and Ninth Symphonies) inspired Mendelssohn to explore *cyclic* formal and motivic procedures for the rest of his life, Todd points out elements of the song in all four movements of the quartet, and he underscores Felix's unabashed allusions to passages from Beethoven's quartets opp. 95, 132, and 130, and 135.[8] Rosen focuses in particular on the recitative in Beethoven's Quartet in A Minor, Op. 132 (1825) that connects the end of his scherzo movement to the beginning of his finale (example 7.1). For Rosen, the young Mendelssohn's "shameless" imitation of this passage—the introductory opening of his Presto as shown at

Example 7.1. Beethoven, String Quartet in A Minor, Op. 132, recitative as bridge into the finale (fifth movement)

Example 7.2. Mendelssohn, String Quartet No. 2 in A Minor, Op. 13, recitative as introduction to the finale (fourth movement)

example 7.2—prepares a finale in his op. 13 quartet in which the subtlety of motivic transformation is "intellectually breathtaking" but also "deeply expressive": "Far from being a secondhand reproduction of Beethoven's ideas, [Mendelssohn's imitations] are individual and personal—in short, peculiarly Mendelssohnian."[9]

I shall go one step further. The passage at example 7.1 suggests to me that, in the recitative from Beethoven's op. 132 to which Mendelssohn alludes, he hears Beethoven himself alluding, with anguish, to an earlier moment in his life and to a much earlier work—the first movement of his 1802 "Tempest" Sonata (see chapter 2). This inspires Felix to do what Beethoven only hinted at doing in op. 132: to return to the original source and make the allusion overt. By comparing the recitative of the "Tempest" (see example 2.5) with the opening of Mendelssohn's Presto, we can only conclude that a nearly straightforward quotation is at hand, and it is fully reinforced by the choice of the key of D minor. At the *a tempo* in m. 9, Felix even invents a figuration that comes closer to Beethoven's allegro idea in the "Tempest" than anything in the op. 132 passage. The telltale moment in all three passages is, however, the surprising C-major sixth-chord; Beethoven begins his op. 132 recitative with this harmony, whereas Mendelssohn leads to it sequentially, just as Beethoven had done in the "Tempest." In short, with Mendelssohn's A-minor Quartet as well as with others of his works from late 1820s, one might be tempted to speak of Mendelssohn the "Beethovenian."

From the Mozartean late eighteenth century to the death of Beethoven in 1827, the European cultural, political, aesthetic, philosophical, and musical landscape had of course radically changed. But from a music-compositional perspective, just one name dictates why *no one*, not even Mendelssohn, could "become a second Mozart" with impunity by the mid-nineteenth century, and that name is, as usual, Beethoven. Indeed, for post-Beethovenian composers of "the Romantic generation," to be compared with Mozart in any way other than as a *Wunderkind* would sooner or later amount to being branded as conservative, classicist, and thus old-fashioned rather than forward-looking—epithets that were all eventually applied condescendingly to Mendelssohn. And yet, as early as 1783, it was Beethoven himself, at age thirteen, who, according to his teacher Christian Gottlob Neefe, would most likely become "a second Mozart"; we know that, in the years that followed, Beethoven's debt to the younger composer remained outstanding (see chapter 3). Let us remember Count Waldstein's assurance to the young Beethoven upon his departure from Bonn to Vienna: "With the help of assiduous labor you shall *receive Mozart's spirit from Haydn's hands.*" For Elaine Sisman, that phrase "refers to the sense of lineage both conceptual and practical that places Beethoven in a musical culture already fully fledged in its genres and expressive possibilities."[10] As an expansive interpretation, this view cannot be denied, but we are left struggling to articulate those elusive *spiritual* qualities that characterize "Mozart's spirit."

Generalities seem inadequate. Commentators often advance such terms as "poise," "balance," "clarity," "craftsmanship," and, again, "Mozartean grace," to capture what makes even Mozart's darkest and most complex music sound as if it has been conjured by "the little magician" he was once called as a child—conjured as if effortlessly and with an irrepressible self-confidence. On the other hand, by the mid-nineteenth century "Mozart's spirit" had also become synonymous with "classical," as opposed to "romantic," these terms having taken on a strong dialectical role in philosophy and the visual arts. In music, no composer before Haydn and Mozart had done more than they to absorb the tendencies of their era and create music that would retrospectively define the notion of "classical form." And so, although comparisons between Mendelssohn and Mozart usually begin with their similarities as child prodigies, Mendelssohn became "Mozartean" first and foremost because of his "profound debt to classical models and his consummate and original command of sonata form."[11]

Musicologists and critics such as Leon Botstein, whom I have just quoted, have taken the lead in substantiating this justifiable claim, while also pointing to Mendelssohn's large-scale formal innovations, especially in the domain of cyclic techniques. Among North American music theorists, the predominant approach to Mendelssohn has been Schenkerian, as anticipated by Heinrich Schenker himself, in his *Der Tonwille* and in *Free Composition*.[12] For example, Carl Schachter and Allen Cadwallader have published studies of several of Mendelssohn's *Songs without Words*, giving attention to elements of form as the product of tonal processes and rhythmic conflicts.[13] William Rothstein's chapter on *Songs without Words* in his *Phrase Rhythm in Tonal Music*, from 1989, offers the most extensive study of "phrase expansion" and "deceptive recapitulations."[14] But Mendelssohn's *Songs without Words* has served as the almost exclusive genre of choice for these Schenkerians, including Schenker. As for Mendelssohn's chamber and symphonic works, there seems to be a dearth of effort on the part of theorists and analysts of form to ask such questions as, How does Mendelssohn construct his themes, and on what grounds might they be compared with Mozartean classical models?[15] In these areas, this chapter attempts to break some new ground. I begin by turning to Mendelssohn's D-minor Piano Trio, Op. 49, with reference to the opening of his first movement. In doing so, I pursue two characteristic features of Beethoven's music and post-Beethovenian instrumental music in general, both explored in earlier chapters: the tremendous expansion of late eighteenth-century theme- types, and the tendency of Mendelssohn's music to invite our perception of form as a dialectical process.

The Piano Trio, Op. 49: Opening

In an overview of Mendelssohn's chamber music, Thomas Schmidt-Beste notes with an exclamation mark that "the first movement of op. 49 is 616 bars long!"[16] An initial observation about this movement must be that it is technically only half that length: within his Molto allegro ed agitato tempo, Mendelssohn unquestionably asks his performers and score readers to recognize that the content of two notated measures stands for that of only one "real" measure, as represented by the formula $R = 2N$.[17] The composer's first basic idea and its varied repetition, over the span of mm. 1–8, thus give to the cellist and pianist a brooding "four-bar" presentation phrase, and what follows, with its faster-moving bass line, provides the continuation to a half cadence (mm. 15–16), completing an "eight-measure" sentence notated in sixteen bars (example 7.3).

Example 7.3. Mendelssohn, Piano Trio No. 1 in D Minor, Op. 49, first movement, mm. 1–40

With the violinist's upbeat into m. 17, the motivic work gets fully under way: as highlighted with brackets in the score, the violin's ascending interval of the sixth twice expands upon the cellist's initial rising fourth. This new idea takes a sequence within an ascending-step pattern, and then all three instruments join forces to strive for a cadence. In short, Mendelssohn's opening sentence is "becoming" an *antecedent type* (it ends with a half cadence) relative to the *continuation* now at hand. Had an authentic cadence been achieved at mm. 31–32, a well-balanced "sixteen-bar" *hybrid* type of theme—*antecedent + continuation*—would have resulted[18] But the cadence is *abandoned* when the cadential six-four at mm. 29–30 fails to resolve; as we shall see, this event motivates the first of an extraordinary series of expansions. The repetition of the cadential idea extends the hybrid theme, while allowing for the upbeat gesture now to rise through a full, climactic octave. The perfect authentic cadence (PAC) achieved at m. 39 presumably closes the main theme, but even that cadence might be misleading.

Mendelssohn's thematic process thus far might profitably be compared with that of the opening of another movement in D minor—one in which, like Mendelssohn's but more so, the quiet pulsating of a syncopated rhythm lends urgency and mystery to the theme. I refer to one of the three concertos Mendelssohn performed most frequently throughout his career, Mozart's Concerto in D Minor, K. 466. As shown at example 7.4, this opening theme, like Mendelssohn's prior to his repetition of the cadential idea, spans the length of sixteen real measures, here notated as such. Mozart's theme-type is less complex than Mendelssohn's, though hardly less effective: a straightforward sixteen-bar sentence—presentation + continuation—achieves its elided PAC on the downbeat of the sixteenth bar. The duration of the passage in real time is roughly the same as for Mendelssohn's at mm. 1–39.

Among the many ways in which Mozart's and Mendelssohn's opening themes create such different effects within their respective genres, their scope and their different formal functions must be counted, for these play a critical role. As the orchestral MT within the opening ritornello, Mozart's theme returns in its original, tightly knit form to mark the beginning of the recapitulation; it also reappears directly after the soloist's alternative MT within the solo exposition, where a half-cadential ending and a standing-on-the-home-dominant (at mm. 108–14), as substitutes for the original authentic cadence, now allow the theme to serve as the exposition's nonmodulatory transition. This latter change of function notwithstanding, in all three appearances Mozart's theme stands as discrete, complete, and self-contained. By contrast, with his opening hybrid structure, Mendelssohn may only have begun to complete the MT of his sonata exposition; in the passage that follows (example 7.5), he will repeatedly ask us retrospectively to reconsider the formal functions of the materials we hear.

What Carl Schachter has called "consecutive downbeat bars" gives us one way of interpreting the new idea at mm. 39–41.[19] It is difficult either to hear or to perform the downbeat of m. 40 as anything other than the strong first beat of a "real" measure at mm. 40–41; this would rule out the idea of an elided cadence at m. 39, but it would also mean that the final cadential measure of Mendelssohn's opening theme—m. 39—is only "one half-bar" in length. The effect of a sudden new burst of energy results, and these are typical characteristics of the beginning

Example 7.4. Mozart, Piano Concerto in D Minor, K. 466, first movement, mm. 1–17

of a classical transition function.[20] On the other hand, when the pianist's new, miniature-sentential phrase reaches an imperfect authentic cadence at m. 47 and then begins to repeat that phrase, the prospect of an antecedent-consequent plan arises.[21] Could this be a second main theme (MT²)? To be sure, we are still in the home key. The shift into the subdominant (at mm. 53–55) might suggest the expansion of a consequent, but it could also signal that we are really in the thick of a modulatory transition after all. And yet, a sequential repetition at mm. 56–59 carries the music right back onto the home dominant (at m. 58), and then a bravura standing-on-that-dominant-seventh ensues, thus undermining the notion that a MT² could achieve proper closure.[22] For those of us who hear only a "half-bar" at m. 39, Mendelssohn now demonstrates the value and flexibility of the $R = 2N$ technique by giving one extra notated bar at m. 64 (indicated at mm. 62–64 as "1–2–3"), thus allowing the cellist's canonic imitation to "catch up" with the violin, restoring odd-numbered measures as accented (David Temperley's "odd-strong"

Example 7.5. Mendelssohn, op. 49, first movement, mm. 39–77

Example 7.5. cont.

pattern),[23] and "stretching" this climactic dominant prolongation. The tumultuous return of the opening theme at m. 67 would certainly seem to cancel the idea that we have just heard a transition. Rather, and at least for a short moment, it would appear that this passage has served as a highly dynamic contrasting middle section (B)—ultimately dominant-oriented—within a much expanded MT that has taken on a *small-ternary* design (A–B–A′).

But one more reinterpretation will be required. At mm. 67–74 we hear the opening theme's presentation phrase, with its original cello melody now in the pianist's bass: but already in the middle of that phrase, a new harmonization gives direction toward a sequential repetition in the subdominant, and after that point in this exposition, Mendelssohn leaves his home key for good. A dominant arrival in the new key, the minor dominant (v), is gained at what I take to be an *elided* downbeat of m. 91 (example 7.6), and then yet another expansion arises. Over the extent of a broad dominant prolongation that stretches to m. 119, the composer introduces a passage that, despite its popularity to the present day, does not formally qualify as a "theme" in the strict classical sense: it only prolongs the dominant. To commemorate this often-sung passage (with words drawn, no less, from Rodgers and Hammerstein),[24] I shall dare to refer to it as a Mendelssohnian "standing-on-the-dominant theme"—a miniature-sentential phrase whose pseudo "half cadence" at m. 99 invites a repetition followed by fragmentation and, finally, liquidation. When there is nothing left of this unforgettable pseudo-theme save for the written-out trill in the piano, the composer's first true secondary theme enters—in the major (rather than minor) dominant.

Put simply, and now returning to m. 67, what we have here is a much elaborated example of the type of main theme in which a potential small-ternary reprise retrospectively "becomes" the beginning of the true transition (A′ ⇒ transition). Haydn and others had explored this maneuver decades earlier, and a case for the same was made in reference to Schubert's *Lebensstürme* Sonata for Four Hands (see chapter 6); like Schubert, Mendelssohn brings to the procedure considerable expansion and a much intensified post-Mozartean dynamic.[25] William Caplin gives as one example from Beethoven the main theme of the finale of his early Piano Sonata in C, Op. 2, No. 3 (1794–95); about this opening, and, I take it, about all such openings, Caplin concludes that "it is not possible, even in retrospect, to identify a convincing end point for the main theme."[26] This is surely the case in Mendelssohn's Trio, and it is fully reinforced in his MT recapitulation. There, a new, inward-looking cadenza for the piano leads through an Adagio to a fermata at mm. 392–96, just prior to the return of the cadential phrase from mm. 25–32, and then, as is customary for him within recapitulations, the composer makes a gigantic cut, altogether removing the authentic cadence heard at m. 39 and allowing his repeated cadential phrase to lead directly into the pseudo-"standing-on-the-dominant theme," now in the home key (example 7.7).

Chapters 1 and 2 examined Carl Dahlhaus's position that Beethoven's "Tempest" Sonata marks the beginning of his ever-increasingly processual approach to form, and I identified in both Dahlhaus's and Adorno's writings on Beethoven a strong post-Hegelian bent. For these two Beethoven-Hegelians, as well as for their forerunner—the Hegel-influenced theorist A. B. Marx—it would, I trust, be not only

Example 7.6. Mendelssohn, op. 49, first movement, mm. 87–121

Example 7.7. Mendelssohn, op. 49, first movement, mm. 399–424

impossible but also inappropriate to determine an "end-point" for Mendelssohn's MT: to invoke a recurring expression in this volume, his cadence at m. 39 may *not yet* be the end of his theme, but shortly after the reprise of his opening idea at m. 67, we are *no longer* within MT territory. Now, readers knowledgeable about Mendelssohn know that both Hegel, as a distinguished professor at the University of Berlin, and Marx, who became the editor of the *Berliner allgemeine musikalische Zeitung* in 1824, were frequent visitors at the home of the well-to-do Mendelssohns during their son's youth. Felix even attended Hegel's lectures on aesthetics at the university during the winter 1828–29, though he balked at Hegel's dialectical view that music since the "classical" period in art history had declined.[27] Around 1824 Marx began to replace Zelter as the single strongest musical influence upon the young composer. In fact, Marx takes the greatest credit for Felix's first intense engagement with Beethoven's music during that year, and his belief that pure instrumental music should express extramusical ideas inspired Felix in 1826 to recast the first draft of his Overture to *A Midsummer Night's Dream*, in order more colorfully to portray the full cast of Shakespeare's disparate characters. An estrangement between Marx and Mendelssohn eventually occurred, but not until 1839.[28] In the light of these remarkable connections, it would please me immensely if I could claim that Mendelssohn's tendency toward processual form—at the least, his capacity for obfuscating some of the formal boundaries that are so clearly articulated in earlier classical styles—were somehow a *direct product* of his relations with Hegel and Marx. But I cannot do this in good faith. Instead, I hold only that, with unparalleled brilliance, he absorbed such procedures—latent or manifest— from Haydn, Mozart, and especially Beethoven, if not also from the musical and cultural *Zeitgeist* in which he thrived.

The Octet, Op. 20

Benedict Taylor disagrees. In his 2008 article about Mendelssohn's Octet, Taylor proposes what I should perhaps have been emboldened to advance in this study: as "one of the first and most important compositions in cyclic form" (yes, the completion of the Octet in 1825 precedes that of Schubert's 1828 E-flat Piano Trio, discussed in chapter 6),[29] Mendelssohn's Octet "enacts an organic, evolving spiral that is not only strongly 'Hegelian' but also comparable to the broad temporal dynamism theorized by Goethe and seen, arguably, in *Faust*."[30] Citing the work of John E. Toews and others on musical historicism, Taylor sees historical self-consciousness as "one of the defining characteristics of Mendelssohn's age," and the Octet as the first work that fully articulates "this modern conception of subjectivity" in music—"the music's apparent ability to reflect on its own history."[31] Hegel's 1807 *Phenomenology of Spirit*, in which is found one of M. H. Abrams's supreme examples of the circular structure, or "circuitous journey,"[32] serves as the work with which the Octet "forms notable correspondences": the finale and the opening movement of the Octet merge into one another, "tying up the work with a return full-circle in an ecstatic meeting of parts and whole," and thus paralleling the structure of Hegel's philosophy as "a circle, or more precisely a spiral, moving out dialectically from an initial unity through contradiction and returning to a recognition and awareness of the self."[33]

But Taylor acknowledges that "when taken to an extreme the connection between Mendelssohn and Hegel inevitably falters": the analogy between the two "becomes strained" when one considers "fundamental differences between the two figures and their attitudes to history"—in particular, their differing views about "artistic progress."[34] For Taylor, this is the point where Goethe, "waiting patiently in the wings," steps in. As Felix's friend and spiritual mentor ever since their famous first meeting in 1821, Goethe shared with both Hegel and, later, Mendelssohn a distrust of "what they saw as the spiritual and emotional immaturity of Romanticism" (as opposed to "Classicism"). For both Goethe and Hegel, "the problem of humanity's relationship to time, the intersection of the temporal and the eternal, the contingent and the absolute, was a paramount question"; for Goethe, "[h]istory and artistic tradition are conceived as the constituents of a dynamic process, each part of which is imbued with both continuity and an ongoing organic growth and development from what has preceded it, in a vision not unlike that of Hegel." But by contrast with Hegel, "the past, for Goethe, never is and can never be superseded." Likewise, for Mendelssohn, "there are no completely new paths in music, only a 'continuation slightly farther' down the one true path."[35]

The centerpiece of Taylor's essay is his analysis of the Octet. Drawing extensively upon the analytic work of Greg Vitercik[36] but in less detail and within the broader agenda summarized above, Taylor sets out to show that the Octet "operates like a large interconnected organic system embodying its own internal teleology and generative process."[37] Evidence provided by both Vitercik and Taylor in support of this view is impressive indeed. In that the view itself rests upon a processual interpretation of specific means whereby the composer's ingenious motivic and harmonic transformations yield enormous postclassical formal expansions, the work of both authors greatly contributes to my own. In turn, I think that Taylor's notion of a merging of the Octet's finale and its opening movement—a "return full-circle"—can be strengthened, or at least more richly clarified. Vitercik persuades me that the "elusive process of motivic transformation" within the Octet's Scherzo (third) movement "hinges on what appears to be a completely insignificant detail within the main theme."[38] In the pages that follow here, only a detail—in this case, a purely foreground harmonic/contrapuntal progression—serves as the anchor of my argument. To uncover the detail, I reverse the direction of Taylor's and Vitercik's analyses, by first turning to a formal and motivic overview of Mendelssohn's brilliant presto finale, and then working my way back to his opening movement.

The finale

Vitercik, Taylor, and earlier writers about the Octet are right to suggest that the finale's large-scale form is "irregular." In particular, Vitercik compares the finale's exposition with typical rondo expositions in Mozart's concerto finales (where the rondo refrain is usually "followed by a string of accessory ideas"), and he concludes that, "in the strangely hectic way the themes tumble out on each other's heels," Mendelssohn's exposition seems more closely related to opening ritornellos in baroque concertos. Taylor adopts Vitercik's labels (*a*, *b*, *c*, and *d*) for the "four main elements" of the exposition and presents them as reproduced, with my annotations, at figure 7.1. Element *a* is, of course, the subject of the composer's *fugal* exposition (not to be confused with sonata exposition), with entries for all eight instruments.

Taylor proposes that the opening fugal presentation leaves "little potential for development." But the fugal opening of the Allegro molto finale of Beethoven's String Quartet in C, Op. 59, No. 3 (1806)—a sonata-form movement, and maybe

Figure 7.1. Adapted from Benedict Taylor, "Musical History and Self-Consciousness in Mendelssohn's Octet, Op. 20," *19th-Century Music* 32/2 (2008): 131–59 (example 10, 114). © 2008, The Regents of the University of California. Used by permission. All rights reserved. Annotations added.

an inspiration for Mendelssohn here—provides evidence to the contrary, and, as we shall see, so does Mendelssohn's Octet. Like Beethoven's, Mendelssohn's fugal exposition serves as his initiating MT. His authentic cadence at m. 25 elides with a repeated four-bar codetta—element *b*—that audaciously borrows the most famous melody from the "Halleluja" Chorus in Handel's *Messiah* ("And he shall reign…"); the version of this idea that comes closest to Handel's original becomes the joyous topic for imitative counterpoint at the start of the "development" (mm. 213ff.).

Mendelssohn's codetta-salute to Handel leads directly into element *c*—the beginning of a foot-stomping, *fortissimo* MT^2, still in the home key. Through a common variant of the ascending-step sequence, this theme tenaciously treks its way upward in pure octave doublings and then gains a V4/2-chord that prepares a cadential progression whose authentic cadence is confirmed with another pair of codettas. Shown as element *d*, the first violin's melody within the repeated four-bar codetta consists of a variant of the opening fugue subject, newly harmonized. The definitive feature of the codetta will be its opening progression: the prolongational I–(vi)–I^6, after which the cadential ii6/5–V^7–I effects closure. Readers are asked to *remember* this progression, because Mendelssohn's Octet is remembering it from over a great span of musical time, and because it will not be forgotten on the final page of this magnificent work.

The modulating transition that now begins at m. 63 seems overdue (example 7.8; note the progression I–(vi)–[V^7]–V). More surprising, its half cadence (at m. 73), followed by a standing-on-the-new-dominant, serves only to prepare a varied return of the rambunctious MT^2-materials (at m. 89), now in the secondary key—V (B♭). From the processual perspective, then, a transposition and transformation of the original MT^2 now serves as the first secondary theme (ST^1), thus somewhat obscuring this formal boundary and giving a new twist to conventional "monothematic" classical procedures, whereby the *opening* main-theme materials reappear to initiate ST^1. On the other hand, both this ST^1 and its ever more animated repetition (beginning at m. 105), with its hocket exchange in the four violins, have abandoned the opening unison character of MT^2 in favor of a dizzying imitative texture that features, first, the ascending fourth from the opening of the Handel codettas (element *b*), now filled in with passing quarter notes, and then fragments of the fugue subject in eighth notes.[39] An evaded cadence at m. 120 motivates a twelve-bar expansion of the repeated ST^1. The elided authentic cadence at m. 133 then initiates what could well have served as the closing section (CS) of this exposition (example 7.9), marked especially by its exquisite plagal ending (mm. 143–45). But a much expanded and heightened repetition of this passage (mm. 145–65) invites the idea of "CS $\Rightarrow$ ST^2," reserving the true codettas for the quiet, shorter phrases at mm. 165–76. These give way to what becomes a retransition (mm. 177–88), carried by solo first violin, into a return of the fugal MT^1 and its codettas in the home key; the clear beginning of a development section ensues (at m. 213). In short, the expansive ST-group has in the end succeeded in balancing the unusually lengthy home-key materials (*a*, *b*, *c*, and *d*) of the opening, and thus far we have every right to imagine that Mendelssohn's finale is following, though erratically, the formal path of the sonata-rondo.

But the many readers for whom the Octet, Op. 20, is one of the greatest chamber works of all time probably know that our young composer has much grander plans for the remainder of his finale—as Vitercik puts it, "plans that reflect its position as the last stage of the work as a whole; little of what happens from here on is what could be expected to happen."[40] Octet aficionados will surely remember that, over the course of what continues to behave like a development, and as if at first coming out of the blue, the opening four-bar phrase of the third-movement

Example 7.8. Mendelssohn, Octet in E-flat Major, Op. 20, finale, mm. 63–69

Example 7.9. Mendelssohn, op. 20, finale, mm. 132–47

Scherzo begins to *intrude* upon this finale, thus insinuating into this work an overt *formal* cyclicism (see chapter 6 and table 6.1) as the outcome of Mendelssohn's motivically cyclic process. Much has been made of the idea that here Mendelssohn emulates the most famous precedent for this cyclic recall—the return, within the finale, of the second main idea in the Scherzo of Beethoven's Fifth Symphony. But Taylor cites Charles Rosen's shrewd assessment of the two entirely different effects: "Rather than occurring after a fermata, bringing the movement to a momentary halt [as in Beethoven's Fifth], the cyclical interruption [in Mendelssohn's finale] is 'integrated seamlessly into the texture.'"[41] What naturally contributes to the seamlessness has been the ever-increasing pervasiveness of the motive of ascending fourth, initially from $\hat{5}$ to $\hat{1}$ within its defining tonal context: as the head motive of the Scherzo, this figure first appears within the finale at the head of the Handel quotation (element *b*), then emerges with frisky grace-notes at the beginning of the transition (example 7.8), and then becomes transformed via passing tones within ST[1], while always keeping in close touch with the Handel idea throughout the ST-group.

Of the three returns of the Scherzo's opening, the last serendipitously finds the Scherzo's original key of G minor (example 7.10). Here, as if carefully planned all along, the ST[1]-melody, borrowed from MT[2], becomes the bass line for the Scherzo phrase, which is thus impelled, now *fortissimo*, to adopt the earlier theme's ascending sequence. Invertible counterpoint reverses the bass and soprano at m. 303, but this does not halt the ongoing sequential ascent until its point of departure—G minor, now about to serve as the clear mediant of the home key—has been regained at m. 313. A virtuoso "Jupiter" Symphony-like motivic display in five-part counterpoint (at mm. 314–20) then leads, via descending fifths, to the home tonic at m. 321, but like the E♭ harmony bypassed in the ascent at mm. 307–8, this arrival is simply not strong enough or long enough to sustain the impression of the beginning of a recapitulation. In fact, the content at mm. 321–26 offers nothing more than a reference to the codettas from the end of the fugal MT[1] (at mm. 25 ff.). And, as Vitercik puts it: "In the shadow of the disorienting events of the preceding 48 measures...it is not surprising that [this] passage tumbles on with barely a moment's hesitation, settling onto a dominant pedal six measures later."[42]

Stretching all the way from m. 327 to the I[6]-chord at m. 355, the dominant pedal deals the final blow to expectations that a sonata-rondo form will be fulfilled, and now the term "irregular" comes into full force as a description of Mendelssohn's utterly *sui generis* design. We will wait in vain for a home-key return of MT[1]—hardly appropriate or necessary in light of the near omnipresence of that theme's continuous eighth-note patterns. And when our ST[1] returns at mm. 339–55 (example 7.11), the dominant pedal disqualifies this event as a regular sonata-form ST recapitulation both in and on the tonic (after all, MT[2], upon which ST[1] is based, received full home-tonic closure in the exposition). And yet, the enormous *Steigerung* created by the stepwise *fortissimo* ascent of ST[1] through the entire octave from $\hat{1}$ to $\hat{8}$ would seem to *demand* a resolution to a definitive root-position tonic when the climactic $\hat{8}$ is achieved at m. 355. An evaded cadence cannot technically be claimed here—there has been no preceding

Example 7.10. Mendelssohn, op. 20, finale, mm. 291–307

3rd return of Scherzo (in g)

cadential progression—but the impact of the I⁶-chord, rather than root tonic, is so powerful, so shocking, that the effect of evasion cannot be denied.

The first-inversion tonic at m. 355 initiates what Taylor regards as the beginning of Mendelssohn's coda.[43] By contrast, I hear that chord as yet another ploy, and a classical favorite of Mendelssohn's, for delaying his coda and achieving a formal expansiveness that, by this point within the finale, would seem to have no limit. As has been amply demonstrated, cadential progressions within classical and later styles are most frequently initiated by tonic harmony *in first inversion*, "often accorded emphasis as a sign that a cadential progression is under way."[44] Mendelssohn's I⁶-chord is no exception: beneath a vaguely familiar, yet "new," slower-moving idea in the first violin, as combined with the fugal eighth-note materials, the first-inversion tonic moves at m. 359 to a tonicized subdominant—

Example 7.11. Mendelssohn, op. 20, finale, mm. 339–75

always full of promise as a pre-dominant cadential harmony but, relative to the preceding twenty-eight-bar dominant pedal, coming *too soon* for a cadence. The IV-chord simply passes through the noncadential V6/5 to root tonic, after which we are right back on the I⁶-chord at m. 367. Only here will that harmony truly initiate a cadential progression, whose cadential tonic is achieved, with little fanfare, at m. 370–71 (example 7.11). By playing down this long-awaited authentic clo-sure, the composer can now motivate, *con fuoco*, a varied repetition of the entire passage, backing up to the I⁶-chord from m. 355; when the PAC is again gained and now elided at m. 387, the ensuing, quiet, sixteen-bar tonic pedal clarifies that the coda has finally begun.

As for the resultant form of the finale, a backward glance reveals that the cadential tonic achieved at m. 387 has been the first home-key tonic which, from the Schenkerian or formal perspective, can claim a structural status subsequent to the sonata-rondo-like return of the home-key fugal MT prior to the beginning of the apparent development. What pretended, then, to be a development section never reached an ending—an arrival on the home dominant, followed by a reca-pitulation. Instead, the entire section from the return of the fugal MT at m. 189 to the beginning of the coda at m. 387 has become a gigantic "second part," with the traditional large-scale Schenkerian "interruption" (*Unterbrechung*) on the structural dominant falling at the end of the exposition, rather than at the end of "the development." But if we regard the coda (mm. 387–429) as a true postca-dential, "after-the-end" event, then the two huge parts nearly balance one another in length (part I: 188 mm.; part II, 198 mm.), and this observation might shed new light on the cuts that the composer made within part II when he revised the Octet.⁴⁵ Much more important, however, as stressed by both Vitercik and Taylor, is that what I call part II radically departs from conventional formal processes for the purpose of a revelation: the finale has been leading with ever-increasing clarity toward "a synthesis of the separate parts of the Octet, where beginning and end are one."⁴⁶

Thus far the only "separate part" to have made an overt return within the finale has been the third-movement Scherzo phrase. At the beginning of the coda (for Taylor, its second part; mm. 387–402), Taylor hears (but I do not) a rhythmic and harmonic reference to the opening of the second-movement Andante, whose source for him can in turn be found at the beginning of the first movement's development section.⁴⁷ For the circle to close, it is now time for an even more explicit return to materials of the first movement, and Mendelssohn does not dis-appoint. The reference he chooses has been noted as "transparent";⁴⁸ for listeners who, like me, have heard that reference without the help of prior analytic com-mentaries, this description will seem right. In the final stage of the finale's coda, shown at example 7.12, the composer transparently and triumphantly recalls the first movement's unforgettable closing section (CS), first heard at the end of that movement's sonata exposition, and reproduced at example 7.13 in the home key, from the end of the recapitulation.

Let us look closely at these two passages. As the jubilant climax of the recapitulation, the CS in the first movement (example 7.13) succeeds perhaps most especially by virtue of its simplicity: within its first four-bar phrase, the cellos reiterate the well-known ascending head motive of the movement's MT, while the first violin just marches upward through a slower-moving arpeggiation of the tonic triad—Î-3̂-5̂—and then embellishes 5̂ with its upper neighbor 6̂ before descending back to Î. In support of the violinist's arpeggiated ascent is the prolongational progression I–(vi)–I⁶, a "classic"

Example 7.12. Mendelssohn, op. 20, finale, m. 402 to end

Example 7.13. Mendelssohn, op. 20, first movement, mm. 266–78

solution for the harmonization of $\hat{1}$–$\hat{3}$–$\hat{5}$, or $\hat{1}$–$\hat{1}$–$\hat{5}$, with bass and soprano moving in contrary motion, and with the vi-chord, as tonic substitute, subdividing the bass's descent by sixth.[49] Note the sharp *sf* diminished-seventh chord against the neighbor-tone $\hat{6}$, and then its resolution to V, as the phrase leads into an exultant, embellished repetition. Evaded cadences then allow the last fragment of the phrase to take two "one-more-time" repetitions—a device that Mendelssohn seems to have adored throughout his career.

The I–(vi)–I⁶ motion is of course the progression that readers have been asked to remember. We observed its role, at figure 7.1, as the harmonic basis of element *d*—the codettas within the finale that follow upon the first appearance of the foot-stomping MT²; and we have now identified its most palpable source within the first movement. But this cyclic recall has been made even richer by a clever revision of the fugue subject that the progression supports: my voice-leading annotations in figure 7.1, at *d*, propose that the shape of the revised subject now skeletally outlines the melody from the first movement's CS: $\hat{1}$–$\hat{3}$–($\hat{5}$)–$\hat{6}$–$\hat{5}$–$\hat{1}$. As within that distant passage, the phrase here is four bars long; once again, it is immediately repeated (mm. 55–58), and once again, a repeated two-bar fragment then creates an acceleration, this time through rhythmic diminution (mm. 59–62).

We turn now to the concluding section of the finale's coda, and thus to the high point of the complete Octet, as shown at example 7.12. By comparing that passage with the one in figure 7.1, at *d*, we know immediately that, within the finale proper, this splendid final page clearly recapitulates the MT^2- codettas from the exposition (they were not heard in the recapitulation). But here a slower-moving melody in the second and third violins shadows the fugue subject while unequivocally recalling the melody of the CS in the first movement, complete with its original opening progression—I–(vi)–I⁶—and its fragmentation. All of this leads to the plagal progression heard only twice earlier, at the end of the finale's exposition, which now reemerges, much extended, to serve as a final, radiant benediction.

And yet, something about this conclusion continues to haunt. Why does this particular ending seem so entirely appropriate, as if there could be no other possible closer for the Octet? If, for Taylor, "the beginning and end are one," if there is a "return full-circle," then how is this achieved? Taylor would seem to rest his case upon the "fusion" of first- and last-movement themes traced above; he describes the "accompaniment" within the passage at example 7.12 as "adumbrating a harmonic progression familiar from the very first measures of the composition," but he defers to Vitercik as to what that progression might be.[50] Perhaps both authors have been impelled, like me, to seek an answer by listening to the finale's coda and then imagining the work to start all over again, at the top of the opening movement, shown at example 7.14.

Example 7.14. Mendelssohn, op. 20, first movement, opening

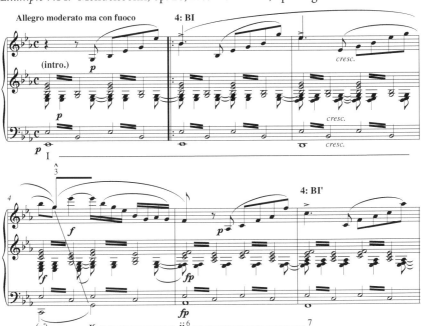

The opening of the first movement

For Vitercik, the first nine measures of this opening provide the progression that will govern "every level of the structure of the first movement": I–vi–ii–V–I.[51] Over the course of the movement, Vitercik identifies ever larger expansions of this progression, in which the ii-chord plays the leading role, with the vi-chord altered to serve as its tonicizing dominant. A comparable progression (with tonicized IV substituting for vi and ii) returns for Vitercik within the second part of the *finale*, now serving as "an enormous tonic cadence covering 108 measures—slightly more than one quarter of the movement's entire length."[52] Oddly, this "cadence" begins for Vitercik with the E♭ harmony "so precariously attained in m. 321,"[53] and it bypasses the I⁶-chord at m. 355 (example 7.11) that so strongly undermines the effect of an ongoing cadential progression. A simpler, alternative harmonic reading of the first movement's opening measures can, I think, restore some of the magic invested within that much later I⁶-chord, while attributing to Mendelssohn even greater transformative cyclic ingenuity in the realm of harmony. At long last, I turn to the local detail toward which I have been striving.

What has always been the most thrilling feature of the first movement's main theme for me is its opening stepwise descent in the bass. As shown in example 7.14, this majestic line moves in broad whole notes from the sustained opening tonic through the resonantly dissonant passing-tone D♮ to the vi-chord at m. 4. But here the primary tone of the movement—$\hat{3}$—arises as the goal of the middleground *Anstieg* (initial ascent), nested within the faster-moving ascending arpeggiations of the repeated head motive. The harmonic support for $\hat{3}$ is not the subdividing vi-chord, but rather the tonic in first inversion to which the submediant passes. Thus, Vitercik's fine analysis notwithstanding, vi does not progress directly to ii at mm. 4–5; instead, the I⁶-chord in m. 4 anchors the primary tone and completes our not-to-be-forgotten progression, I–(vi)–I⁶.[54] This is of course the progression that opens the closing section of the first movement, the MT²-codettas in the finale, and the last stage of the finale's coda. In short, those three passages simplify, clarify, and *compress* the very opening progression of the piece! When we return full circle from the end of the Octet to its beginning, that progression becomes the most perceptible and compelling link for me.

As for the metaphor of the circle, Taylor vacillates about whether the "structure of Hegel's philosophy is a circle, or more precisely a spiral." We will surely agree that the metaphor of "spiral" better captures Mendelssohn's extraordinary achievement. As Taylor puts it: "The closing section of the finale contains both the first movement and finale together, yet it is neither one exactly. The music merges the two, dissolving their individual identities simultaneously and hence transcending them."[55]

The ramifications of the opening I–(vi)–I⁶ progression for later moments in the Octet are both wide-ranging and transcendental in nature. Although the I⁶-chord takes structural priority over the submediant in m. 4, we can now interpret several of Vitercik's expanded "I–vi–ii–V–I" progressions within this first movement as moments where the original passing vi-chord "becomes" VI, now serving as V/ii and thus leading directly to ii. The beginning of the transition, initiated by a return of the opening theme, as shown at example 7.15, is a case in point. Nor should it be regarded as mere coincidence that a sequence to the submediant (G minor ⇒ G major) within the secondary key (V = B♭) constitutes the first motion away from the new tonic within the exposition's ST (beginning at m. 68), or that the home-key submediant (C minor) announces the beginning of the development section's forceful first core (at mm. 137–38), thus anticipating the key of the Andante second movement. At the end of the first movement, a final reinterpretation of the vi-chord occurs within the return of the MT in the very last phrase of the coda: here the bass line's stepwise descent now carries the vi-chord directly to the dominant on its way to the final authentic close. It is, however, within the modulating ST of the Scherzo movement that the opening I–(vi)–I⁶ progression reemerges in its most wondrous form. As shown at example 7.16, now a stepwise descending bass line in B♭ (III) undeniably recalls the bass descent of the first movement's MT. Once again the bass

Example 7.15. Mendelssohn, op. 20, first movement, mm. 34–45

Example 7.16. Mendelssohn, op. 20, Scherzo (third movement), mm. 24–32

passes through the vi-chord, but its continued descent fills in the motion to what, in the first movement, is I⁶. The astonishing D-major harmony that serves as the goal of this phrase can be understood as Mendelssohn's iridescent transformation of the original tonic in first inversion: I⁶ has become the major mediant, itself soon to serve as the home dominant in G minor, for a repeat of the Scherzo's exposition. "Stroke of genius" seems all too lame in the face of such precocity.

More on Mendelssohn's Codas: Overture to *A Midsummer Night's Dream* and the Scherzo of the D-minor Piano Trio

With the Octet, the idea of Mendelssohn as either the "Mozartean" or the "Beethovenian" already seems questionable. This sixteen-year-old has already found his own voice—entirely personal, expansive, ebullient, and original. We love and admire his music today not nearly as much for its "Mozartean grace" as for what makes it uniquely Mendelssohnian. Still, attempts to pinpoint what is Mendelssohnian about Mendelssohn have been no less challenging than efforts to define "Mozartean grace." Perhaps the codas in the first and last movements of the Octet point us to at least one signature characteristic of Mendelssohn's style in general.

Even within works that do not strive toward culminating cyclic conclusions, Mendelssohn often reserves his codas for markedly Mendelssohnian breakthroughs—surprises, moments of sudden revelation. As with the Octet, these tend to result from the emergence and final transformation of a motive or idea hitherto concealed or introduced much earlier and then allowed to slip beneath the radar. Moments like these can be climactic, but just as often they can simply seem like the bestowal of a blessing, gestures that exalt the completed work and allow it to close in a quiet glow; and they can seem to arise with the apparent effortlessness of Mozart.

An example comes from Mendelssohn's second masterpiece, and it will most likely be familiar. As many before me have noted, the coda of his Overture to *A Midsummer Night's Dream*, from 1826, brings a final, unforgettable transformation of the descending-fourth motive E-to-B that has permeated the entire work. In his *Free Composition*, Schenker traces occurrences of the motive within the overture's sonata exposition. As reproduced at figure 7.2a, Schenker's examples demonstrate "*concealed* repetitions via augmentation," as opposed to "motive repetitions in the usual sense."[56] R. Larry Todd's examples, reproduced, with my formal and analytic annotations, at figure 7.2b, support Todd's observation that transformations of the descending tetrachord "all spring from the magical wind chords [which], like a motto, frame the overture and mark the recapitulation." Todd identifies Mendelssohn's final transformation in the coda as a probable quotation from another work inspired by Shakespeare's play—Carl Maria von Weber's opera *Oberon*;[57] note that Mendelssohn's harmonic progression opens with his very own I–(vi)–I⁶, introduced at Todd's example *c*! Todd admirably emphasizes the notion of metamorphosis, Shakespeare's central idea in the play and Mendelssohn's motivic modus operandi.

Figure 7.2a. From Heinrich Schenker, *Free Composition* (*Der freie Satz*) (New York: Longman, 1979), Supplement: Musical Examples, fig. 119, 9.

Ex. 5.11: Mendelssohn, *A Midsummer Night's Dream Overture*, Op. 21 (1826), motives

a)

Intro.: the "magical wind chords"

b)

MT¹: "elves"

c)

MT² ⟹ Trans.: "court of Athens"

d)

ST¹: "pairs of lovers"

e)

ST²: the "braying" Bottom

f)

CS: "royal hunting party of Theseus and Hippolyta"

Ex. 5.12a: Weber, *Oberon* (1826), Act II, Mermaid's Song

and___ the last faint light of the   sun___ hath fled!___
(IV) ————————— I ———— V ———— 7   I

Coda: the final transformation

Ex. 5.12b: Mendelssohn, *A Midsummer Night's Dream Overture*, Op. 21 (1826), Coda

I — (vi) ————————— I⁶ ———— V ———— 7   I

Figure 7.2b. From R. Larry Todd, *Mendelssohn: A Life in Music* (Oxford: Oxford University Press, 2003), 163, 167. Annotations added.

As a second example, I return to the D-minor Piano Trio, this time to the Scherzo (third) movement, in D major. From within this sonata-rondo-like form, example 7.17 shows a passage at the end of a very rich and complex development section. Within a whirlwind of developmental activity based exclusively upon the opening of the rondo refrain (MT), the four-bar *pianissimo* idea that the piano

Example 7.17. Mendelssohn, Piano Trio No. 1 in D Minor, Op. 49, Scherzo (third movement), mm. 98–119

introduces at m. 101 sneaks in unannounced, as if from another musical world. I do not attempt to indicate where the pianist's phrase begins—is it at m. 101, or has the phrase perhaps already gotten under way, via elision in the foregoing bar? The preceding phrase rhythm suggests the latter, but the pianist might be hard-pressed to perform the downbeat of m. 101 as anything but a new beginning. Whatever the case, the strings pick up this new slower-moving phrase and give it a varied repetition, after which the pianist takes one more turn, facilitating a gradual linear ascent in the soprano to the E♮ on the V-of-v-chord at m. 112. Then, just as quickly as it slipped in, this new idea disappears. In the passage preceding this excerpt, we can search for some kind of warning—perhaps a little hint—that something new is about to emerge. The best I can offer is the rhythm of the cellist's bass line beginning at m. 78, as indicated with the arrow in example 7.18.

Example 7.19 begins with the bridge into the coda, and then comes the passage that provoked my original fascination with Mendelssohn's coda transformations. It turns out that the surprising new idea from within the development was a concealed, long-range preparation for one of Mendelssohn's most inspired conclusions. Now the strings reshape that idea's melody, repeat it, and add a new cadential phrase, to complete the only tightly knit thematic structure in the movement—an eight-bar sentence whose cadence is achieved at m. 164. It is worth noting, however,

Example 7.18. Mendelssohn, op. 49, Scherzo, mm. 74–84

Example 7.19. Mendelssohn, op. 49, Scherzo, mm. 153–73

that, in fulfillment of its role as a "coda theme," this hybrid begins on the cadence-initiating I⁶-chord, and thus its complete harmonic content offers nothing more than an expanded cadential progression. For pianists, the opportunity to give a full repetition to this enchanting new theme can be a blissful performance experience. That might partly be because, when one reaches the coda, the difficult pianistic work of the movement has nearly been completed, with only that tricky final sixteenth-note ascent to go at the end—Mendelssohn's insignia "elfin" ascent into the ether.

One might argue that, with his wonderful coda ideas, Mendelssohn confirms his status as the "Mozartean." Consider Mozart's transformative codas in, for example, (1) the first, second, and fourth movements of his "Dissonance" String Quartet, K. 465; (2) the Adagio movement of his String Quintet in G Minor, K. 516; (3) the superb Neapolitan-oriented coda in the finale of his C-minor Concerto, K. 491; and (4) both the *Romanze* movement and the finale of his D-minor Concerto, K. 466. And then, of course, there is Beethoven. Among the many codas by him that bring forth surprisingly "new" materials, I think especially of the coda in the finale of his Cello Sonata in A Major, Op. 69 (1807–8).[58] Perhaps Mendelssohn remembers this coda when, in his Violin Concerto, Op. 64 (1844), he transforms his cyclically all-pervasive neighbor $\hat{6}$–$\hat{5}$ motive to produce the glorious new cadential outburst we hear toward the end of his finale.

For Charles Rosen, the eventual "decline in Mendelssohn's prestige may prove comprehensible if we reflect that in the late nineteenth century the foundation of his fame rested principally on the oratorios and the *Songs without Words.*" The latter have "a Mozartean grace without Mozart's dramatic power, a Schubertean lyricism without Schubert's intensity. If we could be satisfied today with a simple beauty that raises no questions and does not attempt to puzzle us, the short pieces would resume their old place in the concert repertoire. They charm, but they neither provoke nor astonish."[59] Leon Botstein strikes back. For Botstein, we have only to recognize that, as an ideology, "'classicism,' inclusive of the neoclassical movements in architecture and the visual arts," guided Mendelssohn "throughout his life, often in conjunction with the sensibilities of Romanticism...his musical achievement, taken on its own terms and not from within the paradigm of Romanticism, turns out to have been greater than the notion of mere aesthetic simplicity." Mendelssohn's music "retains the capacity to provoke and astonish in ways that were lost on successive nineteenth-century generations, particularly those profoundly influenced by Wagner."[60]

Mendelssohn's reputation gets caught in the crossfire. Drawing especially upon the aesthetics of Moses Mendelssohn, Botstein contends that, like his grandfather, the composer faithfully upheld the humanistic, civic role of music as a means of creating solidarity and commonality within the formation of a community. For this to be accomplished, "music must possess a wide-ranging capacity to elicit response. Its form and content must reach the audience, unambiguously, in musical terms. A surface that to us might seem lacking in complexity and ambiguity, that does not 'puzzle' or 'raise questions' arbitrarily or capriciously, is precisely what Mendelssohn sought."[61] In short, for neither Rosen nor Botstein does Mendelssohn's music "puzzle" or "raise questions," their differences in opinion resting in the end on the idea of questions raised *arbitrarily* or *capriciously*.

My focus in this chapter upon just two of Mendelssohn's works—his earliest masterpiece and his "mid-career" Trio—hardly provides the grounds for grandiose claims either in support of or against the conflicting views of Rosen and Botstein. But in the case of both those works, I lay claim to the view that the composer's expansive, processual approaches to the treatment of form, motive, and harmony are not without their profound complexities and ambiguities, that his transformations within those domains certainly provoke, astonish, and raise questions, and that perhaps the best word for describing the emergence of the "coda theme" in the Scherzo of the op. 49 Trio is "capricious," in the most delightful sense. As we learn from his "secret" exchange with his sister about the Octet (see note 41), Mendelssohn was not above withholding secrets. Whether or not the secrets within his music eventually reveal themselves with the "simplicity" and "transparency" that Botstein applauds, to search for where they hide can be a thrilling effort to uncover the workings of a "little magician"—the aspect of Mendelssohn's musical character that perhaps, above all, warrants his reputation as "a second Mozart."

CHAPTER Eight

... Sed Non Eodem Modo

Chopin's Ascending-Thirds
Progression and His Cello
Sonata, Op. 65

Overview with Respect to Chopin's Genres

It has long been noted that something rather drastic happened to European common-practice tonality over the course of the nineteenth century and into the twentieth. Depending on one's rhetoric, either the blame or the credit goes first of all to what we know as *mediants*, or "third relations." For example, Charles Rosen holds that "[t]he attempt of the early nineteenth century to substitute third or mediant relationships for the classical dominant amounted to a frontal attack on the principles of tonality, and it eventually contributed to the ruin of triadic tonality."[1] By contrast, David Kopp *celebrates* direct chromatic third relations as "the cornerstone" of what he calls "common-tone tonality"—the first step toward "fully normalized" chromatic, rather than diatonic, "harmonic spaces" in nineteenth-century music.[2] In his account of how and why *direct* third-related progressions gain ascendancy in the nineteenth century, Kopp must, however, follow Rosen in gauging their ever-growing independence from the all-powerful tonic-dominant axis. Thus, both Rosen and Kopp, among others, share a common bond with Harald Krebs. Krebs's Schenkerian-based dissertation from 1980 demonstrates that, whereas mediant harmonies in works by Haydn, Mozart, and Beethoven tend to be employed within the controlling domain of large-scale I–III–V, V–III–I, V–III–V, and V–VI–V progressions, Schubert and Chopin begin to use mediants in new "oscillatory," "circular," and ultimately "tonic-replacing" ways.[3]

My project in this chapter is considerably less ambitious than Krebs's, while also indebted to his as a point of departure. I approach the works of just one composer—Chopin. Rather than including what we often still call "submediants," I focus upon diatonic and chromatic *upper* mediants, and I address harmonic progressions that fundamentally take only one direction—they ascend. In other words, I explore *the ascending-thirds progression* within Chopin's oeuvre, and I strive to show that one of its specific types—the I–III–V motion—is so ubiquitous in his works as to warrant the title "Chopin's signature progression." Put briefly, I engage with a type of progression that firmly remains within the domain of the tonic-dominant axis; in doing so, I argue that Chopin's extraordinarily innovative harmonic language is all the more impressive for the extent to which it generally thrives within that domain.

Those familiar with Schenkerian theory will of course recognize that the I–III–V–I progression plays a determinative role in the later stages of Heinrich Schenker's thought. As shown at figure 8.1, from his *Free Composition*, Schenker's premier examples of first-level middleground *Ursatz* forms feature the bass arpeggiation (*Bassbrechung*) of the tonic as "chord of nature," within which the tonic in first inversion *or* the chord of the mediant—altered, no less—serves as a "*third-divider*." That the bass motion of the I–III–V–I progression arpeggiates tonic harmony naturally explains why it serves as Schenker's "organic" prototype for all other *Ursatz* forms; in this light, however, we might be surprised to note that, of the many graphs and schemas of excerpts and complete movements found in *Free Composition*, relatively few—roughly twenty-seven—offer first- or later-level middlegrounds, or even more local examples, of straightforward I–III–V bass arpeggiations. Among these, I count at least ten drawn upon works by Chopin.

Two such graphs, shown at figure 8.2, address one of Chopin's most famous pieces, his Polonaise in A Major, Op. 40, No. 1, from 1838. As an introduction to the type of progression I survey, as one example of Schenker's various approaches to mediant harmonies, and as a first effort to place Chopin's ascending-thirds progressions within the context of both his formal designs and their expressive content, let us consider the opening of this piece (example 8.1).

As with so many opening themes from virtually every one of Chopin's genres, this theme takes the form of a sentence: a basic idea and its immediate, varied repetition yield a four-bar tonic-prolonging presentation, and the shift to the dominant of the chromatically altered *major* mediant at m. 5 coincides with the beginning of the continuation, in which the sequential repetition of the basic idea drives onward to the authentic cadence at m. 8. In Schenker's foreground graph, shown in figure 8.2a, he interprets the III♯-chord as dependent upon the supertonic to which it leads, specifically because, whereas upper mediants share scale-degree $\hat{3}$ with the tonic and can thus prolong it, the supertonic supports the *Urlinie*'s descent to scale-degree $\hat{2}$ on its way to $\hat{1}$. In Schenker's graph of the complete movement, shown in figure 8.2b, the Roman numeral III♯ disappears altogether from the analysis. But no one, surely not even Schenker, would deny that Chopin's exultant III-chord not only supports the arrival of the primary tone $\hat{3}$ in its obligatory register but also provides the defiant, heroic outburst that clinches the character of his theme. The arrow from figure 8.2a to figure 8.1 points to the schema that Schenker's foreground graph most closely resembles.

Chopin's dance genres abound with openings that feature sentences, or large-scale antecedents and consequents structured as sentences, in which the I–III–V ascending-thirds progression guides the harmonic direction. For examples, we can turn to his very first published mazurka, and then to one of his last. As shown in example 8.2, the presentation phrase within the first of the op. 6 mazurkas, from 1830, arrives on the diatonic mediant by means of a sequential repetition of the basic idea: V^7–I,

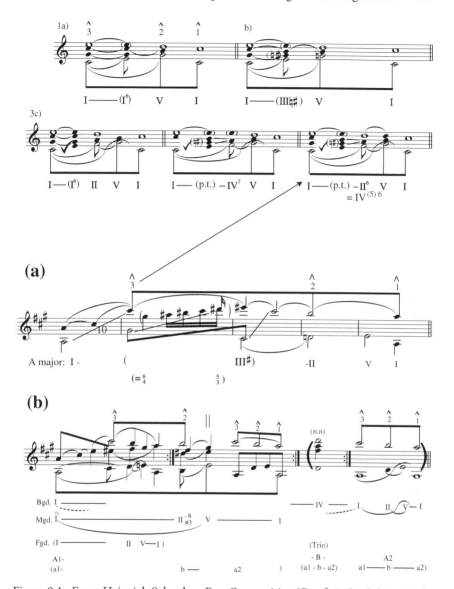

Figure 8.1. From Heinrich Schenker, *Free Composition* (*Der freie Satz*) (New York: Longman, 1979), Supplement: Musical Examples, excerpts from fig. 15.

Figure 8.2. From Schenker, *Free Composition* (*Der freie Satz*) (New York: Longman, 1979), Supplement: Musical Examples: (a) fig. 56, 2e; (b) fig. 40, 1.

Example 8.1. Chopin, Polonaise in A Major, Op. 40, No. 1, mm. 1–8

[V⁷]–III. It might then be the role of the continuation phrase to carry the progression upward to the dominant. But, in an oft-noted contrapuntal passage that Jim Samson has called "prophetic"[4]—exemplifying another characteristic Chopin pattern—the continuation slides downward in parallel tenths, with all voices moving by semitone; the interval of a third from III to V thus inverts to become a sixth. As a result, no cadence ensues at m. 8, and the reason is obvious: in that this eight-bar antecedent begins off-tonic, as V⁷–i, the consequent will do the same, so that, as William Rothstein has explained, the end of the antecedent and the beginning of the consequent overlap.[5] To this we can add that the i–III–V–i progression reaches its completion only at m. 10. The consequent within what becomes a sixteen-bar period regains the mediant at m. 12 and now lovingly dwells upon it (at mm. 13–14), but then the continuation moves on to complete a second i–III–V–i progression.[6]

As proposed in example 8.3, familiarity with the op. 6 mazurka might shed some light on what makes the initial sixteen-bar period of Chopin's A-minor

Example 8.2. Chopin, Mazurka in F-sharp Minor, Op. 6, No. 1, mm. 1–16

Mazurka, Op. 17, No. 4, composed just three years later, both novel and already nostalgic. My "recomposition" here suggests that, at the basis of the presentation phrase in this piece, the ascending i–III–V–i progression is again promised, but this time denied. Over the course of his antecedent, Chopin chooses instead to compose out his long, slow-moving chromatic descent in the bass from 1̂ to 5̂—the bass line whose long-standing associations with lament so touchingly lend to this mazurka its sorrowful tone. In this light, and instead of further destroying what may be some readers' favorite mazurka, as it is mine, I refrain from further recomposition after m. 8.[7]

With example 8.4, we move prematurely to the last year of Chopin's life, and to the second of the op. 67 mazurkas, published posthumously in 1855. Within the A-section of this ternary form, we again hear the off-tonic V⁷–i beginning and the sequential repetition of the initial two-bar idea moving to the mediant; but now the completion of the i–III–V–i progression already occurs at the beginning of a notably *post*classical "continuation," in which, rather than, say, beginning with

Example 8.3. Chopin, Mazurka in A Minor, Op. 17, No. 4, mm. 1–14

fragmentation, the composer simply cycles back to his opening idea and extends its tonic with a repeated plagal progression whose the effect is postcadential. The subdominant at m. 8 beautifully prepares the return of the dominant at the beginning of the consequent, and the sixteen-bar period concludes with the first and only genuine cadence in the theme. In the light of other, earlier mazurkas whose openings or middle sections highlight the ascending-thirds progression (see table 8.1), I am tempted to hear this mazurka as a reminiscence, as Chopin's fond farewell to a genre that he had admirably served.

Example 8.4. Chopin, Mazurka in G Minor, Op. 67, No. 2, mm. 1–19

Table 8.1 Other Mazurkas Whose A-Sections or Trios Open with or Highlight the I–III–V Ascending-thirds Progression

Op. 17, No. 2, in E Minor (1833)

The sentential antecedent and consequent within the A-section move via descending fifths from i to III, then V⁷—I at the beginning of the continuation, which concludes with HC (antecedent), then PAC (consequent).

Op. 17, No. 3, in A-flat (1833)

Within the Trio, in ♭VI (= E), the sentential antecedent features model/sequence as I–iii–V (pseudo-interruption); the I–iii–V7–I motion is completed in the consequent. (See Schenker 1979, fig. 30a.)

Op. 24, No. 4, in B-flat Minor (1833)

Within the A-section as rounded binary, *a* and *a'* (with written-out repetitions) feature model/sequence as i–III–v, then PAC via V7–i.

(continued)

Table 8.1 *Cont.*

Op. 41, No. 4, in C♯ Minor (1838–39)

> The A-section within the A–B–A′ form features a "sixteen-bar" sentence (notated as 32 bars; $R = 2N$) featuring i (model)–III (sequence)–V6/5 (not root)–I, then vi–V7–I (continuation to PAC). The continuation is then repeated.

"Notre Temps" in A Minor (c. 1839)

> Within the A–B–A′ form, part 1 of the small-binary A-section features (V7)–i (model), [V7]–III (sequence), and then a repetition; the periodic part 2 provides III–V (antecedent: HC); i–V–i (consequent: PAC).

Op. 59, No. 1, in A Minor (1845)

> Within the A-section, the sentential *a* unfolds as (V7)–I (four-bar CBI), [V7]–III (four-bar sequence), and then [V7]–V; iv–V7–i (compressed continuation to PAC).

Op. 63, No. 2, in F Minor (1846)

> Within the A–B–A form, A takes the design of a sixteen-bar period, with (V7)–I, [V7]–III then leading through ♭II⁶ to the HC; the consequent substitutes iv on its way to the PAC.

Mazurka Op. 68, No. 2, in A Minor (c. 1827)

> An A–B–A′ form, with the A-section as a rounded binary: *b* stands on III and connects back to *a*′ via III–V7–i. The B-section takes the form of a small binary in the tonic major: part 1 ends in iii; part 2 then begins with (ii)–V7–I and continues with a sustained tonic pedal.

Mazurka Op. 68, No. 3, in F (c. 1830)

> Within the small-ternary A-section, *b* stands on V/vi = III. The return to *a*′ completes III–V7–I. (The Trio is in Lydian IV = B♭.)

This list does *not* include the countless internal instances of the ascending-thirds sequence within the mazurkas, nor does it include mazurkas, such as op. 67, no. 2, in which a fundamental I–III–V–I *Bassbrechung* would obtain over the span of the complete movement.

We might also be tempted at this point to wonder if Chopin's polonaises and mazurkas point to the possibility that there is something distinctly "Polish" about sequences that feature the I–III–V progression.[8] Whether or not this could be the case, the period at example 8.5 that opens his Waltz Op. 64, No. 2 (1846–47), of *Les Sylphides* fame, tells us that he did not resist that type of sequence even when he was working within the most pan-European, and ultimately Viennese, of dance genres. Here, within a two-bar hypermeter (two notated bars behave as one "real" bar, as discussed in chapter 7), the sentential antecedent begins, admittedly, with a repetition of the basic idea sequenced *downward*, to the submediant. But the continuation phrase (mm. 9–16) transforms and fragments the opening idea, treating this to a sequence in the mediant and then proceeding to an arrival on the tonicized dominant seventh at m. 15–16, thus traversing the i–III–V7 path but now effecting an interruption. The chromatic link into what clearly functions as a consequent in the next sixteen bars warrants the introduction of a new, colloquial term for the analysis of form in Chopin's music and that of some of his contemporaries: my term is "the nineteenth-century half cadence" (19cHC)—a local

Example 8.5. Chopin, Waltz in C-sharp Minor, Op. 64, No. 2, mm. 1–32

form-defining arrival on the dominant that, unlike the typical goal of classical half cadences, includes its seventh. Chopin's consequent (mm. 17–32) reaches the *mediant as seventh-chord* through a descending-fifths sequence and arrives at an authentic cadence in m. 32.

Once we begin to listen for the ascending-thirds sequence in Chopin's repertoire, we discover that it pervades every one of Chopin's genres, and this certainly includes another genre especially associated with German-Viennese music —the multimovement sonata. Along with the four minor-mode opening themes considered thus far, the beginning of the finale from Chopin's Sonata in B Minor, Op. 58 (1844)—its rondo refrain—exemplifies his preference for the traditional *diatonic* mediant when drawing upon the i–III–V progression in minor-mode contexts (example 8.6). Within Chopin's $R = 2N$ notation, the magnificent "four-bar" introduction crescendos toward this theme's presentation phrase, which then, partly by dint of its *subito* soft dynamic, its low register, and its triplets, seems as if to roll its way through the ascending-thirds sequence, with marked pauses for breath on, first, the diatonic mediant, and then the dominant. Chopin's continuation (not shown) immediately completes the i–III–V–i progression; it then proceeds by prolonging the tonic through a descending-fifths motion, by stalling with repeated fragments on the tonic, by descending chromatically in tenths back to the dominant, and by concluding "too soon," as the result of an elided authentic cadence that simultaneously initiates a varied repetition of the theme. Though this opening might invoke the tarantella, the movement itself is not a stylized dance—its irregular eleven-bar continuation (= 5½ hypermeasures) pays no heed to the dancer's dependency upon predictable four-bar units. The repetition of the theme does indeed "normalize" the original continuation; example 8.6 shows this regularized, eight-bar unit. But this example indicates as well that precisely where a now-regular "eight-bar" sentence might have been completed, Chopin *abandons* the cadence, initiates a "new" cadential progression (mm. 44–47), and then *evades* the cadence, motivating a "one-more-time" repetition whose Picardie tonic-major closure elides into this movement's contrasting theme. These expansion techniques unquestionably smack of Beethovenian sonata procedures within secondary themes. We can note not only that Chopin already implements them within his opening rondo refrain but also that his ascending-thirds sequence has had no trouble finding its home within the sonata genre.

Unlike most classical five-part rondos, Chopin's finale offers only one contrasting section, or "couplet." Thus, in crude letter names, the overall plan would be A–B–A′–B′–A″–coda—the postclassical form favored by Schubert and discussed in reference to the Andante movement of his E-flat Piano Trio (see chapter 6). To the question whether, in Chopin's finale, such a plan should technically be regarded as a rondo, his answer is yes: this is the plan he employs in both of his independent rondos, op. 5 and op. 16, in the last movement of his F-minor Concerto, Op. 11, specifically designated "Rondo," and also in his Nocturne in D-flat Major, Op. 27, No. 2. However, as the first B-section of his B-minor Sonata finale reaches its end, what might have seemed like an example of William Caplin's "subordinate-theme complex"—a characteristic plan for the first couplet of both rondos and sonata-rondos—breaks from that plan and insists upon a retrospective reinterpretation.[9]

As shown at example 8.7, Chopin opens his B-section with what will surely sound like a transition—and one that will now genuinely leave the home key. Like the rondo refrain, the new passage begins with an ascending-thirds sequence; as if again to imbue the sonata genre with his own voice, Chopin now demonstrates one of the ways his I–III–V–I progression can work within the tonic *major* mode. We reach the diatonic iii—the D♯-minor chord—at m. 57, but the real goal of the sequence is the D♯-*major* triad on the downbeat of m. 60, and during its four-bar prolongation, the E♮s

Example 8.6. Chopin, Sonata in B Minor, Op. 58, finale, mm. 1–53

Example 8.7. Chopin, op. 58, finale, mm. 52–90

Example 8.7. cont.

within the turns around D♯ lend to this major III♯-chord the apparent function of V/ vi. Sure enough, what could have been a vi-chord appears at m. 64; but, as a dominant seventh, this chord bypasses the region of G♯ minor and instead initiates a descending-fifths sequence right back to the diatonic iii at m. 68. A loose, modulatory sentential process—presentation plus continuation—has been completed; now this process will begin again, picking up where the presentation left off at m. 60. Yet another sequence follows, with the ongoing I–iii–V progression achieving its dominant at m. 76. Here the new waltz-like material, with its initial stability in the key of the dominant major—F♯ major—undeniably suggests the beginning of a secondary theme. But then the eight-bar waltz passage veers directly back into, of all keys, the home tonic B major. At this point the prospect of a closed sonata or sonata-rondo secondary theme all but vanishes, and when the home tonic becomes transformed into the dominant of E minor, we understand why: Chopin will bring back his complete rondo refrain in the key of the subdominant. Yet, before doing this, he has in fact composed out the I–iii–V–I progression over the span of his entire B-section (see figure 8.3).

One more word about Chopin's B-minor finale, with reference to example 8.8. Through the magic of a dominantseventh that becomes an augmented-sixth chord, the subdominant version of the rondo refrain slips with abandon into a return of the B-section in E♭ major—thus, again, the major III(♯)-region, enharmonically standing in for D♯ major. As a result, when the rondo refrain returns in the home key for the last time, the long-range tonal plan from B′ through the final A-section becomes III–V–i. If, in the end, we dare to privilege Chopin's glorious B-section in III over his subdominant refrain, a Schenkerian-like view of the long-range tonal plan might look like the one I offer at figure 8.3. Given that this movement ends in the tonic B major, my long-range *major*-mode *Bassbrechung* seems appropriate.

Example 8.8. Chopin, op. 58, finale, mm. 137–44

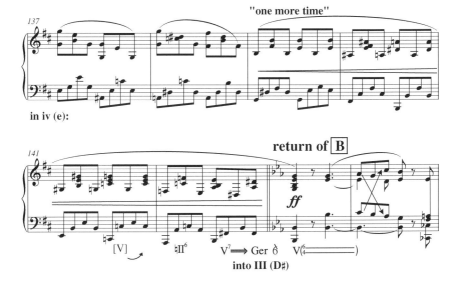

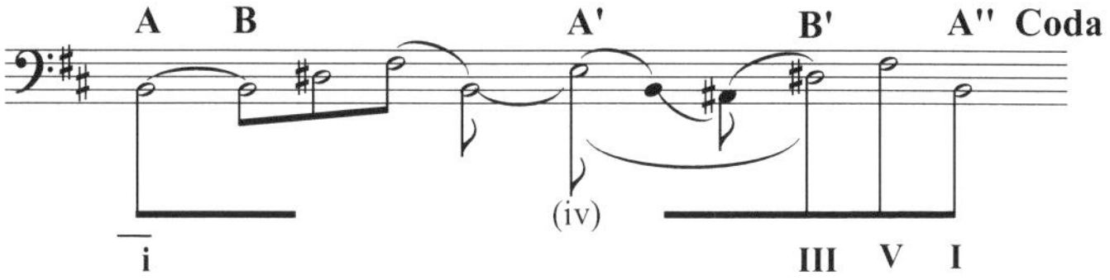

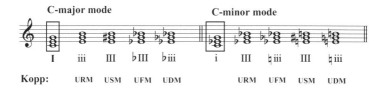

A   B   A'   B'   A'' Coda

(iv)

i   III   V   I

Figure 8.3. Chopin, op. 58, finale, long-range tonal plan.

Thus far, we have seen Chopin employ the I–III–V progression in three differ-ent harmonic ways: his minor-mode mazurkas consistently incorporate the diatonic mediant; his Polonaise in A major bursts into the mediant major; and his sonata finale exploits both. This should be the moment for taking stock of the full range of upper mediant-types available within the major and minor modes. Relative to the keys of C major and C minor, I present the eight possibilities in figure 8.4, and I coordinate these with Kopp's names and their abbreviations.[10] Whereas Kopp strives for what he regards as unbiased, neutral terms, my Schenkerian "bias" and my particular focus upon variants of the I–III–V progression require the retention of Roman numerals. As throughout this study, I adopt Donald Francis Tovey's lowercase numerals for minor triads; I also adopt Schenker's method of using literal, rather than symbolic, accidentals for indicating chromatic alterations within individual keys.

There is simply no question that the types of mediants observed in our exam-ples thus far are Chopin's preferences. To my knowledge, Kopp is right to claim that what he calls the upper and lower disjunct mediants (UDM and LDM) are less used until later in the nineteenth century.[11] But his analysis of Chopin's strange and won-derful B-major Mazurka, Op. 56, No. 1 (1843) demonstrates Chopin's symmetrically planned visits to four chromatic third-related keys all in one short piece—the keys of both the lower and the upper flat and sharp mediants (LFM, LSM, UFM, and USM).[12] As early as 1798, Beethoven took an experimental journey in his Piano Sonata, Op. 13 ("Pathétique")—from C minor into E♭ minor on his way to the ordinary diatonic

C-major mode   **C-minor mode**

I   iii   III ♭III ♭iii   i   III ♮iii III ♮iii

Kopp: URM   USM   UFM   UDM   URM   UFM   USM   UDM

URM = Upper Relative Mediant (two common tones)
USM = Upper Sharp Mediant (one common tone)
UFM = Upper Flat Mediant (one common tone)
UDM = Upper Disjunct Mediant (no common tones)

Figure 8.4. Summary of upper mediant relations, as defined by David Kopp, *Chromatic Transformations in Nineteenth-Century Music* (Cambridge: Cambridge University Press, 2002).

mediant. Beethoven and Schubert notwithstanding, trips to the upper flat mediant within ascending-thirds progressions in *minor* modes (UFM = iii) still seem rare, well into the 1830s. Chopin provides at least one example, from the contrasting middle section of his Etude in A Minor, Op. 25, No. 4 (1835–37).

Example 8.9 begins toward the end of the A-section of this piece, with its authentic cadence in the (back-relating) minor dominant. Section B opens with a two-bar model tonicizing the diatonic submediant (VI); its sequence down a third nearly places us, for just a split second, in the region of Kopp's upper disjunct mediant—D♭ major, relative to A minor. But the root triad in that "key" fails to materialize; instead we move into the extremely remote region of A♭ (a semitone below the home tonic), and then an ascending-step sequence leads circuitously to a cadential progression in C minor (mm. 29–30)—the upper flat mediant, iii. What follows until the return of the A-section can simply be described as repeated cadential gestures (motivically drawn from those in the A-section) and then codettas, all fundamentally "standing on" this chromatic mediant. A Picardie transformation of the iii-chord at m. 35 cancels the E♭s and allows for the retransition into the A′-section to be made by means of the conventional diatonic minor-mode progression III–V–i. But the prolonged C-minor harmony in mm. 30–34 surely points ahead to Chopin's greater derring-do with chromatic third-relations in his later works.

Scholars of classical form know well that B-sections of small ternaries, minuets, and scherzos, as well as development sections within sonata-form movements, tend to feature prolongations of the home dominant as their goal, thus expressing the formal function of standing on the dominant.[13] It is also well known that Haydn, Mozart, Beethoven, and others all occasionally implemented the technique of arrival and standing on the "wrong" dominant—usually V/vi.[14] Nor does one need to be reminded that the V/vi-chord is equivalent to major III in both the major and minor modes; thus, when a root-position home dominant arises as a connective to the tonic at the beginning of the reprise, the III–V–I progression will emerge. In his A-minor etude, Chopin must, in the end, resort to this progression: the two cross-relations that result when a C-*minor* chord moves directly to an E-major chord would clearly have been out of bounds for him. But he seems to have been extremely fond of composing contrasting middle sections that end by "standing on" major III in the guise of V/vi, and many of these yield local or long-range I–III–V–I progressions. Let me offer two examples—both, coincidentally, in the key of B major, a Chopin favorite.[15]

Example 8.10 comes from the trio within the composer's First Scherzo, in B Minor, Op. 20, from around 1835. Within the tonic major, the trio as a whole takes the form of a rounded binary, with a written-out repetition *b* + *a′*.[16] Example 8.10 shows the consequent phrase of the first *a*-section followed by section *b* and its return to *a′*. It has been well documented that the music of the trio's *a*-section is based upon a traditional Polish carol but that the *b*-section is strictly Chopin's. Given this context, I find it hardly coincidental that here is the moment in which Chopin introduces a variant of his "signature" progression. A melodic reference to the ascending-thirds sequence (note the melodic ascent from B to D♯ to F♯) carries the beginning of the *b*-section from the subdominant through a

Example 8.9. Chopin, Etude in A Minor, Op. 25, No. 4, mm. 17–41

stepwise-ascending bass motion to an arrival on V/vi at m. 328. Now an exquisitely poignant half-diminished seventh-chord[17] serves as neighbor to the III⁷-chord in disguise, until, at the end of this eight-bar "standing-on-III" phrase, the home dominant releases the tension and moves to the tonic at the beginning of *a′*, thus completing the local I–III–V7–I progression.

Example 8.10. Chopin, Scherzo in B Minor, Op. 20, mm. 310–38 (from the Trio)

As shown at example 8.11, the basic structure of the opening eight-bar sentence in Chopin's Nocturne in B Major, Op. 32, No. 1 (1837) bears a remarkable resemblance to that of the A-major Polonaise (example 8.1). But one could hardly ask for a greater contrast in affect, thus the title of this chapter—*sed non eodem modo* (from the epigraph of Schenker's *Free Composition*, "but not in the same way"). Here, at m. 6, the tonicized move into the *diatonic* mediant coordinates with a *stretto* that presses on with a *crescendo* to the supertonic and then falls into silence; it is as if a beautiful, tender dream has been disrupted by the darkest of preconscious thoughts. The cadence at mm. 7–8 manages to suppress the anxiety, but not for good; that same disturbing gesture will return to close the nocturne's small-ternary section A.

The form of this nocturne is unusual for Chopin: let us describe it as a large-scale binary followed by a repetition of part II (labeled B), just slightly embellished. Part II begins with a new, repeated idea in the dominant; when this is sequenced down a third (example 8.12), we are again in the realm of the diatonic mediant—

Example 8.11. Chopin, Nocturne in B Major, Op. 32, No. 1, mm. 1–10

Example 8.12. Chopin, op. 32, No. 1, mm. 25–43

D♯ minor. A new model and its sequence (mm. 27–30) do their best to pull away from that region, only in the end to find the submediant (G♯ minor) and settle upon its dominant; the mediant minor has become the mediant major III. A transposition of the opening idea from part I's contrasting middle (see mm. 8–10, example 8.11) transforms that originally cheerful thought into something again quite troubling. The disturbance cannot be contained; again, and now for the third time in this piece, the *stretto* irrupts. Again, the gentle cadential idea breaks the silence and attempts to console; this time it tries even harder—an evaded cadence at m. 37 motivates a new five-bar phrase, rich and full with the *fioritura* at m. 39 and the expansive trill into the cadence at mm. 40–41. Within the repetition of part II (B′), the same passage recurs, but now containment is no longer a possibility. Jim Samson proposes that the *stretto* interruptions "can hardly prepare us for the coda, with its ominous drumbeat and dramatic recitative."[18] I beg to differ: in this nocturne the I–iii–ii6–V–I progression and the unusual form have been put to the task of warning us four times that the gentle dream will fail, in the end, to serve as the guardian of untroubled sleep.[19]

This is the moment to acknowledge that the role of mediants and the ascending-thirds progression in Chopin's music will not be news to numerous Chopin scholars, and especially to those who have written about the three large works that explore a so-called "two-key scheme," thus demonstrating "directional tonality": in the case of all three of these pieces—the Second Scherzo, Op. 31, the Second Ballade, Op. 38, and the Fantasy, Op. 49—the two keys in question are related by a diatonic relative third.[20] The work of one such scholar in particular provides the groundwork for mine. In his 1989 dissertation and then in an essay from 1992, John Rink traces Chopin's gradual shift after around 1830 from "closed, symmetric harmonic foundations (such as I–IV–I and i–III–i)" toward more "dynamic" background progressions, including multiple types of I–III–V–I, I–IV–V–I, and I–II–V–I.[21] In his 1993 study titled "Schenker and Improvisation," Rink describes one of his hypothetical background structures for Chopin's early drafts of the Polonaise-Fantasy, Op. 61, as "based on an underlying progression similar to countless others used by Chopin—i–III–V"; here Rink clarifies that the Polonaise-Fantasy's ultimate background progression—I–♭III–V–I—"has a structural function nowhere else in Chopin's music *except* in the contemporaneous *Barcarolle*" (both works were completed in 1846).[22] Finally, Rink's Cambridge Music Handbook on Chopin's piano concertos carefully documents the outstanding role of embedded and long-range I–III–V–I progressions within the first and last movements of both opp. 21 and 11.[23] This brings me to Chopin's sonata-form movements in general, and to his Cello Sonata, Op. 65, in particular.

It is a commonplace that, from the Schenkerian perspective, *any minor-mode* sonata-form movement in which the exposition's secondary theme (or group) takes the traditional key of the diatonic mediant will most likely have a background i–III–V–I tonal plan: in this scenario, the structural dominant will be achieved, as usual, toward the end of the development, and the recapitulation, fundamentally in the home key, will complete the long-range background progression. Now, *all* of Chopin's mature works within the sonata tradition—and I include here his two concertos along with his two piano sonatas and the Cello Sonata—carry titles that designate a minor mode, and the first movements of all of these introduce secondary themes in the relative major, that is, the diatonic mediant. In short, *all* of his first-movement sonata forms, or variants of that plan, rest upon a fundamental i–III–V–i *Bassbrechung*.[24]

It happens that two of Chopin's first-movement sonata forms employ the I–III–V progression even more intensely: in these movements the composer creates what we colloquially call a "three-key exposition," better understood as a *modulating secondary theme*. The first of these movements opens Chopin's earliest piano concerto, in F Minor, Op. 21, completed in 1829; the other movement is the opening Allegro moderato of his Sonata for Piano and Violoncello, Op. 65 (1845–46)—his last published work. As compared with his piano sonatas, the Cello Sonata has received relatively little analytic attention, and reactions to this piece have been, shall we say, mixed. This chapter thus proceeds by examining the role of the Cello Sonata within Chopin's ascending-thirds tradition and taking a fresh look at its Largo movement.

First Movement of the Cello Sonata: Allegro Moderato

Opinions about the Cello Sonata have run the gamut from enormous failure to acknowledged success. In 1890 Frederick Niecks described this piece as "hardly anything else but…painful effort…the first and last movements are immense wildernesses with only here and there a small flower."[25] Jeffrey Kallberg has regarded the sonata as "a fine work that nonetheless falters."[26] By contrast, for Charles Rosen, but with no further comment, the work is an "undervalued masterpiece."[27] From Chopin's own remarks about this work, and from the more than one hundred pages of sketches he left behind,[28] it has seemed that no other project gave him greater anguish—and this during the period of his estrangement with George Sand, not to mention his ever failing health.

Commentaries about the Cello Sonata tend to fall within studies that compare formal and motivic aspects of the work with those of Chopin's two mature piano sonatas. In a chapter titled "German Dialogues," Jim Samson sees these three sonatas as Chopin's "most direct response to the achievements of the German Classical tradition"; following Józef Chomiński, Samson credits these works, in varying degrees, with a synthesis of Chopin's earlier accomplishments within a distinctly Austro-German framework.[29] Samson applauds the Cello Sonata's "continuously evolving, organically growing shapes,"[30] its remarkable range of contrapuntal textures within a duo medium that Chopin had not explored since his early years, and its astonishing "spirit of renovation and renewal."[31] Samson notwithstanding, discussions of the Cello Sonata consistently take short shrift as compared with the piano sonatas, and the relatively rare performances of this piece are special events, indeed.

I wish to shed new light on how the Cello Sonata responds to the German sonata tradition in a language that is uniquely Chopin's. By 1838 Robert Schumann could proclaim: "Chopin can hardly write anything now but that we feel like calling out in the seventh or eighth measure, 'It is by him!' "[32] In the opening of the first movement of this sonata, we might already make that call earlier (example 8.13). Although Chopin's meter is duple rather than triple, his upbeat dotted rhythms, shifted to the downbeat at m. 4, instantly evoke the proud rhetoric of his polonaises and some of his mazurkas. More telltale, if subtler, is the entry of the mediant harmony and then the dominant on the downbeats of mm. 3 and 4. This first phrase locally anticipates the long-range tonal path of the first movement's exposition, its local progression into the core of the development, the overall i–III–V–i *Bassbrechung* that spans the complete movement, and Chopin's original plan for the tonal course of the four-movement sonata as a whole.

Example 8.13. Chopin, Sonata for Piano and Violoncello in G Minor, Op. 65, first movement, mm. 1–10

My analytic overlay in example 8.13 acknowledges that a best interpretation of the mediant harmony in this case might be as a "divider" on the way to the surprising iv⁶-chord, rather than as a divider from tonic to dominant, but the direct motion from tonic to mediant at mm. 2–3 and the climactic dominant-seventh arrival at m. 4 surely look forward to the exposition's forthcoming tonal plan. This opening phrase serves as a motivic matrix—a veritable *Grundgestalt*—in other ways as well. The neighbor motion marked "x" in example 8.13 adopts the dotted rhythm in m. 4, prepares the cellist's first entry at m. 8, and ultimately pervades not only this movement but also the following three, as demonstrated by Józef Chomiński.[33] Moreover, within the initial idea at mm. 1–2, the melody places its greatest stress upon the tones of the descending arpeggiation 3̂–1̂–5̂; whether or not this contour is an "inverted" and reordered transference to the melody of the ascending i–III–V harmonic progression, it most certainly generates the next two most prominent thematic ideas of the exposition—the beginning (at m. 24) of what seems at first like a second main theme (MT²), shown in example 8.14, and the opening (at m. 69) of the first secondary theme (ST¹), in example 8.15.

Example 8.14. Chopin, op. 65, first movement, mm. 24–28, 36–39

At m. 36 (example 8.14) the pianist's sequential repetition of the apparent MT² idea, now in the subdominant, asks that we retrospectively reinterpret the formal function of this passage as a whole: it would seem that MT² is processually becoming a transition. But by the end of its passionate journey—so wonderfully rich in contrapuntal dialogue and motivic development—we are still fundamentally in the home key, as confirmed by a standing-on-the-home-dominant (at mm. 53–60). So it is that a nonmodulating transition motivates the new, hushed, *dolce* passage shown at example 8.15. This turns out to be the composer's last opportunity for a move into the mediant; through a striking change of texture, dynamic, and even, by implication, tempo, Chopin also invites us to hear the *dolce* passage as an introduction to the first secondary theme.

Example 8.15. Chopin, op. 65, first movement, mm. 60–78, 89–92

Example 8.15. cont.

ST¹ takes the form of a sixteen-bar period, with an exchange of parts—from piano to cello—for the much expanded consequent. This will be Chopin's modulating secondary theme: although it begins in the mediant (B♭ major), its emphatic *pesante* cadence will close in the dominant minor (D minor), thus completing the exposition's underlying i–III–v progression and eliding into a second ST—one that will confirm the key of the dominant minor and provide a tumultuous closure therein. The opening of ST¹ already predicts the long-range modulation: its antecedent and consequent begin with an ascending-*step* sequence whose goal, at m. 73, is the mediant within B♭, but also the tonic in D minor.

I shall not attempt to account here for how Chopin's development section eventually finds its way to the home dominant and prepares a recapitulation of both secondary themes in the home key, but I offer two additional observations about this opening movement. First, Chopin's signature progression makes a local appearance at the beginning of his development (example 8.16a); this time the I–III–v progression overshoots its goal and settles upon ♮VII (F major) for the return of the cadenza gesture from the opening of the movement. Second, at the very end of the movement (example 8.16b), the cellist twice repeats the approach to the final cadence, the second time proclaiming in diminution the original descending 3̂–1̂–5̂ outline of the movement's opening melodic idea. The pianist's codettas then dramatically underscore that arpeggiation, now descending through two octaves from $\hat{1}$ to $\hat{3}$, and reinforcing the $\hat{3}$–$\hat{1}$–$\hat{5}$ pattern en route. By these means, the composer's last, full-scale essay involving the ascending-thirds progression comes melodically full circle in its final descent.

Example 8.16. Chopin, op. 65, first movement: (a) mm. 113–20; (b) mm. 223 to end

Third Movement of the Cello Sonata: Largo

In his review of Ferdinand Gajeweski's introduction to the facsimile *Worksheets to Chopin's Violoncello Sonata*, Jeffrey Kallberg criticizes the omission of cellist Auguste Franchomme's copy of the cello part, signed as dictated to him by his friend Chopin himself. According to Kallberg, this copy contains "a hint that at one time the sonata's Largo [movement] preceded the Scherzo in the large-scale design of the work."[34] Had Chopin not relinquished that plan, the long-range tonal progression over the course of his four movements would have served as his career's most broad-ranging application of the ascending-thirds progression: i (first movement, in G minor)–III (Largo, in B♭ major)–v (Scherzo, in D minor)–i (rondo Finale). In the end, the appearance of the Largo as the third, rather than second, movement of the cycle conforms with the position of Chopin's slow movements in all of his earlier four-movement works, including the Sonata Op. 4 and the Piano Trio Op. 8, from his Warsaw years. But in this case the placement of the Largo seems especially significant. From within a work undoubtedly composed as Chopin's tribute to his closest non-Polish friend, the Largo emerges as the expressive core of the cycle—the moment in which Chopin as pianist and Franchomme as cellist enter into their most intimate exchange. In my effort to capture something of the unique nature of one of Chopin's "German Dialogues," I engage here in my own dialogue with W. Dean Sutcliffe, whose inspired and detailed 1999 essay on the Largo warrants recognition and invites debate.[35]

Sutcliffe's study addresses the widely held view that, for better or worse, Chopin's "late style" evinces a renewed interest in "counterpoint" of the type inspired by J. S. Bach. For Sutcliffe, Chopin's counterpoint in the Largo is, however, "of a different order, involving the disposition of different compositional parameters such as phrase structure, harmony, and texture."[36] In Sutcliffe's account, one result is a considerable ambiguity in respect to the overall *form* of the movement. For example, in the score of the movement at example 8.17, we can note that, beginning with its eighth-note motion in m. 1, the cellist's tender, *cantabile* opening melody returns at pitch on the second beat of m. 14. Sutcliffe hears this moment as a "reprise" within what he perceives, "in crude thematic terms," as a possible "ABAB-coda" form; but he acknowledges that this reprise is "unsatisfactory"—it is "severely undermined" by the "mysterious augmented sixth" on the downbeat of m. 14, which "is then sidestepped rather than resolved." Moreover, having posited the idea of a contrasting B-section, Sutcliffe challenges us to struggle with him in determining where it begins and ends: "If we try to determine the precise boundary between the end of the first A section of the movement and the onset of B, we find it not so much difficult as impossible."[37]

To Sutcliffe's "counterpoint of parameters," I add one parameter that he does not discuss: as proposed by my rebarrings at example 8.17, this parameter is *meter*. Sutcliffe mentions that Chopin's 3/2 meter is "a decidedly unclassical one"—a detail that, along with others, suggests an "explicit return to baroque practice."[38] I go further: another baroque-like detail might be the pervasiveness of just one single idea in this movement—the one announced by the two instruments in the notated

Example 8.17. Chopin, op. 65, Largo

Example 8.17. cont.

mm. 1–2. Chopin's unusual choice of the 3/2 meter enhances the continuously varied repetitions of that idea by allowing his harmonic rhythm to effect a *hemiola* alternation of duple and triple groupings—2/2 alternating with 3/2. An awareness of these metric shifts can, I think, shed some light on Chopin's *sui generis* form, and their consideration might be useful for performers of the movement.

By *conducting* mm. 1–14 of the Largo, we can consider the possibility that Chopin's opening idea actually projects a "3-bar" unit in 2/2 meter, arriving on the half cadence in the notated m. 2. When the cellist and pianist exchange their melody and bass lines, the repetition of the "three-bar" idea (at mm. 3–4) might suggest a sentential presentation, of the kind identified in some of my earlier examples; we might thus expect a continuation, beginning at m. 5. Here the destabilizing shift to the Ab-major sixth-chord confirms our expectations, but the cellist's version of the original opening idea remains a "three-bar" unit, this time tonicizing C minor (vi). At m. 7, the pianist echoes just a fragment of that idea, and now, for the first time, the perceived meter changes to the notated 3/2 meter, thus creating a shorter, more urgent one-bar gesture. What follows—the poignant, ever-intensifying sequential dialogue between the two instruments—will then be heard in 3/2 all the way to the downbeat of m. 14, where the shock of the inverted augmented-sixth chord suggests a critical impasse in the dialogue. This is the point beyond which, whatever the question or topic of discourse might have been, there is no choice but to abandon the discussion, thus the shift back into 2/2. In short, there is no "B-section" here—no standard dominant arrival to announce its conclusion. Instead, we have only a potential first part within a small-binary form, but one whose non-ending simply initiates a cautious starting again—an extraordinary obliteration of formal boundaries, and one that might invite comparison with the cyclical first part of Robert Schumann's "Warum?" from his *Phantasiestücke*, Op. 12 (1837). Like Schumann, Chopin does not answer the question "why."

Sutcliffe astutely notes that the move from the dominant at m. 15 into the *subito forte* Ab-major chord at m. 16 recapitulates that same connection at mm. 4–5 (the root progression is by ascending third). Another role reversal gives this Ab-major gesture to the pianist, after which the cellist takes the lead. From this point forward, the 3/2 meter will be retained into the final bar, and the instrumental dialogue from the first part will be expressed entirely by the cello, as it presses within a crescendo to its *forte* apex, the high G♮ that unleashes an impassioned cadenza in m. 21. The tonic in first inversion (I^6) on the downbeat of m. 22 characteristically promises the beginning of a cadential progression, but at m. 24, where the two instruments once again exchange parts, I hear only a "one-more-time" repetition, of the type motivated by an evaded cadence, rather than by authentic closure. In short, a coda does not emerge, nor can there be one in this movement, because everything must remain open for the event of m. 25. Here, as Sutcliffe says, "for the first and only time in the movement, both cello and piano deliver melodic lines simultaneously"; "they perform a duet that sounds frankly operatic."[39] I hear this moment as a deeply heartfelt coming together—a musical embrace so powerful that it might even reflect Chopin's motivation to persevere with the completion of the Cello Sonata at all costs, for the sake of his beloved cellist friend. With the exquisite Ab in m. 26—the tone that has played such a prominent harmonic role throughout (see the circled tones in example 8.17)—the final two bars cycle back to the opening progression of the movement, withholding closure until the last downbeat, and thus prolonging a moment of utmost intimacy to the very end.

For performers of Chopin's piano music, nothing could be more unique about the Cello Sonata than this singular opportunity to *perform Chopin* in dialogue with another instrumentalist, and no movement encapsulates the dialogic nature of the work as much as the Largo. Of the many ways, then, in which Chopin's "German dialogue" is also his "Chopin dialogue," two of these—his signature ascending-thirds progression and his profoundly personal slow-movement design—emerge as central to this work.

CHAPTER Nine

Coming Home

This final chapter originated as a keynote address I was invited to present at the twenty-sixth annual meeting of the Society for Music Theory, in Madison, Wisconsin, November 2003. It was a clever idea for the program committee of that society to choose a speaker who would be virtually "coming home" to give her address; I am a native of the state of Wisconsin. To say the obvious, my topic shamelessly took its cue from that committee. More to the point, my work on this study as a whole represents a particular kind of homecoming: when I turned to matters involving the European repertoire of the early nineteenth century, I was coming home in no small measure to some of the music with which I had grown up, especially at the keyboard. My effort in chapter 6 to examine formal processes in Schubert's music that enact a "turning inward" was motivated as much as anything by a private question: why have I always felt so very much at home with Schubert? A similar question lies at the heart of this chapter: here I seek musical answers for why the closing moments in many of Robert Schumann's compositions would seem for me to evoke the idea of yearning to "come home."

Of course, there is a manifest way in which most tonal pieces end by "coming home": they tend to end in their "home key." Just why that expression has become such a commonplace is a topic in its own right, and one that many have undoubtedly pondered.[1] Who would deny that the metaphor of the tonic as "home key," though admittedly bound to a Western music-theoretical tradition, must have something to do with a sentiment shared by other cultures over many centuries. "Home" is not just the place where we now live; it is also the place where we first lived, and thus it is the source of everything that our childhood meant to us. Individuals whose childhoods were destroyed by abuse or deprived of love and respect are not likely to want to return home. But for those who were fortunate, childhood was the Garden of Eden before the Fall—the time when we trusted that our parents loved us unconditionally, when we believed that we would always be safe in their care.

Time and place tend to merge here. For this small-town American, childhood was the place where an out-of-tune Chickering piano shared the living room with an early version of the television, where we children played softball after school in the open lot next door, where, to this day, a solitary close-position minor triad in the middle register invokes the warning of the freight train that would come through town in the middle of the night. But "home" need not be a particular place; for nomadic cultures, perhaps home is simply the comfort of food, family, and sleep at the end of the day. Nor must home necessarily be associated with a particular time; for those who have never left home, it might seem timeless. No wonder the stability and sense of completeness that tonic closure can convey has become associated with one of the most potent and often consoling words in any language.

And yet, leaving home, rather than staying home, has long been the norm for young adults, and there is nothing essentially modern, or American, about this. If the Trojan War occurred, then Homer's legendary Ulysses may have left home in the twelfth century B.C., to fight the battle and then to delay his return for many years. The history of so many civilizations is the tale of one migration, voyage, crusade, expedition, exodus, emigration, expulsion, and deportation after another. In our last century alone—ravaged by civil wars, military coups, totalitarian regimes, home-lessness, two World Wars, and threats of a third—the plight of individuals as exiles or emigrants has yielded a powerful genre of its own in all the arts. To name some of the most well-known contributors, I think of Vladimir Nabokov's poignant *Speak, Memory*; of various poems and essays by Joseph Brodsky; of the writings of Thomas Mann, Theodor Adorno, Edward Said, Milan Kundera, Eva Hoffman, and W. G. Sebald.[2] Adorno once wrote, "For a man who no longer has a homeland, writing becomes a place to live."[3] Whether or not the work of composers, performers, and music theorists reflects their status as émigrés, I think of Rachmaninov, Stravinsky, Horowitz, Schoenberg, Bartók, Krenek, Hindemith, Kurt Weill, Hanns Eisler, Miklós Rózsa, Bruno Walter, Otto Klemperer, Rudolf Réti, and the Schenkerians Felix Salzer, Hans Weisse, Ernst Oster, and Oswald Jonas.[4] Consider the photographic series called "Exiles" by the Czechoslovakian Josef Koudelka, or the photos of global and national migrations by the Brazilian Sebastião Salgado.[5] Or consider the 2003 film *Rabbit-Proof Fence*, in which three small "half-caste" Aborigine girls, abducted in the 1930s for the "betterment" of Australian society, escape and walk some 1,500 miles along the fence, to find their way home.[6] If there is one thing that studies of dispossession would seem to share, it is the message that home is never the same once we leave it, especially if we never manage to return.

I am particularly concerned here with what "home" might have meant to Austrians and Germans in the early decades of the nineteenth century. By 1815 the Congress of Vienna had marked the end of the Napoleonic Wars and established a German Confederation under Austrian control. But now, as Nicholas Marston puts it, "the repressiveness of Metternich's police state created a heightened sense of separation between public and private spheres of action and expression."[7] In his memoir of 1872, Schubert's friend Eduard von Bauernfeld looks back on life in Vienna in the 1820s and says: "The police in general and censorship in particular weighed on us all like a monkey we could not get off our back."[8] Within this corrupt urban environment, where overcrowding and disease were everywhere and death was a daily event, where your neighbor might turn out to be a spy, home became sacred; it was the one place of refuge, comfort, and privacy, the safe haven where secrets could be shared, and where the piano could accommodate performances of music from the genres that "turn inward." The bürgerlich homemaker was of course the woman of the house, who usually stayed at home, and to whom the *pater familias* could retreat from public life at the end of the day; for men, "family and home became the symbol of peace, tranquility, privacy, and male authority."[9]

In this light, it is especially touching to note that, of the many lodgings Franz Schubert shared with friends, none lasted long enough to be called his home. This detail is one of the many pointing to the likelihood that Schubert himself identified with the protagonist who sings "Ich bin ein Fremdling überall" ("I am a stranger everywhere") in the song "Der Wanderer" (D. 489), from 1816—the year of Schubert's first departure from his father's home.[10] As the composer of song cycles, and as one who tremendously admired Conradin Kreutzer's setting (1818) of Ludwig Uhland's *Wanderlieder* poems (1813), Schubert might easily have jumped onto the Uhland type of *Wanderlieder* bandwagon. In the grand *Bildungsgeschichte* tradition of, for example, Goethe, Tieck, Novalis, and Eichendorff, Uhland's wanderer undertakes the quintessential German Romantic quest for self-awareness; his journey away from home both mirrors and enables the psychological process of coming to grips with absence, self-division, and alienation. The last song of the Uhland/Kreutzer cycle is called "Heimkehr"—"homecoming"; through the act of coming home, Uhland's wanderer achieves resolution and attains a higher level of appreciation for the loved one he had left behind.[11] By contrast, Wilhelm Müller's young man in *Die schöne Müllerin*, having left his home, ends his own life when his beloved becomes unattainable, and Müller's wanderer in *Die Winterreise*, far from going home, ends by identifying with a homeless street musician, the hurdy-gurdy player. *These* are the poetic cycles that occupied Schubert. Indeed, it may well be that Schubert's most meaningful homecoming took place in the story he titled "Mein Traum," posthumously discovered and published, incidentally, by none other than Robert Schumann. As discussed in chapter 6, Schubert's document, in first-person narrative, portrays him as returning to what seems like a true home only after the second of two exiles—long, long years in a distant land; only at the end of the story does he find himself transported back to a father who is now loving and weeping, and to the sensation of eternal bliss.[12] But remember: this was only a dream.

Like Schubert, Schumann was not encouraged by his family to pursue a musical career. His decision in 1830 to abandon the study of law in favor of music alienated him from his entire family and gave his mother a "broken heart"—these words from the woman to whom he was the most intensely attached.[13] When, at age eighteen, Schumann departed from his childhood home in Zwickau to enter law school in the big city of Leipzig, his first letter to his mother expresses what certainly sounds like a touch of homesickness: "I long with all my heart to return to my quiet home where I was born and have spent happy days in nature. Nature, where can I find it here? Everything is so artificial: there are no hills, no valleys, no woods."[14] Although Schumann returned home often enough over the years to come, there are three occasions on which his absence from home must surely have seemed strange, and maybe these hark back to the two great losses he faced in his fifteenth year—the death of his older sister, possibly by suicide, and the death of his father just ten months later. Perhaps because home had become painfully, even obsessively, associated with death for him, he could not bring himself to attend the funeral either of his brother Julius in 1833 or of his mother in 1836, and he arrived home too late for his brother Eduard's funeral in 1839. On that return, he recorded the impression that his hometown "was now completely extinct."[15] When death comes to our childhood home, what might once have been idyllic can become the primal site of loss and greatest sadness.

It is well known that the year 1840 became Schumann's *Liederjahr*, his "Year of Song." This was the year that would eventually bring a successful outcome to the lawsuit against Clara Wieck's father that Robert and Clara had initiated for legal permission to marry. A hiatus in the formal proceedings against Wieck, and one during which Clara would be on tour in northern Germany, found Robert suddenly producing song after song in rapid succession—nearly 125 songs by the end of the year. John Daverio asserts that many of these, though by no means all, may be viewed as "musical missives to the distant beloved, much like the piano music of the middle and later 1830s."[16] In fact, it was Clara herself who selected the twelve poems from Joseph von Eichendorff's collected edition that would become the basis for the song cycle Robert regarded as his "most profoundly romantic"—the Eichendorff *Liederkreis*, Op. 39.[17] At a time when Clara was away from home, and estranged from the father who ruled there, while Robert longed for the home he hoped soon to create with Clara, it may be no coincidence that the song eventually to become the first of the cycle speaks of homelessness, and that the cycle's most celebrated song enacts a transcendental flight "nach Haus."

Robert Schumann—"Mondnacht," from *Liederkreis*, Op. 39

I refer to the first of two songs (nos. 1 and 8) titled "In der Fremde" and to Song No. 5, the ravishingly beautiful "Mondnacht," in the key of E major. Readers who know Patrick McCreless's essay on the Eichendorff *Liederkreis* or David Ferris's study of the same, or those who have studied Charles Burkhart's superb analysis of "Mondnacht," in the 1990 volume of *Schenker Studies*, may wonder why I would find reason to revisit this song.[18] I do so because none of these authors asks the questions I wish to raise. From the striking manner in which Schumann sets Eichendorff's final words, "nach Haus," what might we imagine that these words meant for Schumann? To what extent might the closing moments of his song hold the key to his reading of the poem as a whole?

Excerpts from Schumann's setting of "Mondnacht" will be found at example 9.1; Eichendorff's poem and a translation follow here.

"Mondnacht"	*"Moonlit Night"*
Es war, als hätt' der Himmel	It was as if the heaven
Die Erde still geküsst,	had quietly kissed the earth,
Dass sie im Blüthen-Schimmer	so that she, in the shimmer of blossoms,
Von ihm nur träumen müsst'.*	must dream only of him.
Die Luft ging durch die Felde	The breeze went through the fields,

Die Aehren wogten sacht,	the ears of corn swayed gently,
Es rauschten leis' die Wälder,	the woods rustled softly,
So sternklar war die Nacht.	the night was starry and clear.
Und meine Seele spannte	And my soul spread
Weit ihre Flügel aus,	its wings wide,
Flog durch die stillen Lande,	flew through the quiet land,
Als flöge sie nach Haus.	as if it were flying home.
—*Joseph von Eichendorff*	—*Translation by David Ferris*[19]

*Schumann changed Eichendorff's "nun" to "nur" in line 4.

Example 9.1. Robert Schumann, *Liederkreis*, Op. 39, Song 5, "Mondnacht"

Example 9.1. cont.

As shown in the score and at figure 9.1, Schumann responds to Eichendorff's three-stanza poem by anticipating what became known as the *Reprisenbar form*[20]—a variant of the venerable A–A′–B scheme, whereby, in this case, an introduction and then a single pair of phrases (4 + 4; labeled *a*), repeated (*a′*), provide the material for both of the A-sections and the final section of B. Why this bar-form

***Reprisenbar* form:**

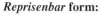

A_____ A'_____ B _____ Coda

	Intro.	*a*	*a'*	Intro.	*a*	*a'*	*b*	*a''*	
mm.	1-6	7-14	15-22	23-28	29-36	37-44	45-52	53-61	61-68

Figure 9.1. "Mondnacht," overview of the formal design.

variant? Schumann's rationale is no less elegant for being easily understood. In Eichendorff's first two stanzas, we have nothing more, or less, than a hushed, shimmering, moonlit Caspar David Friedrich landscape, in which, as if (*es war, als hätt'*) once upon a time, heaven and earth embrace one another in a kiss and the gentlest of breezes provides the only motion. By contrast, the third stanza mobilizes the poem—it carries us first inward, then outward and upward into the starry night: as if present all along, a first person emerges, and now this soul gains wings, like the soul in Plato's *Phaedrus*; expanding its wings, the soul "flies through the quiet land, *as if* it were flying home." If ever the third stanza of a three-part poem were to beg in its musical setting for change and a new direction, here it is.

Like the sixth and seventh songs of this *Liederkreis*, "Mondnacht" makes a drastic departure "from normal compositional practice," to quote Charles Burkhart. The complete song is based upon "the incomplete progression V–I, that is, on a harmonic foundation that lacks the normal initial tonic," and thus the song exemplifies in its entirety what Heinrich Schenker called an "auxiliary cadence." For Burkhart, the only *structural* home-tonic resolution comes "precisely on the last word, 'Haus' [home]"; in short, exclaims Burkhart, "the poem seems almost to have been written for the very purpose of being recomposed in terms of an auxiliary cadence!"[21] Burkhart's exquisite series of voice-leading graphs explores this point on multiple levels of structure; with his permission, I reproduce two of his graphs—the one representing "foreground," and level (c) of his three "early levels"—at figure 9.2, a and b. All of the Roman numerals in Burkhart's graphs except for the enlarged ones—V–(II)–V–I—have been added by me.

In figure 9.2a as well as in the score starting at m. 7, it should be clear that, on the most foreground level, a descending-fifths sequence—[V6/5]–ii; V6/5–I—composes out Burkhart's more middleground ii–V progression. This in turn serves to prolong the background dominant over the span of the first vocal phrase, and then again through each of its repetitions. Burkhart observes that in fact the ii–V progression already appears over the dominant pedal in the pianist's introduction; this is just one of several astonishing ways in which the introduction anticipates the essential motivic components of the song proper. To the three motives that Burkhart identifies, I have applied the following labels in the score at example 9.1: *x*, for the neighbor motion C♯-to-B that establishes the primary tone $\hat{5}$; *y*, for the descending-third motion <F♯–E–D♯>, which recurs in the pseudo-bass (lowest) voice at mm. 8–9; and *z*, for the implied descending fourth <B–A–G♯–F♯>, which returns as the primary descent $\hat{5}–\hat{4}–\hat{3}–\hat{2}$ beneath the vocal line, as a "cover-tone voice," over the span of mm. 5–13.[22] Most remarkable is the manner in which the piano's introduction portrays the forthcoming metaphor of the first stanza. The pianist's two

Figure 9.2. Graphs by Charles Burkhart, "Departures from the Norm in Two Schumann Songs," in *Schenker Studies*, ed. Hedi Siegel (Cambridge: Cambridge University Press, 1990), 152, 148. Reproduced with kind permission; foreground harmonic analysis added. (a) foreground; (b) early level c.

hands begin far apart, within the extremes of bass and soprano register, but then they *converge* in the middle register and descend together. The image of the masculine "heaven"—*Der Himmel*, or, rather, the rays of the moon itself—descending as if in wedded bliss to kiss the feminine "earth," *Die Erde*, and to set her aglow with dreams, must have been particularly moving to Robert and Clara, as they awaited the verdict that would determine the direction of their lives together. In a letter from Robert to Clara in April 1838, we even learn that Robert regarded the word "Ehe"—"marriage"—to be a "musical word"; its pitch equivalent is <E–B–E>, as heard at mm. 10–11 in the bass and as <B–E–B> at the word "die Erde."[23]

Clearly, the momentous effect of section B, which begins at m. 45, has everything to do with the static quality of the dominant prolongation throughout sections A and A′. After forty-six measures of hovering on dominant harmony, the motion to V⁷-of-IV at m. 47 comes on the word "spannte" as if to expand the tonal realm; here the radiant return of the introductory gesture, now in its highest register, miraculously creates the illusion of "stretching" the phrase over the great vocal divide between "spannte" and "weit" that ignores Eichendorff's poetic enjambment. When the subdominant at m. 51 moves to the motivically crucial supertonic, the ii-chord at m. 53, the opening vocal phrase now begins for the first and only time directly on that harmony, and this time it behaves like the consequent phrase that we might have expected all along: via hemiola at mm. 57–59, the singer now takes the descent "home" to scale-degree 1̂ that has been avoided until the end.[24]

As if in contradiction, the word "Haus" coincides for the pianist *not* with the cadential tonic, but rather with an inverted form of the secondary dominant that seems to have sent the soul into orbit at m. 47—the V⁷-of-IV. In technical terms, an evaded cadence occurs at m. 59, and this is followed by the plagal progression IV–I. Burkhart's foreground graph at figure 9.2a clearly displays this delayed arrival on root tonic at m. 61, but figure 9.2b suggests that, on the background level, he understands the delay to be the composing-out of a cadential tonic already fundamentally in effect at the word "Haus" in m. 59; surely Schenker would have concurred. By contrast, David Ferris hears the passage at hand as a "weakening of the harmonic progression"; this, in coordination with the "disjunction between vocal melody and accompaniment" at m. 59, creates an "open ending" for him.[25] Both authors address what Burkhart describes as the "typically Eichendorffian idea of Man's yearning to be at one with Nature"—a benign Nature, within which the protagonist "moves toward a new state of being or a deepening of experience."[26] But Ferris sees Schumann's "open ending" as capturing something of Eichendorff's intimation that the epiphanic flight of the soul can only be elusive, unreal, and transitory. For Ferris, Eichendorff's "allusion to the soul's return home makes it clear that, within his earthly life, the narrator cannot achieve the convergence for which he yearns"; this will happen only in death.[27] In other words, and unless I have misunderstood, "nach Haus" conveys a certain resignation, if not disappointment, in Ferris's view.

For me, Schumann's treatment of those highly charged words—"nach Haus"—has always conveyed something quite different: there is something about moving *beyond* the goal of the home tonic, only then to settle upon it, that seems to make this arrival all the more powerful, satisfying, and transcendental. Schumann's coda unquestionably confirms that, even if this is just a dream, the soul has arrived at the very place toward which it strove. Fragments of the introductory gesture in the middle and low registers, and then a final liquidation of these, now all transposed into the domain of the home key, suggest that the wings of the soul now fold inward and come to rest. Here is a "nach Haus" that is *even better* than the childhood Garden of Eden we left behind, regardless of whether we can ever reclaim it, or recreate it, on this earth. In another letter from 1838, Robert writes to Clara: "If I could only be as truly devoted as I was in childhood—I was really a happy child then, assembling chords at the piano, or picking flowers outside.... But one grows older. Now I want to play with you, the way angels do together, from eternity to eternity.”[28] Perhaps for Robert in the spring of 1840, still struggling to gain Clara's hand, Eichendorff's “nach Haus” meant being at home for a blissful eternity with Clara.

Robert Schumann—“Widmung,” from *Myrthen*, Op. 25

Friedrich Wieck managed to sustain the legal battle against his daughter and Robert for an entire fourteen months, but by August of 1840 Wieck's *de facto* admission of defeat was made official, and now the wedding plans could get under way. Already by April of that year, Robert had completed a collection of songs to be presented to Clara as a wedding present; on September 7, five days before the wedding, Robert paid for a “lavishly bound copy” of that collection; its title is *Myrthen* (myrtles, after the flower traditionally associated with German weddings), and it is dedicated “To my beloved bride.”[29] Appropriately, the first song of the group sets a poem by Friedrich Rückert titled “Widmung”—“Dedication”; a reduction of that song is given at example 9.2. Here follow the text and my translation.

“Widmung”

Du meine Seele, du mein Herz,	You my soul, you my heart,
Du meine Wonn', o du mein Schmerz,	you my rapture, O you my grief,
Du meine Welt, in der ich lebe,	you my world, in which I live,
Mein Himmel du, darein ich schwebe,	you my heaven, in which I soar,
O du mein Grab, in das hinab	O you my grave, in which
Ich ewig meinen Kummer gab.	I have eternally buried my sorrow.
Du bist die Ruh', du bist der Frieden,	You are repose, you are peace,
Du bist der Himmel mir beschieden.	you were granted to me by heaven.
Dass du mich liebst, macht mich mir wert,	That you love me gives me self-worth,
Dein Blick hat mich vor mir verklärt,	your gaze has in my eyes transfigured me,
Du hebst mich liebend über mich,	by loving, you raise me above myself,
Mein guter Geist, mein bessres Ich!	my good spirit, my better self!

—*Friedrich Rückert*

There is hardly any mystery as to who is the “du” to whom Robert Schumann addresses Rückert's wonderful outpouring—“Du meine Seele, du mein Herz, du meine Wonn', o du mein Schmerz.” Nor is it surprising that Schumann's music transforms Rückert's nonstanzaic, one-part poetic form into a musical small ternary (A–B–A′). Rückert's change of tone—or dynamic, as it were—at “Du bist die Ruh', du bist der Frieden” so beautifully invites Schumann's shift into the serene dream-world of ♭VI at the beginning of his B-section in m. 14 (enharmonic E major, relative to the home tonic of A♭); his reprise of Rückert's opening four lines then inspires him to close the A′-section by jumping to the last, and most moving, line of the poem, “Mein guter Geist, mein bessres Ich!” But like “Mondnacht,” “Widmung” takes an especially remarkable turn at its very end, and here there might be some mystery.

Example 9.2. Robert Schumann, *Myrthen*, Op. 25, Song 1, "Widmung" (reduction to twostaves)

Example 9.2. cont.

My analytic overlay in the score at example 9.2 makes a claim for scale-degree 3̂—the C♮ on the first "Du"—as primary tone. Natural 3̂ moves by implication to ♭3̂, the enharmonic B♯, at the beginning of the B-section. And then, in one of Schumann's most breathtaking retransitions, the neighbor-tone C♯ over the A-major chord in m.25 becomes the D♭ of m. 26, while an unexpected descent via augmented fourth in the bass carries the harmony from the Neapolitan to the home dominant seventh. Within the four-bar "standing-on-the-dominant-pedal" phrase that follows, the stunning suspended grace-note in m. 27 suggests that the pianist's voice nearly falters in anticipation of the singer's "mein guter Geist." At the cadential close of the reprise in mm. 38–39, analysts will be hard-pressed to find a fundamental *Urlinie* descent within the vocal part; instead, the voice reaches upward to regain the F♯, thus fulfilling its prominent role in mm. 4, 9, 32, and 37. Finally, just what does the pianist's coda have to do with this song?

Although I have seen nothing in print about this, I know I am not the only listener who hears Schumann alluding in his coda to the opening of Schubert's well-known "Ave Maria" (example 9.3). Why does Schumann do this? The obvious first answer—a prayer to Clara as virgin saint, the holy mother of God—may be the least interesting. Two additional ideas come to mind. First, it happens that, as a concert pianist in Berlin during the winter of 1839–40, Clara frequently performed Franz Liszt's 1838 transcription of Schubert's song, often on demand; we know this from her letters to Robert.[30] Like the many other messages in music that Robert was in the habit of sending to Clara, his allusion to "Ave Maria" might thus have been an especially private and professionally complimentary one. Second, there may have been another dedicatee lurking behind the tones of Schumann's coda, and that would be Schubert himself—the composer whom Schumann loved the most, and to whom he may have been the most indebted. Even at the end of Schumann's short life, just before his suicide attempt and his demand to be committed to an asylum, what brought him one glorious moment of happiness was the delusion that Schubert himself had appeared to him and given him a magnificent melody, for a set of variations.[31]

Example 9.3. Schubert, "Ellen's Gesang III: Hymne an die Jungfrau (Ave Maria)," mm. 3–4

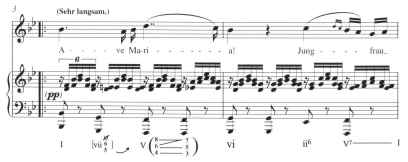

As for the structural role of Schumann's coda, we might note that the twice-heard "Ave Maria" melody, though technically just a turn around scale-degree Î (the A♭), itself alludes to the middleground $\hat{3}$–$\hat{2}$–$\hat{1}$ descent at the end of the A-section in mm. 12–13. We would have good reason to expect that a similar descent might provide the fundamental melodic closure of the song proper, but this is missing from the vocal line at m. 38, having been transferred to the pianist's tenor voice. Thus, whether or not Schumann's coda "comes home" to both Clara and Schubert, it does indeed subtly accomplish a melodic "homecoming"—the one that, with such declamatory verve, the vocal line withholds. And yet, when we compare Schumann's harmonization of "Ave Maria" with Schubert's, we discover much greater dissonance in Schumann's version: note that the almost completely chromatic, lament-like descent in the bass provides the opportunity for a new inversion of the half-diminished ii^7-chord previously heard at the word "Schmerz" in mm. 5 and 33. Rückert reminds us that there can be great pain in love; one senses that Schumann, just now on the verge of creating a life with Clara, had the prescience and wisdom to anticipate something of both the joy and the sorrow they would share.

Here, then, is another closing moment in Schumann that retrospectively seems to encapsulate the expressive core of the piece, but it does so as if by standing outside the piece, for the purpose of reflecting upon it. We can come closer to capturing what happens here if we compare such closings with some of those great heroic struggles to victory, those progressive trajectories, those willful end-oriented works, often cyclic, that so many nineteenth-century composers, including Schumann, explored in the aftermath of Beethoven. By contrast, the closings and codas that I examine here are quiet, rather than climactic, events; the quietness is not atypical of codas in general, but not a requirement of them. The coda in "Widmung" is not set up to serve as the goal to which everything is directed, but it nevertheless brings the song "home," by virtue of both its structure and its deeply reflective, allusive character.

Clara Schumann—"Die stille Lotosblume," Op. 13, No. 6

A counterexample will now be useful, and I choose another song—this one in the same key, A♭ major, but this one by Clara herself. Let us consider the ingenious but entirely different ending and overall shape that emerges in Clara's setting, excerpted at example 9.4, of Emanuel Geibel's poem "Die stille Lotosblume," shown below with my translation. Upon Robert's encouragement, and now in the role of Clara Schumann, rather than Clara Wieck, she composed this song in 1842 and published it the following year, as the last of her Six Songs, Op. 13.

"Die stille Lotosblume"

Die stille Lotosblume	The silent lotusblossom
Steigt aus dem blauen See,	rises from the blue lake,

| Die Blätter flimmern und blitzen | the leaves glisten and flash, |
| Der Kelch ist weiss wie Schnee. | the chalice is white as snow. |

Da giesst der Mond vom Himmel	There the moon from heaven pours
All seinen gold'nen Schein,	all his golden shine,
Giesst alle seine Strahlen	pours all his rays
In ihren Schoss hinein.	into her lap.

Im Wasser um die Blume	In the water around the flower
Kreiset ein weisser Schwan,	circles a white swan,
Er singt so süss, so leise	he sings so sweetly, so softly,
Und schaut die Blume an.	and looks at the flower.

Er singt so süss, so leise	He sings so sweetly, so softly,
Und will im Singen vergehn.	and wants to perish in singing.
O Blume, weisse Blume,	Oh flower, white flower,
Kannst du das Lied verstehn?	can you understand the song?

—*Emanuel Geibel*

One of Robert's own songs in his *Myrthen* collection is his setting of a poem by Heinrich Heine called, simply, "Die Lotosblume" (Op. 25, No. 7). From Heine as well as Geibel, one learns that the exotic, feminine-gendered lotus blossom prefers the moonlight to the morning sun; only at night does she rise up from the lake. Her delicate snow-white "chalice" suggests virginity, but the masculine-gendered moon knows how to make love to her. In Geibel's poem a third party enters the scene—a swan who yearns to rival the moon as suitor; it would appear that the swan knows how to communicate only through song. We do not know who raises the question at the end of Geibel's last stanza—"Oh flower...can you understand the song?" Does the swan finally speak, or are these more likely the words of a narrator? Either way, the lotus blossom offers no answer, and so the swan's song was probably in vain. To underscore the ambiguity, Clara reverses the V-to-I harmonic path that Robert took in his "Mondnacht," and the outcome is even bolder: Clara Schumann's song ends on the dominant seventh.

To be more precise, Clara's ending is her beginning: what returns in her final two bars is her initial two-bar introduction, with its elegant appoggiatura-chord embellishment of the dominant seventh. To be sure, the introduction serves as the upbeat to an unequivocal structural tonic in m. 3. But then both the antecedent phrase in mm. 3–6 and the continuation in mm. 7–10 lead to a half cadence (a "nineteenth-century half cadence" at m. 10), and the latter even specifically brings back the introductory progression (shown with brackets and an asterisk in the score). From this point forward, that progression will emerge as a kind of matrix, or referential source.

Geibel's second stanza takes a repetition of the music for his first, such that a varied strophic form seems under way; but the pianist's interlude at mm. 18–21 extends the dominant seventh as goal, while introducing a new, double-neighbor figure that allows for pitch-specific returns of the introductory progression in diminution. The original antecedent phrase returns yet again at mm. 22–25, but then a new model-sequence phrase (mm. 26–29) carries us via descending step into the distant, inward realm of ♭III (C♭ major), the key for the swan's song. At this point the strophic form opens into something more comparable to the bar form—A–A–B, as in "Mondnacht"; although an entire fourth stanza awaits its

Example 9.4. Clara Schumann, Op. 13, No. 6, "Die stille Lotosblume"

Example 9.4. cont.

setting, Geibel's third and fourth stanzas are combined, for good textural reasons, to create just one expansive third part. Note that the material of the pianist's interlude becomes pervasive from m. 30 onward.

It goes without saying that nothing could be more diametrically opposed to the notion of "coming home" in tonal music than a piece that refuses to achieve tonal closure, but nothing could have been more appropriate in the context of Geibel's poem. Like the swan who circles round and round the flower, singing for all his life but going nowhere, Clara's song ends by coming full circle, by floating back to where it began. There can be no homecoming here, no resolution, because the poem itself ends midstream: we will never know whether the lotus blossom succumbs to the swan or remains indifferent to him. It is tempting to propose that Clara Schumann's ending is even more daring than her husband's at the end of the first song of his cycle *Dichterliebe*: whereas Robert's concluding dominant seventh in F♯ minor is given a fleeting, albeit false, sense of resolution at the beginning of his second song, in A major, Clara's "Die stille Lotosblume" is the very last song in a group of six. There is no indication that Clara thought of her op. 13 collection as a "cycle"—to be performed complete, with Song 6 as the last; moreover, historians have stressed that even those opuses by Robert that we have come to think of as song cycles, or piano cycles, were hardly ever performed as such during his lifetime.[32] But unless a performance of "Die stille Lotosblume" were to be followed by *something*, preferably in A♭ major, its ending is unsettling.

Clara's song demonstrates just one of various ways in which the closing of a movement can avoid creating the effect of a homecoming. Let me stress that in no way do I equate mere home-tonic cadential closure—a staple of the tonal repertoire—with "coming home." On the contrary, for example, Robert's "Ave Maria" moment serves as a *post*cadential postscript to his song's definitive cadence. Nor do "homecomings" require the formal setting of a coda. The arrival "nach Haus" in "Mondnacht" coincides with the act of closing, rather than with the coda that follows. On the matter of "homecoming" as closure or postclosure, the next piece I consider might be a genuine borderline case.

Robert Schumann—*Arabeske*, Op. 18

I turn to the very first piece by Robert Schumann that I studied as a young pianist—his *Arabeske* in C Major, Op. 18, from 1839. The closing passage of the *Arabeske* might also very well be the original source of my fascination with closings in Schumann that would seem to evoke longings to "come home." The passage in question is shown at example 9.5; note that Schumann marks this not as a "Coda," but rather "Zum Schluss." In his "performer's analysis" of the *Arabeske*, from 1996, Charles Fisk reminds us that in translation "Zum Schluss"—"In closing"— "suggests the idea of cadential articulation much more strongly than does the term 'coda'—'tail'"; in other words, "Zum Schluss" implies the process of moving toward closure, rather than of reflecting upon a closure already achieved.[33] Like me, Fisk hears this passage as one that brings resolution, particularly in the realm

Example 9.5. Robert Schumann, *Arabeske*, Op. 18, m. 209 to end

of register; he also holds that the passage "still searches for something," that it even "pleads" to "keep the music open."[34] I shall amplify Fisk's views, while introducing a few of my own.

First to the matter of register, as this relates to formal design. The *Arabeske* takes the form of a modest, five-part rondo—A–B–A–C–A; it is thus most likely the "*Rondolette*" that Robert tells Clara he has composed, in a letter from Vienna during his six-month stay there in 1838–39.[35] As shown in the score at example 9.6, the rondo refrain itself—the A-section—is cast as a small ternary. The refrain opens with a presentation-type phrase whose model-sequence design allows the theme to strive upward to the high G♮ at m. 8. As 5̂, this tone *in that register* becomes the primary tone of the movement, but there is no *Urlinie*-like descent from it in the passage that follows. We might want to tease out a descent in the lower register over the span of the cadential phrase (mm. 9–12) and its varied repetition (mm. 13–16; see my effort to do so), but the retention of scale-degree $\hat{5}$ at the cadence suggests that fundamental closure has not been achieved.

At mm. 17–24, a short, wistful, contrasting-middle phrase twice explores the mediant, E minor (iii), but then twice moves with a *ritardando* to the tonicized dominant. After this, the entire first part of the rondo refrain returns without

Example 9.6. Schumann, op. 18, mm. 1–26

alteration. And that is exactly what will happen with each subsequent appearance of the complete refrain: the passage at mm. 1–40 will return unchanged. Word has it that Schumann often sat dreamily at the keyboard and played favorite passages of his music over and over again; it seems that he invites us to do precisely the same with his rondo theme.

As Fisk observes, the first episode, the Minore I that begins at m. 41 (example 9.7), opens by transforming the E-minor idea at m. 17 and then repeating it twice, "each time more intensely, as if the music cannot get away from it."[36] The first part of Minore I quickly regains the primary tone G♮, now as $\hat{3}$ within E minor, and then provides a stepwise descent from it, in tenths with the bass; but the descent passes through F♮ rather than F♯, and the goal of the descent is the implied D♯ at the Phrygian half cadence in m. 48. Pretending to be a refrain within a littler rondo-within-the-rondo, the opening phrase of Minore I returns twice; in fact, the episode ends with that phrase, again arriving at the half cadence in E minor at m. 88. If the Minore I has introduced a "conflicting stratum of experience" relative to the more serene rondo refrain, then the retransition that follows (end of example 9.7) attempts a reconciliation.[37] But the effort seems arduous, and maybe even unsuccessful: everything about this passage—its constant fluctuations in tempo, its loose model-sequence design, its utterly unstable tonal plan, its unresolved dominant sevenths and six-four chords—conveys the effect of a precarious groping toward an unclear goal. Indeed, as the ultimate harmonic link back to the rondo refrain, the Neapolitan at m. 101 appears *pianissimo* out of the blue; it is approached via tritone in the bass. When the refrain finally gets under way again at m. 105, there is the sense that a very dark cloud has lifted.

Fisk hears a synthesis of the rondo theme, the first episode, and the retransition within the Minore II, which begins at m. 144 (example 9.8)[38] Begging his pardon, I sense even greater conflict here. Now we have the first unaccompanied *forte* version of the rondo theme's initial upbeat gesture—the arabesque-like flourish of neighbor motive with grace-note. Its dotted rhythm pervades this episode's accompaniment; what results is a gruff, defiant character, until here quite foreign to the movement. The first part of this episode begins and ends in the submediant, A minor, and then it takes a repetition. The second part (mm. 153–60), also repeated, forcefully works its way through an ascending-fifths sequence to close in E minor (iii). The final part (mm. 161–68) acts as a "pseudo-reprise": it recapitulates the opening of the episode, but does so in the "wrong" key—E minor, rather than A minor. One advantage of the "wrong" key is that it permits the primary tone G♮ to be regained at m. 163, after which a supported $\hat{3}$–$\hat{2}$–$\hat{1}$ descent in E minor brings us to the authentic cadence in m. 167, with E♮ in the soprano. And then the rondo theme returns for the last time. But for the *first* time, the E♮ at the end of Minore II supplies the hitherto unstated tone that leads to the theme's F♮ in its fourth bar.

Finally, let us return to "Zum Schluss" (example 9.5). The slower-moving half-note rhythm of its soprano melody, reverberating in syncopation an octave below, undoubtedly refers back to that troubled retransition (at example 9.7). But here the tonal tension of that earlier passage is being resolved: like a typical coda, the "Zum Schluss" passage follows upon a final cadence in the home key, and there will be

Example 9.7. Schumann, op. 18, mm. 41–48, 89–105

no further departures from that key. Remember, however, that the refrain's final cadence does not sufficiently complete an *Urlinie* descent from the high G♮. In particular, a supported E♮, 3̂, is nowhere to be heard, except in the lower register at m. 204 (as at m. 12, example 9.6). Surely that factor explains in part what makes the appoggiatura motion <E–D> in the higher register at the beginning of "Zum Schluss" seem so "right" and yet so poignant. Perhaps now an *Urlinie* descent will be completed from the E, and thus maybe this passage, like the coda in the first movement of Beethoven's "Waldstein" Sonata, will be the type of coda that does not really stand outside the fundamental structure of the movement as a whole; in short, perhaps that is what "Zum Schluss" means here.

Could it be that the <E–D> gesture, thrice repeated and each time expanded, with each of its tones taking dissonant support, pleads *not* to "keep the music open," but rather to achieve a close—that is, to bring the music "home"? Listen

Example 9.8. Schumann, op. 18, mm. 145–69

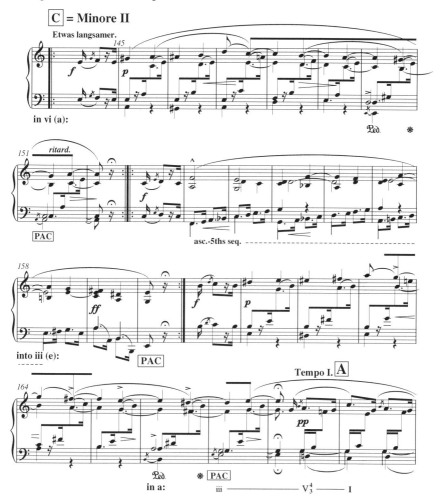

especially to the extraordinary effect of release and relief, when, finally, at mm. 215–16, the <E–D> motive—augmented, no less—at least attains a half cadence. In the final phrase, the music does indeed find a C♮ at m. 219, but the submediant harmony here denies this tone a structural role, and the melody moves back into the lower register. One last, heart-rending appoggiatura chord at m. 221 underscores an augmentation in the soprano of the rondo refrain's upbeat neighbor-note motive, <G–A–G>, and then the original motive itself returns to lift the soprano right back to the starting point of "Zum Schluss," the E♮. So much, then, for an *Urlinie* closure; here is a closing that remains melodically open. In his commentary about the plight of the main character in Ludwig Tieck's novel *Franz Sternbalds Wanderungen*, literary critic Marshall Brown says: "There *is* no return home in this world, there is only moving forward. And moving forward means moving away from home and childhood, away from idyllic, self-centered ease, and out into the complexities of the world."[39] The "Zum Schluss" passage of the *Arabeske* seems to know this; it yearns to close, but in the end it finds the courage to point away from home and into the future.

An irony here is that the *Arabeske*, Op. 18, has been regarded by some as verging on *Hausmusik*—music for performance in the home, rather than in the concert hall or the salon; one of the reasons I was playing the *Arabeske* at an early age is because it is not at all technically difficult. By 1839 Clara, ever shrewd (even at age twenty) about what audiences wanted to hear her play, found herself begging Robert to write simpler, more accessible piano music—"easily understandable, and something without titles…not too long and not too short."[40] Anthony Newcomb has argued that around this time Robert himself came to recognize the need to change direction: the intensely subjective, often "eccentric," technically demanding, sometimes harmonically "harsh" and rhythmically experimental piano works of his youthful 1830s were just not selling, nor would even Clara risk trying to present them to an unprepared public.[41] It happens, however, that, among the works by Robert Schumann listed at table 9.1 as candidates for further investigation into closings that suggest "coming home," two of these—the *Fantasie* in C Major, Op. 17, and the slightly later *Davidsbündlertänze*, Op. 6[42]—exemplify the undeniably romantic style Robert eventually felt obliged to modify. In particular, there is no other piece by Robert Schumann that more consummately proceeds in a trajectory toward "home" than his *Fantasie*, Op. 17. Moreover, as Berthold Hoeckner claims, the *Fantasie* has "enjoyed perhaps the richest reception of any romantic piano work, having become, in a sense, a monument to Romanticism. Interpretations of especially the first movement have drawn upon quintessential categories of romantic aesthetics: fragment, *Witz*, and arabesque."[43] One of the many contributions that Hoeckner's work on the *Fantasie* makes is his critical engagement with the views of an illustrious list of writers since the late 1980s who have addressed (or readdressed) this piece; these include John Daverio, Linda Roesner, Charles Rosen, Anthony Newcomb, and Nicholas Marston, whose Cambridge Music Handbook on the *Fantasie*, from 1992, is invaluable. Readers may be well acquainted both with Schumann's *Fantasie* and with the work

Table 9.1 Closings in Robert Schumann's Music That Suggest "Coming Home": Other Candidates

Fantasie in C Major, Op. 17 (1836), discussed in this chapter.

Davidsbündlertänze, Op. 6 (1837):
    Coda of No. 14 (in E-flat major)
    No. 18 (final movement, in C): Motto—"Quite superfluously, Eusebius added the
        following, but his eyes spoke of great bliss."

Kinderszenen, Op. 15 (1838):
    No. 13 (final movement): "Der Dichter spricht"

Dichterliebe, Op. 48 (1840):
    Song 18 (last song), "Die alten, bösen Lieder"—piano postlude (quotes the postlude
        from Song 12, "Am leuchtenden Sommermorgen")
    Piano Quintet in E-flat Major, Op. 44 (1842): Finale

of some one or more of those writers. But since no other work by Schumann could serve so fully as a culminating example of my topic, I address it here.

Robert Schumann—*Fantasie*, Op. 17

Schumann composed the first version of this work as a "Sonata for Beethoven," in the hope that money from its sales could be contributed toward the monument of Beethoven that was to be erected in Bonn. But the inception of the work, in 1836, also coincided with the period of greatest estrangement between Robert and Clara; her father had insisted that she return all of Robert's letters and never see him again. Two years later, and now referring to the work as a "fantasy," Robert tells Clara that its first movement, originally titled "Ruins," is "probably the most passionate thing I have ever written—a deep lament for you."[44] Although there remain a few doubting Thomases,[45] most connoisseurs of the *Fantasie* have long agreed that the first movement makes reference to, by drawing upon, the beginning of the last song from Beethoven's cycle *An die ferne Geliebte*, shown at example 9.9. Those familiar with Beethoven's work will recall that this is the cycle in which the poet strives to surmount the spatial and temporal distance between himself and his beloved, by singing songs of love and then asking her to sing them back to him. Accordingly, the last song not only begins with a variant of the first song but then also cyclically recapitulates that song, at the very point where the poet trusts that his loved one has also begun to sing. Schumann's allusion to Beethoven's cycle creates the perfect union of professional goal and private aspiration: he pays tribute to Beethoven by quoting him, but at the same time he has Beethoven's distant beloved secretly refer to Clara, to whom he sends all his love and sorrow through this music.[46]

Hoeckner goes further than anyone to date in tracing fragments of both the first and the last of Beethoven's songs within Schumann's first movement.[47] I focus

Example 9.9. Beethoven, *An die ferne Geliebte*, Op. 98, opening of Song 6 (the original key is E-flat major)

only on the two most prominent ideas that Schumann appropriates, the ones labeled *a* and *b* in Beethoven's score in example 9.9. I have reversed *a* and *b* here, because that is what Schumann did. At Beethoven's *a*, note especially the motion through the interval of a fifth upward to and then down from the A♭, $\hat{6}$, as harmonized by the progression from ii6/5–V. Shown in example 9.10, the opening melodic idea (*a*) of the main theme of Schumann's first movement draws only upon Beethoven's descending fifth from $\hat{6}$, but Schumann preserves the progression ii⁷-to-V⁷ over a dominant pedal. Beethoven's opening *b*-melody becomes the melodic component of Schumann's cadential idea, which strives to modulate toward closure in the dominant at m. 17. An evaded cadence motivates the cadential idea to press again towards closure, now in rhythmic diminution; this time an imperfect authentic cadence (IAC) in V is locally achieved, but the immediate transformation of the tonicized dominant into a home dominant seventh reinterprets that goal as a half cadence in the home key.[48]

The large-scale *sui generis* form of the *Fantasie*'s first movement has been endlessly debated. But perhaps some will agree that a sonata-like transition begins at m. 29 and leads to the first stage (at m. 41) of a two-part, modulating secondary theme, whose initial key—D minor—surely refers back to that marvelous ii-chord over dominant pedal at the movement's opening. Certainly the key of D minor helps to sustain focus upon the A♮ with which the main theme began, now even giving it consonant support. New forms of first *a* and then *b* provide the melodies of this secondary theme, and then much intensified passagework in octaves carries us from deep within the piano's lower register to its highest point thus far, ushering in the second stage of the secondary theme—in the subdominant (F), the least "classical" of secondary regions (example 9.11). Now an exquisite new harmonization and texture for *a* leads to what, in a letter of 1838 to Clara, Robert described as the melody he liked "the most" (at mm. 65–67).[49] There is no wonder why: here the simplification of the accompaniment (from turbulent sixteenths to quiet eighth notes) allows for the *a*-idea's overlapping imitative dialogue within the secondary theme's D-minor stage to become gentler and more intimate, as if the thoughts of two have become one. (Robert's favorite moment coincides with, as I hear it, an arresting ii4/2 chord, over implied dominant pedal, whose bass tone F♮ hovers, unresolved except by transfer to the soprano at m. 67.) Now the *b*-idea and its embellished repetition, as if improvised, then imitated (mm. 69–72), submit to *ritardandos* that suggest words beginning to fail. Efforts to reinvigorate the dialogue only lead to a heart-rending exchange—first an Adagio in the alto register, and then another in the soprano, this one abandoning all hope of closure on the poignant diminished-seventh chord at mm. 80–81.

By far the most remote, even disguised, version of the *b*-idea (at mm. 157–60) interrupts the narrative of the famous *Im Legendenton* (not shown)—the central passage that has thwarted sonata-form interpretations of the movement. When *a* enters (mm. 181–94), in the high register within the dream world of the Neapolitan, it recaptures and transforms the overlapping dialogue from within the secondary theme. After the *Im Legendenton* reaches its stoic conclusion ("Yes, and this is the way the story ended"), a recapitulation of sorts begins with the transition materials from the exposition, and then the two-fold secondary theme returns transposed

Example 9.10. Robert Schumann, *Fantasie* in C Major, Op. 17, first movement, mm. 1–21

Example 9.11. Schumann, op. 17, first movement, mm. 60–83

down a step; that is, it begins in the home tonic minor and now moves into E♭ major—Beethoven's original home key in *An die ferne Geliebte*. For those on the inside track, the fundamental direction of the movement now begins to emerge; everything is leading inexorably to a revelation at the very end. The Adagio at m. 295 quotes the *b*-idea in its clearest, most Beethoven-like form, and in doing this, it closes the movement with the first and *only* authentic cadence in C major (example 9.12). Charles Rosen puts it best: Schumann does not just allude to Beethoven's ideas; he *absorbs* these, to the point where it sounds as if he had composed them himself. The allusion to Beethoven within the Adagio "appears not as a reminiscence of another composer, but as at once the source and the solution of everything in the music—up to that final page … the entire movement … is a preparation for, and development of, the concluding phrase," "which serves as the point of rest and the center of gravity."[50] In short, here is Schumann's most complex, most elaborate "homecoming," second only to the one he will achieve at the end of his *Fantasie* as a whole.

Example 9.12. Schumann, op. 17, first movement, m. 295 to end

Schumann originally planned to recapitulate the end of his first movement at the end of his last movement, but he changed his mind. Rosen insists on the effectiveness of Schumann's original plan and performs the last movement accordingly. I vote on Schumann's ultimate ending, shown at example 9.13. No blatant cyclicism here; instead, something much more moving—for its subtlety, and because now the music celebrates a homecoming over the distant span of the complete three-movement work. A circle within a circle is closed: the texture and harmonic progression beginning at m. 130 bring us back to the beginning of the movement (example 9.14), and the pervasive neighbor motion <G–A–G> clearly remembers the opening of the first movement. It even regains the register of that initial A♭, whose appearances in so many different contexts throughout the piece suggest to me that this tone is the technical representative of the secret "leiser Ton" from the poem of Friedrich Schlegel with which, as a motto, Schumann prefaced the *Stichvorlage* of his first movement in 1838.[51] The end of the *Fantasie* may just be one of the great musical homecomings of all time.

In his comparison of the healthy, successful Biedermeier career of Felix Mendelssohn and the troubled one of Robert Schumann, Michael P. Steinberg sees "two different sides of subjectivity in music: coherent versus fragmented subjectivity, in the first case an ability to build a fluid ego between the poles of private and public, Jewish and Gentile, masculine and feminine [Mendelssohn]; in the second case a cultural and psychological defeat to the pressures of an emerging,

Example 9.13. Schumann, op. 17, finale, m. 127 to end

Example 9.14. Schumann, op. 17, opening of finale

essentializing ideology of identity [Schumann]."[52] For Steinberg, Schumann thus represents the "spiritually homeless," for whom identity *is* the ideology: "Bourgeois identity and respectability, and masculine propriety and control were clearly concerns for Schumann in ways they do not seem to have been for Mendelssohn." As a result, "Schumann does not seem to develop a coherent subjective voice that is allegorized in music. Specifically, intimacy and privacy are split off from the public and rhetorical." Such piano works as the "esoteric" *Fantasie* are for Steinberg "the site of the private, the secret, the *heimlich*, and thereby also of the *unheimlich*, or uncanny and terrifying."[53]

Yes, Schumann's music knows the terror of the *unheimlich*, and for good personal as well as cultural reasons: from his late teens onward, he lived in the terror of going mad one day. And, yes, music like the *Fantasie* is wildly esoteric. One of the many gripping details about Schumann is that the music pianists in particular regard as some of his greatest ever written was later dismissed by him as "immature and unfinished"; in 1843 he says, "[T]he man and the musician in me were always trying to express themselves simultaneously; no doubt that remains so, although I have learned to control myself and also my art better."[54] Steinberg notwithstanding, the closing moments of no other composer before Schumann would seem to know better how to convey a longing for home, and sometimes its imaginative attainment, even if, as Georg Lukács has said, "longing has never had a home."[55] And so I relish this opportunity, at the end of my study, to come home to Schumann.

NOTES

Chapter 1

1. Theodor W. Adorno, *Beethoven: The Philosophy of Music*, ed. Rolf Tiedemann (Stanford: Stanford University Press, 1998), xi (hereafter cited as Adorno, *Beethoven*). Adorno, *Beethoven: Philosophie der Musik*, ed. Rolf Tiedemann (Frankfurt am Main: Suhrkamp, 2nd ed., 1994): "Wir verstehen nicht die Musik—sie versteht uns. Das gilt für den Musiker so gut wie für den Laien. Wenn wir sie uns am nächsten meinen, dann spricht sie uns an und wartet mit traurigen Augen, daß wir ihr antworten" (15). Tiedemann reports that Adorno's statement, in the earliest of his notebooks containing his fragments on Beethoven, appears directly before the first note explicitly dealing with the composer.

2. Tiedemann, in Adorno's *Beethoven*, xii. Tiedemann's observation must surely draw upon the following, from Adorno's *Philosophy of Modern Music* (New York: Seabury, 1973): "The material transformation of those elements responsible for expression in music...has today become so radical that the possibility of expression itself comes into question...the mere idea of humanity, or of a better world no longer [has] any sway over mankind—though it is precisely this which lies at the heart of Beethoven's opera" (19).

For Stephen Hinton, in his "Adorno's Unfinished *Beethoven*" (*Beethoven Forum* 5[1996]), other factors might explain why Adorno did not complete the Beethoven book. Given that his projected [*Beethoven:*] *Philosophie der Musik* and his *Philosophie der neuen Musik* are "both predicated on a nineteenth-century, essentially Beethovenian paradigm of musical processuality or temporality, on the one hand, and the postulate of subjective authenticity, on the other," Adorno's *Philosophie der Musik* had already "fed directly into his philosophy of new music" (149). Moreover, in that Adorno's "deep attachment to the classical tonal repertory is tempered by the ideological reservations of a critical theorist," those reservations "may well have prevented him from bringing the project to fruition. In several respects he didn't need to. He utilized much of the Beethoven material in lectures and other publications" (153). Finally, and here in resonance with Tiedemann's view, Hinton proposes that Adorno "may even have been hampered, as a sociologist, by the evident nostalgia he expressed for the golden age of bourgeois humanism, or at least felt unable to strike a satisfactory balance between musical enthusiasm and historical critique" (153).

3. Adorno, *Beethoven*, 14, 13, emphasis added (from a 1939 notebook). Adorno, *Beethoven: Philosophie der Musik*: "Beethovens Musik ist die Hegelsche Philosophie: sie ist aber zugleich wahrer als diese" (36). "Die Beethovensche Einheit ist demgegenüber eine, die sich in Gegensätzen bewegt, d. h. deren Momente als einzelne begriffen einander zu widersprechen scheinen. Darin liegt nun aber der Sinn der Beethovenschen Form als eines Prozesses, daß durch die unablässige 'Vermittlung' zwischen den einzelnen Momenten und schließlich durch den Vollzug der Form als ganzer die scheinbar einander entgegengesetzten Motive in ihrer Identität begriffen werden" (35).

4. We learn from Adorno in 1964 that he regarded his essay "Schubert," written at the age of twenty-five (it originally appeared in *Die Musik* 21/1, 1928), to be his "first comprehensive…study of the meaning of music" (cited in Jonathan Dunsby and Beate Perrey, introduction to "Schubert (1928)," *19th-Century Music* 29/1 [2005], 3). That essay, discussed in chapter 5 of this volume, concludes with the following: "Schubert's music brings tears to our eyes.…This is music we cannot decipher, but it holds up to our blurred, over-brimming eyes the secret of reconciliation at long last" (Adorno, "Schubert (1928)," trans. Dunsby and Perrey, 14). In Adorno's Beethoven fragments, no composer next to Beethoven receives greater attention than Schubert. There, and to a greater degree than in "Schubert," his music tends to serve as a foil to Beethoven's. For example: "Banalities, that is, the mere structures of tonality, are to be found in [Beethoven's] work as much as in Schubert…in Beethoven there is a dynamic, which strives towards a goal and reflects the effort to reach it. Hence, the accents point beyond themselves to the whole, whereas those in Schubert merely remain where they are" (Adorno, *Beethoven*, 51; from 1939). And: "The flagging of energy to be found in Schubert and Schumann is the price exacted for the attempted transcendence of form. More form is less. This flagging—in Schubert the unfinished works, in Schumann the mechanical element—is the first manifestation of the decay of music as an objective language" (Adorno, *Beethoven*, 73–74; from 1939). Or: "The truly characteristic element of Schumann—and then of Mahler and Alban Berg—is the inability to hold themselves back, the tendency to give, to throw themselves away. Here the Romantic principle means to give up the ownership aspect of experience, indeed the self" (Adorno, *Beethoven*, 155; from 1942). These quotations hardly do justice to Adorno's ideological outlook on nineteenth-century music, but they point to some of his central concerns.

5. Hinton, "Adorno's Unfinished *Beethoven*," 151.

6. Adorno, *Beethoven*, 14, 8. Adorno, *Beethoven: Philosophie der Musik*: "Humanität bei [Beethoven] heißt: so sollst du dich verhalten wie diese Musik sich verhält. Anweisungen zu einem aktiven, tätigen, sich entäußernden, dabei nicht engen, und solidarischen Leben" (28).

7. See, for example, Leon Plantinga, *Romantic Music: A History of Musical Style in Nineteenth-Century Europe* (New York: Norton, 1984), 5–13; Carl Dahlhaus, *Nineteenth-Century Music* (Berkeley: University of California Press, 1989), 49–51; Richard Taruskin, *The Oxford History of Western Music*, vol. 2: *The Seventeenth and Eighteenth Centuries* (Oxford: Oxford University Press, 2005), 497–504, 571, 607.

8. For Lydia Goehr: "Trying to live on musical commissions and public engagements was extremely difficult. As part of an infant class, composers were subject to new marketing constraints and unstable social forces of which they had no previous experience. However musical works and their composers were being conceived 'in the books', they required publishing houses, performing bodies, and a paying public to sustain their worldly existence. But most of these institutions were newly born themselves, and were therefore unable or unwilling as yet to treat composers in a consistent and fair manner." *The Imaginary Museum of Musical Works: An Essay in the Philosophy of Music* (Oxford: Oxford University Press, 1992), 210.

9. Immanuel Kant, *Kritik der Urteilskraft*, ed. Gerhard Lehmann (Stuttgart, 1966), part 1, book 1, section 13, as translated by Peter le Huray and James Day in *Music and Aesthetics in the Eighteenth and Early-Nineteenth Centuries*, ed. le Huray and Day (Cambridge: Cambridge University Press, 1988), 159.

10. Heinrich Christoph Koch, *Versuch einer Anleitung zur Composition* (3 vols.; Leipzig: A. F. Böhme, 1782–1793; reprint, Hildesheim: Olms, 1969). See Mark Evan Bonds, *Wordless Rhetoric: Musical Form and the Metaphor of the Oration* (Cambridge, MA: Harvard University Press, 1991), 2, 4, 53.

11. The formation of a musically educated public became an aspiration within a "public sphere of discourse" emerging in earnest toward the end of the eighteenth century. Following

upon numerous studies concerning the formation of the German musical canon, David Gramit's *Cultivating Music: The Aspirations, Interests, and Limits of German Musical Culture, 1770–1848* (Berkeley: University of California Press, 2002) addresses a wealth of source materials (e.g., from music journals, studies of vocal pedagogy, and articles about concerts) that contributed toward the institutionalizing of a culture of "serious" music in German-speaking Europe. "Both the aspirations of German musical culture and the defining boundaries that its advocates set for it were inseparably intertwined with the interests of music as a field of social practice, and the entire project hinged on the acceptance of music as essential to the cultivation of fully human individuals, the *Bildungsideal* so central to the self-identity of the German bourgeoisie" (2).

12. Heinrich Christoph Koch, *Kurzgefasstes Handwörterbuch der Musik* (Leipzig: J. F. Hartknoch, 1807; reprint, Hildesheim: Olms, 1981); see Bonds, *Wordless Rhetoric*, 126.

13. Bonds, *Wordless Rhetoric*, 5. And thus: "It is convention, in fact, that ensures the intelligibility of genius" (120), for which reason Bonds laments the long-standing "attitude of implicit disdain in musical scholarship toward the study of convention" (51).

14. John Neubauer, *The Emancipation of Music from Language: Departures from Mimesis in Eighteenth-Century Aesthetics* (New Haven, CT: Yale University Press, 1986).

15. Carl Dahlhaus, *The Idea of Absolute Music* (Chicago: University of Chicago Press, 1989), 3 (emphasis added).

16. Friedrich Schlegel, *Kritische Friedrich-Schlegel-Ausgabe*, vol. 2: *Charakteristiken und Kritiken I* (Munich, Paderborn, and Vienna: Ferdinand Schöningh, 1967), 254: "Alle *reine* Musik muß philosophisch und instrumental sein (Musik fürs Denken)" (a literary notebook entry of 1797). "Wer aber Sinn für die wunderbaren Affinitäten aller Künste und Wissenschaften hat, wird…eine gewisse Tendenz aller reinen Instrumentalmusik zur Philosophie an sich nicht unmöglich finden. Muß die reine Instrumentalmusik sich nicht selbst einen Text erschaffen? und wird das Thema in ihr nicht so entwickelt, bestätigt, variiert und kontrastiert, wie der Gegenstand der Meditation in einer philosophischen Ideenreihe?" (from *Athenäum Fragmente*, no. 444, 1798), as translated by le Huray and Day in *Music and Aesthetics*, 247.

17. See Neubauer, *The Emancipation of Music*, 195.

18. Goehr, *The Imaginary Museum*, 149.

19. Goehr, *The Imaginary Museum*, 152. For a critique of Goehr's reading of the work-concept in respect to baroque musical culture in general and J. S. Bach's music in particular, see Harry White, "'If It's Baroque, Don't Fix It': Reflections on Lydia Goehr's 'Work-Concept' and the Historical Integrity of Musical Composition," *Acta Musicologica* 69/1 (1997): 94–104.

20. Goehr, *The Imaginary Museum*, 242, 174, 224–25.

21. Goehr, *The Imaginary Museum*, 218–23.

22. Goehr, *The Imaginary Museum*, 249. See also J. Peter Burkholder, "Museum Pieces: The Historicist Mainstream in Music of the Last Hundred Years," *Journal of Musicology* 2/2 (1983): 115–34.

23. Goehr, *The Imaginary Museum*, 239, 164.

24. On Reicha and Momigny, see Ian Bent, *Analysis*, Norton/Grove Handbooks in Music (New York: Norton, 1987), 16–22; and Scott Burnham, "Form," in *The Cambridge History of Western Music Theory*, ed. Thomas Christensen (Cambridge: Cambridge University Press, 2002), 883–87.

25. Goehr, *The Imaginary Museum*, 208.

26. William E. Caplin, *Classical Form: A Theory of Formal Functions for the Instrumental Music of Haydn, Mozart, and Beethoven* (New York: Oxford University Press, 1998).

27. In *Classical Form* (265n.46) Caplin thanks me for recommending the use of the "becoming" symbol. James Hepokoski and Warren Darcy also adopt the symbol, but they

incorrectly attribute the origin of its use in discussions of formal function to Caplin; see Hepokoski and Darcy, *Elements of Sonata Theory: Norms, Types, and Deformations in the Late-Eighteenth-Century Sonata* (Oxford: Oxford University Press, 2006), 53n.4.

28. See especially the essay collection *Beyond Structural Listening? Postmodern Modes of Hearing*, ed. Andrew Dell'Antonio (Berkeley: University of California Press, 2004).

29. From William Caplin: "To speak of a 'first-time' listening experience is not necessarily to refer literally to the initial hearing of the piece. Even a well-known work can be experienced by a listener as if it were being heard for the first time" (*Classical Form*, 282n.47). For Adorno on listening both "forward and backward," see chapter 2 of this volume.

30. Carl Dahlhaus, *Ludwig van Beethoven: Approaches to His Music* (Oxford: Clarendon, 1991), 180. Dahlhaus, *Ludwig van Beethoven und seine Zeit* (Laaber: Laaber-Verlag, 1987) (hereafter *LvB*): "Überlieferte Schemata stellten für Beethoven gleichsam einen Gegenstand des Komponierens dar: Sie wurden weder übernommen noch verworfen, sondern als 'Material' benutzt, das durch den Zusammenhang, in den es geriet, seine Funktion wechselte. Rudimente einer langsamen Einleitung…ändern ihren Sinn, ohne daß jedoch die Erinnerung an die ursprüngliche Funktion ausgelöscht wäre…Und die Ambiguität setzt beim Hörer, den Beethoven 'impliziert,' sowohl Traditionsbewußtsein als auch die Fähigkeit voraus, über das Gewohnte hinauszugehen" (222).

31. In two of his works Dahlhaus provides as many as five discrete but similar discussions of Beethoven's op. 31, no. 2: in *Nineteenth-Century Music*, 13–15; and in *Ludwig van Beethoven*, 6–7, 89, 116–18, 169–71. See also his "Zur Formidee in Beethovens d-moll-Sonate opus 31,2," *Die Musikforschung* 33 (1980): 310–12. Dahlhaus's numerous references in *Ludwig van Beethoven* to August Halm's *Von zwei Kulturen der Musik* (1913) with regard to op. 31, no. 2 suggest how much his interpretation of its first movement owes to Halm's (see Dahlhaus, *Ludwig van Beethoven*, 6, 82, 89, 98, 203). For Dahlhaus on the subject of Halm, see "'Von zwei Kulturen der Musik': Die Schlussfuge aus Beethovens Cellosonate opus 102,2," *Die Musikforschung* 31 (1978): 397–405. See also Lee A. Rothfarb, *August Halm: A Critical and Creative Life in Music* (Rochester: University of Rochester Press, 2009), 93, 167, 255n.2.

32. Dahlhaus, *Ludwig van Beethoven*, 116–17 (emphasis added). Dahlhaus, *LvB*: "Die thematische Struktur des ersten Satzes aus Beethovens *d-moll-Sonate* opus 31,2 ist seit Jahrzehnten Gegenstand einer Kontroverse, die unabschließbar erscheint, solange man die Widersprüche, die zwischen Motivik, Syntax und Harmonik bestehen…durch einseitige Akzentuierung des einen oder des anderen Moments zu unterdrücken versucht, statt sie als Vehikel einer Dialektik zu begreifen, durch die sich in der musikalischen Vorstellung die Form des Satzes als Transformationsvorgang konstituiert" (153).

33. Dahlhaus, *Ludwig van Beethoven*, 89, 169, 170 (emphasis added). Dahlhaus, *LvB*: "Der Streit…ist sinnwidrig [nonsensical], weil er eine Entscheidung fordert, wo die Pointe der Komposition in der Nicht-Entscheidbarkeit—in einer als ästhetische Qualität aufzufassenden Ambiguität—besteht" (210–11). "Der Anfang des Satzes ist *noch nicht* Thema, der Evolutionsteil ist es *nicht mehr*…Indem aber Beethoven die 'Setzung' der Themen vermeidet und von einer Vorform sogleich zu einer entwickelnden Ausarbeitung übergeht, *erscheint die Form in einem emphatischen Sinne als Prozeß*" (211–12; emphasis added). For the "not yet—no longer" construction, see also *Ludwig van Beethoven*, 117, as well as Dahlhaus, *Nineteenth-Century Music*, 15.

34. Friedrich Schlegel, *Kritische Schriften* (Munich: Deutscher Taschenbuch, 1972) 38–39 (from *Athenäum Fragmente*, no. 116): "Die romantische Poesie ist eine progressive Universalpoesie…Die Romantische Dichtart ist noch im Werden; ja das ist ihr eigentliches Wesen, daß sie ewig nur werden, nie vollendet sein kann" (38–39), as translated by Arthur O. Lovejoy, *Essays in the History of Ideas* (Baltimore: Johns Hopkins Press, 1948), 226.

John Daverio clarifies that "becoming" for Schlegel refers here to the incompletion not of the individual poem, but rather of the *whole* of modern poetry, which strives to achieve but also to surpass the perfect wholeness of the body of ancient (classical) poetry through a "boundlessly developing *classicism*" and through "its self-mirroring structure." See Daverio, *Nineteenth-Century Music and the German Romantic Ideology* (New York: Schirmer, 1993), 157–58. In other words, individual artworks will manifest becoming to the extent that, like classical poems, they embrace or reflect one another but also raise that reflection "to a higher power, as if multiplying it in an endless series of mirrors" (from Schlegel, *Athenäum Fragmente*, no. 116, cited in Daverio, 156).

35. Hegel: "[D]ie Sache ist noch nicht in ihrem Anfang, aber er ist nicht bloß ihr Nichts, sondern es ist schon auch ihr Sein darin. Der Anfang ist selbst auch Werden, drückt jedoch schon die Rücksicht auf das weitere Fortgehen aus." G. W. F. Hegel, *The Encyclopaedia Logic (with the Zusätze): Part I of the Encyclopaedia of Philosophical Sciences with the Zusätze* (Indianapolis: Hackett, 1991), 143 (from "First Subdivision of the *Logic*: The Doctrine of Being," par. 88). For an excellent overview of Hegel's *Logic* and its role as a source for Adorno's central concepts, see Michael Spitzer, *Music as Philosophy: Adorno and Beethoven's Late Style* (Bloomington: Indiana University Press, 2006), 48–53.

36. About *aufheben*, the editorial committee that published the first edition of Hegel's *Werke* provided the following addition (*Zusatz*): "At this point we should remember the double meaning of the German expression '*aufheben*'. On the one hand, we understand it to mean 'clear away' or 'cancel,' and in that sense we say that a law or regulation is cancelled (*aufgehoben*). But the word also means 'to preserve,' and we say in this sense that something is well taken care of (*wohl aufgehoben*). This ambiguity in linguistic usage, through which the same word has a negative and a positive meaning, cannot be regarded as an accident nor yet as a reason to reproach language as if it were a source of confusion. We ought rather to recognise here the speculative spirit of our language, which transcends the 'either-or' of mere understanding" (Hegel, *The Encyclopaedia Logic*, 154; see also 146).

The conventional translation into English of Hegel's *aufheben* is "sublation." For a fine glossary in English of Hegelian terms, including *aufheben*, with reference to Michael Inwood's *A Hegel Dictionary* (Oxford: Blackwell, 1992), see Barbara Titus, "Conceptualizing Music: Friedrich Theodor Vischer and Hegelian Currents in German Music Criticism, 1848–1887" (D.Phil. diss., University of Oxford, 2005), Appendix I.

37. See, for example, W. H. Auden's ascription of becoming to all music, in "Notes on Music and Opera," within his collection *The Dyer's Hand and Other Essays* (1948) (New York: Vintage, 1989), 465–74. As a counterexample, see Leonard B. Meyer's several superb discussions of the Romantic "openness and continuousness of Becoming" as these relate philosophically and ideologically to what he calls "implied," or "emergent" (versus "syntactic") structures in nineteenth-century music from Beethoven through Mahler and beyond, in *Style and Music: Theory, History, and Ideology* (Philadelphia: University of Pennsylvania Press, 1989), 324, 197–200, 264, 325–26.

38. Bonds, *Wordless Rhetoric*, 1, 13–14.

39. Dahlhaus, *Ludwig van Beethoven*, 114. Dahlhaus, *LvB*: "Der Vorgang selbst ist vielmehr—paradox ausgedrückt—das Resultat" (150).

40. See Janet Schmalfeldt, "Towards a Reconciliation of Schenkerian Concepts with Traditional and Recent Theories of Form," *Music Analysis* 10/3 (1991): 233–87.

41. Heinrich Schenker, *Free Composition (Der freie Satz)* (New York: Longman, 1979), 5.

42. Arnold Schoenberg, *The Musical Idea and the Logic, Technique, and Art of Its Presentation* (New York: Columbia University Press, 1995), 45, from "German Texts of Unpublished *Gedanke* Manuscripts Referred to in the Commentary, Manuscript No. 11 [undated], *Der Musikalische Gedanke; seine Darstellung und Durchführung*," 424.

43. For a background on ideological sources of the tension between Schenkerian and formal theorists, see Schmalfeldt, "Towards a Reconciliation," 233–34. See also Nicholas Cook, *The Schenker Project: Culture, Race, and Music Theory in* Fin-de-siècle *Vienna* (Oxford: Oxford University Press, 2007), especially 285–96.

44. I refer to Helmut Federhofer, *Beiträge zur musikalischen Gestaltanalyse* (Graz: Akademische Druck-u. Verlagsanstalt, 1950); Felix Salzer, *Structural Hearing: Tonal Coherence in Music* (New York: Dover, 1962; orig. publ., 1952); Allen Forte and Steven E. Gilbert, *Introduction to Schenkerian Analysis* (New York: Norton, 1982); David Neumeyer and Susan Tepping, *A Guide to Schenkerian Analysis* (Englewood Cliffs, NJ: Prentice-Hall, 1992); Allen Cadwallader and David Gagné, *Analysis of Tonal Music: A Schenkerian Approach*, 3rd ed. (New York: Oxford University Press, 2011). See also William Rothstein, *Phrase Rhythm in Tonal Music* (New York: Schirmer Books, 1989).

45. Cadwallader and Gagné, *Analysis of Tonal Music* (1st ed., 1998), 223.

46. I paraphrase my account of Schenker's views about form in Schmalfeldt, "Towards a Reconciliation," 234.

47. Schenker, *Free Composition*, 131.

48. In my first published essay, on performance-analysis relations (revisited in chapter 5 of this volume), as well as in my study of Berg's op. 1, I presented Schenkerian voice-leading graphs but also invoked formal concepts developed by Schoenberg and his proponents. See Schmalfeldt, "On the Relation of Analysis to Performance: Beethoven's Bagatelles Op. 126, Nos. 2 and 5," *Journal of Music Theory* 29/1 (1985): 1–31; and "Berg's Path to Atonality: The Piano Sonata, Op. 1," in *Alban Berg: Historical and Analytical Perspectives*, ed. David Gable and Robert P. Morgan (Oxford: Clarendon Press, 1991), 79–109. In Schmalfeldt, "Cadential Processes: The Evaded Cadence and the 'One More Time' Technique" (*Journal of Musicological Research* 12 [1992]: 1–52), I propose that a much-needed revisionist approach to the theory of cadence rests in part on the willingness of Schenkerians to acknowledge that "the Schenkerian perception of structural levels depends no less heavily on the concept of cadence than does the formal perception of such 'foreground' entities as phrase, theme, theme-group, section, and part" (12). Finally, see my "Towards a Reconciliation."

Among the many subsequent integrative studies that should be cited here, a notable example is Peter H. Smith's *Expressive Forms in Brahms's Instrumental Music: Structure and Meaning in His* Werther *Quartet* (Bloomington: Indiana University Press, 2005). Smith strives to integrate Schenkerian and Schoenbergian concepts by means of what he calls "dimensional counterpoint": "A movement's form consists of the total structure that emerges through a *counterpoint of musical dimensions*. These dimensions…can be reduced to three main categories: thematic design, key scheme, and tonal structure" (31). See also Kevin Swinden, "Toward Analytic Reconciliation of Outer Form, Harmonic Prolongation and Function," *College Music Symposium* 45 (2005): 108–23.

49. Charles J. Smith, "Musical Form and Fundamental Structure: An Investigation of Schenker's *Formenlehre*," *Music Analysis* 15/2–3 (1996), 196–97, 270 (Smith's emphasis), 280 (my emphasis). Says Smith: "Having narrowly defined 'form' in structural (i.e. primarily harmonic) terms, I can hardly act surprised that form turns out to be essentially synonymous with structure" (279).

50. Peter Smith has, however, not been silent; for a thorough-going critique of Charles Smith's proposals, see Peter H. Smith, *Expressive Forms in Brahms's Instrumental Music*, 49–54, 58–60.

51. Cook, *The Schenker Project*, 289. Cook discusses Charles Smith's revision of Schenker's graph, in *Free Composition*, figure 152/1, for Robert Schumann's "Wenn ich in deine Augen seh' "—Song 4 from *Dichterliebe*.

52. Gianmario Borio, "Schenker versus Schoenberg versus Schenker: The Difficulties of a Reconciliation," *Journal of the Royal Musical Association* 126 (2001), 251.

53. Cook, *The Schenker Project*, 140, 294.

54. Cook, *The Schenker Project*, 295.

55. Cook, *The Schenker Project*, 295–96.

56. See Forte and Gilbert, *Introduction to Schenkerian Analysis*, 135.

57. For example, in a section labeled "Some Schenkerian Implications," Hepokoski and Darcy compare their secondary-theme (S-) paradigms with Schenker's background view of sonata form as an interruption structure, and they devise the term "ZPAC" for referring to the expositional perfect authentic cadence in the dominant that would correspond with the completion of the linear fifth-progression (*Zug*) prolonging $\hat{2}$ at the interruption. The authors then weigh the complex, often nonidentical, relationship of the Schenkerian ZPAC to their own concept of EEC—"essential expositional closure," understood as "the first satisfactory PAC in the key of the dominant." See Hepokoski and Darcy, *Elements of Sonata Theory*, 147–49.

58. James Webster, "*Formenlehre* in Theory and Practice," in *Musical Form, Forms & Formenlehre: Three Methodological Reflections*, ed. Pieter Bergé (Leuven: Leuven University Press, 2009), 123, 125, 128. Webster refers to Kurt Westphal, *Der Begriff der musikalischen Form in der Wiener Klassik: Versuch einer Grundlegung der Theorie der musikalischen Formung* (Leipzig: Breitkopf & Härtel, 1935; 2nd ed., Giebig über Prien am Chiemsee: Katzbichler, 1971). See also Webster, "Sonata Form," *New Grove* (rev. ed., 2001), vol. 23, 687–701. In his *Haydn's "Farewell" Symphony and the Idea of Classical Style* (Cambridge: Cambridge University Press, 1991), Webster says: "As this volume amply testifies, I am in fundamental sympathy with Schenkerian analysis. At the same time, I am skeptical" (53).

59. Webster, "*Formenlehre*," 128–29.

60. James Hepokoski, "Sonata Theory and Dialogic Form," in Bergé, *Musical Form, Forms & Formenlehre*, 70–71.

61. Hepokoski and Darcy, *Elements of Sonata Theory*, 8.

62. William E. Caplin, "What Are Formal Functions?" in Bergé, *Musical Form, Forms & Formenlehre*, 25.

63. Adorno, *Beethoven*, 70 (emphasis added). Adorno, *Beethoven: Philosophie der Musik*: "Bestimmte Ausdruckskonfigurationen gehören bei Beethoven bestimmten musikalischen Symbolen...Woher aber nehmen sie die fast unbegreifliche Kraft, jene auch wirklich zu übermitteln? Das ist eine der zentralsten Fragen. Ich kann mir einstweilen die Antwort nicht anders vorstellen, als daß der Ursprung des Bedeutens bei Beethoven in rein musikalischen Funktionen liegt, die sich dann im je fungierenden, versprengten Mittel sedimentieren und ihm als Ausdruck zufallen. Aber freilich—gehen nicht diese Funktionen selbst wieder auf Ausdruck zurück?" (110).

64. Adorno, "On the Problem of Musical Analysis," trans. Max Paddison, in Adorno, *Essays on Music* (Berkeley: University of California Press, 2002), 177–78. Paddison first published his translation in *Music Analysis* 1 (1982): 169-87.

65. Friedrich Blume, *Classic and Romantic Music: A Comprehensive Survey* (New York: Norton, 1970), 146, 103.

66. For the distinction between "process" and "product," see Scott Burnham, *Beethoven Hero* (Princeton, NJ: Princeton University Press, 1995): "Beethoven's music is thus heard to embody the form of artistic mimesis newly privileged in the late eighteenth century: the imitation of *natura naturans*, or the process of nature, supersedes that of *natura naturata*, the product of nature. Such an emphasis also reflects the way views of the self and human nature had changed by 1800" (118–19). Burnham portrays Beethoven's sonata-form movements in the heroic style as entailing "the sustained experiential intensity of continuous

renewals" created by "a flexible and often far-reaching rhythm of action and reaction, down-beat and upbeat." "Such a process corresponds not only to the Idealist dialectic of opposi-tional conflict but also to the typically conflicted nature of the self-conscious hero of German classical drama, living between the polar forces of deed and reflection" (119).

67. As two early examples pertinent to this study, the titles of the following speak for themselves: Boris Vladimiroch Asafiev, *Die musikalische Form als Prozess* (1976; Russian, 1963); and David B. Greene, *Temporal Processes in Beethoven's Music* (1982). See James Robert Tull, "B. V. Asaf'ev's 'Musical Form as a Process': Translation and Commentary" (Ph.D. diss., Ohio State University, 1977).

68. Anthony Newcomb, "Those Images That Yet Fresh Images Beget," *Journal of Musicology* 2/3 (1983), 227, 232 (emphasis added).

69. Newcomb, "Those Images," 234–36. Newcomb refers to, among others, Frank Kermode, *The Sense of an Ending: Studies in the Theory of Fiction* (1979); E. H. Gombrich, *Art and Illusion: A Study in the Psychology of Pictorial Representation* (1961); Edward T. Cone, "Beyond Analysis" (1967); and Cone, "Three Ways of Reading a Detective Story—Or a Brahms Intermezzo" (1977). Cone's articles have been reprinted in Edward T. Cone, *Music: A View from Delft*, selected essays, ed. Robert P. Morgan (Chicago: University of Chicago Press, 1989).

70. Janet Schmalfeldt, "Form as the Process of Becoming: The Beethoven-Hegelian Tradition and the 'Tempest' Sonata," in *Beethoven Forum* 4 (1995): 37–71.

71. Newcomb, "Those Images," 237 (emphasis added).

72. Among Newcomb's later articles, the following address aspects of narrativity and processual form in Robert Schumann's music: Anthony Newcomb, "Once More 'Between Absolute and Programme Music': Schumann's Second Symphony," *19th-Century Music* 7/3 (1984): 233–50; and Newcomb, "Schumann and Late Eighteenth-Century Narrative Strategies," *19th-Century Music* 11/2 (1987): 164–74. In my "Towards a Reconciliation" (236–37), I suggest that Newcomb's call for a "formulation of narrative paradigms" in music, as "a series of functional events in prescribed order," had already been answered in part by Arnold Schoenberg, in his *Fundamentals of Musical Composition* (New York: St. Martin's, 1967); as mentioned, Schoenberg's ideas about formal function have since then been fully developed by Caplin in his *Classical Form*.

73. David Lewin's "Music Theory, Phenomenology, and Modes of Perception" first appeared in *Music Perception* 3/4 (1986): 327–92; it has been reprinted in Lewin, *Studies in Music with Text* (Oxford: Oxford University Press, 2006), 53–108. Lewin refers to Edmund Husserl, *The Phenomenology of Internal Time Consciousness* (1964). Among writers who have developed phenomenologically oriented approaches to temporality in music, Lewin discusses the work of Judith Lochhead, Thomas Clifton, Taylor Greer, Nicholas Cook, James Tenney, Jonathan Kramer, Lewis Rowell, Christopher Hasty, Marvin Minsky, and Eugene Narmour.

In his critical reflections on Rose Rosengard Subotnik's critique of "structural listening," Martin Scherzinger brings David Lewin's 1986 article into contact with the work of Jacques Derrida: "Although they are described in a style quite remote from Derrida, Lewin's irreduc-ibly temporalized perceptions approximate the workings of Derrida's deconstructive phe-nomenological inquiries, especially his discussion of the sign's *temporization* (or the becoming-time-of space)—a notion that he also borrows from Husserl." Scherzinger, "The Return of the Aesthetic: Musical Formalism and Its Place in Political Critique," in Dell'Antonio, *Beyond Structural Listening?*, 262.

74. Izchak Miller, *Husserl, Perception, and Temporal Awareness* (1984), 2–3, as cited in Lewin, "Music Theory," 53.

75. Lewin, "Music Theory," 56.

76. Lewin, "Music Theory," 59.

77. Lewin, "Music Theory," 94–96.

78. Lewin takes exception to the notion that composers make choices or decisions: "a composer should never be thinking 'shall it be this *or* that'; he should only be thinking 'shall it be *this*?' If the answer is 'no,' he must work with the material, whether by intuition or elbow grease, until the question once more presents itself: 'now, shall it be *this*?' and so on, until all shall be as it is" (David Lewin, "Behind the Beyond: A Response to Edward T. Cone," *Perspectives of New Music* 7 [1968–69], 66). On this point I take sides with Cone, who, in his reply to Lewin, argues: "the observer is not always an artist, but the artist is always an observer.... How, then, can [Lewin] insist that 'the artist does not 'decide, he *knows*.'... Perhaps painter-as-creator 'knows,' but painter-as-critic must question, just as composer-as-critic says to himself 'this isn't working.'" Edward T. Cone, "Mr. Cone Replies," op. cit., 71.

79. According to Carl Czerny, Beethoven made the following remark to his violinist friend Wenzel Krumpholz "around 1803": "Ich bin nur wenig zufrieden mit meinen bisherigen Arbeiten. Von heute an will ich *einen neuen Weg* einschlagen" (Czerny, *Erinnerungen aus meinem Leben* [1842], ed. Walter Kolneder [Strasbourg: P. H. Heitz, 1968], 43; emphasis added). Given that the compositions Czerny associates with this remark are the piano sonatas opp. 28 (1801) and 31 (1802), Leon Plantinga suggests that "the year in question was more likely 1802" (Plantinga, *Beethoven's Concertos: History, Style, Performance* [New York: Norton, 1999], 344n.40). About the difficulty of interpreting Beethoven's similar, documented remark in an 1802 letter to Breitkopf and Härtel, where the composer refers to the "wirklich ganz neue Manier" of his Variations Opp. 34 and 35 (both from 1802), see William Kinderman, *Beethoven* (Berkeley: University of California Press, 1995), 51–52. James Hepokoski registers his skepticism about the significance of Beethoven's "new path"; see Hepokoski, "Approaching the First Movement of Beethoven's *Tempest* Sonata through Sonata Theory," in *Beethoven's "Tempest" Sonata: Perspectives of Analysis and Performance*, ed. Pieter Bergé, Jeroen D'hoe, and William E. Caplin (Leuven: Peeters, 2009), 185n.8. By contrast, Kinderman holds that Beethoven's "innovative presumption [his allusion to a "new manner" in his variations of 1802] is actually confirmed by the musical content" (Kinderman, *Beethoven*, 52).

Chapter 2

1. "That is, no one actually believes [Hegel's] central ontological thesis, that the universe is posited by a Spirit whose essence is rational necessity." Charles Taylor, *Hegel* (Cambridge: Cambridge University Press, 1975), 538. Taylor nonetheless delivers this verdict in a chapter that asks, "Why at the same time is his philosophy highly relevant to our time in a whole host of ways?" (538).

2. See Susan McClary, *Feminine Endings: Music, Gender, and Sexuality* (Minneapolis: University of Minnesota Press, 1991), 69, 127–30, and 156.

3. See Richard Rorty, "The Intellectuals at the End of Socialism," *Yale Review* 80 (1992): 1–16. Speaking of Kant as well as Hegel, Michael Spitzer writes: "It might not be immediately obvious what relevance these two eighteenth-century philosophers can have for us today. Nevertheless, Kant—arguably the foremost Western thinker since Aristotle—has never really gone away, and Hegel, after a long eclipse in the Anglo-American tradition, has leapt back to life in the work of contemporary philosophers such as Charles Taylor and Robert Brandom." *Music as Philosophy: Adorno and Beethoven's Late Style* (Bloomington: Indiana University Press, 2006), 273. Spitzer refers to Taylor's *Hegel*, cited in note 1 above, and to Robert Brandom, "Some Pragmatist Themes in Hegel's Idealism" (1999).

4. In particular, Carl Dahlhaus's death in 1989 elicited numerous tributes, retrospectives, and critical essays. See especially Philip Gossett, "Carl Dahlhaus and the 'Ideal Type,'" *19th-Century Music* 13/1 (1989): 49–56; James Hepokoski, "The Dahlhaus Project and Its Extra-musicological Sources," *19th-Century Music* 14/3 (1991): 221–46; and the review essays by Hermann Danuser, John Daverio, and James Webster on Dahlhaus's *Ludwig van Beethoven und seine Zeit* and his *Ludwig van Beethoven*, edited by Michael C. Tusa, in *Beethoven Forum* 2 (1993): 179–227.

The following studies, essay collections, and translations around the turn of this century attest to a vigorous renewal of interest in Adorno's thought: Max Paddison, *Adorno's Aesthetics of Music* (Cambridge: Cambridge University Press, 1993); Paddison, *Adorno, Modernism and Mass Culture* (London: Kahn & Averill, 1996); Robert W. Witkin, *Adorno on Music* (London: Routledge, 1998); Adorno, *Beethoven: The Philosophy of Music* (Stanford: Stanford University Press, 1998) (see chapter 1 of this volume); Nigel Gibson and Andrew Ruben, eds., *Adorno: A Critical Reader* (Oxford: Wiley-Blackwell, 2002); Adorno, *Essays on Music* (2002). See also Charles Rosen, "Should We Adore Adorno?" *New York Review of Books*, October 24, 2002.

5. Carl Dahlhaus, *The Idea of Absolute Music* (Chicago: University of Chicago Press, 1989), 42.

6. E. T. A. Hoffmann, review of Beethoven's Fifth Symphony (1810), *Schriften zur Musik: Aufsätze und Rezensionen* (Darmstadt: Wissenschaftliche Buchgesellschaft, 1979), 36: "Haydn fasst das Menschliche im menschlichen Leben romantisch auf…Mozart nimmt mehr das Übermenschliche, das Wunderbare, welches im innern Geiste wohnt, ins Anspruch. Beethovens Musik bewegt die Hebel des Schauers, der Furcht, des Entsetzens, des Schmerzes, und erweckt jene unendliche Sehnsucht, die das Wesen der Romantik ist." Translation by Mark Evan Bonds, in his *Music as Thought: Listening to the Symphony in the Age of Beethoven* (Princeton, NJ: Princeton University Press, 2006), 35–36. See also E. T. A. Hoffmann, *Musical Writings: "Kreisleriana," "The Poet and the Composer," Music Criticism* (Cambridge: Cambridge University Press, 1989), 238.

7. Dahlhaus, *The Idea of Absolute Music*, 57. For a superb analysis of Hoffmann's review, see Bonds, *Music as Thought*, chap. 3, "Listening to Truth: Beethoven's Fifth Symphony."

8. Bonds, *Music as Thought*, 56.

9. Robert C. Solomon, *In the Spirit of Hegel: A Study of G. W. F. Hegel's "Phenomenology of Spirit"* (New York: Oxford University Press, 1983), 99. According to Bonds: "Whether Hoffmann knew Hegel's *Phenomenology of Spirit* directly cannot be documented, but the treatise had already attracted intense attention by the time Hoffmann set to work on his review of Beethoven's Fifth Symphony…Jean Paul was one of the work's most enthusiastic early reviewers. Hoffmann's knowledge of this work can be reasonably inferred for a person of his education and professional training as a jurist" (*Music as Thought*, 136n.30). The Hegel-Hoffmann connection runs in both directions; James H. Donelan argues that, in Hegel's series of lectures on aesthetics, the first of which he gave in 1818, "Hegel was responding to contemporaneous statements on the importance of music by E. T. A. Hoffmann, among others" (*Poetry and the Romantic Musical Aesthetic* [Cambridge: Cambridge University Press, 2008], xv).

10. See Robin Wallace, *Beethoven's Critics: Aesthetic Dilemmas and Resolutions during the Composer's Lifetime* (Cambridge: Cambridge University Press, 1986), 45–53, 126–43; and Scott Burnham, "Aesthetics, Theory and History in the Works of Adolph Bernhard Marx" (Ph.D. diss., Brandeis University, 1988), 29, 54.

11. The quotation appears in Michael Ermarth, *Wilhelm Dilthey: The Critique of Historical Reason* (1978), as cited in Burnham, "Aesthetics, Theory and History," 242.

12. See Burnham, "Criticism, Faith, and the *Idee*: A. B. Marx's Early Reception of Beethoven," *19th-Century Music* 13 (1990): 183–92.

13. G. W. F. Hegel, *Phenomenology of Spirit* (Oxford: Oxford University Press, 1977), 6.

14. Burnham, "Aesthetics, Theory and History," 240–41.

15. Solomon, *In the Spirit of Hegel*, 196. My discussion here should have alerted Benedict Taylor and Stephen Rumpf that I am not among those who "connect the notion of an irresistible linear teleology to Hegelian views of history," as Taylor's citation of my 1995 version of this chapter suggests, in reference to Rumpf. See Taylor, "Musical History and Self-Consciousness in Mendelssohn's Octet, Op. 20," *19th-Century Music* 32/2 (2008): 141–42n.34; and Stephen Rumpf, *Beethoven after Napoleon: Political Romanticism in the Late Works* (Berkeley: University of California Press, 2004): 212–20.

16. Rose Rosengard Subotnik, *Developing Variations: Style and Ideology in Western Music* (Minneapolis: University of Minnesota Press, 1991), 17.

17. "Durch die Form ist der Inhalt des Geistes bestimmt worden, durch sie ist er dem Verstand erfassbar." A. B. Marx, "Die Form in der Musik," in *Die Wissenschaften im neunzehnten Jahrhundert*, ed. Johannes Andreas Romberg, vol. 2 (Leipzig: Romberg's Verlag, 1856), 26 (cited in Burnham, "Aesthetics, Theory and History," 97). Burnham provides a complete translation of Marx's "Die Form in der Musik" in A. B. Marx, *Musical Form in the Age of Beethoven: Selected Writings on Theory and Method* (Cambridge: Cambridge University Press, 1997), 55–90.

18. Scott Burnham, "The Role of Sonata Form in A. B. Marx's Theory of Form," *Journal of Music Theory* 33/2 (1989): 251.

19. G. W. F. Hegel, *The Encyclopaedia Logic (with the Zusätze): Part I of the Encyclopaedia of Philosophical Sciences with the Zusätze* (Indianapolis: Hackett, 1991), 203. Discounting Hegel, Burnham turns to Schelling's idea of a "polar tension between a positive force (infinite motion) and a negative force" for a reminiscence of Marx's outlook on the relation of content to form ("Aesthetics, Theory and History," 97).

20. Birgitte Plesner V. Moyer, "Concepts of Musical Form in the Nineteenth Century with Special Reference to A. B. Marx and Sonata Form" (Ph.D. diss., Stanford University, 1969), 73–74.

21. See Heinrich Schenker, *Free Composition (Der freie Satz)* (New York: Longman, 1979), 131 (quoted in chapter 1 of this volume).

22. Burnham, "The Role of Sonata Form," 249.

23. Burnham, "The Role of Sonata Form," 252 (emphasis added).

24. Burnham, "The Role of Sonata Form," 261–64, 263. The paragraph quoted in full originally appears in Burnham, "Aesthetics, Theory and History," 125–26.

25. For an interpretation of the particular path taken by each of the authors mentioned above, see M. H. Abrams, *Natural Supernaturalism: Tradition and Revolution in Romantic Literature* (New York: Norton, 1971), chap. 4: "The Circuitous Journey: Through Alienation to Reintegration."

26. I paraphrase Abrams (*Natural Supernaturalism*, 233) here, substituting "musical form" for "religion" in his discussion.

27. "The formation of the *Hauptsatz* is the first product of the *Idee*, of the mood—in short, of the impulse for the composition that is to come into being. It determines all that follows." A. B. Marx, *Die Lehre von der musikalischen Komposition, praktisch-theoretisch*, 2nd ed., vol. 3 (Leipzig: Breitkopf and Härtel, 1841), 259. Compare Marx's statement with the following from Arnold Schoenberg: "Music of the homophonic-melodic style of composition, that is, music with a main theme . . . produces its material by, as I call it, *developing variation*. This means that variation of the features of a basic unit produces all the thematic formulations which provide for fluency, contrasts, variety, logic and unity, on the one hand, and character, mood, expression, and every needed differentiation, on the other hand—thus elaborating the *idea* of the piece." "Bach" (1950), in *Style and Idea: Selected Writings of Arnold*

Schoenberg, ed. Leonard Stein (New York: St. Martin's, 1975), 397. For an authoritative account of Schoenberg's conception of *Grundgestalt*, see Patricia Carpenter, "*Grundgestalt* as Tonal Function," *Music Theory Spectrum* 5 (1983): 15–38. For an analytic application of the concept as inextricably associated with "developing variation," see Janet Schmalfeldt, "Berg's Path to Atonality: The Piano Sonata, Op. 1," in *Alban Berg: Historical and Analytical Perspectives*, ed. David Gable and Robert P. Morgan (Oxford: Clarendon Press, 1991), 79–109.

28. From Adorno, "Schubert (1928)," in which "Das Beethovensche Muss" is translated by Jonathan Dunsby and Beate Perrey as "Beethovenian 'fate' " (13).

Notions of a determinative initial "theme" appear in rhetoric-oriented music-theoretical literature long before Marx. For example, in his *Dictionnaire de musique* (1768), Jean-Jacques Rousseau at first treats the term "sujet" as if comparable in music to the "subject" or "topic" of an oration—"the idea that serves as the basis of all the others" (as quoted in Carl Dahlhaus, *Ludwig van Beethoven: Approaches to His Music* [Oxford: Clarendon, 1991], 144; my translation).

29. A. B. Marx, "Als Recension der Sonate, Op. 111 von L. v. Beethoven," *Berliner allgemeine musikalische Zeitung* (1824), quoted in Burnham, "Criticism, Faith, and the *Idee*," 185.

30. Burnham, "Criticism, Faith, and the *Idee*," 187.

31. Arthur Schopenhauer, *The World as Will and Representation* (New York: Dover, 1966), vol. 2, 448–49.

32. Patricia Carpenter, "Musical Form and Musical Idea: Reflections on a Theme of Schoenberg, Hanslick, and Kant," in *Music and Civilization: Essays in Honor of Paul Henry Lang*, ed. Edmond Strainchamps and Maria Rika Maniates (New York: Norton, 1984), 396.

33. Schoenberg, "National Music (1)" (1931), in *Style and Idea*, 171. Nicholas Cook notes that "the Hegelian frame of reference is self-evident" in the following statement, from Schoenberg's *Harmonielehre*: "[E]ven if our tonality is dissolving, it already contains within it the germs of the next artistic phenomenon. Nothing is definitive in culture; everything is only preparation for a higher stage of development, for a future which at the moment can only be imagined, conjectured." Schoenberg, *Theory of Harmony* (1911), 97, cited in Cook, *The Schenker Project*, 310.

34. Arnold Schoenberg, *Fundamentals of Musical Composition* (New York: St. Martin's Press, 1967), 8; and "On revient toujours" (1948), in *Style and Idea*, 108–9. See also the quotation from Schoenberg in note 27 above.

35. Schoenberg, "National Music (2)" (1931), in *Style and Idea*, 174.

36. The quoted passages in this paragraph are from Adorno, *Philosophy of Modern Music* (New York: Seabury Press, 1973), 55, 74 (emphasis added), 61.

37. Adorno, *Philosophy of Modern Music*, 42.

38. "In early childhood [composers] adjusted to the goings-on around them; later they are moved by ideas expressing their own, already socialized form of reaction. Even individualistic composers from the flowering of the private sphere, men like Schumann and Chopin, are no exceptions; the din of the bourgeois revolution rumbles in Beethoven, and in Schumann's *Marseillaise* quotations it echoes, weakened, as in dreams. The subjective mediation, the social element of the composing individuals and the behavior patterns that make them work so and not otherwise, consists in the fact that the compositorial subject, however necessarily it may mistake itself for a mere being-for-itself, constitutes a moment of the social productive forces." Theodor W. Adorno, *Introduction to the Sociology of Music* (New York: Seabury Press, 1976), 211. See also Subotnik, *Developing Variations*, 19.

39. Subotnik, *Developing Variations*, 21.

40. Adorno, *Sociology of Music*, 210 (emphasis added).

41. Adorno, *Philosophy of Modern Music*, 74.

42. Richard Leppert, in Adorno, *Essays on Music*, ix.

43. Subotnik, *Developing Variations*, 19. But one cannot fault Adorno for having never tried to explain "mediation"; see the chapter with that title in his *Sociology of Music*, 194–218.

44. Adorno, "On the Problem of Musical Analysis," in *Essays on Music*, 164. See Rose Rosengard Subotnik, "Toward a Deconstruction of Structural Listening: A Critique of Schoenberg, Adorno, and Stravinsky," in *Explorations in Music, the Arts, and Ideas: Essays in Honor of Leonard B. Meyer*, ed. Eugene Narmour and Ruth A. Solie (Stuyvesant, NY: Pendragon, 1988), 87–122; a revised version of this essay appears in Subotnik, *Deconstructive Variations: Music and Reason in Western Society* (Minneapolis: University of Minnesota Press, 1996). At no point in her 1988 essay or her 1996 revision does Subotnik refer to Adorno's lecture on analysis under discussion here. In that lecture as well as in other writings by Adorno, one finds that the term "structural listening" (*strukturelles Hören*) is Adorno's own, rather than Subotnik's, as she would seem to imply (see "Toward a Deconstruction," 88; *Deconstructive Variations*, 148). Adorno may in turn have known Felix Salzer's Schenkerian-oriented *Strukturelles Hören: Der tonale Zusammenhang in der Musik* (1952), first published in English as *Structural Hearing: Tonal Coherence in Music* by Charles Boni (New York: Dover, 1962).

In her 2004 "Afterword: Toward the Next Paradigm of Musical Scholarship," in *Beyond Structural Listening?*, ed. Andrew Dell'Antonio (Berkeley: University of California Press, 2004), 279–302, Subotnik offers a "time lapse" retrospective on the motivations for her 1988 essay and argues that new "deconstructive objections" to her critique and its objects, as "older notions of structural listening," have conflated the critique itself with the concepts she criticizes, "all under the rubric of a (somewhat enlarged) notion of structural listening" (283): "My original essay made clear the value I attached to structural modes of listening even as I pleaded for the enlargement of musical study through the development of other modes. I have not changed my mind on this matter" (284). Subotnik finds Robert Fink's essay in this collection so compelling "that it just about succeeds in melting one's [my] resistance to reading about sharps and flats" (292).

45. See Adorno, "On the Problem of Musical Analysis," in *Essays on Music*, 171, for all quotations in this paragraph. As with all of Adorno's published ideas about Beethoven and Hegel cited or discussed thus far, sources for this late proclamation about coherence and "Becoming" can be found in his much earlier preparatory notes for the Beethoven book that he never completed (see chapter 1 of this volume). For one example among many, in a notebook from 1940 Adorno writes: "Beethoven's achievement lies in the fact that in his work—and in his alone—the whole is never external to the particular but emerges solely from its movement, or, rather, is this movement. In Beethoven there is no mediation *between* themes, but, as in Hegel, the whole, as pure becoming, is itself the concrete mediation" (*Beethoven: The Philosophy of Music*, 24). Adorno, *Beethoven: Philosophie der Musik* (Frankfurt am Main: Suhrkamp, 2nd ed., 1994): "Das Gelingen bei Beethoven besteht darin, daß bei ihm, und ihm allein, das Ganze niemals dem Einzelnen äußerlich ist sondern allein aus dessen Bewegung hervorgeht oder vielmehr diese Bewegung ist. Es wird bei Beethoven nicht vermittelt *zwischen* Themen, sondern wie bei Hegel ist das Ganze, als reines Werden, selber die konkrete Vermittlung" (49).

46. Adorno, *Beethoven: The Philosophy of Music*, 180.

47. Theodor W. Adorno, *Hegel: Three Studies* (Cambridge, MA: MIT Press, 1993), 133–34. Adorno, *Drei Studien zu Hegel* (Frankfurt: Suhrkamp, 1963): "Insofern die Reflexion jeden Begriffs, regelmäßig verbunden mit der Reflexion der Reflexion, den Begriff durch den Nachweis seiner Unstimmigkeit sprengt, affiziert die Bewegung des Begriffs stets auch

das Stadium, dem sie sich entringt. Der Fortgang ist permanente Kritik des Vorhergehenden, und solche Bewegung ergänzt die synthetisch fortschreitende" (122–23).

48. Adorno, *Hegel: Three Studies*, 136. Adorno, *Drei Studien*: "Die Musik des Beethovenschen Typus, nach deren Ideal die Reprise, also die erinnernde Wiederkehr früher exponierter Komplexe, Resultat der Durchführung, also der Dialektik sein will, bietet dazu ein Analogon, das bloße Analogie überschreitet" (124).

49. For examples from British scholars since 1965, see Philip Barford, "The Approach to Beethoven's Late Music," *Music Review* 30 (1969): 106–17; and Christopher Ballantine, "Beethoven, Hegel and Marx," *Music Review* 33 (1972): 35–46. Neither author refers to Adorno's work.

50. Adorno, *Hegel: Three Studies*, 137. Adorno, *Drei Studien*: "Vielleicht hilft zum Verständnis dieser Analogie wie zum innersten Hegels, daß die Auffassung der Totalität als der in sich durch Nichtidentität vermittelten Identität ein künstlerisches Formgesetz aufs philosophische überträgt" (124–25).

51. Adorno, *Hegel: Three Studies*, 135, 123. Adorno, *Drei Studien*: "man muß Hegel lesen, indem man die Kurven der geistigen Bewegung mitbeschreibt, gleichsam mit dem spekulativen Ohr die Gedanken mitspielt, als wären sie Noten" (112).

52. Adorno, *Hegel: Three Studies*, 136. Adorno, *Drei Studien*: " Auch hochorganisierte Musik muß man mehrdimensional, *von vorwärts zugleich und rückwärts hören*. Das erheischt ihr zeitliches Organisations-prinzip: Zeit ist nur durch Unterschiede des Bekannten und nicht schon Bekannten, des Dagewesenen und des Neuen zu artikulieren; Fortgang selber hat zur Bedingung ein rückläufiges Bewußtsein. Man muß einen ganzen Satz kennen, in jedem Augenblick des Vorhergehenden retrospektiv gewahr sein. Die einzelnen Passagen sind als dessen Konsequenzen aufzufassen, der Sinn abweichender Wiederholung ist zu realisieren, das Wiedererscheinende nicht bloß als architektonische Korrespondenz, sondern als zwangvoll Gewordenes wahrzunehmen" (124; emphasis added).

Already from Adorno's notebook from 1944: "Beethoven's music is immanent in the same way as is philosophy, bringing forth itself. Hegel, who has no concepts outside philosophy, is, in that sense, likewise concept-less in face of the 'heterogeneous continuum.' That is to say, his ideas, like those of music, are explained only by each other. This idea must be followed up exactly, since it leads to the innermost depths" (Adorno, *Beethoven: The Philosophy of Music*, 12). Adorno, *Beethoven: Philosophie der Musik*: "Die Musik Beethovens ist immanent wie die Philosophie, sich selbst hervorbringend. Hegel hat auch keinen Begriff außerhalb der Philosophie und ist in gewisser Weise gegenüber dem heterogenen Kontinuum auch begriffslos, d. h. seine Begriffe nur durch sich selber erklärt wie die musikalischen. Dies muß genau verfolgt werden und führt ins Innerste" (33).

53. Stephen Hinton, "The Conscience of Musicology: Carl Dahlhaus (1928–89)," *Musical Times* 130 (1989): 737. For Dahlhaus's critique of the "trivialization" that Adorno's "dictate of the historically necessary" underwent in the 1950s, see Dahlhaus's introduction to a translated excerpt from Adorno's *Philosophie der neuen Musik*, in *Contemplating Music*, ed. Ruth Katz and Carl Dahlhaus (Stuyvesant, NY: Pendragon Press, 1993), vol. 4, 113–15.

54. Carl Dahlhaus, "Zu Adornos Beethoven-Kritik," in *Adorno und die Musik*, ed. Otto Kolleritsch, vol. 12 (Graz: Universal Edition, 1979), 170, 178.

55. Dahlhaus, *Ludwig van Beethoven*, 4–5, 31, 34–35. Dahlhaus, *Ludwig van Beethoven und seine Zeit* (Laaber: Laaber-Verlag, 1987) (hereafter *LvB*): "Das Publikum, für das Beethoven die Sonata [op. 81a] bestimmte...war eine anonyme Öffentlichkeit, nicht ein geschlossener Freundeszirkel, wie er Carl Philipp Emanuel Bach vorschwebte, als er davon sprach, daß ein Komponist, um andere zu rühren, selbst gerührt sein müsse. Und in dem Maße, in dem der sympathisierende, an der Person des Komponisten Anteil nehmende

Kreis zum 'Publikum' wurde, trennte sich das ästhetische Subjekt immer entschiedener vom biographischen" (64).

56. Dahlhaus, *Ludwig van Beethoven*, 36, 41, 15.

57. Dahlhaus, *Ludwig van Beethoven*, 35, 6. See also Dahlhaus's "What Is 'Developing Variation'?" (1984), in Carl Dahlhaus, *Schoenberg and the New Music* (Cambridge: Cambridge University Press, 1987), 128–33.

58. Dahlhaus, *Ludwig van Beethoven*, 41–42. Dahlhaus, *LvB*: "Erst in der Reflexion—der Brechung vom Objekt her—wird das Subjekt für sich selbst erkennbar...Is nun aber—ideengeschichtlich—die Subjekt-Objekt-Dialektik eine Entdeckung der Zeit um 1800, so ist es nicht überraschend, daß das im musikalischen Formprozeß immer wieder—und nicht allein bei der Werkentstehung ein für allemal—tätige Subjekt erst bei Beethoven zu sich selbst gekommen zu sein scheint. Das ästhetische Subjekt ist gewissermaßen das im Werk überdauernde, ihm als 'Energeia' einbeschriebene kompositorische Subjekt" (71–72).

59. Dahlhaus, *Ludwig van Beethoven*, 42. Dahlhaus, *LvB*: "Und aus der Reflektiertheit des Kompositionsprozesses resultiert wiederum die Forderung einer analogen Reflektiertheit des musikalischen Hörens, wie denn nicht der Kompositionsprozeß, sondern allein die ihn spiegelnde Rezeption—als Verhältnis zwischen dem tönenden Objekt und dessen Wahrnehmung—rekonstruierbar ist. Das ästhetische Subjekt ist also weder die empirische Person des Komponisten noch die des Hörers, sondern ein imaginäres Subjekt, das eine Vermittlungsinstanz zwischen der werkkonstituierenden Tätigkeit des Komponisten und der nachvollziehenden des Hörers darstellt" (72).

60. Dahlhaus, *Ludwig van Beethoven*, 113, 120, 115. Dahlhaus's "Form as Transformation" was first published as "Musikalische Form als Transformation: Bemerkungen zur Beethoven-Interpretation," in *Beethoven-Jahrbuch* 9 (Bonn: Beethovenhaus, 1977).

61. Dahlhaus, *Ludwig van Beethoven*, 114, 118 (emphasis added). Dahlhaus, *LvB*: "...so wenig geht musikalische Form in der Eindeutigkeit auf, die sie schließlich erreicht oder zu erreichen scheint. Die 'eigentliche' Bedeutung, die sich am Ende zeigt, ist vielmehr—paradox ausgedrückt—lediglich Bestandteil eines über sie hinausgreifenden Gesamtsinns, der die 'uneigentlichen', vom Bewußtsein zurückgelassenen, aber nicht vergessenen Bedeutungen mit einschließt. *Der Weg, nicht dessen Ende, ist das Ziel*" (155; emphasis added).

62. Dahlhaus, *Ludwig van Beethoven*, 116.

63. Dahlhaus, *Ludwig van Beethoven*, 163, 160, 164. Dahlhaus's "Eine wenig beachtete Formidee" (included in Dahlhaus's *LvB* as "Eine vergessene Formidee" and translated as "A Forgotten Formal Idea" in *Ludwig van Beethoven*, 159–65) first appeared in *Analysen: Beiträge zu einer Problemgeschichte des Komponierens. Festschrift für Hans Heinrich Eggebrecht zum 65. Geburtstag*, ed. Werner Breig, Reinhold Brinkmann, and Elmar Budde (Weisbaden: Steiner, 1984), 248–56.

64. Dahlhaus, *Ludwig van Beethoven*, 164–65. Dahlhaus, *LvB*: "[S]ondern daß es auch möglich ist, den inneren Konnex vom Ende her zu begreifen: einem Ende, in dem gewisser-maßen die zurückliegenden Motive und Teilmomente aufeinandertreffen zu einer musika-lischen Konfiguration, die insofern ein 'Ereignis' darstellt, als in dem Licht, das sie zurückwirft, frühere Vorgänge als Bestandteile einer 'Geschichte' sichtbar werden" (205–06).

65. Schoenberg, "Brahms the Progressive" (1947), in *Style and Idea*, 407 (cited in Dahlhaus, *Ludwig van Beethoven*, 37).

66. Dahlhaus, *Ludwig van Beethoven*, 36–37. Dahlhaus, *LvB*: "Entscheidend ist nicht, entgegen Schönbergs Auffassung, eine abstrakte, vom Formgrundriß logelöste 'Logik' der Motiventwicklung, sondern deren Vermittlung mit den Funktionen und Stationen eines Formprozesses" (67).

67. Dahlhaus, *Ludwig van Beethoven*, 42 (emphasis added). Dahlhaus, *LvB*: "Wenn Beethoven im ersten Satz der *Es-Dur-Klaviersonate* opus 31,3 die Sonatenform einer

'Reflexion' unterwirft—und zwar dadurch, daß sich der Anfang des Satzes, scheinbar eine Introduktion, nachträglich als Hauptthema erweist, und daß die Fortsetzung (T. 18), die wie eine Überleitung wirkt und in der Reprise auch als solche fungiert, von einer Evolutionspartie (T. 33), die als 'eigentliche' Überleitung gelten muß, aus ihrer Rolle verdrängt wird—, so macht er die musikalische Form als vom Subjekt konstituiert kenntlich: 'Introduktion,' 'Hauptthema' und 'Überleitung' erweisen sich als Kategorien, die nicht am Objekt 'gegeben' sind, sondern an das tönende Gebilde 'herangetragen' werden. Bei unreflektiertem Formverständnis ist sich das Subjekt seiner konstituierenden Tätigkeit nicht bewußt; es versteht sich als Rezeptionsorgan für ein fest umrissenes 'Ding' mit bestimmten 'Eigenschaften.' Erst die Zumutung, *Kategorien auszutauschen*, bringt dem Hörer seine Subjektivität als Konstituens des Formprozesses zu Bewußtsein" (72; emphasis added).

Concerning Beethoven's "reflecting nature," Dahlhaus cites Ludwig Finscher, "Beethovens Klaviersonata opus 31,3," in *Festschrift für Walter Wiora* (1967), 385–96.

68. Dahlhaus, *Ludwig van Beethoven*, 117. Dahlhaus, *LvB*: "Der Anfang der Sonate ist motivisch locker gefügt und sowohl harmonisch als auch syntaktisch 'offen,' so daß er zunächst als Introduktion, nicht als Exposition eines Themas erscheint" (153).

69. Carl Dahlhaus, *Nineteenth-Century Music* (Berkeley: University of California Press, 1989), 14.

70. Dahlhaus, *Ludwig van Beethoven*, 89. For Dahlhaus on the various views about "theme" mentioned above, see 46, 121, 126, 123.

71. Dahlhaus, *Ludwig van Beethoven*, 99.

72. Dahlhaus, *Ludwig van Beethoven*, 106–7 (in the essay "Introduction and Coda").

73. "[L]ike the difference between coda and codetta, a slow introduction differs from a thematic introduction with respect to both its location in the structural hierarchy and the complexity of its formal organization. A thematic introduction resides on the hierarchical level comparable to that of a basic idea, contrasting idea, cadential idea, and codetta. This short unit is normally supported by a tonic prolongation and generally has no melodic profile." William E. Caplin, *Classical Form: A Theory of Formal Functions for the Instrumental Music of Haydn, Mozart, and Beethoven* (New York: Oxford University Press, 1998), 203; see also 15.

74. Citing instances of recitative in *Don Giovanni*, Richard Kramer reminds us that, "[i]n Mozart, the first-inversion triad establishes the new scene, always a shift from the tonal space and formal closure of the scene preceding." Thus with Beethoven: "To *begin* a sonata in this way is to evoke the aura of dramatic action under way. No earlier sonata by Beethoven—and none by Mozart or Haydn—begins with so radical an opening; the only gambit comparable to it is Emanuel Bach's Sonata in F, with its fragile opening phrases in C minor and D minor." *Unfinished Music* (New York: Oxford University Press, 2008), 193.

75. The convention of referring to op. 31, no. 2 as the "Tempest" Sonata originates with the well-known report made by Beethoven's friend and amanuensis, the notoriously unreliable Anton Schindler. Upon asking Beethoven for the "key" to the piano sonatas op. 31, no. 2 and op. 57, Schindler claims that Beethoven replied, "Just read Shakespeare's *Tempest*." See Anton Felix Schindler, *Beethoven as I Knew Him* (1860) (Chapel Hill: University of North Carolina Press, 1966), 406. Timothy Jones proposes that Schindler's anecdote "might be seen as forming part of the power play of cultural politics in the 1840s": Beethoven's "repeated references to covert Shakespearian programmes in his works [were] grist to the mill of critics and biographers who wished to bolster his cultural authority by yoking it with the supreme figure in the European literary pantheon." *Beethoven: The "Moonlight" and other Sonatas, Op. 27 and Op. 31* (Cambridge: Cambridge University Press, 1999), 45. For an effort to relate Shakespeare's play to the composer's own life circumstances during the years

1802–4, see Theodore Albrecht, "Beethoven and Shakespeare's *Tempest*: New Light on an Old Allusion," in *Beethoven Forum* 1 (1992): 81–92.

In his "Primitive Encounters: Beethoven's 'Tempest' Sonata, Musical Meaning, and Enlightenment Anthropology" (*Beethoven Forum* 6, 1998), Lawrence Kramer places Beethoven's "tempest series" (the piano sonatas op. 10, no. 1, op. 13, op. 31, no. 2, and op. 57) within the Enlightenment project of "speculative anthropology or 'universal history,'" fundamental to which the "primitive encounter ... of a civilized person with someone closer to the state of nature"—a "cultural primitive" or, say, the victim of a tempest—elicits sympathy for the sufferer that in turn "produces subjectivity by taking the other into the self" (42–43, 47). "By this account, sympathy with suffering is the origin of both human subjectivity and social bonding" (46). In Kramer's account of the first movement of the "Tempest" Sonata, the voice of the sufferer, "the voice as plaint, as call for sympathy" (58), is heard within the recitatives at the beginning of the recapitulation: they insert themselves "in the sympathy-forged chain of response and appeal that Rousseau postulates for melody. They both express a deep solicitude and summon the listener to respond solicitously" (57).

Richard Cohn suggests with insight that the "motivic story" he tells about the first movement of Beethoven's "Tempest"—a story of "concealed introversion and its registral migrations"—might be considered in light of Shakespeare's verses for the shipwrecked Ferdinand in Act I, Scene 2 of *The Tempest*: "Where should this music be? i' th' air or th' earth?/ . . . But 'tis gone./ No, it begins again." See Cohn, "'This music crept by me upon the waters': Introverted Motives in Beethoven's 'Tempest' Sonata," in *Engaging Music: Essays in Music Analysis*, ed. Deborah Stein (New York: Oxford University Press, 2005), 234–35.

As for the veracity of Schindler's report, and, by extension, its applications to op. 31, no. 2, Richard Kramer summarizes: "The questioning continues. We can be certain only that answers will not be forthcoming" (*Unfinished Music*, 203).

76. I am indebted to William Caplin for noting that the introductions in Beethoven's op. 78 and Chopin's op. 35 serve different formal functions—the former as a slow introduction, the latter as a thematic introduction. See William E. Caplin, "Beethoven's *Tempest* Exposition: A Springboard for Form-Functional Considerations," in *Beethoven's "Tempest" Sonata: Perspectives of Analysis and Performance*, ed. Pieter Bergé, Jeroen D'hoe, and William E. Caplin (Leuven: Peeters, 2009), 90n.12. My point here is that, as "first-time" listeners wait to hear what will happen after the fermata at m. 2, they might expect *either* type of introduction to be unfolding.

77. Leon Plantinga, *Romantic Music: A History of Musical Style in Nineteenth-Century Europe* (New York: Norton, 1984), 32; Dahlhaus, *Ludwig van Beethoven*, 174.

78. Schoenberg, *Fundamentals of Musical Composition*, 20–24, 58–81.

79. William E. Caplin, "Funktionale Komponenten im achttaktigen Satz," *Musiktheorie* 1 (1986): 241–43. Caplin acknowledges Erwin Ratz's contribution to the concept of formal function in general and his clarifications of Schoenberg's views on the sentence in particular; see Ratz, *Einführung in die musikalische Formenlehre: Über Formprinzipien in den Inventionen und Fugen J. S. Bachs und ihre Bedeutung für die Kompositionstechnik Beethovens* (Vienna: Universal, 1973). Caplin further discusses the sentence in his "The 'Expanded Cadential Progression': A Category for the Analysis of Classical Form," *Journal of Musicological Research* 7 (1987): 218–19; he devotes his chap. 3 in *Classical Form* to the sentence.

For a discussion of examples of the theme-type that Schoenberg called the "sentence" as found in the treatises of Johann Philipp Kirnberger, Joseph Riepel, and Heinrich Christoph Koch, see Janet Schmalfeldt, "Cadential Processes: The Evaded Cadence and the 'One More Time' Technique," *Journal of Musicological Research* 12 (1992): 50n.19. I attempt to establish correlations between characteristic features of the sentence and Schenkerian models in

Schmalfeldt, "Towards a Reconciliation of Schenkerian Concepts with Traditional and Recent Theories of Form," *Music Analysis* 10/3 (1991), 233–87.

80. In his critique of earlier analyses of the "Tempest," Ludwig Misch proposes as much—namely, that "the complex of the first six bars (in spite of the two-tempo structure, which is misleading at first glance) may well be a 'theme.'" "(*To be conscious of this, just imagine that bars 7 to 20 have been deleted.*)" Ludwig Misch, *Beethoven Studies* (Norman: University of Oklahoma Press, 1953), chap. 5, "The 'Problem' of the D Minor Sonata (Op. 31, No. 2)," 44 (emphasis added). For Misch, the "structural idea of the movement" rests upon the antithesis *largo-allegro* as a dualism of this theme, whereby "the contrast, which we otherwise usually find in the relationship between [*Hauptsatz* and *Seitensatz*], is anticipated *in nuce*. Therefore in accordance with the logic and economy of Beethoven's structural methods, it is neither necessary nor possible to introduce a second theme" (51–52).

81. Carl Dahlhaus, "Satz und Periode: Zur Theorie der musikalische Syntax," *Zeitschrift für Musiktheorie* 9/2 (1978): 16–26, and *Ludwig van Beethoven*, 117.

82. Caplin, "The 'Expanded Cadential Progression,'" 216. In the glossary for *Classical Form*, Caplin gives the following: "theme—A unit consisting of a conventional set of initiating, medial, and ending intrathematic functions. It must close with a cadence" (257).

83. For a full-length discussion of correspondences between Schoenberg's notion of "theme" and Schenker's "complete middleground harmonic-contrapuntal structure," see my "Towards a Reconciliation." In the making of my graphs for the exposition of the "Tempest," I had access to Edward Laufer's unpublished graph for the development and the beginning of the recapitulation, as presented by him on March 16, 1985, at the Schenker Symposium (Mannes College of Music, New York) in a paper titled "Parenthetical Passages." Laufer presented similar graphs in his lecture titled "Some Development Sections and the Study of Voice Leading," at Yale University on April 26, 1988. I am deeply grateful to Edward Laufer for his suggestions concerning Beethoven's exposition. Roger Kamien has kindly informed me that neither Laufer's nor my work fundamentally contradicts his own graphs for the beginning of the exposition and the recapitulation of the "Tempest," as presented in his "Aspects of the Recapitulation in Beethoven Piano Sonatas," *The Music Forum*, ed. Felix Salzer, vol. 4 (New York: Columbia University Press, 1976), 228–35.

84. Dahlhaus, *Ludwig van Beethoven*, 118.

85. See, for example, Donald Francis Tovey, *A Companion to Beethoven's Pianoforte Sonatas* (London: Associated Board of the Royal Schools of Music, 1931), 122.

86. My graphing method in example 2.4 for showing $\hat{5}$–$\hat{4}$–$\hat{3}$–$\hat{2}$ descents at mm. 75–87 attempts to capture the discontinuous, *disruptive* effect of the evaded cadences; see Schmalfeldt, "Cadential Processes," 35–42. By contrast, Richard Cohn hears continuous, repeated $\hat{5}$–$\hat{4}$–$\hat{3}$–$\hat{2}$–$\hat{1}$ motions—descending "fifth-fills"—in counterpoint with ascending fifth-fills containing an augmented second. For Cohn, the "motivic source for the movement," that is, the source for the two fifth-spans as well as for a third motive (the stepwise span through a diminished fourth), is the passage in diminuendo at mm. 133–37, toward the end of the development—the place where Beethoven would seem to "turn down the flame at the very moment that the pot is about to brim over" ("'This music crept by me upon the waters,'" 230, 227–28). The descending $\hat{5}$–$\hat{4}$–$\hat{3}$–$\hat{2}$–$\hat{1}$ motive makes its initial appearance in mm. 2–4 (see example 2.1).

87. Ratz, *Einführung in die musikalische Formenlehre*, 25.

88. Through the alignment of voice-leading graphs for mm. 1–21 and mm. 143–71, Roger Kamien has demonstrated that "the recapitulation is an extraordinary variation of the opening thirteen bars of the exposition" ("Aspects of the Recapitulation in Beethoven Piano Sonatas," 228; see also 229–35). Edward Laufer's unpublished graphs of the recapitulation (see note 83 above) confirm Kamien's viewpoint while underscoring Laufer's position that

the recapitulative passage at mm. 143–70 serves in the poetic if not technical sense as a "parenthetical return"—one that connects the home dominant of m. 121 with the same at m. 171.

89. Kramer, "Primitive Encounters," 55. In response to Kramer, one might say that the turbulence of the Allegro at mm. 3–6 retrospectively *suppresses* the "voice" invoked by the recitative-like opening rolled chord. The only chance for the voice to be heard, and then only as if from a distance, will be when the stormy music temporarily subsides into the recitatives, for the last time, only then to regain its annihilating intensity.

90. Wilhelm Furtwängler, *Ton und Wort: Aufsätze und Vortage* (1954), as cited in Allen Forte, "Schenker's Conception of Musical Structure," *Journal of Music Theory* 3 (1959): 2.

91. Janet Schmalfeldt, "Form as the Process of Becoming: The Beethoven-Hegelian Tradition and the 'Tempest' Sonata," in *Beethoven Forum* 4 (1995): 37–71.

92. Caplin, "Beethoven's *Tempest* Exposition," 87–125; and James Hepokoski, "Approaching the First Movement of Beethoven's *Tempest* Sonata through Sonata Theory," in *Beethoven's "Tempest" Sonata: Perspectives of Analysis and Performance*, ed. Pieter Bergé, Jeroen D'hoe, and William E. Caplin (Leuven: Peeters, 2009), 181–212. Included along with Caplin's and Hepokoski's articles in this collection are essays about the "Tempest" by Pieter Bergé and Jeroen D'hoe, Scott Burnham, Poundie Burstein, Kenneth Hamilton, Robert Hatten, William Kinderman, William Rothstein, Douglass Seaton, and Steven Vande Moortele. Page numbers from *Beethoven's "Tempest" Sonata* for quotations from Caplin's and Hepokoski's essays are cited in parentheses in my text.

93. James Hepokoski and Warren Darcy, *Elements of Sonata Theory: Norms, Types, and Deformations in the Late-Eighteenth-Century Sonata* (Oxford: Oxford University Press, 2006), 24.

94. Two additional factors "problematize any [secondary-theme] claim" for Hepokoski: the "non-S character" of the passage beginning at m. 42, and its "back-reference" to the rhythm (i.e., motivic content) of the opening Allegro idea. A "convincing S-character" should display a "marked thematic contrast (often in the direction of the more *legato* and lyrical), dynamic change, and so on" (198–99). These observations point to a fundamental divergence of Sonata Theory from Caplin's theory, in which "the formal function of an individual group does not depend on its motivic content.... a single motive can saturate a musical composition without obscuring the form, precisely because motives carry little in the way of functional implications" (Caplin, *Classical Form*, 4).

95. With Hepokoski's claim that "equally convincing arguments [in support of 'process'] can be, and have been, made on behalf of hundreds of similarly processual examples from, say, Mozart and (especially) Haydn (a master of *Fortspinnung* motivic elaboration)" ("Approaching the First Movement," 186), he suggests that he does not acknowledge the distinction between analyses of *motivic* transformation and observations about processual *formal* reinterpretation—Dahlhaus's fundamental concern.

96. Richard Kramer, *Unfinished Music*, 186. Kramer refers to Barry Cooper, *Beethoven and the Creative Process* (1990), 183–90.

97. Kramer, *Unfinished Music*, 171, 201, 193 (see note 74 above).

98. See Caplin, *Classical Form*, 205 and 280n.34.

99. Early in "Beethoven's *Tempest* Exposition," (88), Caplin recommends Ludwig Misch's essay, "The 'Problem' of the D Minor Sonata" (see note 80 above), for a summary of views about the opening of the "Tempest" as introduction. Misch takes issue in particular with analyses by Theodore Frimmel, Arnold Schmitz, Hugo Riemann, Wilibald Nagel, Hugo Leichtentritt, and Karl Blessinger. Hepokoski proposes that Dahlhaus's reading of the transition—"indeed, that whole interpretive tradition"—may have originated with A. B. Marx (my premier Beethoven-Hegelian), who marks m. 21 with the description, "Jetzt erst tritt

der Hauptsatz, aus dem Largomotiv erwachsen." Marx, *Ludwig van Beethoven: Leben und Schaffen* (1908), as cited by Hepokoski, "Approaching the First Movement," 186n.10.

100. Caplin ("Beethoven's *Tempest* Exposition," 91n.13) cites Leonard B. Meyer, "A Universe of Universals," *Journal of Musicology* (1998).

101. As the manifestation of a "looser" formal organization in mm. 21–41 of the "Tempest," Caplin points to Beethoven's use of a four-bar compound basic idea (CBI) and its repetition within the potential sixteen-bar sentential plan, and he notes that sixteen-bar sentences do not occur in the main themes of the composer's piano sonatas prior to the first movement of op. 28; rather, sixteen-bar sentential designs more commonly arise in transitions (and in secondary themes); see Caplin, "Beethoven's *Tempest* Exposition," 91–92n.15. To be sure, in Beethoven's first three piano concertos—opp. 19, 15, and 37—the opening tutti themes of all three first movements feature sixteen-bar sentences; the main theme of his First Symphony, Op. 21 (1799–1800) expands upon the sixteen-bar sentence, with its CBI and repetition extended to a full six measures each. But the different characters and social roles of concertos and symphonies relative to piano sonatas must be acknowledged, and none of these sixteen-bar sentences anticipates the dark and stormy music of the "Tempest." Perhaps worth mentioning is that the piano sonatas to follow in immediate succession after the op. 31 set— the "Waldstein," Op. 53, and the "Appassionata," Op. 57—both open with main themes modeled upon the sixteen-bar sentence. Listeners for whom the beginning of the transition in the "Tempest" could initially sound like the beginning of a main theme might be influenced by their familiarity with Beethoven's later as well as earlier works. Just the same, Caplin's point is well taken.

102. While acknowledging the "distinctly introductory character" of the opening of Beethoven's op. 31, no. 3, Caplin stresses that he is "not aware of any analysts being tempted, as they are with the 'Tempest,' to recognize a genuine introduction there" (Caplin, "Beethoven's *Tempest* Exposition," 95). As Caplin might have expected, Dahlhaus is one analyst who succumbed to the temptation; see my quotation above (p. 37) from Dahlhaus's *Ludwig van Beethoven*.

103. That the "Tempest" heralds Beethoven's later explorations of new ways in which to create formal ambiguities in the openings of his first movements is well substantiated in Benedict Taylor, "The Problem of the 'Introduction' in Beethoven's Late Quartets," *Ad Parnassum* 3/6 (2005): 45–64. In this study of the composer's "Galitzin" quartets, opp. 127, 132, and 130, with a focus upon the first movement of op. 127, Taylor investigates "a characteristic feature of Beethoven's late works"—"the strange ambiguity and interplay between what is a slow introduction and what is alternatively an allegro first subject/exposition 'proper'" (45). As with the "Tempest," all three of these quartets open with a "slow-fast thematic complex"; and highly individualized returns of this "bi-segmented" complex at large-scale formal boundaries (e.g., at the beginning of the development and at the "false recapitulation" in op. 127) retrospectively undermine the perception of the slow segment as a genuine introduction, rather than as an integral component of the main theme, while raising the question whether these movements have begun to deform the processual, "dynamic" sonata forms of Beethoven's earlier works in favor of more static "rotational," or "strophic," formal designs (48–49, 60–64).

Caplin notes that "the strategy of opening a sonata-form exposition with a main theme that embodies qualities of a slow introduction proved to be highly influential." Among examples, he cites Schubert's String Quintet in C and the *Unfinished* Symphony ("Beethoven's *Tempest* Exposition," 95). To these works by Schubert, I shall add his Piano Sonata in A Minor, Op. 42, D. 845; see chapter 5 of this volume.

104. See Caplin, *Classical Form*, 102.

105. With his two new moments for retrospective formal reinterpretation (at mm. 42–49 and at mm. 75–87), and in light of his adoption in *Classical Form* of my symbol for "becomes" (⇒) as a means of signaling form-functional reinterpretations, Caplin may be justified in

raising an eyebrow ("Beethoven's *Tempest* Exposition," 116n.46) over the contrasting characterizations of our respective analytic approaches assigned to the two of us by Michael Spitzer. For Spitzer, "there are not one but 'two' Hegels—a 'left' and a 'right'—which take their cue from the two [temporal] moments of the dialectic, negation and synthesis." In Spitzer's analogy, Schoenberg, Ratz, and Caplin are "right Hegelians": they move "from right to left," starting with the static "end-point"—the synthesis, as represented by established classical formal conventions—and working back to examine the processual (negation) stages through which the synthesis has been achieved. Spitzer portrays Dahlhaus and me as "left Hegelians": moving "from left to right," we "prefer to see formal functions not as stable entities [syntheses], . . . but as expressions of a thematic process undergoing developing variation." See Spitzer, *Music as Philosophy*, 241–42. (See also my comments above, p. 25, about the debate among Hegelian scholars concerning Hegel's "end-point.") Although Spitzer associates the "right Hegel" with Hegel's reactionary political rationalization of the Prussian state as a historical necessity, Caplin and I should surely not assume that Spitzer intends to impose political overtones upon us as music theorists. All the same, Caplin certainly does not regard himself as a "Hegelian," nor do I claim to be one. In this study I simply identify a Beethoven-Hegelian tradition and attempt to extend its values with respect to the perception of musical form as process. On the other hand, with his application of Adorno's Hegelian-informed concepts to the interpretation of Beethoven's late style, Spitzer emerges as Dahlhaus's clearest successor within the pantheon of Beethoven-Hegelians.

106. Schmalfeldt, "Cadential Processes," 35.

107. The graph at example 2.4 now all the more strongly resembles the graph of Chopin's Etude in E-flat Minor, Op. 10, No. 6 presented as example 11b in my "Cadential Processes" article (40); in both cases I argue for the prolongation of the cadential dominant whose resolution to the tonic is disrupted and delayed. As explained in that article (35), I opt for square brackets, rather than parentheses, in representing "one-more-time" repetitions: by borrowing square brackets from the tradition in literature for signaling explanatory additions within a cited text, I emphasize that "one-more-time" repetitions, far from serving as parenthetical statements or mere interpolations, play an essential foreground role in the characterization of formal, dynamic, and dramatic processes.

108. *Ludwig van Beethoven: The Op. 31 Piano Sonatas*, Richard Goode, pianist. Elektra Nonesuch 9 79212-2 (recorded October 1983 at the American Academy and Institute of Arts and Letters, New York City).

109. *Four Piano Sonatas on Period Instruments*, Malcolm Bilson, pianist, Claves (ASIN: B00005B7LL), 2002; and *Beethoven: Piano Sonatas No. 1, 14, 17, 28*, Malcolm Bilson, pianist, Claves CD 2104 (2002).

110. For more debate about Beethoven's "Tempest" Sonata among Caplin, Hepokoski, and me, see *Music Theory Online* 16.2 (2010). This volume reproduces a special session held at the 2009 annual meeting, in Montréal, of the Society for Music Theory; the session was organized by the society's Committee on the Status of Women, and it focused upon my work. The papers on Beethoven's "Tempest" that Caplin and Hepokoski kindly agreed to present within the session drew in part from their articles in *Beethoven's "Tempest" Sonata*; my response to their papers incorporated materials from the final section of this chapter.

Chapter 3

1. James Webster, *Haydn's "Farewell" Symphony and the Idea of Classical Style* (Cambridge: Cambridge University Press, 1991), 355, 358, 356. See also Webster, "The Concept of Beethoven's 'Early' Period in the Context of Periodizations in General," *Beethoven*

Forum 3 (1994): 1–27; "Haydn's Symphonies between *Sturm und Drang* and 'Classical Style': Art and Entertainment," in *Joseph Haydn Studies*, ed. W. Dean Sutcliffe (Cambridge: Cambridge University Press, 1998), 28–45; "Between Enlightenment and Romanticism in Music History: 'First Viennese Modernism' and the Delayed Nineteenth Century," *19th-Century Music* 25/2–3 (2001–2): 108–26; and "The Eighteenth Century as a Music-Historical Period?", *Eighteenth-Century Music* 1/1 (2003): 47–60.

2. Webster, *Haydn's "Farewell" Symphony*, 341–43, 352. Taking Charles Rosen's *The Classical Style: Haydn, Mozart, Beethoven* (1971) as points of departure and return, Webster addresses Adolf Sandberger's "Zur Geschichte des Haydnschen Streichquartetts" (*Altbayerische Monatsschrift* 2 [1900], 224–65) and then refers back to the stylistic "periods" and "schools" introduced in 1834 by Raphael Georg Kiesewetter (in his *Geschichte der europäisch-abendländischen oder unsrer heutigen Musik*) as well as to selected twentieth-century writings about Haydn and Viennese Classicism by, among others, Guido Adler, Wilhelm Fischer, Alfred Einstein, Friedrich Blume, Ludwig Finscher, and Jens Peter Larsen.

3. In disputing "the tradition of Haydn's having failed to understand Beethoven's music, at least through 1802," Webster argues that "the role of Romantic musical aesthetics in the rise of this anecdotal tradition must at least be noted. By the 1830s, when the mainstream of this tradition originated . . . Haydn's reputation was already well on its way toward the now debased myth of 'Papa Haydn' from whose debilitating influence we still have not entirely freed ourselves. Schumann's notorious epithet for Haydn, 'gewohnter Hausfreund,' dates from 1841; Marx's 1850 biography of Beethoven (I, 21–24) offers an appalling example of the contempt for and misunderstanding of Haydn that could arise in this atmosphere. The other side of the coin was the veneration of Beethoven as a revolutionary and of his works as the evolutionary goal of Western music. Under such conditions, it must have been all too easy to portray Haydn as the unwitting dupe of the impatient Beethoven." "The Falling-out Between Haydn and Beethoven," in *Beethoven Essays: Studies in Honor of Elliot Forbes*, ed. Lewis Lockwood and Phyllis Benjamin (Cambridge, MA: Harvard University Press, 1984), 27.

4. Webster, *Haydn's "Farewell" Symphony*, 10; see also 123. Webster uses the terms "through-composed" and "cyclic integration" with the following connotations: "'through-composed' for dynamic or gestural phenomena (run-on movements, recalls, unresolved instabilities, lack of closure, and so forth); 'cyclic integration' or 'organization' for aspects of musical construction and technique (commonalities of material, tonal relations, and the like). But in Haydn these domains cannot be meaningfully dissociated, and the reader must not expect total consistency of usage" (7–8).

5. Webster, *Haydn's "Farewell" Symphony* (chap. 5), 123–25. Webster refers to Donald Francis Tovey's writings in general and cites the following: Edward T. Cone, *Musical Form and Musical Performance* (1968); Rosen, *The Classical Style*; Leonard B. Meyer, *Explaining Music: Essays and Explorations* (1973); Fred Everett Maus, "Music as Drama," *Music Theory Spectrum* 10 (1988) (Maus's focal point is the opening of Beethoven's String Quartet Op. 95); and Carolyn Abbate, "What the Sorcerer Said," *19th-Century Music* 12/3 (1989). More astonishing than the absence of Haydn's music in narrative studies is that Webster's own book was the very first comprehensive analytic monograph on a multimovement work by Haydn (see *Haydn's "Farewell" Symphony*, 7).

6. Webster, *Haydn's "Farewell" Symphony*, 368, 370. Having so firmly proclaimed the greater coherence of Haydn's "Farewell," Webster himself seems caught by surprise: "(This point admittedly takes some getting used to. I myself recently opined that it was 'ironic' that Haydn should have outdone Beethoven in this respect. But no irony is entailed; in his music, such integration was always possible)" (370). Kerman's views about Beethoven's

Fifth as cited by Webster are from Joseph Kerman and Alan Tyson, "Beethoven, Ludwig van," in *The New Grove Dictionary of Music and Musicians* (London: Macmillan, 1980), vol. 2, 354–94.

7. Webster, *Haydn's "Farewell" Symphony*, 371. The quoted materials by Lawrence Kramer are from his *Music and Poetry: The Nineteenth Century and After* (1984), 234–35. In his review of Webster's book, W. Dean Sutcliffe pays Webster the following well-deserved compliment: "An unofficial critical consensus seems to direct that it is bad taste, or simply misguided, to equate Haydn with the likes of Bach or Beethoven as a creative genius; Webster's refusal to remain with the bounds of 'good taste' in his assessment represents a major step forward" (*Music Analysis* 13/1 [1994], 131).

8. Elisabeth Eleonore Bauer, *Wie Beethoven auf den Sockel kam: Die Entstehung eines musikalischen Mythos* (Stuttgart and Weimar: J. B. Metzler, 1992); Scott Burnham, *Beethoven Hero* (Princeton, NJ: Princeton University Press, 1995); Tia DeNora, *Beethoven and the Construction of Genius: Musical Politics in Vienna, 1792–1803* (Berkeley: University of California Press, 1995); David B. Dennis, *Beethoven in German Politics, 1870–1989* (New Haven, CT: Yale University Press, 1996); Leon Botstein, "The Search for Meaning in Beethoven: Popularity, Intimacy, and Politics in Historical Perspective," in *Beethoven and His World*, ed. Scott Burnham and Michael P. Steinberg (Princeton, NJ: Princeton University Press, 2000); Stephen Rumph, *Beethoven after Napoleon: Political Romanticism in the Late Works* (Berkeley: University of California Press, 2004); Mark Evan Bonds, *Music as Thought: Listening to the Symphony in the Age of Beethoven* (Princeton, NJ: Princeton University Press, 2006); and Michael Spitzer, *Music as Philosophy: Adorno and Beethoven's Late Style* (Bloomington: Indiana University Press, 2006).

9. Lewis Lockwood, "Beethoven before 1800: The Mozart Legacy," *Beethoven Forum* 3 (1994): 44.

10. Lockwood, *Beethoven: The Music and the Life* (New York: Norton, 2003), 57.

11. Lockwood, *Beethoven*, 59–60; Lockwood, "Beethoven before 1800," 49, 51–52.

12. Lockwood, "Beethoven before 1800," 39–40; Lockwood, *Beethoven*, 57–60.

13. Elaine Sisman, "'The Spirit of Mozart from Haydn's Hands': Beethoven's Musical Inheritance," in *The Cambridge Companion to Beethoven*, ed. Glenn Stanley (Cambridge: Cambridge University Press, 2000), 52; for references to studies on Beethoven's modeling procedures, see 312nn.24–25.

14. Sisman, "The Spirit of Mozart," 52. Sisman's example concerns differences in opinion between Douglas Johnson and Basil Smallman on models for Beethoven's Piano Trio in C Minor, Op. 1, No. 3; see 312n.26.

15. Sisman, "The Spirit of Mozart," 54–56.

16. Sisman, "The Spirit of Mozart," 46, 50.

17. The Quartet Op. 33, No. 3 may be best known by its nickname, *der Vogel* ("Bird"). It was originally published, by Artaria in 1782, as the fourth quartet within op. 33's group of six.

18. Daniel Heartz, *Haydn, Mozart and the Viennese School 1740–1780* (New York: Norton, 1995), 400.

19. In Webster's view, "during these years of declining powers [i.e., between 1800 and 1804], Haydn resented not only Beethoven's 'arrogance' and lack of gratitude, but perhaps also his success in continuing to push forward into new domains of music—domains that he believed would have lain open to him if only his health had not failed" (Webster, "The Falling-out Between Haydn and Beethoven," 28).

20. See especially Gretchen A. Wheelock's engaging discussion of the op. 33 quartets in *Haydn's Ingenious Jesting with Art: Contexts of Musical Wit and Humor* (New York: Schirmer Books, 1992), 14–15, and chap. 5 (90–115).

21. Webster, *Haydn's "Farewell" Symphony*," 163, 131. For Webster's views on op. 33, no. 3, and on the even more destabilized opening of op. 33, no. 1, see 127–31, 143; Webster's table 5.2 (132) lists "Off-tonic openings in [fifteen] Haydn symphony movements (through 1774)."

22. Richard Kramer, *Unfinished Music* (New York: Oxford University Press, 2008), 195.

23. As noted by Daniel Heartz, in both the Scherzando Allegretto (second) movement and the finale of op. 33, no. 3, Haydn "begins by having ii follow I" (*Mozart, Haydn and Early Beethoven 1781–1802* [New York: Norton, 2009], 319). As if to ensure that we notice this advance toward *motivic cyclicism* (see chapter 6 of this volume)—that is, toward Webster's "through-composition," his "integration of the cycle"—Haydn begins the compound basic idea of his Scherzando Allegretto on the inverted tonic (I^6); his consequent begins on ii^6. Webster comments on the "off the tonic" openings of these movements in *Haydn's "Farewell" Symphony*, 212.

24. For examples, consider the robust four-part textures in the first-movement openings of all but the first and second of Haydn's earlier six quartets op. 20 and the openings of the op. 33 quartets, nos. 2, 5, and 6.

25. See William E. Caplin, *Classical Form: A Theory of Formal Functions for the Instrumental Music of Haydn, Mozart, and Beethoven* (New York: Oxford University Press, 1998), 127.

26. Mark Evan Bonds, "The Sincerest Form of Flattery? Mozart's 'Haydn' Quartets and the Question of Influence," *Studi musicali* 22 (1993): 381. For Bonds: "Only in m. 18 do we arrive at a statement squarely in C major. The rhythm becomes more propulsive, the phrases more connected, all four voices participate in the texture, and we at last have a sense that the piece has 'begun'" (381).

27. Webster, *Haydn's "Farewell" Symphony*, 128.

28. James Hepokoski and Warren Darcy's reference to the end of this development section underscores our different approaches to the interpretation of formal boundaries that have been blurred. From the following, it would seem that these authors pinpoint the beginning of Haydn's recapitulation *only* at m. 111: "Also possible are developments that end by tonicizing the minor-mode mediant with a iii:PAC, then proceed to the tonic recapitulation by inflecting the fifth of iii up a half-step (the familiar 5–6 shift) to produce the tonic, thus bypassing a strong dominant, although a brief passage of fill might allude *en passant* to the otherwise 'missing' dominant.... A virtually pure example (though mediated by a brief V4/3) may be found in the first movement of Haydn's Quartet in C, op. 33 no. 3, 'Bird,' mm. 108–11" (*Elements of Sonata Theory: Norms, Types, and Deformations in the Late-Eighteenth-Century Sonata* [New York: Oxford University Press, 2006], 203). Webster makes a distinction between "the thematic reprise (equivalent to m. 1)" that begins at m. 108 and the arrival of the tonic C major in m. 111, "the equivalent of m. 4" (*Haydn's "Farewell" Symphony*, 143). For Richard Kramer, "the moment of recapitulation" would seem to come at m. 108—"at this E with focused intensity...as a naked fifth...then absorbed in the sleight-of-hand return to C major" (*Unfinished Music*, 195; see Kramer's fine graphic summary, 197). My expression "retransition ⇒ recapitulation" eschews the choice of a single point of recapitulation, while lending greater support than does Webster in this case to the idea that "form-as-process" techniques are germane to Haydn's music.

29. In his article about Dahlhaus's *Ludwig van Beethoven*, Webster finds it "refreshing that Dahlhaus links Beethoven's thematic-developmental treatment of sonata form to Haydn's, in opposition to 'architectonic' procedures...obviously, if tacitly, associated with Mozart." But "even the approving references to Haydn turn out to be mere window dressing: more often, Dahlhaus retails the old dogma that it was Beethoven who first problematized musical form, who first composed 'against' the conventions of this time" ("Dahlhaus's *Beethoven* and the Ends of Analysis," *Beethoven Forum* 2 [1993], 211–12).

30. For Hepokoski and Darcy, the convention of a distinct ending for transitions defines the "two-part exposition," in which the transition leads to a medial caesura; see my discussion of this concept in chapter 2 of this volume.

31. See Janet Schmalfeldt, "Towards a Reconciliation of Schenkerian Concepts with Traditional and Recent Theories of Form," *Music Analysis* 10/3 (1991): 260.

32. See Caplin, *Classical Form*, 235 and 237, and Hepokoski and Darcy, *Elements of Sonata Theory*, 398 and 404: the exposition within a sonata-rondo form is *never* repeated, and it is *always* followed by a retransition to the return of the rondo refrain. However, for Hepokoski and Darcy, the finale of Haydn's Trio is a "perfect example" of "playful" Type 3 finales [normative sonata forms] "that have the rondo character (the rondo 'attitude')—or the Type 4 blend [sonata-rondo]—very much on their minds, referencing it in flavor if not in structure" (399).

33. See Wheelock, *Haydn's Ingenious Jesting with Art*, chap. 7, "The Paradox of Distraction."

34. With "codettas ⇒ transition," I assign a new name to Caplin's "false closing section," in which "codettas appear at first to have a post-cadential function in relation to the main theme, but they are then understood retrospectively to initiate…the transition proper" (*Classical Form*, 129). Caplin and I are clearly referring to the same processual technique, with the difference being simply that, for me, there is nothing "false" about the codettas. They begin by functioning as such; they relinquish that role only when, or after, we perceive *in time* that the process of their becoming the beginning of a transition has been under way. The same goes for another of the four ways in which, for Caplin, a transition might begin— "with the opening material of the main theme" (127–28). Typically, this is the familiar case whereby the main theme ends with a half cadence, and the transition then begins as if it would be a consequent, thus "consequent ⇒ transition" for me.

35. All four series of Haydn's piano trios from 1794–95 (with three trios per series) were dedicated to women; the last set, in which the C-major Trio is the first of the group, was dedicated to Therese Jansen Bartolozzi, who "could have become a professional per-former like her teacher Clementi or her friend Dussek," were it not that this "was considered socially demeaning and was eschewed by most women (other than singers)" (Heartz, *Mozart, Haydn and Early Beethoven*, 515).

36. See Caplin, *Classical Form*, 201–2, and 280n.29. For Hepokoski and Darcy, Haydn's finale, like the first movement of Beethoven's "Tempest" Sonata, would provide an example of the "continuous," rather than two-part, exposition: no medial caesura and thus no secondary theme.

37. I take a more playful (and processual) view of Haydn's exposition than does Caplin: my "false start" at m. 54 is, *tout court*, the beginning of Caplin's subordinate theme 1 (ST[1]) (Caplin, *Classical Form*, 280n.29).

38. Compression is in order not only in light of a relatively lengthy development but also because a substantial coda will ensue. Thus, the recapitulation begins not with the complete small-ternary main theme, but only with its "rondo refrain." The transition takes a new excursion through the subdominant to prepare the home dominant, but then the highly abbreviated version of the secondary theme leads directly to the closing section, which in turn prepares the coda.

39. As noted by Mary Hunter, in "Haydn's London Piano Trios and His Salomon String Quartets: Private vs. Public?" (in *Haydn and His World*, ed. Elaine Sisman [Princeton, NJ: Princeton University Press, 1997]), "it is a truism of the Haydn literature that the six string quartets of 1793 are 'public' pieces, while the twelve late piano trios of 1795–96 belong to a 'private' musical sphere" (103). Hunter breaks down these absolute categories by proposing a "private/public continuum" in which the two social spheres are strongly interdependent.

As examples, she cites the "public" gesture of the "fanfare arpeggio" at the beginning of the first movement of the C-major Trio and the "orchestral" effect, comparable to similar gestures in the quartets, of the tutti tremolo in the coda of the finale under discussion (107). On the other hand, Hunter proposes that: "In general, the trios model the act of performance as more continuous with the act of composition than do the quartets" (110). In the case of the ST within the C-major Trio's finale, with its "false start," its "one more time" repetition, and its "detour," my characterization lends support to Hunter's position: here it is as if the pianist, clearly in charge (the string parts carry a minimal role), highlights "the comic or capricious potential of the act of performance" (119).

40. See especially Leon Plantinga, *Clementi: His Life and Music* (London: Oxford University Press, 1977), 5–6.

41. On the "false-recapitulation effect," see Hepokoski and Darcy, *Elements of Sonata Theory*, 221–28. Caplin's examples of the "false recapitulation" all occur in a nontonic key (*Classical Form*, 159, 225, 238, 277n.58). See Mark Evan Bonds, "Haydn's False Recapitulations and the Perception of Sonata Form in the Eighteenth Century" (Ph.D. diss., Harvard University, 1988). For a refutation of the concept in the light of eighteenth-century theoretical writings, see Peter A. Hoyt, "The 'False Recapitulation' and the Conventions of Sonata Form" (Ph.D. diss., University of Pennsylvania, 1999).

42. For example, only the secondary theme in the home key recurs in the second parts of the first movements of Clementi's very early WO 14 (1768), of his revised Oeuvre 1, No. 2 (1780–81), and of his op. 10, no. 1 (1783).

43. Hepokoski and Darcy regard the appearance of Clementi's main theme (primary theme = P) in the dominant minor as the beginning of a "recapitulatory rotation": "Simpler, more schematic examples of recapitulatory rotations that begin in V following a development may be found in the first movements of Clementi's Piano Sonata in F Minor, op. 13 no. 6, and Schubert's Symphony No. 4 in C Minor, D. 417. Both composers were attracted to unorthodox, sometimes flagrantly transgressive, tonal layouts in their sonata forms, and in this case the structures of the two pieces are (coincidentally?) similar" (*Elements of Sonata Theory*, 277).

44. In particular, Tim Carter's discussion of the Act I Trio, like mine, proposes a sonata-form interpretation. Our divergences in respect to formal functions within that plan yield different views about Mozart's dramatic design and its implications. See Tim Carter, *W. A. Mozart: Le Nozze di Figaro* (Cambridge: Cambridge University Press, 1987), 95–104.

45. For the superb idea of an orchestral "cue" at the beginning of Mozart's Trio, see David Lewin, "Music Analysis as Stage Direction," in *Music and Text: Critical Inquiries*, ed. Steven Paul Scher (Cambridge: Cambridge University Press, 1992), 163–76 (reprinted in Lewin, *Studies in Music with Text* [Oxford: Oxford University Press, 2006], 19–30). Lewin's portrayal of the Count in need of a cue leans heavily on the notion that the "dominant-to-tonic cadence on 'sento' is somehow weak and unconvincing" (167). Other theorists, including myself, would offer weight to Lewin's view by arguing that the V7–I progression at mm. 1–5 cannot be construed as a "cadence" of any kind: there has been neither the implication of a cadential function nor a preceding cadential progression, even if one tries to find this by backing up to the last six bars of the preceding recitative, as does Carter, in his *W. A. Mozart: Le Nozze di Figaro*, 95. See Caplin, *Classical Form*, 42–43; and Caplin, "The Classical Cadence: Conceptions and Misconceptions," *Journal of the American Musicological Society* 57/1 (2004): 51–117.

46. In contrast with the Count's opening "angry interjections in dotted rhythms," Basilio provides "the first material with any shape to it"—"a mincing *alla breve*"—for Wye Jamison Allanbrook: "Characters who use the dignified *alla breve* usually put the brakes on more restless rhythms, moving serene and sedate through the most snarled of imbroglios ... Basilio

is on the contrary a spiteful lightweight, with his high tenor voice and his habit of giving every second measure of the *Alla breve* a mincing feminine ending; his assumed dignity is a mock of dignity itself." *Rhythmic Gesture in Mozart: Le Nozze di Figaro and Don Giovanni* (Chicago: University of Chicago Press, 1983), 89. The rhythm of Allanbrook's "feminine ending" is Basilio's sanctimonious appropriation of the Count's rhythm at mm. 5, 7, and 9.

David Lewin was among the first of several to note that Basilio's music (my TR-theme) "recomposes" the opening of Cherubino's aria "No so più, cosa son, cosa faccio," the preceding number in Act I. For Lewin, this appropriation implies that Basilio must have eavesdropped on Cherubino's performance; "knowing or strongly suspecting that Cherubino is presently hiding somewhere in the room, [Basilio] is now making sure that Susanna knows his suspicion and suspects his certain knowledge." Thus "Mozart's Basilio goes far beyond Beaumarchais's and Da Ponte's" (Lewin, "Music Analysis as Stage Direction," 174–75, 168).

47. In Allanbrook's view: "Susanna, in the trio victim and pursued, is given little other material of any substance. Instead her music provides the transition from one harmonic place to another" (*Rhythmic Gesture in Mozart*, 91). We can endow Susanna with greater manipulative resourcefulness by noting that the new material she initiates at m. 24, with its agitated eighth notes, begins *directly* in the sonata's secondary key, the dominant—albeit in its minor, rather than major, mode. As outlined here in table 3.1, two cadential phrases work to bring this full-fledged ST[1] to a close: the deceptive cadence at m. 40 motivates a repetition that arrives at the elided authentic cadence at m. 43. Thus the passage at mm. 24–43 does not carry the role of a mere transition; Basilio's half cadence at m. 23 has already served as the definitive departure from the home tonic.

48. In Carolyn Abbate's *Unsung Voices: Opera and Musical Narrative in the Nineteenth Century* (Princeton, NJ: Princeton University Press, 1991), the Count's recitative within the Trio is portrayed as "axiomatic for operatic narrating in the nineteenth century"—that is, for the type of scene that offers a "monaural" report, while also reflecting upon "the greater performance in which it is embedded" (62–63). The Count gives a report about yesterday's event, but he also pantomimes this: "[T]he coincidence of narrating and enactment has, in fact, created a reflexive moment of peculiar force, for the Count's act of narrating seems to engender the disaster of which it tells" (64). It is the shift from accompanied recitative (mm. 121–28) to the Count's appropriation of Basilio's TR-theme (mm. 129–38) by which "*the music itself* returns precisely at the reflexive moment in the narration, as if to underscore a conjunction both rich and unstable. It is only *in retrospect* [emphasis added] that we hear how the entire recitative whispers sounds from the number, as in the first measures: chords interspersed with talk, but cast into a timbral and gestural recollection of the trio's opening *Tosto andate* (low strings, rumbling with B♭ third figures).... Thus the narration in the Figaro trio dissembles; it plays at monaural narration (straight information, straight recitative) as it builds to a moment at which its reflexivity is revealed as if by magic, and the Count's narrating produces Cherubino out of a chair" (64, 66). As will be noted, I shall offer additional reasons why it is *Basilio*'s music that creates the reflexivity.

49. Carter and I hold differing views on this point. For him, "the return to the home key, B flat major, emphasizes the fact that despite all these events things have hardly changed— the trio scarcely advances the action of the opera—and that we are in effect back where we started in terms of the overall plot" (*W. A. Mozart: Le Nozze di Figaro*, 102).

50. Siegmund Levarie, *Mozart's "Le Nozze di Figaro": A Critical Analysis* (New York: Da Capo Press, 1977), 57. Carter's "joke on our expectations" is the beginning of the "false recapitulation" at m. 101 (*W. A. Mozart: Le Nozze di Figaro*, 101).

51. Mozart's treatment of the TR-theme points to a pervasive technique in classical and later music—the return of materials in contexts wherein their original formal function has changed. As one of countless examples, in the first movement of Mozart's Violin Sonata in

E Minor, K. 304, the standing-on-the-dominant material at mm. 9–12, which functions as the *contrasting middle* (*b*-section) of the small-ternary MT, recurs (transposed) to serve as the *beginning* of ST² (at mm. 59–67); within the development section, the original material returns, now to mark the *end* of the retransition (for which reason it is eliminated within the recapitulation of the MT). Standing-on-the-dominant materials are especially "mobile" in this respect. In that elsewhere within this volume I apply the concept of "becoming" *only* to cases wherein retrospective form-functional reinterpretation is invited over the course of a *single* passage (rather than in later recurrences of that passage), my processual interpretation of Basilio's TR-theme stretches beyond my own conceptual boundaries. Here, however, my maneuver seems justified; I try to capture the changing functions of a theme established in association with a *single* character—Basilio, the chameleon whose verbal maneuvers in this Trio control the dramatic action and thus the formal process.

52. As for the influence of Haydn, Mozart, and Clementi upon Beethoven, Maynard Solomon's comments provide a good summary: "Mozart's influence, which had shaped many of the Bonn works, remained fundamental during the early Vienna years, especially in Beethoven's chamber music for strings and for winds. The absence of personal competition in relation to Mozart permitted Beethoven to express sublimated adoration for the Salzburg master, seeking to become his musical heir, while still sensing the futility of striving for a perfection that had already been attained.... Haydn was the main focus of Beethoven's anxieties, for he was seeking to find a personal voice in a world thoroughly dominated by the older master. Muzio Clementi, too, seems to have caused Beethoven some disquiet: on Clementi's visit to Vienna in 1804, Beethoven refused to make a first call on [him], with the result that the two composers studiously avoided each other." *Beethoven*, 2nd rev. ed. (New York: Schirmer Books, 1998), 128–29.

53. Burnham, *Beethoven Hero*, 64–65.

Chapter 4

1. Franz Gerhard Wegeler and Ferdinand Ries, *Biographische Notizen über Beethoven* (Coblenz, 1838), 82–83; as cited in Alexander Thayer, *Thayer's Life of Beethoven,* rev. and ed. Elliot Forbes (Princeton, NJ: Princeton University Press, 1967), 332.

2. See Thayer, *Thayer's Life of Beethoven*, 333. Within my first presentation of the paper that serves as the basis of this chapter, at the 2005 International Orpheus Academy for Music Theory, in Ghent, violinist Ann Vancoillie brilliantly reenacted Bridgetower's improvised cadenza and performed many other excerpts from the first movement of op. 47 with me. In subsequent presentations of the paper, violinists Rebecca Ansel (School of Music, Ithaca College, 2005), Karma Tomm (Tufts University, 2006), and Peter Zazofsky (School of Music, Boston University, 2006) kindly adopted Vancoillie's role. I am profoundly grateful to these four superb violinists for having helped me bring the memory of George Bridgetower alive.

3. As cited in Sieghard Brandenburg, "Zur Textgeschichte von Beethovens Violinsonate Opus 47," *Musik, Edition, Interpretation: Gedenkschrift Gunthers Henle*, ed. Martin Bente (Munich: Henle, 1980), 111. Others have claimed in passing, but without further discussion, that Beethoven wrote his op. 47 sonata for Bridgetower; see, for example, Josephine R. B. Wright, "George Polgreen Bridgetower: An African Prodigy in England 1789–99," *Musical Quarterly* 66 (1980): 65; Ann-Louise Coldicott, "Beethoven's Musical Environment," in *The Beethoven Compendium: A Guide to Beethoven's Life and Music*, ed. Barry Cooper (London: Thames and Hudson, 1991), 88–89; and Barry Cooper, "Who's Who of Beethoven's Contemporaries," in *The Beethoven Compendium*, 43.

4. Elliot Forbes, in *Thayer's Life of Beethoven*, 333.

5. Brandenburg, "Zur Textgeschichte," 113. The translation is mine, with the gracious help of my colleague Mark DeVoto.

6. From the *Allgemeine musikalische Zeitung*, August 28, 1805, cols. 769–72, as cited in Suhnne Ahn, "Beethoven's Opus 47: Balance and Virtuosity," in *The Beethoven Violin Sonatas: History, Criticism, Performance*, ed. Lewis Lockwood and Mark Kroll (Urbana and Chicago: University of Illinois Press, 2004), 81n.18.

7. F. G. Edwards, "George P. Bridgetower and the Kreutzer Sonata," *Musical Times* 49 (1908): 302–8; Wright, "Bridgetower: An African Prodigy," 67.

8. Edwards, "George P. Bridgetower," 302–3.

9. Clifford D. Panton, *George Augustus Polgreen Bridgetower, Violin Virtuoso and Composer of Color in Late 18th Century Europe* (New York: Edwin Mellen Press, 2005), 8. As acknowledged by Panton, Bridgetower's correct year of birth was confirmed by Betty Matthews, Honorary Archivist for the Royal Society of Musicians ("Letters to the Editor: George Bridgetower," *Musical Times* 122 [1981]: 85).

10. Panton, *Bridgetower*, 5–6, 19–22. As cited by Wright ("Bridgetower: An African Prodigy," 68–69), Hans Volkmann provided evidence that Bridgetower's father probably emigrated, or escaped, to Europe from Barbados (Volkmann, *Beethoven in seinen Beziehungen zu Dresden* [Dresden, 1942], 151). Wright and Panton point out that the name Bridgetower suggests the Barbados seaport of Bridgetown (see Panton, *Bridgetower*, 5). As Panton says, "[I]t would have been very natural for an African to adopt the name of either a place or a family to which he may have been sold" (6).

11. Edwards, "George P. Bridgetower," 303.

12. Edwards, "George P. Bridgetower," 303. "Son talent, aussi vrai que précose, est une des meilleures réponses que l'on puisse faire aux Philosophes qui veulent priver ceux de sa Nation et de sa couleur, de la faculté de se distinguer dans les Arts." Daniel Heartz reports that Bridgetower's Paris début, "at the age of ten," occurred at the Concert Spirituel on April 13, 1789 (*Mozart, Haydn and Early Beethoven 1740–1780* [New York: Norton, 1995], 442).

13. According to Heartz (*Mozart, Haydn and Early Beethoven*, 443), Bridgetower performed a violin concerto on the sixth concert of Johann Peter Salomon's 1791 series in London, in the Hanover Square Rooms on April 15, 1791. Haydn's first appearance in Salomon's concerts, at the keyboard over one of his symphonies, occurred on March 12, Salomon's first concert (438).

14. See Wright, "Bridgetower: An African Prodigy," 79, 70.

15. Edwards, "George P. Bridgetower," 305.

16. Beethoven, *The Letters of Beethoven* (London: Macmillan, 1961), vol. 1, no. 74 (p. 75).

17. Thayer, *Thayer's Life of Beethoven*, 72, 134.

18. See Maynard Solomon, *Beethoven*, 2nd rev. ed. (New York: Schirmer Books, 1998), 77–79. Thayer quotes Carl Czerny (in his contribution to Cocks's *London Musical Miscellany*, August 2, 1852) as follows: "In whatever company he might chance to be, [Beethoven] knew how to produce such an effect upon every hearer that frequently not an eye remained dry, while many would break out into loud sobs; for there was something wonderful in his expression in addition to the beauty and originality of his ideas and his spirited style of rendering them" (*Thayer's Life of Beethoven*, 185).

19. Rudolph Réti, *Thematic Patterns in Sonatas of Beethoven* (New York: Da Capo Press, 1992), chap. 14, "The Thematic Pitch of the *Kreutzer* Sonata," 145–65; Owen Jander, "The 'Kreutzer' Sonata as Dialogue," *Early Music* 16 (1988): 34–49.

20. Ahn, "Beethoven's Opus 47," 64. See also Suhnne Ahn, "Genre, Style, and Compositional Procedure in Beethoven's 'Kreutzer' Sonata, Opus 47" (Ph.D. diss., Harvard University, 1997).

21. See Samuel Wesley's appreciation of Bridgewater's performances of "the matchless and immortal solos of Sebastian Bach," as cited in Edwards, "George P. Bridgetower," 305. As of this writing, it cannot be verified that Bridgetower had already begun to perform Bach's unaccompanied sonatas, or that Beethoven knew them, by 1803. I am grateful, however, to Su Yin Mak for having placed me in touch with Benedict Cruft, violinist and Dean of Music at the School of Music, Hong Kong Academy for Performing Arts; Cruft kindly informed me that Bach's unaccompanied violin sonatas were first published by Simrock in 1802, thus opening up the possibility that Bridgetower gained this first edition when he arrived on the continent that year and thus that he might even have played some of Bach's sonatas for Beethoven.

22. To quote Max Rostal, in his *Beethoven, The Sonatas for Piano and Violin: Thoughts on their Interpretation* (New York: Toccata Press, 1985): "For most violinists this unaccompanied beginning seems a nightmare. A rendition which is truly persuasive in its interpretation demands here enormous concentration and inner calm: like a prologue, it immediately proclaims a great work; indeed, it must announce the necessary atmosphere already with the very first chord" (120). I thank violinist Karma Tomm for offering the following technical observations about the violinist's opening phrase: string crossings between the second and third beats of m. 1 make it difficult to sustain the effect of legato; moreover, extensions in the left hand when moving between those same two beats make for difficulty in accurate intonation (fingers 1 and 2 on F♯–D, to fingers 2 and 4 on D–B). In combination, these two techniques call for intense focus and control.

23. I am indebted to William Rothstein, who, in response to an earlier version of my graph at example 4.3b, kindly offered me a different view of the long-range connection from F at m. 19 to E at m. 27—one that I attempt to represent here. At example 4.3b, level 2 proposes that Beethoven's actual outer-voice counterpoint is a variant of the simpler motion in which the bass ascends in tenths with the upper voice; level 3 summarizes the fundamental progression as ii–V⁷–I in C (III). One remarkable implication of this reading is that the *only* structural home-tonic harmony within Beethoven's main theme is the tonic that marks the cadence at m. 44!

24. William E. Caplin, *Classical Form: A Theory of Formal Functions for the Instrumental Music of Haydn, Mozart, and Beethoven* (New York: Oxford University Press, 1998), 207–8. Caplin notes that: "Problematic in this interpretation, of course, is the lack of tonic prolongation at the end of the presentation" (207). The same must be said for the presentation (at mm. 19–36) within Beethoven's Presto main theme.

25. Caplin, *Classical Form*, 203.

26. Donald Francis Tovey proclaimed the novel major-to-minor motion within the op. 47 introduction as "one of the landmarks in musical history" (*Essays in Musical Analysis: Chamber Music* [London: Oxford University Press, 1944], 135). William Drabkin examines the validity of Tovey's observation in his survey of intra- and inter-movement tonal plans in works by Mozart and Haydn that "are concerned with the relationship of minor to major." See William Drabkin, "The Introduction to Beethoven's 'Kreutzer' Sonata: A Historical Perspective," in *The Beethoven Violin Sonatas: History, Criticism, Performance*, ed. Lewis Lockwood and Mark Kroll (Urbana and Chicago: University of Illinois Press, 2004), 83–107. As Drabkin notes, the one "frequently invoked" precedent for Beethoven's permanent shift from major to minor *within* an opening Adagio arises in Mozart's remarkable Violin Sonata in G Major, K. 379 (1781); but Drabkin is reluctant to regard Mozart's Adagio as an introduction (88). This Adagio promises to be a self-contained sonata form in G major, complete with a repeated exposition. A development section arrives on the home dominant, followed by a standing-on-that-dominant that now inflects the minor mode; in the place of a recapitulation, a full-fledged sonata-form Allegro ensues in G minor. In debate with Drabkin (and in apparent agreement with Lewis Lockwood; see his "Beethoven before 1800," 48) I suggest that here might be a case of the incomplete "slow movement ⇒ Introduction"; Mozart's

innovative request for retrospective reinterpretation seems undeniable. The second movement of K. 379, in variation form, restores the tonic major. For later, more straightforward examples of "slow movement ⇒ Introduction," see Beethoven's "Waldstein" Piano Sonata in C Major, Op. 53, and his Sonata for Piano and Cello in A Major, Op. 69.

Coincidentally, Mozart, like Beethoven with his op. 47, barely managed to complete K. 379 the night before its première: "but in order to be able to finish it, I only wrote out the accompaniment for Brunetti and retained my own part in my head." Mozart, *The Letters of Mozart and His Family*, April 8, 1781, to his father (no. 397), as cited in Maynard Solomon, *Mozart: A Life* (New York: HarperCollins, 1995), 309, 564n.27.

27. See, for instance, Réti, *Thematic Patterns*, 153.

28. Lawrence Kramer, *After the Lovedeath: Sexual Violence and the Making of Culture* (Berkeley: University of California Press, 1997), 82, 215. Kramer regards the "second theme" at mm. 91–116 as one that defers the continuation of the "first theme." In short, he does not note that the "first theme" has closed in m. 45.

29. From within Beethoven's piano sonatas, for example, the rolled B♭ chord at the beginning of the slow movement of the "Tempest" Sonata unequivocally recalls the rolled chord with which the first movement begins (as well as the other rolled chords within that movement—at m. 7, at the beginning of the development section, and within the recapitulation). The opening stepwise descent in D major from $\hat{5}$ to the octave below at the beginning of the "Pastorale" Piano Sonata, Op. 28 (1801) looks forward to the simpler, shorter descent, now fundamentally from $\hat{5}$ to $\hat{1}$, within the initial basic idea of the finale. This relatively strong connection might retrospectively give substance to the idea that the fleeting stepwise $\hat{5}$-to-$\hat{1}$ descent at the beginning of the Andante, in D minor, relates to the openings of both the first and last movements in op. 28.

30. Réti, *Thematic Patterns*, 158–59.

31. Kramer, *After the Lovedeath*, 41.

32. Leo Tolstoy, *The Kreutzer Sonata and Other Stories*, trans. David McDuff (Harmondsworth: Penguin Books, 1985), 96–98; and Tolstoy, *The Kreutzer Sonata and Other Stories*, trans. Louise and Aylmer Maude and J. D. Duff (Oxford: Oxford University Press, 1997), 144, 145.

33. Kramer, *After the Lovedeath*, 79.

34. Richard Leppert, *The Sight of Sound: Music, Representation, and the History of the Body* (Berkeley: University of California Press, 1993), 176.

35. Kramer, *After the Lovedeath*, 238. An exception is the case of Regina Strinasacchi (1761–1829), the brilliant and famous young Mantuan violinist for whom Mozart composed his Violin Sonata in B-flat, K. 454, and with whom he premièred that work at the Kärntnertortheater in the presence of Emperor Joseph II on April 28, 1784. I am grateful to several colleagues, and in particular to Elaine Sisman, for alerting me to the phenomenon of Strinasacchi.

36. See Beethoven, *The Letters of Beethoven*, nos. 74 and 75 (91–92).

37. See Brandenburg, "Zur Textgeschichte," 114.

38. Thayer, *Thayer's Life of Beethoven*, 333.

39. See Solomon, *Beethoven*, 169–70.

40. Rita Dove, distinguished U.S. Poet Laureate (1993–95), has taken this opportunity; see her poem "The Bridgetower" (*New Yorker* 2008) and her *Sonata Mulattica* (2009).

Chapter 5

1. Jim Samson, "Analysis in Context," in *Rethinking Music*, ed. Nicholas Cook and Mark Everist (Oxford: Oxford University Press, 1999), 49.

2. Schmalfeldt, "On the Relation of Analysis to Performance: Beethoven's Bagatelles Op. 126, Nos. 2 and 5," *Journal of Music Theory* 29/1 (1985): 1–31.

3. See Lawrence Rosenwald, "Theory, Text-setting, and Performance," *Journal of Musicology* 11/1 (1993), 69; Joel Lester, "Performance and Analysis: Interaction and Interpretation," in *The Practice of Performance: Studies in Musical Interpretation*, ed. John Rink (Cambridge: Cambridge University Press, 1995), 198; and Nicholas Cook, "Analysing Performance and Performing Analysis," in *Rethinking Music*, ed. Nicholas Cook and Mark Everist (Oxford: Oxford University Press, 1999), 246.

4. My live performance of Beethoven's op. 126 was broadcast in 1984 by the Canadian Broadcasting Corporation (CBC) in Montréal.

5. In this respect I would seem to be an exception to John Rink's rule that "the division into split personalities hardly reflects how most musicians operate." Rink, "Analysis and (or?) Performance," in *Musical Performance: A Guide to Understanding*, ed. John Rink (Cambridge: Cambridge University Press, 2002), 36.

6. See, for example, Suzanne Cusick, "Feminist Theory, Music Theory, and the Mind/ Body Problem," *Perspectives of New Music* 32/1 (1994): 8–27. Cusick discusses Fanny Hensel's Piano Trio in D Minor.

7. "If nothing else, it must be remembered that musical 'feeling' for the performer is an amalgam of emotion and intelligence, of response and control, of empathy and command, of the autonomic and proprioceptive (to use more technical physiological terms). To put this point at its simplest but also its most profound, and in a way that we can all somehow grasp, 'feeling' is an amalgam of being and doing." Jonathan Dunsby, "Performers on Performance," in *Musical Performance: A Guide to Understanding*, ed. John Rink (Cambridge: Cambridge University Press, 2002), 226.

8. Authors frequently cited in this respect are Eugene Narmour, "On the Relationship of Analytical Theory to Performance and Interpretation," in *Explorations in Music, the Arts, and Ideas*, ed. Eugene Narmour and Ruth A. Solie (Stuyvesant, NY: Pendragon, 1988), 317–40; and Wallace Berry, *Musical Structure and Performance* (New Haven, CT: Yale University Press, 1989).

9. Lester, "Performance and Analysis," 197.

10. Cook, "Analysing Performance and Performing Analysis," 247, 242–44, 255–58.

11. "Indeed, the public may be surprised to find that performance itself typically occupies a rather small part of performers' attention. Actual performance is the tip of an iceberg of performers' practice and rehearsal, which in countless different ways is the 'analytical' level of music-making, the time when everything is put in place mentally and physically for the on-stage 'calculation' that has but one opportunity to be right. Otherwise, one is 'just playing.'" Dunsby, "Performers on Performance," 232–33.

12. See Carolyn Abbate, "Music—Drastic or Gnostic?", *Critical Inquiry* 30/3 (2004): 505–36.

13. Neurologist and music lover Oliver Sacks has awakened the general public to an interest in the phenomenal, and often inexplicable, musical skills and powers that he proposes may be innate in all of human nature, including musicians, patients, and everyone else. See his *Musicophilia: Tales of Music and the Brain* (New York: Vintage Books, 2007).

14. Maurice J. E. Brown, with Eric Sams (Work-List), *The New Grove Schubert* (New York: Norton, 1983), 49–50 (first published in *The New Grove Dictionary of Music and Musicians*, 1980). See also William Kinderman, "Schubert's Piano Music," in *The Cambridge Companion to Schubert*, ed. Christopher H. Gibbs (Cambridge: Cambridge University Press, 1997), 157–59.

15. For a probing discussion of Schubert's unfinished Sonata in F Minor, D. 625 (from the summer of 1818), see Richard Kramer, *Unfinished Music* (Oxford: Oxford University Press, 2008), 325–28.

16. Otto Erich Deutsch, *Schubert: A Documentary Biography* (reprint, New York: Da Capo Press, 1977), 264–65.

17. John M. Gingerich, "Schubert's Beethoven Project: The Chamber Music, 1824–1828" (Ph.D. diss., Yale University, 1996), 124.

18. The seminal essay on Schubert's sexuality and his illness is by Maynard Solomon, "Franz Schubert and the Peacocks of Benvenuto Cellini," *19th-Century Music* 12/3 (1989): 193–206. For responses to this study, see *19th-Century Music* 12/1 (1993), a special issue titled "Schubert: Music, Sexuality, Culture," edited by Lawrence Kramer, which includes articles by Rita Steblin, Maynard Solomon, Kristina Muxfeldt, and David Gramit, with commentaries by Kofi Agawu, Susan McClary, James Webster, and Robert Winter.

19. Deutsch, *Schubert: A Documentary Biography*, 338–40.

20. See the title of Gingerich's dissertation, note 17 above.

21. Charles Fisk, *Returning Cycles: Contexts for the Interpretation of Schubert's Impromptus and Last Sonatas* (Berkeley: University of California Press, 2001), 203, 271–77, 283.

22. Carl Dahlhaus, *Ludwig van Beethoven: Approaches to His Music* (Oxford: Clarendon, 1991), 170; see chapter 2 of this volume.

23. A clear and impressive precedent for this discussion is Janet M. Levy's "Beginning-ending Ambiguity: Consequences of Performance Choices," in *The Practice of Performance: Studies in Musical Interpretation* (Cambridge: Cambridge University Press, 1995), 150–69. Levy explores "functional ambiguities" in passages from Haydn, Mozart, and Beethoven that suggest "*double entendres,*" "puns," and formal "overlaps" ("dovetailed *processes*"). For Levy, these cases of ambiguity "need not—indeed should not—be resolved. The choice of the performer to let ambiguity 'live' releases the power to shape and enrich musical experience" (168). By contrast, instances of cadential ambiguity in Schubert's op. 42 under consideration here would seem to require either/or, rather than both/and, choices for the pianist.

24. See William E. Caplin, "The Classical Cadence: Conceptions and Misconceptions," *Journal of the American Musicological Society* 57/1 (2004): 86–96.

25. Andreas Staier, fortepiano (Teldec 0630-11084-2, 1996); Maurizio Pollini (Deutsche Grammophon LP 2530 473).

26. Richard Goode (Elektra Nonesuch 79271-2, 1993); András Schiff (London/Decca 440 305-2, 1993).

27. For the small binary as a common type of theme, see William E. Caplin, *Classical Form: A Theory of Formal Functions for the Instrumental Music of Haydn, Mozart, and Beethoven* (New York: Oxford University Press, 1998), chap. 7. For the distinction between "cadential" and "postcadential," see Caplin, "The Classical Cadence," 89–96.

28. See Steven Laitz, "The Submediant Complex: Its Musical and Poetic Roles in Schubert's Songs," *Theory and Practice* 21 (1996): 123–65. Laitz identifies the $\hat{5}$–$\sharp\hat{5}$–$\hat{6}$ motive and its retrograde in major, minor, and relative- and parallel-key contexts. See also Jeremy Day-O'Connell, "The Rise of $\hat{6}$ in the Nineteenth Century," *Music Theory Spectrum* 24/1 (2002): 35–67, for the history and "reception," in both theory and practice, of $\hat{6}$ (and its relation to $\hat{5}$) in the major scale; and Day-O'Connell, *On Pentatonicism from the Eighteenth Century to Debussy* (Rochester, NY: University of Rochester Press, 2007).

29. A famous precedent for this pitch-specific clash arises at mm. 276–79 in the development section of the first movement of Beethoven's Third Symphony. See also the beginning of Beethoven's second main theme (MT[2]), m. 32, in the finale of his Quartet in A Minor, Op. 132, composed, like Schubert's op. 42, in 1825.

30. William Rothstein, "Analysis and the Act of Performance," in *The Practice of Performance: Studies in Musical Interpretation*, ed. John Rink (Cambridge: Cambridge University Press, 1995), 202.

31. The name "omnibus" for the progression with chromatic voice exchange heard in Schubert's mm. 36–37 originates in a paper by Victor Fell Yellin in 1972 (Yellin traces his awareness of the term to Roger Martinez of the University of San Juan); see Yellin, *The Omnibus Idea* (Warren, MI: Harmonie Park Press, 1998). See also Paula J. Telesco, "Enharmonicism and the Omnibus Progression in Classical-Era Music," *Music Theory Spectrum* 20/2 (1998): 242–79.

32. See Janet Schmalfeldt, "Cadential Processes: The Evaded Cadence and the 'One More Time' Technique," *Journal of Musicological Research* 12 (1992): 1–52. In classical styles, it is unusual, however, for the "one-more-time" technique to effect a backing-up all the way to the beginning of a theme.

33. Peter H. Smith, "Structural Tonic or Apparent Tonic?: Parametric Conflict, Temporal Perspective, and a Continuum of Articulative Possibilities," *Journal of Music Theory* 39/2 (1995): 273–74.

34. For "core" and "pre-core," see Caplin, *Classical Form*, chap. 10, "Development," 141–55. Caplin's glossary gives the following: "core—A themelike unit of a development consisting of a relatively large model (4–8 mm.), one or more sequential repetitions, fragmentation, a concluding half cadence (or dominant arrival), and a postcadential standing on the dominant" (254); "pre-core—The initial unit of a development section, preceding a core or core substitute" (256). Caplin's terms draw upon Erwin Ratz's "core of the development" (*Kern der Durchführung*), in his *Einführung in die Musikalische Formenlehre: Über Formprinzipien in den Inventionen und Fugen J. S. Bachs und ihre Bedeutung für die Kompositionstechnik Beethovens* (Vienna: Universal, 1973), 33.

35. Kramer, *Unfinished Music*, 359.

36. Adopting Alfred Brendel's insight "To wander is the Romantic condition" as a motto (*Music as Sounded Out: Essays, Lectures, Interviews, Afterthoughts* [1990], 86), Richard Kramer presents a brilliant case for the view that, in the op. 42 sonata, as with the unfinished sonatas D. 571, D. 625, and D. 840 (the "Reliquie"), Schubert manifests "a profound disquiet at the idea of reprise. One senses a reluctance to return—an unwillingness to celebrate [like Beethoven] the advance to the tonic, to concede, in the return to the opening music of the sonata, that this music is *about* the tonic.... The return home, a return imposed by the deepest theoretical conditions of sonata, is now questioned at its root, probed, problematized" (*Unfinished Music*, 259–61). I cannot describe Schubert's hard-earned achievement of the structural, recapitulatory tonic at m. 186 as a "celebration," but here, as well as in his coda (to be discussed), the ever-increasing intensity with which he advances to the home tonic suggests the portrayal of a willful determination to gain the goal rather than simply probe the problem. I hold as well that Schubert's recapitulatory strategy in this movement cannot be fully addressed outside the context of his opening measures.

37. Scott Burnham, "Landscape as Music, Landscape as Truth: Schubert and the Burden of Repetition," *19th-Century Music* 29/1 (2005): 40.

38. Theodor Adorno, "Schubert (1928)," *19th-Century Music* 29/1 (2005): 11.

39. Jonathan Dunsby and Beate Perrey, introduction to Adorno, "Schubert (1928)," 4.

40. Rolf Tiedemann also proposes that Adorno is probably referring here to the Sonata op. 42; see his comment in Adorno, *Beethoven: The Philosophy of Music* (Stanford: Stanford University Press, 1998), 236n.264.

41. Adorno, "Schubert (1928)," 11.

42. Adorno, "Schubert (1928)," 11.

43. Richard Leppert, "On Reading Adorno Hearing Schubert," *19th-Century Music* 29/1 (2005): 58.

44. For Adorno, "the countless anecdotes that tell us of the premonitions of death that Schubert the person may have had are of hardly any significance. Much more important is

his choice of texts.... Remember that both of the great cycles are stimulated by poems in which again and again images of death appear before the person who sees them and who wanders among them as demeaned as the Schubert of *Lilac Time*" (Adorno, "Schubert (1928)," 10).

45. Gingerich, "Schubert's Beethoven Project," 231–32.

Chapter 6

1. Ludwig van Beethoven, *The Letters of Beethoven* (London: Macmillan, 1961), no. 228; *Ludwig van Beethoven: Briefwechsel, Gesamtausgabe* (1996---), "no. 408 (November 22 [not 2], 1809)," as cited in Maynard Solomon, *Beethoven* (New York: Schirmer Books, 1998), 53 and 439n.20.

This chapter is an expanded version of the keynote address I presented at the Sixth Conference of the Dutch Society for Music Theory, in Utrecht on February 20, 2004. I am grateful to Bert Mooiman for assisting me on that occasion in the performance of Schubert's *Allegro* in A Minor for Four Hands (*Lebensstürme*), and for the superb performances of excerpts from Schubert's Piano Trio in E-flat Major provided by three students from the Utrecht School of the Arts.

2. "das Moralische Gesetz in uns, u. der gestirnte Himmel über uns' Kant!!!" For the apparent source of this entry in Beethoven's conversation book, and for its potential relevance to his *Missa solemnis* as well as other works from the 1820s, see William Kinderman, *Beethoven* (Berkeley: University of California Press, 1995), 238–39, 281–82.

3. Charles Taylor, *Sources of the Self: The Making of the Modern Identity* (Cambridge, MA: Harvard University, 1989), 364–65.

4. See Taylor, *Sources of the Self*, 111–14. See also James H. Donelan, *Poetry and the Romantic Musical Aesthetic* (Cambridge: Cambridge University Press, 2008), in which the chief topic is Romantic "self-consciousness." For Donelan, this concept "emerged as the central principle of Idealist epistemology in a demonstrable progression from Kant's distinction between a priori and empirical knowledge, to Fichte's assertion of the self-positing subject, and from there to Hölderlin's and Hegel's (and possibly Schelling's) reworking of the idea in their early joint project in aesthetics, the *Systemprogramm* fragment" (xiii).

5. M. H. Abrams, *The Mirror and the Lamp: Romantic Theory and the Critical Tradition* (London: Oxford University Press, 1953). See also Abrams, *Natural Supernaturalism: Tradition and Revolution in Romantic Literature* (New York: Norton, 1971).

6. Taylor, *Sources of the Self*, 369.

7. Taylor, *Sources of the Self*, 374–75.

8. Taylor, *Sources of the Self*, 377; for the dissolving of a distinction between the ethical and the aesthetic, see 373.

9. From E. T. A. Hoffmann's review of Beethoven's Fifth Symphony in *Musical Writings: "Kreisleriana," "The Poet and the Composer," Music Criticism* (Cambridge: Cambridge University Press, 1989), 239 (see chapter 2 of this volume).

10. This was the dedicatory message to Archduke Rudolphe that Beethoven wrote on the autograph score of his *Missa Solemnis*; see Solomon, *Beethoven*, 272.

11. Friedrich Schiller, "Über Matthissons Gedichte" (1794), in his *Werke und Briefe* (Frankfurt/Main: Deutscher Klassiker Verlag, 1988–2004), vol. 8, 1024–25: "Nun besteht aber der ganze Effekt der Musik...darin, die inneren Bewegungen des Gemüts durch analogische äussere zu begleiten und zu versinnlichen....Dringt nun der Tonsetzer und der Landschaftmaler in das Geheimnis jener Gesetze ein, welche über die innern Bewegungen des menschlichen Herzens walten,...so wird er aus einem Bildner gemeiner Natur zum

wahrhaften Seelenmaler." As cited and translated in Mark Evan Bonds, "Idealism and the Aesthetics of Instrumental Music at the Turn of the Nineteenth Century," *Journal of Musicology* 50/2–3 (1997), 400, and in Bonds, *Music as Thought: Listening to the Symphony in the Age of Beethoven* (Princeton, NJ: Princeton University Press, 2006), 18, and 124n.40 (emphasis added).

12. Johann Gottfried Herder, *Kalligone* (1800), pt. 2, in his *Sämmtliche Werke* (Berlin: Weidmann, 1877–1913), vol. 22, 187: "Denn sie [Musik] ist Geist, verwandt mit der grossen Natur innersten Kraft, der Bewegung." As cited and translated in Bonds, "Idealism," 409, and in Bonds, *Music as Thought*, 25, and 127n.67 (emphasis added).

13. August Wilhelm Schlegel, *Vorlesungen über schöne Literatur und Kunst* (1801–2), Erster Teil: *Die Kunstlehre*, in his *Kritische Ausgabe der Vorlesungen*, vol. 1: *Vorlesungen über Ästhetik I (1798–1803)* (Paderborn: Ferdinand Schöningh, 1989), 375: "[Musik] selbige ohne Bezug auf Gegenstände bloss nach ihrer Form in unserm inner Sinn darstellt; und lässt sie…in reinerem Aether athmen." As cited and translated in Bonds, "Idealism," 405, and in Bonds, *Music as Thought*, 21, and 126n.52 (emphasis added).

14. Susan McClary, *Conventional Wisdom: The Content of Musical Form* (Berkeley: University of California Press, 2000), 71, 73.

15. McClary, *Conventional Wisdom*, 102.

16. McClary, *Conventional Wisdom*, 105 (emphasis added).

17. McClary, *Conventional Wisdom*, 118–19, 122.

18. Lawrence Kramer, *Franz Schubert: Sexuality, Subjectivity, Song* (Cambridge: Cambridge University Press, 1998), 28, 5.

19. Kramer, *Franz Schubert*, 28.

20. Kramer, *Franz Schubert*, 10, 29–31, 21, 32.

21. Maurice J. E. Brown, with Eric Sams (Work-List), *The New Grove Schubert* (New York: Norton, 1983), 64; Alfred Einstein, *Schubert: The Man and His Music* (Frogmore: Panther, 1971; orig. publ., 1951), 315.

22. Just whether the expanded cadential idea beginning at m. 7 leads to a half cadence or results in an evaded cadence is a matter of debate. If we hear the dominant as the goal, we hear a half cadence, yet the hypermetric strong-bar stress on the cadential six-four at m. 9 and its resolution to a dominant-seventh chord perhaps more strongly suggest that an authentic cadence is being promised but denied. By "deleting" the silence and imagining the first bar of m. 12 to begin, via cadential elision, directly at m. 11, we can more fully appreciate the potency of the silence itself. Performers who wish to project the effect of an evaded cadence at mm. 9–11 will want to minimize a *ritardando* at m. 10, as if pressing on but then being caught by surprise at the absence of authentic closure. For other examples in which performers are "in charge" of conveying potential closure or the lack therefore, see the discussion of Schubert's A-minor Piano Sonata, Op. 42, in chapter 5 of this volume.

23. Problematic in this interpretation, from the perspective of the *classical* small ternary form, is the following: "An examination of the classical repertory reveals that the contrasting middle [B-section] never elides with the exposition [A-section]" (William E. Caplin, *Classical Form: A Theory of Formal Functions for the Instrumental Music of Haydn, Mozart, and Beethoven* [New York: Oxford University Press, 1998], 75). Given the immediate introduction of MT²'s basic idea in the bass at m. 23, then imitated in the alto at m. 24, I cannot deny the effect of elision at the beginning of m. 23. On this basis, Caplin has suggested (private exchange) that what follows, at mm. 23–36, might be regarded as the first part of a *two-part transition*, the second of which occurs over the span of mm. 37–59ff. But he and I agree that the idea of *two* nonmodulating transitions in this exposition complicates the process. I shall hold, then, that Schubert's unusual, postclassical procedure can best be

compared with the case in which the potential A´-section of a MT small-ternary form becomes the beginning of the "real" transition, thus "A´ ⇒ transition."

24. The quadruple counterpoint has been noted in Brian Newbould, *Schubert: The Music and the Man* (Berkeley: University of California Press, 1997), 400.

25. Schubert's earlier instance is in the first movement of his unfinished "Reliquie" Sonata in C Major, D. 840 (1825), not published until 1861; the modulating ST^1 in this major-mode movement begins in B minor—that is, vii♯5. See Newbould, *Schubert*, 393; see also Kramer, *Unfinished Music*, for whom the return to B minor and then B major within the development is suggestive "of *Aufhebung*, in all the senses comprised in that Hegelian concept: at once of elevation (even in the mystical sense) and dissolution" (353).

26. On this point, see Margaret Notley, "Schubert's Social Music: The 'Forgotten Genres,'" in *The Cambridge Companion to Schubert*, ed. Christopher H. Gibbs (Cambridge: Cambridge University Press, 1997), 148.

27. Thomas Christensen, "Four-Hand Piano Transcription and Geographies of Nineteenth-Century Musical Reception," *Journal of the American Musicological Society* 52/2 (1999): 284–85, 276. See also Philip Brett, "Piano Four-Hands: Schubert and the Performance of Gay Male Desire," *19th-Century Music* 21/2 (1997): 149–76.

28. Kramer, *Franz Schubert*, 29.

29. Robert Schumann, *On Music and Musicians* (New York: McGraw-Hill, 1946), 121.

30. See Scott Burnham, *Beethoven Hero* (Princeton, NJ: Princeton University Press, 1995); and Karol Berger, "Beethoven and the Aesthetic State," *Beethoven Forum* 7 (1999): 43. See also Berger, *Bach's Cycle, Mozart's Arrow: An Essay on the Origins of Musical Modernity* (Berkeley: University of California Press, 2007), 340.

31. The process by which "slow movement ⇒ Introduction" can be considered a reversal of the technique whereby "Introduction ⇒ MT." See references to other examples in chapter 4, note 26.

For a discussion of the song cycle *An die ferne Geliebte* (1816), Beethoven's only vocal essay in "formal cyclicism," see chapter 9 this volume. Elaine Sisman addresses this piece and the two additional works of 1815–16—op. 102, no. 1, and op. 101— in which Beethoven explores "intermovement returns"; see Sisman, "Memory and Invention at the Threshold of Beethoven's Late Style," in *Beethoven and His World*, ed. Scott Burnham and Michael P. Steinberg (Princeton, NJ: Princeton University Press, 2000), 51–87. It should be clear that Sisman's table 1 (52) and my table 6.1 were conceived independently, their similarities notwithstanding. Whereas I include works in which slow introductions would initially seem to function as independent movements, Sisman's table 1 purports to list only those pieces with "thematic returns that take place between movements" (Sisman, "Memory and Invention," 52); thus, she does not include Beethoven's String Quartet Op. 18, No. 6 (*La malinconia*), instead grouping that work with others (op. 13, op. 70, no. 2, op. 130, and op. 135) in which the composer brings back a slow introduction within the *same* movement (53). As an apparent exception, Sisman's table 1 includes op. 110, even though the author acknowledges that "the return of the Arioso dolente and fugue are virtually part of the same movement" (79). More important, Sisman's essay places all of Beethoven's formally cyclic works within the context of "overlapping domains of fantasy, image, invention, and memory" (58), whereas I am particularly concerned with works that feature recollections within finales of slow movements as moments of interiority.

32. Berger, "Beethoven and the Aesthetic State," 38, 36; Berger, *Bach's Cycle*, 334–35.

33. Note J. W. N. Sullivan's observation about Beethoven's last quartets, as applied by William Kinderman to op. 110: the whole work seems to "radiate, as it were, from a central experience." Kinderman, "Integration and Narrative Design in Beethoven's Piano Sonata in A-flat Major, Opus 110," *Beethoven Forum* 1 (1992), 112.

34. See Kinderman, "Integration and Narrative Design," 124.

35. "Se solen sjunker ner" was either composed or notated and arranged from folk sources by Isaak Albert Berg. It has been reproduced in Stephen E. Hefling and David S. Tartakoff, "Schubert's Chamber Music," in *Nineteenth-Century Chamber Music*, ed. Stephen E. Hefling (New York: Routledge, 2004), 117–18; the source is Manfred Willfort, "Das Urbild des Andante aus Schuberts Klaviertrio Es-Dur, D 929," *Österreichische Musikzeitschrift* 33 (1978). Benta Bob's translation appears in Hefling and Tartakoff, "Schubert's Chamber Music," 116.

36. Lawrence Kramer, *Musical Meaning: Toward a Critical History* (Berkeley: University of California Press, 2002), 265; Kramer, *Franz Schubert*, 158; Leo Treitler, "Language and the Interpretation of Music," in *Music and Meaning*, ed. Jenefer Robinson (Ithaca, NY: Cornell University Press, 1997), 47.

37. Kramer, *Franz Schubert*, 158. In his *Musical Meaning*, Kramer makes the correct association—of the Swedish song with the Andante's main theme (265).

38. Maynard Solomon, "Franz Schubert's 'My Dream,'" *American Imago* 38 (1981): 137–54; Charles Fisk, *Returning Cycles: Contexts for the Interpretation of Schubert's Impromptus and Last Sonatas* (Berkeley: University of California Press, 2001), 8–10. For the full text of Schubert's "Mein Traum" in translation, see Otto Erich Deutsch, *Schubert: A Documentary Biography* (reprint, New York: Da Capo, 1977), 226–28.

39. Fisk, *Returning Cycles*, 111, 278–82. As further examples, Fisk mentions the slow movements of Schubert's String Quartet in G Major (D. 887; 1826) and the piano sonatas in C major (D. 840; 1825), D major (D. 850; 1825), and G major (D. 894; 1826).

40. For a comparable formal and dramatic design, see Schubert's Impromptu in C Minor, Op. 90 (D. 899; 1827).

41. Newbould, *Schubert*, 372.

42. Treitler, "Language and the Interpretation of Music," 47; Kramer, *Franz Schubert*, 158.

43. Kramer, *Franz Schubert*, 157.

44. The descending leaps within both the Andante idea and the finale's ST[1] in fact pervade and characterize what I regard as the finale's ST[2] (mm. 121–37) and ST[3] (mm. 137–63, EC). Consider, for example, the basic idea of ST[2] in the violin at mm. 121–24, where the upbeat-downbeat descending leaps now ever more strongly invoke the initial falling third of the Andante's cadential idea.

45. See John Gingerich, "Schubert's Beethoven Project: The Chamber Music, 1824–1828" (Ph.D. diss., Yale University, 1996), chap. 6: "Narrative Strategy and 'Heavenly Length': The Two Last Movements of the E-flat Piano Trio" (338–63). For a recording of Schubert's uncut version of the finale, Gingerich cites the Golub-Kaplan-Carr Trio, *Schubert Works for Piano Trio* (New York, 1988; Arabeske Z6580-2). The Mozartean Players (Harmonia Mundi, HCX 3957095; 1995, 2001) and the Altenberg Trio Wien (Vanguard Classics, 99134; 1996) have also recorded the uncut version.

46. Kramer, *Franz Schubert*, 167, 155, 158, 171.

Chapter 7

1. Robert Schumann, "Trio für Pianoforte mit Begleitung," in *Gesammelte Schriften über Musik und Musiker*, 5th ed., Martin Kreisig (Leipzig 1914), I, 500; as translated in Schumann, *On Music and Musicians* (New York: McGraw-Hill, 1946), 217.

2. Goethe's pronouncement appears in Karl Mendelssohn-Bartholdy, ed., *Goethe and Mendelssohn (1821–1831)* (1970; orig. publ. 1874), 17, as cited in R. Larry Todd, *Mendelssohn:*

A Life in Music (Oxford: Oxford University Press, 2003), 89. Todd's account (87–89) of Felix's two "trials" draws upon a report by one of the attendants, Ludwig Rellstab, in his *Aus meinem Leben* (Berlin, 1861), vol. 2, 135–48.

3. Heinrich Heine, "Dritter Brief aus Berlin," *Sämtliche Werke*, ed. K. Briegleb (Munich, 1959), vol. 2, 59 (June 7, 1822), as cited in Todd, *Mendelssohn*, 104.

4. Charles Rosen, *The Romantic Generation* (Cambridge: Harvard University Press, 1995), 569.

5. Richard Taruskin, *The Oxford History of Western Music*, vol. 3, *The Nineteenth Century* (Oxford: Oxford University Press, 2005), 179; Robert Levin (with Yehudi Wyner), in a recorded radio interview with Cathy Fuller on Boston's WGBH station, February 2005. In an essay during Mendelssohn's birth-year bicentennial in 2009, Alex Ross celebrates "the most amazing child prodigy in music history" but adds, "'What about Mozart,' you may ask?" Ross then cites a variant of Goethe's pronouncement quoted above, noting that Goethe "gave the palm to young Felix." See Ross, "The Youngest Master: Mendelssohn at Two Hundred," *New Yorker*, February 23, 2009: 77.

6. Todd, *Mendelssohn*, 49.

7. Todd, *Mendelssohn*, 44, 57, 49.

8. Todd, *Mendelssohn*, 176–79. See also R. Larry Todd, "The Chamber Music of Mendelssohn," in *Nineteenth-Century Chamber Music*, ed. Stephen E. Hefling (New York: Routledge, 2004), 185–88. Greg Vitercik gives a detailed critical account of "the relation, on almost a moment-by-moment basis," between Mendelssohn's op. 13 and Beethoven's op. 132; see Vitercik, *The Early Works of Felix Mendelssohn: A Study in the Romantic Sonata Style* (Philadelphia: Gordon and Breach, 1992), 227–67.

9. Rosen, *The Romantic Generation*, 575–78, 570.

10. Elaine Sisman, "'The Spirit of Mozart from Haydn's Hands': Beethoven's Musical Inheritance," in *The Cambridge Companion to Beethoven*, ed. Glenn Stanley (Cambridge: Cambridge University Press, 2000), 45 (see the discussion of her essay in chapter 3 of this volume). For further interpretation of Waldstein's statement relative to Haydn, see Sisman, "'The Spirit of Mozart from Haydn's Hands,'" 50–51, and Lockwood, "Beethoven before 1800: The Mozart Legacy." *Beethoven Forum* 3 (1994): 42–43.

11. Leon Botstein, "Neoclassicism, Romanticism, and Emancipation: The Origins of Felix Mendelssohn's Aesthetic Outlook," in *The Mendelssohn Companion*, ed. Douglass Seaton (Westport, CT: Greenwood Press, 2001), 1.

12. Heinrich Schenker gives complete graphs of Mendelssohn's *Songs without Words*, Op. 30, No. 6 and Op. 67, No. 6, in *Der Tonwille*, vol. 10 (Vienna: Universal Edition, 1924), 25–29, 30–33; in *Free Composition* (*Der freie Satz*) (New York: Longman, 1979), Schenker returns to op. 30, no. 6 and also refers to passages from the Overture to *A Midsummer Night's Dream* (see below), the Wedding March from the Incidental Music, the *Song without Words* Op. 62, No. 6, and the Symphony in A Minor, Op. 56.

13. In "Rhythm and Linear Analysis: Aspects of Meter," *Music Forum* 6/1 (1987), Carl Schachter analyzes Mendelssohn's *Song without Words* Op. 102, No. 4; he addresses op. 62, no. 1 in "The Triad as Place and Action," *Music Theory Spectrum* 17/2 (1995): 152–58. Both of these articles have been reprinted in Schachter, *Unfoldings: Essays in Schenkerian Theory and Analysis*, ed. Joseph N. Straus (New York: Oxford University Press, 1999). Allen Cadwallader has offered analyses of the *Songs without Words* Op. 62, No. 1 and Op. 85, No. 1; see his "Form and Tonal Process: The Design of Different Structural Levels," in *Trends in Schenkerian Research*, ed. Allen Cadwallader (New York: Schirmer Books, 1990), 1–21. See also Allen Cadwallader and David Gagné, *Analysis of Tonal Music: A Schenkerian Approach*, 3rd. ed. (New York: Oxford University Press, 2011), 271–81 (on op. 62, no. 1).

14. William Rothstein, *Phrase Rhythm in Tonal Music* (New York: Schirmer Books, 1989), chap. 6, "Mendelssohn: *Songs without Words*" (183–213).

15. Two exceptions to this claim are Greg Vitercik's *The Early Works of Felix Mendelssohn* and an article by Julian Horton and Paul Wingfield titled "Norm and Deformation in Mendelssohn's Sonata Forms," in *Mendelssohn Perspectives*, ed. Jacqueline Waeber and Nicole Grimes (Aldershot: Ashgate, forthcoming).

16. Thomas Schmidt-Beste, "Mendelssohn's Chamber Music," in *The Cambridge Companion to Mendelssohn*, ed. Peter Mercer-Taylor (Cambridge: Cambridge University Press, 2004), 145.

17. On the distinction between "a *real*, experiential measure and a *notated* measure," see William E. Caplin, *Classical Form: A Theory of Formal Functions for the Instrumental Music of Haydn, Mozart, and Beethoven* (New York: Oxford University Press, 1998), 35. The case of $R = 2N$ has often been confused with the phenomenon of "hypermeter," defined by David Temperley as "meter above the level of the measure" (i.e., the *real* measure) and examined by numerous theorists in recent decades. See Temperley, "Hypermetrical Transitions," *Music Theory Spectrum* 30/2 (2008): 305–25. Temperley himself does not distinguish between the two phenomena; for example, his discussion of Andrew Imbrie's, Heinrich Schenker's, Justin London's, and his own views on a "hypermetric shift" in a passage from the development section of the first movement of Beethoven's Fifth Symphony does not acknowledge the $R = 2N$ factor in this movement (see "Hypermetrical Transitions," 314–16).

18. On hybrid theme types, see Caplin, *Classical Form*, chap. 5.

19. Schachter, "Rhythm and Linear Analysis: Aspects of Meter," 39 (reprinted in Schachter, *Unfoldings*, 104).

20. See the discussion of transitions in chapter 2, 54–55.

21. It is the imperfect authentic cadence at m. 47 that retrospectively encourages the perception, at least for me, of a phrase beginning at m. 40, rather than at m. 39: the span at mm. 40–47 yields a regular "four-bar" phrase (notated as eight bars), with its "odd-strong" "third" bar marked by the change of texture at m. 44.

22. As indicated in example 7.5, I identify a "premature dominant arrival" at m. 58: "A dominant arrival that appears before the end of the prevailing melodic-motivic and phrase-structural processes" (Caplin, *Classical Form*, 256).

23. See Temperley, "Hypermetrical Transitions," 305.

24. "When the dog bites, when the bee stings," from "My Favorite Things," *The Sound of Music* (1959).

25. For earlier examples of A´ ⇒ transition, see the finale of Haydn's String Quartet in D Major, Op. 20, No. 4 (1772; publ. 1774); the first movement of Mozart's String Quartet in B-flat Major, K. 458 (1784); and the finale of Beethoven's Fourth Piano Concerto, Op. 58 (1805–6). See also the first movement of Schubert's Piano Sonata in B-flat, D. 960 (1828; not published until 1838). The list could go on.

26. Caplin, *Classical Form*, 274n.30.

27. See Todd, *Mendelssohn*, 183. Benedict Taylor reports that "Mendelssohn's notes for these lectures still exist, though they are currently in private hands and scholars have not been given the chance to study them in detail." "Musical History and Self-Consciousness in Mendelssohn's Octet, Op. 20," *19th-Century Music* 32/2 (2008): 134.

28. Todd, *Mendelssohn*, 128, 161, 267. Recall my Hegelian interpretation of Marx's pedagogical methods in chapter 2 (27–28).

29. Mendelssohn's Octet does not precede Schubert's *Wandererfantasie* for piano, composed late in 1822 and published early in 1823. Unlike Schubert's E-flat Piano Trio, the *Wandererfantasie*—a four-movement work forged into a single one—cannot technically be described as formally cyclic (no intermovement thematic returns here), but Schubert's novel

form and the intensity of its explicit *motivic* cyclicism were pathbreaking in 1823. See Charles Fisk, *Returning Cycles: Contexts for the Interpretation of Schubert's Impromptus and Last Sonatas* (Berkeley: University of California Press, 2001), chap. 3, "The Wanderer's Tracks" (60–80).

30. Taylor, "Musical History and Self-Consciousness," 132, 157.

31. Taylor, "Musical History and Self-Consciousness," 134, 133. Taylor refers to John E. Towes, "Musical Historicism and the Transcendental Foundation of Community: Mendelssohn's *Lobgesang* and the 'Christian German' Cultural Politics of Frederick William IV," in *Rediscovering History: Culture, Politics, and the Psyche* (1994); and Towes, *Becoming Historical: Cultural Reformation and Public Memory in Early Nineteenth-Century Berlin* (2004).

32. See M. H. Abrams, *Natural Supernaturalism: Tradition and Revolution in Romantic Literature* (New York: Norton, 1971), chap. 4.

33. Taylor, "Musical History and Self-Consciousness," 133–34, 132, 135.

34. Taylor, "Musical History and Self-Consciousness," 135, 151. About Hegel, Mendelssohn wrote to his sisters on May 28, 1831: "It is unbelievable, Goethe and Thorwaldsen are still living, and Beethoven died only a few years ago, and yet Hegel proclaims that German art is as dead as a rat. *Quod non!* If he really feels thus, so much the worse for him, but when I reflect for a while on his conclusions they appear to me very shallow." *Reisebriefe von Felix Mendelssohn Bartholdy aus den Jahren 1830 bis 1832* (1861), as quoted in Taylor, "Musical History and Self-Consciousness," who then asserts: "Much of Mendelssohn's progress [as exemplified or adumbrated in the Octet?] would stem ultimately from his desire to rebut Hegel's 'conclusions'" (152–53). As discussed in chapter 2 of this volume, the debate continues as to whether Hegel imagined an end-point—that is, whether for him "time and history [and, by extension, the history of art as *Geist*] are completed when *Geist* comes to full self-knowledge, that is, with his own philosophy" (149).

35. Taylor, "Musical History and Self-Consciousness," 135, 154–55.

36. Vitercik, *The Early Works of Felix Mendelssohn*, chap. 3.

37. Taylor, "Musical History and Self-Consciousness," 136.

38. Vitercik, *The Early Works of Felix Mendelssohn*, 104–5; see Vitercik's complete analysis of the Scherzo, 104–20.

39. These observations stand in opposition to Vitercik's view that, within his sonata exposition, "Mendelssohn simply reintroduces the same material over and over" (*The Early Works of Felix Mendelssohn*, 125).

40. Vitercik, *The Early Works of Felix Mendelssohn*, 127.

41. Taylor, "Musical History and Self-Consciousness," 145, citing Rosen, *The Romantic Generation*, 89.

To Rosen's account of Beethoven's Scherzo recall in his finale, let us add the impressions of the character of Helen in E. M. Forster's *Howards End* (New York: Vintage Books, 1921): "[L]ook out for the part where you think you have done with the goblins [in the scherzo] and they come back [in the finale]." For Helen, in the narrator's words, the goblins "merely observed in passing that there was no such thing as splendour or heroism in the world.... Panic and emptiness!... Beethoven chose to make all right in the end.... But the goblins were still there. They could return. He has said so bravely, and that is why one can trust Beethoven when he says other things" (33–34).

I doubt that Helen would have heard goblins in Mendelssohn's Scherzo or in his finale. But as a "secret," told by the composer to his sister Fanny alone, Mendelssohn confided that his Scherzo had been inspired by the *Walpurgisnacht's* Dream episode in Goethe's *Faust*, part I. In Fanny Mendelssohn's words, "one feels so near the world of spirits, lightly carried up into the air; one would like to take up a broomstick and follow the aerial procession"

(Todd, *Mendelssohn*, 149–50, citing Sebastian Hensel, *The Mendelssohn Family (1729–1847) from Letters and Journals* [1882], vol. 1, 131).

42. Vitercik, *The Early Works of Felix Mendelssohn*, 130.

43. Taylor, "Musical History and Self-Consciousness," 146.

44. See Caplin, "The Classical Cadence: Conceptions and Misconceptions," *Journal of the American Musicological Society* 57/1 (2004): "Indeed, following a prolonged root-position tonic [from the beginning of a thematic unit], the appearance of I⁶ to initiate the cadential progression later in a theme helps to lighten the harmonic texture, to provide greater dynamic momentum, and to motivate a return to the stability of the final cadential tonic" (70). See also Caplin, *Classical Form*, 27.

45. As reported by Vitercik, "at some time between 1825 and 1833 [when the Octet appeared in print, in the version discussed here], Mendelssohn subjected the work to a thorough revision that addressed both details of the part-writing and fundamental issues of formal structure…in favor of a more flexible formal design" (*The Early Works of Felix Mendelssohn*, 71–72). Vitercik summarizes Mendelssohn's revisions and considers their purposes.

46. Taylor, "Musical History and Self-Consciousness," 149.

47. Taylor, "Musical History and Self-Consciousness," 147, 142.

48. Taylor, "Musical History and Self-Consciousness," 148.

49. For example, consider the Adagio opening of Mozart's Overture to *The Magic Flute*, to which Mendelssohn, in the same key, may be paying tribute; Mendelssohn too uses the progression with magical results. I am grateful to Mark DeVoto for reminding me about Mozart's Overture. For a more immediate example of the progression at hand, albeit in the minor mode, as i–(VI)–i⁶, see the opening of Mendelssohn's D-minor Piano Trio, at example 7.3.

50. Taylor, "Musical History and Self-Consciousness," 148.

51. Vitercik, *The Early Works of Felix Mendelssohn*, 133; see his discussion of the I–vi–ii–V–I progression in the first movement, 74–85.

52. Vitercik, *The Early Works of Felix Mendelssohn*, 132.

53. Vitercik, *The Early Works of Felix Mendelssohn*, 132.

54. The cellists must ascend to the G♯ as bass of the I⁶-chord in m. 4, rather than continue the traditional downward bass motion characteristic of the progression: the C♯ on the downbeat of that bar is the cello's lowest tone.

55. Taylor, "Musical History and Self-Consciousness," 135, 149.

56. Schenker, *Free Composition*, 99–100.

57. Todd, *Mendelssohn*, 162, 163–65. See also Todd, *Mendelssohn: The "Hebrides" and Other Overtures* (Cambridge: Cambridge University Press, 1993), 52–58.

58. I discuss the coda in the finale of Beethoven's op. 69 in Janet Schmalfeldt, "Cadential Processes: The Evaded Cadence and the 'One More Time' Technique," *Journal of Musicological Research* 12 (1992): 30–34.

59. Rosen, *The Romantic Generation*, 589.

60. Botstein, "Neoclassicism, Romanticism, and Emancipation," 2–3.

61. Botstein, "Neoclassicism, Romanticism, and Emancipation," 18.

Chapter 8

1. Charles Rosen, *The Romantic Generation* (Cambridge, MA: Harvard University Press, 1995), 237.

2. David Kopp, *Chromatic Transformations in Nineteenth-Century Music* (Cambridge: Cambridge University Press, 2002), 1–3. This study provides an account of how theorists from the eighteenth to the twenty-first centuries have treated third relations; it draws upon

David Lewin's "transformational theory" and on the branch of that project known as "neo-Riemannian theory."

3. Harald Krebs, "Third Relations and Dominant in Late 18th- and 19th-Century Music" (Ph.D. diss., Yale University, 1980).

4. Jim Samson, *The Music of Chopin* (Oxford: Clarendon Press, 1994), 112. See also David Beach, "Chopin's Mazurka, Op. 17, No. 4," *Theory and Practice* 2/3 (1977): 12–16; Rosen, *The Romantic Generation*, 421–23; and Joel Lester, "Harmonic Complexity and Form in Chopin's Mazurkas," *Ostinato Rigore: Revue internationale d'études musicales* 15 (2000): 101–20.

5. William Rothstein, *Phrase Rhythm in Tonal Music* (New York: Schirmer Books, 1989), 46–48.

6. Rather than serving as Schenkerian representations of prolonged interval spans, the beamed tones in example 8.2 simply draw attention to the recurring motivic descents within the alto voice from F♯, as noted by Charles Rosen. These give "an individual richness and coherence to the voice leading," but above all, they prepare "the beautiful effect in bars 13 to 15, where the F♮ changes to an F♯ and gives a surprising new meaning to the twice-repeated melodic figure. The subtlest nuances of harmony in Chopin are so powerful because, like this one, they have been prepared contrapuntally many bars in advance" (Rosen, *The Romantic Generation*, 423).

7. As in example 8.2, the beamed tones in mm. 1–6 at example 8.3 highlight a motivic detail: the motion <B–C–D–C> within the inner voice in the introduction at mm. 1–4 recurs in diminution in the soprano at mm. 5–6. See Beach, "Chopin's Mazurka, Op. 17, No. 4," 12–16; see also Allen Forte and Steven E. Gilbert, *Introduction to Schenkerian Analysis* (New York: Norton, 1982), 357–62.

8. About the Mazurka in B-flat Minor, Op. 24, No. 4, Jim Samson says: "The energy of the main theme itself derives from a simple model and sequence technique whose ascending pattern creates three 'incomplete' and only one 'complete' statement. Its alternation of dominant and tonic harmonies in both the major and minor keys is again typical of later mazurkas (Op. 30 No. 4) and it has even been suggested (Paschalow) that this feature has direct origins in folk music" (*The Music of Chopin*, 115; Samson refers to W. Paschalow, *Chopin a polska muzyka ludowa*, [1951]).

9. "The first couplet is normally organized as either a subordinate-theme complex (consisting of a transition, subordinate-theme group, closing section, and retransition) or an interior theme. In the first case, the first refrain and couplet constitute a sonata exposition." William E. Caplin, *Classical Form: A Theory of Formal Functions for the Instrumental Music of Haydn, Mozart, and Beethoven* (New York: Oxford University Press, 1998), 233.

10. See Kopp, *Chromatic Transformations*, 12–13.

11. Kopp, *Chromatic Transformations*, 12.

12. Kopp, *Chromatic Transformations*, 235–40. See also the quirky Mazurka in B Major, Op. 41, No. 2 (1838), wherein a move into first E♭ major (= D♯, Kopp's USM) and then D major (Kopp's UFM) characterizes a varied repetition within the A-section of a loosely defined ternary form.

13. See Caplin, *Classical Form*, 268n.18, for the distinction between dominant prolongation, a type of harmonic progression, and "standing on the dominant," a label of formal function.

14. For examples of this technique, Caplin shows the end of the development in the first movement of Beethoven's "Spring" Violin Sonata in F, Op. 24, and he cites three symphonic works by Haydn; see *Classical Form*, 141–42 and 275n.17. In James Webster's *Haydn's "Farewell" Symphony and the Idea of Classical Style: Through-Composition and Cyclic Integration in His Instrumental Music* (Cambridge: Cambridge University Press, 1991), his

table 5.3 (135) lists "[h]alf-cadence caesuras with remote continuations in Haydn symphony developments through 1774"; all but one of the six caesuras listed as occurring in retransitions feature the "V/vi–I" relationship. See also David Beach, "A Recurring Pattern in Mozart's Music," *Journal of Music Theory* 21/1 (1983): 1–29. Beach's recurring pattern is the large-scale progression V–III♯–I connecting the end of the development section and the beginning of the recapitulation in selected works; III♯ arises as V/vi at the end of the development.

15. See Jean-Jacques Eigeldinger, *Chopin: Pianist and Teacher as Seen by His Pupils*, (Cambridge: Cambridge University Press, 1986), 29, on the key of B major as the one that allows the pianist's right hand to assume "the most convenient, the most natural, the most relaxed position" (100n.30); and William Rothstein, "Chopin and the B-major Complex: A Study in the Psychology of Composition," *Ostinato Rigore: Revue internationale d'études musicales* 15 (2000): 149–72.

16. As is often the case with trios in minuets and scherzos (see Caplin, *Classical Form*, 229), the consequent within the written-out repetition of a′ remains open and "becomes" the retransition to the return of the scherzo.

17. The half-diminished seventh-chord can be considered a referential sonority in the First Scherzo: consider the opening harmony.

18. Samson, *The Music of Chopin*, 90.

19. "In a certain sense all dreams are *dreams of convenience*: they serve the purpose of continuing sleep instead of waking up. *The dream is the guardian of sleep, not its disturber.*" Sigmund Freud, *The Interpretation of Dreams* (1999), 180.

20. Foremost among the many writings about op. 31, op. 38, and op. 49 are the following: Harald Krebs, "Alternatives to Monotonality in Early Nineteenth-Century Music," *Journal of Music Theory* 25/1 (1981): 1–16; and "Tonal and Formal Dualism in Chopin's Scherzo, Op. 31," *Music Theory Spectrum* 13/1 (1991): 48–60; William Kinderman, "Directional Tonality in Chopin," in *Chopin Studies*, ed. Jim Samson (Cambridge: Cambridge University Press, 1988), 50–76; Carl Schachter, "Chopin's Fantasy Op. 49: The Two-Key Scheme," in *Chopin Studies*, 221–53; Rosen, *The Romantic Generation*, passim; and Jim Samson, "Chopin's Alternatives to Monotonality: A Historical Perspective," in *The Second Practice of Nineteenth-Century Tonality*, ed. William Kinderman and Harald Krebs (Lincoln: University of Nebraska Press, 1996), 34–44.

21. John Rink, "The Evolution of Chopin's 'Structural Style' and Its Relation to Improvisation" (Ph.D. diss., University of Cambridge, 1989); and "Tonal Architecture in the Early Music," in *The Cambridge Companion to Chopin*, ed. Jim Samson (Cambridge: Cambridge University Press, 1992), 88. In the latter essay, Rink notes that Chopin's first rondo, published in 1825 as op. 1, "is based on an unorthodox (but entirely logical) tonal scheme divided into two phrases," the first of which features "a progression by major third/diminished fourth from C minor (theme A) through E major (theme B – bars 65ff.) and A♭ (theme C – 130ff.) back to C minor for the second statement of theme A (158ff.)" (p. 81). In other words, Chopin's very first opus explores a nondiatonic ascending-thirds progression.

22. John Rink, "Schenker and Improvisation," *Journal of Music Theory* 37/1 (1993): 33, 40.

23. John Rink, *Chopin: The Piano Concertos* (Cambridge: Cambridge University Press, 1997); see the formal outlines for these movements at Rink's figures 4.1, 4.3, 4.5, and 4.7.

24. I contend that this observation holds even for the first movement of Chopin's often-maligned Piano Concerto No. 2, in E Minor, Op. 11 (1830). There, much to the dismay of Niecks, Tovey, Rosen, and others, Chopin stays in the home-tonic minor/major throughout his exposition; but then his *recapitulation* brings back his first secondary theme in the mediant (G major), this time ultimately modulating to close in E minor. In short, Chopin

simply postpones the traditional overall i–III–V–i tonal plan; whether in defiance of tradition or not, he reserves that plan for his recapitulation.

25. Frederick Niecks, *Frederic Chopin as a Man and Musician*, 2nd ed., vol. 2 (London: Novello, 1890), 229.

26. For Jeffrey Kallberg, the cello sonata falters "in attempting to integrate the newly developed style of musical continuity with its unstable, chromatic harmonies into a genre that normally for Chopin featured long passages of stable, diatonic material." "Chopin's Last Style," *Journal of the American Musicological Society* 38/2 (1985); reprinted in Kallberg, *Chopin at the Boundaries: Sex, History, and Musical Genre* (Cambridge, MA: Harvard University Press, 1996), 133.

27. Charles Rosen, "Rehearings: The First Movement of Chopin's Sonata in B-flat Minor, Op. 35," *19th-Century Music* 14/1 (1990): 62; see also Rosen, *The Romantic Generation*, 466.

28. See Ferdinand Gajewski, "Introduction," in *The Work Sheets to Chopin's Violoncello Sonata: A Facsimile* (New York: Garland, 1988).

29. Samson, *The Music of Chopin*, 128, 129; citing Józef Chomiński, *Fryderyk Chopin* (Leipzig: VEB Deutscher Verlag für Musik, 1980) 112–14.

30. Samson, *The Music of Chopin*, 139.

31. Jim Samson, *Chopin* (Oxford: Oxford University Press, 1996), 268.

32. Robert Schumann, *Neue Zeitschrift für Musik* 9 (1838), 179, as translated in Leon Plantinga, *Schumann as Critic* (New Haven, CT: Yale University Press, 1967), 230.

33. Chomiński, *Fryderyk Chopin*, 146.

34. Jeffrey Kallberg, review of *The Work Sheets to Chopin's Violoncello Sonata: A Facsimile*, Introduction by Ferdinand Gajewski, *Notes*, 2nd Ser., 46/3 (1990): 803.

35. W. Dean Sutcliffe, "Chopin's Counterpoint: The Largo from the Cello Sonata, Opus 65," *Musical Quarterly* 83/1 (1999): 114–33.

36. Sutcliffe, "Chopin's Counterpoint," 118.

37. Sutcliffe, "Chopin's Counterpoint," 123, 129.

38. Sutcliffe, "Chopin's Counterpoint," 125.

39. Sutcliffe, "Chopin's Counterpoint," 131.

Chapter 9

1. With his reference to those "great rivals of Western metaphorical thought, the Platonic sun and the Heideggerian home," Michael Spitzer broaches the metaphor of "home" but does not elaborate in reference to "home key." See Spitzer, *Metaphor and Musical Thought* (Chicago: University of Chicago Press, 2004), 341.

2. Vladimir Nabokov, *Speak, Memory: An Autobiography Revisited* (1996). See, for example, Joseph Brodsky's "The Condition We Call Exile," in his *On Grief and Reason: Essays* (1995), 22–34. Among the many writings by Said, Kundera, Hoffman, and Sebald, see Edward W. Said, *The Politics of Dispossession: The Struggle for Palestinian Self-Determination, 1969–1994* (1994) and *Out of Place: A Memoir* (1999); Milan Kundera, *The Book of Laughter and Forgetting* (1996); Eva Hoffman, *Lost in Translation: A Life in a New Language* (1989), *Shtetl: The Life and Death of a Small Town and the World of Polish Jews* (1998), and *After Such Knowledge* (2004); and W. G. Sebald, *The Emigrants* (1996), *Austerlitz* (2001), and *On the Natural History of Destruction* (2003).

3. Theodor W. Adorno, *Minima Moralia: Reflections from Damaged Life* (London: Verso Editions, 1978), 87.

4. Lydia Goehr writes: "For my grandfather, as for others in my family who have lived in countries different from those of their birth, their musical activity has been one of their

strongest connections to home. Unreflectively, 'home' names a place and a life once lived; reflectively, it names a continually transforming set of bonds organized by activities, conversations, and relationships that trace memories of the past, establish patterns of present significance, and suggest desires for the future. 'Home' is largely synonymous with 'family': when a family finds itself in no place in particular, the bonds (musical or otherwise) between its members carry the significance of home." *The Quest for Voice: On Music, Politics, and the Limits of Philosophy* (Berkeley: University of California Press, 1998), chap. 5, "Music and Musicians in Exile: The Romantic Legacy of a Double Life," 176. Drawing on responses from exiled composers to a request for interviews in 1950 by Albert Goldberg of the *Los Angeles Times*, Goehr portrays their world as one that "revealed much more constructive conflict or contrapuntal doubleness than it did either simple logical opposition or harmonious theory" (206).

5. Josef Koudelka, *Exiles* (1997), and Sebastião Salgado, *Terra: Struggle of the Landless* (1997), *Migrations: Humanity in Transition* (2000), and *The Children: Refugees and Migrants* (2000).

6. *Rabbit-Proof Fence* (2003), based on a true story, as told in the book by Doris Pilkington Garama.

7. Nicholas Marston, "Schubert's Homecoming," *Journal of the Royal Musical Association* 125 (2000): 248.

8. Eduard von Bauernfeld, *Erinnerungen aus Alt Wien* (1923), as cited in Leon Botstein, "Realism Transformed: Franz Schubert and Vienna," in *The Cambridge Companion to Schubert*, ed. Christopher H. Gibbs (Cambridge: Cambridge University Press, 1997), 22.

9. Marston, "Schubert's Homecoming," 248.

10. Charles Fisk, *Returning Cycles: Contexts for the Interpretation of Schubert's Impromptus and Last Sonatas* (Berkeley: University of California Press, 2001), 8. In his 1928 essay on Schubert, Theodor Adorno wrote that running throughout Schubert's oeuvre is a "language…in dialect; but it is a dialect from nowhere [without a soil]. It has the flavor of the native [a homeland]; yet there is no such place [homeland], only a memory. He is never further away from that place [native soil] than when he cites it." I combine the translation in Theodor Adorno, "Schubert (1928)," *19th-Century Music* 29/1 (2005): 14 (discussed in chapter 5) with that of Rolf Tiedemann, in Adorno, *Beethoven: The Philosophy of Music* (Stanford: Stanford University Press, 1998), 219n.137.

11. See Barbara Turchin, "The Nineteenth-century *Wanderlieder* Cycle," *Journal of Musicology* 5/4 (1987): 498–525.

12. See chapter 6, p. 147 and note 38. Schubert's wishful happy ending becomes inverted in Marilynne Robinson's novel *Home* (2008). Here a prodigal son and his pious sister return home in their middle age to care for their imperious father, a retired Presbyterian minister facing his final days. As James Wood puts it: "The Boughton children come home to a strange, old-fashioned Iowa town, but the return is hardly the balm it promises to be, for home is too personal, too remembered, too disappointing. Eden is exile, not Heaven" ("Books: Marilynne Robinson's *Home*," *New Yorker*, September 8, 2008, 78). To the bitter end, the father cannot forgive the son for having left home and disgraced the family; the son departs again, without his father's blessing.

13. See Peter Ostwald, *Schumann: The Inner Voices of a Musical Genius* (Boston: Northeastern University Press, 1985), 66–69, 72. For statements in letters to Schumann from his mother, Ostwald cites Georg Eisman, *Robert Schumann: Ein Quellenwerk über sein Leben und Schaffen* (1956), and Eugenie Schumann, *Robert Schumann: Ein Lebensbild Meines Vaters* (1931). See also John Daverio, *Robert Schumann: Herald of a "New Poetic Age"* (New York: Oxford University Press, 1997), 61–62.

14. Robert Schumann, *Jugendbriefe* (Leipzig: Breitkopf & Härtel, 1886), vol. 1, 22–23 (letter of October 24, 1828), as translated in Ostwald, *Schumann*, 34. In a reworking for his

diary of the letter to his mother, Schumann further describes a dream in which his sister-in-law Therese stood before him and softly sang "*süsse Heimath*" (sweet home)—the Adagio ending of a song titled "Heimweh" (homesickness) by Carl Gottlieb Reissiger (op. 50, no. 1); see Berthold Hoeckner, "Schumann and Romantic Distance," *Journal of the American Musicological Society* 50/1 (1997): 83–85, and Hoeckner, *Programming the Absolute: Nineteenth-Century German Music and the Hermeneutics of the Moment* (Princeton, NJ: Princeton University Press, 2002), 71–79.

15. Daverio, *Robert Schumann*, 181, citing and translating Schumann, *Tagebücher, Band II: 1836–1854*, ed. Georg Eisman (Leipzig: VEB Deutscher Verlag für Musik, 1987), 90.

16. Daverio, *Robert Schumann*, 191.

17. Daverio, *Robert Schumann*, 193.

18. Patrick McCreless, "Song Order in the Song Cycle: Schumann's *Liederkreis*, Op. 39," *Music Analysis* 5/1 (1986): 5–28; David Ferris, *Schumann's Eichendorff "Liederkreis" and the Genre of the Romantic Cycle* (Oxford: Oxford University Press, 2000); Charles Burkhart, "Departures from the Norm in Two Songs from Schumann's *Liederkreis*," in *Schenker Studies*, ed. Hedi Siegel (Cambridge: Cambridge University Press, 1990), 146–64.

19. Ferris's translation is in *Schumann's Eichendorff "Liederkreis,"* 144.

20. As discussed by William Rothstein, the term *Reprisenbar* was used by Alfred Lorenz in his *Das Geheimnis der Form bei Richard Wagner* (1924–33). Rothstein defines "Reprisenbar" as "a bar form ending with a melodic return (AABA)," and he likens the form to what he calls a "quatrain" (*Phrase Rhythm in Tonal Music* [New York: Schirmer Books, 1989], 288).

21. Burkhart, "Departures from the Norm," 146–47.

22. Burkhart, "Departures from the Norm," 153.

23. John Daverio, *Crossing Paths: Schubert, Schumann, and Brahms* (Oxford: Oxford University Press, 2002), 75; see Clara and Robert Schumann, *Briefwechsel: Kritische Gesamtausgabe* (Frankfurt: Stroemfeld/Roter Stern, 1984–2001), 145.

24. Charles Rosen sees the phrase at mm. 53–61 as "a consequent to the preceding phrase" (*The Romantic Generation* [Cambridge, MA: Harvard University Press, 1995], 698). Following Arnold Schoenberg's more restrictive notion of antecedent-consequent, I propose that this last vocal phrase serves as a consequent to all earlier vocal phrases *except for* the immediately preceding one: this last phrase begins as a varied repetition of the original at mm. 7–14, but now, rather than reaching only V, it closes on the tonic.

25. Ferris, *Schumann's Eichendorff "Liederkreis,"* 156.

26. Burkhart, "Departures from the Norm," 147, 163–64.

27. Ferris, *Schumann's Eichendorff "Liederkreis,"* 146, 156–57.

28. Ostwald, *Schumann*, 137. See Berthold Litzmann, ed., *Clara Schumann: Ein Künstlerleben nach Tagebüchern und Briefen* (Leipzig: Breitkopf & Härtel, 1925), 166.

29. Daverio, *Robert Schumann*, 194–95, 191.

30. See David Ferris, "Public Performance and Private Understanding: Clara Wieck's Concerts in Berlin," *Journal of the American Musicological Society* 56/2 (2003): 376–77, 380.

31. See Ostwald, *Schumann*, 7; and Daverio, *Robert Schumann*, 457–58.

32. For example, baritone Julius Stockhausen gave the first complete public performance of Schumann's *Dichterliebe* with Brahms as late as 1861, and with Clara in 1862; he later premièred complete public performances of Schumann's *Frauenliebe und Leben*, his Eichendorff *Liederkreis*, and the *Spanisches Liederspiel*. Clara Schumann's first public performance of Robert's piano cycle *Davidsbündlertänze*, Op. 6, did not occur until 1860, and even then she performed only ten of the eighteen dances; although she gave many private performances of Robert's *Carnaval*, Op. 9, and his *Kinderszenen*, Op. 15, her first public presentations of those cycles waited until 1856 and 1868, respectively. See Nancy B.

Reich, *Clara Schumann: The Artist and the Woman*, rev. ed. (Ithaca and London: Cornell University Press, 2001), 208, 259. See also Kristina Muxfeldt, "*Frauenliebe und Leben* Now and Then," *19th-Century Music* 25/1 (2001), 40; Muxfeldt reports that Wilhelmine Schröder-Devrient performed the complete *Frauenliebe* at a private soirée on October 14, 1848.

33. Schumann did not hesitate to use the Latinate term "coda" when this was the formal function he wished to convey. There are passages labeled as codas in the scherzo movements of his First and Second Symphonies, his Piano Quintet, and two of his three Piano Trios (Op. 63 and Op. 80), as well as in the Andante movement in the second of his three String Quartets, Op. 41. More pertinent to the solo piano work under discussion here are the codas designated as such in three of Schumann's *Davidsbündlertänze* (nos. 6, 13, and 17).

34. Charles Fisk, "Performance, Analysis, and Music Imagining, Part I: Schumann's *Arabesque*," *College Music Symposium* 36 (1996): 59–72.

35. See Daverio, *Robert Schumann*, 177.

36. Fisk, "Performance, Analysis, and Music Imagining, Part I," 65.

37. Fisk, "Performance, Analysis, and Music Imagining, Part I," 67.

38. Fisk, "Performance, Analysis, and Music Imagining, Part I," 68: "The music of this episode overlays the melodic motive of Minore I (5–6–5–2–3) with the upbeat-motive and the chromatic ascent from the theme, and then combines this new fusion with a stepwise melodic descent deriving from the transition (mm. 145–49)."

39. Marshall Brown, *The Shape of German Romanticism* (Ithaca and London: Cornell University Press, 1979), 124.

40. As translated in Anthony Newcomb, "Schumann and the Marketplace: From Butterflies to *Hausmusik*," in *Nineteenth-Century Piano Music*, ed. R. Larry Todd (New York: Schirmer Books, 1990), 266.

41. Newcomb, "Schumann and the Marketplace," 268, passim.

42. About the final movement of the *Davidsbündlertänze* and its inscription, Peter Kaminsky has written: "But it would diminish the full richness of the inscription to take it too literally, for the specific manner of that closure in C major is prepared by the process of cross reference over the course of the entire work. There is something subtly ironic about the ending: while it is plausible that *Davidsbündlertänze* could close with the penultimate movement, the final piece adds an entirely new level of structural significance to the preceding movements of the cycle." "Principles of Formal Structure in Schumann's Early Piano Cycles," *Music Theory Spectrum* 11/2 (1989): 224.

43. Hoeckner, "Schumann and Romantic Distance," 109–10. See also Hoeckner's *Programming the Absolute*, chap. 2, "Schumann's Distance."

44. See Nicholas Marston, *Schumann: Fantasie, Op. 17* (Cambridge: Cambridge University Press, 1992), 6.

45. For example, see Newcomb, "Schumann and the Marketplace," 295–96.

46. See Rosen, *The Romantic Generation*, 103.

47. See Hoeckner, *Programming the Absolute*, 100–1 (fig. 2.9).

48. See William E. Caplin on the "reinterpreted half cadence" in *Classical Form: A Theory of Formal Functions for the Instrumental Music of Haydn, Mozart, and Beethoven* (New York: Oxford University Press, 1998), 57. Caplin uses my "becoming" symbol (⇒) to represent this transformation.

49. Clara and Robert Schumann, *Briefwechsel* 2:562, dated June 9, 1838, as cited in Hoeckner, *Programming the Absolute*, 94–95 and 285.n124; also cited in Marston, *Schumann: Fantasie, Op. 17*, 10 and 101n.37.

50. Rosen, *The Romantic Generation*, 103, 101.

51. "Durch all Töne tönet/ Im bunten Erdentraum/ Ein leiser Ton gezogen/ Für den, der heimlich lauschet"—the final quatrain of the ninth poem, "Die Gebüsche," from the

second part of Friedrich Schlegel's cycle *Abendröte*. For a discussion of the significance of Schumann's motto, see Marston, *Schumann: Fantasie, Op. 17*, 37–40.

52. Michael P. Steinberg, "Schumann's Homelessness," in *Schumann and His World*, ed. R. Larry Todd (Princeton, NJ: Princeton University Press, 1994), 54.

53. Steinberg, "Schumann's Homelessness," 65, 54, 67. The *locus classicus* on "*unheimlich*" for Steinberg is of course Sigmund Freud's 1919 essay "The Uncanny" (as cited in his *Collected Papers*, vol. 4 [London, 1925]), in which Freud "defines the uncanny as the opposite of the *heimlich*, 'that class of the terrifying which leads back to something long known to us, once very familiar.' But the opposites converge: 'What is *heimlich* thus comes to be *unheimlich*...something familiar and old-established in the mind that has been estranged only by the process of repression.' The homely is the site also of the unhomely, the uncanny: *heimlich* and *unheimlich* coincide, and that is the root of terror, especially in childhood" (68). See also Michael P. Steinberg, *Listening to Reason: Culture, Subjectivity, and Nineteenth-Century Music* (Princeton, NJ: Princeton University Press, 2004), 122–31 ("Schumann's Uncanny Histories").

54. As quoted in Marston, *Schumann: Fantasie, Op. 17*, 98.

55. As quoted in Stephen Downes, "Kierkegaard, a Kiss, and Schumann's *Fantasie*," *19th-Century Music* 22/3 (1999): 279.

BIBLIOGRAPHY

Abbate, Carolyn. *Unsung Voices: Opera and Musical Narrative in the Nineteenth Century*. Princeton, NJ: Princeton University Press, 1991.

———. "Music—Drastic or Gnostic?" *Critical Inquiry* 30/3 (2004): 505–36.

Abrams, M. H. *The Mirror and the Lamp: Romantic Theory and the Critical Tradition*. Oxford: Oxford University Press, 1953.

———. *Natural Supernaturalism: Tradition and Revolution in Romantic Literature*. New York: W. W. Norton, 1971.

Adorno, Theodor W. *Drei Studien zu Hegel*. Frankfurt: Suhrkamp, 1963.

———. *Philosophy of Modern Music*. Translated by Anne G. Mitchell and Wesley V. Blomster. New York: Seabury Press, 1973. (Orig. publ. as *Philosophie der neuen Musik* [Tübingen: Mohr, 1949].)

———. *Introduction to the Sociology of Music*. Translated by E. B. Ashton. New York: Seabury Press, 1976. (Orig. publ. as *Einleitung in die Musiksoziologie: Zwölf theoretische Vorlesungen* [Frankfurt: Suhrkamp, 1962].)

———. *Minima Moralia: Reflections from Damaged Life*. Translated by E. F. N. Jephcott. London: Verso, 1978. (Orig. publ. 1951.)

———. "On the Problem of Musical Analysis." Translated by Max Paddison (from a tape-recording of Adorno's lecture at the Hochschule für Musik und Darstellende Kunst, Frankfurt am Main, February 24, 1969). *Music Analysis* 1/2 (1982): 169–87.

———. *Hegel: Three Studies*. Translated by Shierry Weber Nicholsen with an introduction by Shierry Weber Nicholsen and Jeremy J. Shapiro. Cambridge, MA: MIT Press, 1993.

———. *Beethoven: Philosophie der Musik*. 2nd ed. Edited by Rolf Tiedemann. Frankfurt am Main: Suhrkamp, 1994.

———. *Beethoven: The Philosophy of Music*. Fragments and texts edited by Rolf Tiedemann; translated by Edmund Jephcott. Stanford: Stanford University Press, 1998.

———. *Essays on Music*. Selected,with introduction, commentary, and notes by Richard Leppert. New translations by Susan H. Gillespie. Berkeley: University of California Press, 2002.

———. "Schubert (1928)." Translated by Jonathan Dunsby and Beate Perrey in *19th-Century Music* 29/1 (2005): 3–14. (Orig. publ. in *Die Musik* 21/1 [1928]. Reprinted in *Moments musicaux: Neu gedruckte Aufsätze 1928–1962* [Frankfurt: Suhrkamp, 1964].)

Agawu, Kofi. *Music as Discourse: Semiotic Adventures in Romantic Music*. Oxford Studies in Music Theory. Oxford: Oxford University Press, 2009.

Ahn, Suhnne. "Genre, Style, and Compositional Procedure in Beethoven's 'Kreutzer' Sonata, Opus 47." Ph.D. diss., Harvard University, 1997.

———. "Beethoven's Opus 47: Balance and Virtuosity." In *The Beethoven Violin Sonatas: History, Criticism, Performance*, edited by Lewis Lockwood and Mark Kroll, 61–82. Urbana and Chicago: University of Illinois Press, 2004.

Albrecht, Theodore. "Beethoven and Shakespeare's *Tempest*: New Light on an Old Allusion." *Beethoven Forum* 1, edited by Christopher Reynolds (1992): 81–92.

Allanbrook, Wye Jamison. *Rhythmic Gesture in Mozart: Le Nozze di Figaro and Don Giovanni.* Chicago: University of Chicago Press, 1983.

Auden, W. H. *The Dyer's Hand and Other Essays* (1948). Edited by Edward Mendelson. New York: Vintage, 1989.

Ballantine, Christopher. "Beethoven, Hegel and Marx." *Music Review* 33 (1972): 35–46.

Barford, Philip. "The Approach to Beethoven's Late Music." *Music Review* 30 (1969): 106–17.

Bauer, Elisabeth Eleonore. *Wie Beethoven auf den Sockel kam: Die Entstehung eines musikalischen Mythos.* Stuttgart and Weimar: J. B. Metzler, 1992.

Beach, David. "Chopin's Mazurka, Op. 17, No. 4." *Theory and Practice* 2/3 (1977): 12–16.

———. "A Recurring Pattern in Mozart's Music." *Journal of Music Theory* 21/1 (1983): 1–29.

Beethoven, Ludwig van. *The Letters of Beethoven*, 3 vols. Translated and edited by Emily Anderson. London: Macmillan, 1961.

Bent, Ian. *Analysis.* Norton/Grove Handbooks in Music. New York: W. W. Norton, 1987.

Bergé, Pieter, ed. *Musical Form, Forms & Formenlehre: Three Methodological Reflections.* Leuven: Leuven University Press, 2009.

Berger, Karol. "Beethoven and the Aesthetic State." *Beethoven Forum* 7, edited by Mark Evan Bonds (1999): 17–44.

———. *Bach's Cycle, Mozart's Arrow: An Essay on the Origins of Musical Modernity.* Berkeley: University of California Press, 2007.

Berry, Wallace. *Musical Structure and Performance.* New Haven, CT: Yale University Press, 1989.

Blume, Friedrich. *Classic and Romantic Music: A Comprehensive Survey.* Translated by M. D. Herter Norton. New York: W. W. Norton, 1970.

Bonds, Mark Evan. "Haydn's False Recapitulations and the Perception of Sonata Form in the Eighteenth Century." Ph.D. diss., Harvard University, 1988.

———. *Wordless Rhetoric: Musical Form and the Metaphor of the Oration.* Cambridge, MA: Harvard University Press, 1991.

———. "The Sincerest Form of Flattery? Mozart's 'Haydn' Quartets and the Question of Influence." *Studi musicali* 22 (1993): 365–409.

———. "Idealism and the Aesthetics of Instrumental Music at the Turn of the Nineteenth Century." *Journal of the American Musicological Society* 50/2–3 (1997): 387–420.

———. *Music as Thought: Listening to the Symphony in the Age of Beethoven.* Princeton, NJ: Princeton University Press, 2006.

Borio, Gianmario. "Schenker versus Schoenberg versus Schenker: The Difficulties of a Reconcilation." *Journal of the Royal Musical Association* 126 (2001): 250–74.

Botstein, Leon. "Realism Transformed: Franz Schubert and Vienna." In *The Cambridge Companion to Schubert*, edited by Christopher H. Gibbs, 15–35. Cambridge: Cambridge University Press, 1997.

———. "The Search for Meaning in Beethoven: Popularity, Intimacy, and Politics in Historical Perspective." In *Beethoven and His World*, edited by Scott Burnham and Michael P. Steinberg, 332–66. Princeton, NJ: Princeton University Press, 2000.

———. "Neoclassicism, Romanticism, and Emancipation: The Origins of Felix Mendelssohn's Aesthetic Outlook." In *The Mendelssohn Companion*, edited by Douglass Seaton, 1–27. Westport, CT: Greenwood Press, 2001.

Brandenburg, Sieghard. "Zur Textgeschichte von Beethovens Violinsonate Opus 47." In *Musik, Edition, Interpretation: Gedenkschrift Gunthers Henle*, edited by Martin Bente, 111–24. Munich: Henle, 1980.

Brendel, Alfred. *Thoughts and Afterthoughts*. Princeton, NJ: Princeton University Press, 1976.

———. *Music as Sounded Out: Essays, Lectures, Interviews, Afterthoughts*. London: Robson Books; New York: Farrar, Straus and Giroux, 1990.

Brendel, Franz. *Geschichte der Musik*. Leipzig: Heinrich Matthes, 1860.

———. "Robert Schumann with Reference to Mendelssohn-Bartholdy and the Development of Modern Music in General (1845)." Translated by Jürgen Thym. In *Schumann and His World*, edited by R. Larry Todd, 317–37. Princeton, NJ: Princeton University Press, 1994. (Orig. publ. in *Neue Zeitschrift für Musik* 22 [1845].)

Brett, Philip. "Piano Four-Hands: Schubert and the Performance of Gay Male Desire." *19th-Century Music* 21/2 (1997): 149–76.

Brown, Marshall. *The Shape of German Romanticism*. Ithaca and London: Cornell University Press, 1979.

Brown, Maurice J. E., with Eric Sams (Work-List). *The New Grove Schubert*. New York: W. W. Norton, 1983.

Burkhart, Charles. "Departures from the Norm in Two Songs from Schumann's *Liederkreis*" ["Mondnacht" and "Schöne Fremde"]. In *Schenker Studies*, edited by Hedi Siegel, 146–64. Cambridge: Cambridge University Press, 1990.

Burkholder, J. Peter. "Museum Pieces: The Historicist Mainstream in Music of the Last Hundred Years." *Journal of Musicology* 2/2 (1983): 115–34.

Burnham, Scott. "Aesthetics, Theory and History in the Works of Adolph Bernhard Marx." Ph.D. diss., Brandeis University, 1988.

———. "The Role of Sonata Form in A. B. Marx's Theory of Form." *Journal of Music Theory* 33/2 (1989): 247–71.

———. "Criticism, Faith, and the *Idee*: A. B. Marx's Early Reception of Beethoven." *19th-Century Music* 13/3 (1990): 183–92.

———. *Beethoven Hero*. Princeton, NJ: Princeton University Press, 1995.

———. "A. B. Marx and the Gendering of Sonata Form." In *Music Theory in the Age of Romanticism*, edited by Ian Bent, 163–86. Cambridge: Cambridge University Press, 1996.

———. "Form." In *The Cambridge History of Western Music Theory*, edited by Thomas Christensen, 881–906. Cambridge: Cambridge University Press, 2002.

———. "Landscape as Music, Landscape as Truth: Schubert and the Burden of Repetition." *19th-Century Music* 29/1 (2005): 31–41.

Cadwallader, Allen. "Form and Tonal Process: The Design of Different Structural Levels." In *Trends in Schenkerian Research*, edited by Allen Cadwallader, 1–21. New York: Schirmer Books, 1990.

Cadwallader, Allen, and David Gagné. *Analysis of Tonal Music: A Schenkerian Approach*, 3rd ed. New York: Oxford University Press, 2011.

Caplin, William E. "Funktionale Komponenten im achttaktigen Satz." *Musiktheorie* 1 (1986): 241–43.

———. "The 'Expanded Cadential Progression': A Category for the Analysis of Classical Form." *Journal of Musicological Research* 7 (1987): 215–57.

———. *Classical Form: A Theory of Formal Functions for the Instrumental Music of Haydn, Mozart, and Beethoven*. New York: Oxford University Press, 1998.

———. "The Classical Sonata Exposition: Cadential Goals and Form-Functional Plans." *Tijdschrift voor Muziektheorie* 6/3 (2001): 195–209.

———. "The Classical Cadence: Conceptions and Misconceptions." *Journal of the American Musicological Society* 57/1 (2004): 51–117.

———. "What Are Formal Functions?" In Bergé, *Musical Form, Forms & Formenlehre* (2009), 21–40.

———. "Beethoven's *Tempest* Exposition: A Springboard for Form-Functional Considerations." In *Beethoven's "Tempest" Sonata: Perspectives of Analysis and Performance*, edited by Pieter Bergé, coedited by Jeroen D'hoe and William E. Caplin, 87–125. Analysis in Context. Leuven Studies in Musicology, vol. 2. Leuven: Peeters, 2009.

Carpenter, Patricia. "*Grundgestalt* as Tonal Function." *Music Theory Spectrum* 5 (1983): 15–38.

———. "Musical Form and Musical Idea: Reflections on a Theme of Schoenberg, Hanslick, and Kant." In *Music and Civilization: Essays in Honor of Paul Henry Lang*, edited by Edmond Strainchamps and Maria Rika Maniates with Christopher Hatch. New York: W. W. Norton, 1984.

Carter, Tim. W. A. *Mozart: Le Nozze di Figaro*. Cambridge: Cambridge University Press, 1987.

Chomiński, Józef. *Fryderyk Chopin*. Translated (from Polish to German) by Bolko Schweinitz. Leipzig: VEB Deutscher Verlag für Musik, 1980.

Chopin, Frédéric. *Chopin's Letters*. Collected by Henryk Opienski; translated by E. L. Voynich. New York: Dover, 1988.

Christensen, Thomas. "Four-Hand Piano Transcription and Geographies of Nineteenth-Century Musical Reception." *Journal of the American Musicological Society* 52/2 (1999): 255–98.

Chua, Daniel. K. L. *The "Galitzin" Quartets of Beethoven*. Princeton, NJ: Princeton University Press, 1995.

Cohn, Richard. "'This music crept by me upon the waters': Introverted Motives in Beethoven's 'Tempest' Sonata." In *Engaging Music: Essays in Music Analysis*, edited by Deborah Stein, 226–35. New York: Oxford University Press, 2005.

Coldicott, Ann-Louise. "Beethoven's Musical Environment." In Cooper, *The Beethoven Compendium* (1991).

Cone, Edward T. *Musical Form and Musical Performance*. New York: Norton, 1968.

———. *The Composer's Voice*. Berkeley: University of California Press, 1974.

———. *Music: A View from Delft*. Selected essays, edited by Robert P. Morgan. Chicago: University of Chicago Press, 1989.

Cook, Nicolas. "Analysing Performance and Performing Analysis." In *Rethinking Music*, edited by Nicholas Cook and Mark Everist, 239–61. Oxford: Oxford University Press, 1999.

———. *The Schenker Project: Culture, Race, and Music Theory in* Fin-de-siècle *Vienna*. Oxford: Oxford University Press, 2007.

Cooper, Barry, ed. *The Beethoven Compendium: A Guide to Beethoven's Life and Music*. London: Thames and Hudson, 1991.

Cusick, Suzanne. "Feminist Theory, Music Theory, and the Mind/Body Problem." *Perspectives of New Music* 32/1 (1994): 8–27.

Czerny, Carl. *Erinnerungen aus meinem Leben* (1842). Edited by Walter Kolneder. Strasbourg: P. H. Heitz, 1968.

Dahlhaus, Carl. "'Von Zwei Kulturen der Musik': Die Schlussfuge aus Beethovens Cellosonate opus 102,2." *Die Musikforschung* 31 (1978): 397–405.

———. "Formenlehre und Gattungstheorie bei A. B. Marx." In *Heinrich Sievers zum 70. Geburtstag*, edited by Günter Katzenberger, 29–35. Tutzing: Hans Schneider, 1978.

———. "Satz und Periode: Zur Theorie der musikalische Syntax." *Zeitschrift für Musiktheorie* 9/2 (1978): 16–26.

———. "Zu Adornos Beethoven-Kritik." In *Adorno und die Musik*, edited by Otto Kolleritsch, 170–79. Studien zur Wertungsforschung, vol. 12. Graz: Universal Edition, 1979.

———. "Zur Formidee in Beethovens d-molle-Sonate opus 31,2." *Die Musikforschung* 33 (1980): 310–12.

───── . "Hegel und die Musik seiner Zeit." *Hegelstudien Beiheft* 22 (1983): 333–50.

───── . "Ästhetische Prämissen der 'Sonatenform' bei Adolf Bernhard Marx." *Archiv für Musikwissenschaft* 41 (1984): 73–85.

───── . *Ludwig van Beethoven und seine Zeit*. Grosse Komponisten und ihre Zeit. Laaber: Laaber-Verlag, 1987.

───── . *Schoenberg and the New Music*. Translated by Derrick Puffett and Alfred Clayton. Cambridge: Cambridge University Press, 1987.

───── . *The Idea of Absolute Music*. Translated by Roger Lustig. Chicago: University of Chicago Press, 1989. (Orig. publ. as *Die Idee der absoluten Musik* [Kassel, 1978].)

───── . *Nineteenth-Century Music*. Translated by J. Bradford Robinson. Berkeley: University of California Press, 1989. (Orig. publ. as *Die Musik des 19. Jahrhunderts*. Vol. 6 of *Neues Handbuch der Musikwissenschaft* [Wiesbaden, 1980].)

───── . *Ludwig van Beethoven: Approaches to His Music*. Translated by Mary Whittall. Oxford: Clarendon Press, 1991.

Daverio, John. *Nineteenth-Century Music and the German Romantic Ideology*. New York: Schirmer Books, 1993.

───── . *Robert Schumann: Herald of a "New Poetic Age."* New York: Oxford University Press, 1997.

───── . "'One More Beautiful Memory of Schubert': Schumann's Critique of the Impromptus, D.935." *Musical Quarterly* 84/4 (2001): 604–18.

───── . *Crossing Paths: Schubert, Schumann, and Brahms*. Oxford: Oxford University Press, 2002.

Day-O'Connell, Jeremy. "The Rise of $\hat{6}$ in the Nineteenth Century." *Music Theory Spectrum* 24/1 (2002): 35–67.

───── . *On Pentatonicism from the Eighteenth Century to Debussy*. Rochester, NY: University of Rochester Press, 2007.

Dell'Antonio, Andrew, ed. *Beyond Structural Listening? Postmodern Modes of Hearing*. Berkeley: University of California Press, 2004.

Dennis, David B. *Beethoven in German Politics, 1870–1989*. New Haven, CT: Yale University Press, 1996.

DeNora, Tia. *Beethoven and the Construction of Genius: Musical Politics in Vienna, 1792–1803*. Berkeley: University of California Press, 1995.

Deutsch, Otto Erich. *Schubert: A Documentary Biography*. Translated by Eric Blom. London: J. M. Dent & Sons, 1946. Reprint, New York: Da Capo, 1977. (Orig. publ. as *Franz Schubert: Die Dokumente seines Lebens*. Munich: O. Müller, 1913–14.)

Donelan, James H. *Poetry and the Romantic Musical Aesthetic*. Cambridge: Cambridge University Press, 2008.

Downes, Stephen. "Kierkegaard, a Kiss, and Schumann's *Fantasie*." *19th-Century Music* 22/3 (1999): 268–80.

Drabkin, William. "The Introduction to Beethoven's 'Kreutzer' Sonata: A Historical Perspective." In *The Beethoven Violin Sonatas: History, Criticism, Performance*, edited by Lewis Lockwood and Mark Kroll, 83–107. Urbana and Chicago: University of Illinois Press, 2004.

Dunsby, Jonathan. "Performers on Performance." In *Musical Performance: A Guide to Understanding*, edited by John Rink, 225–36. Cambridge: Cambridge University Press, 2002.

Eigeldinger, Jean-Jacques. *Chopin: Pianist and Teacher as Seen by His Pupils*. Translated by Naomi Shohet. Cambridge: Cambridge University Press, 1986.

Einstein, Alfred. *Schubert: The Man and His Music*. Translated by David Ascoli. Frogmore: Panther, 1971. (Orig. publ. 1951.)

Edwards, F. G. "George P. Bridgetower and the Kreutzer Sonata." *Musical Times* 49 (1908): 302–8.

Federhofer, Helmut. *Beiträge zur musikalischen Gestaltanalyse*. Graz: Akademische Druck-u. Verlagsanstalt, 1950.

Ferris, David. *Schumann's Eichendorff "Liederkreis" and the Genre of the Romantic Cycle*. New York: Oxford University Press, 2000.

———. "Public Performance and Private Understanding: Clara Wieck's Concerts in Berlin." *Journal of the American Musicological Society* 56/2 (2003): 351–408.

Fichte, Johann Gottlieb. *Introductions to the Wissenschaftslehre and Other Writings (1797–1800)*. Edited and translated by Daniel Breazeale. Indianapolis: Hackett, 1994.

Fisk, Charles. "Performance, Analysis, and Musical Imagining, Part I: Schumann's *Arabesque*." *College Music Symposium* 36 (1996): 59–72.

———. *Returning Cycles: Contexts for the Interpretation of Schubert's Impromptus and Last Sonatas*. Berkeley: University of California Press, 2001.

Forte, Allen. "Schenker's Conception of Musical Structure." *Journal of Music Theory* 3 (1959): 1–30.

Forte, Allen, and Steven E. Gilbert. *Introduction to Schenkerian Analysis*. New York: W. W. Norton, 1982.

Gajewski, Ferdinand. Introduction to *The Work Sheets to Chopin's Violoncello Sonata: A Facsimile*. Music in Facsimile, 3. New York: Garland, 1988.

Gibson, Nigel, and Andrew Ruben, eds. *Adorno: A Critical Reader*. Oxford: Wiley-Blackwell, 2002.

Gingerich, John. "Schubert's Beethoven Project: The Chamber Music, 1824–1828." Ph.D. diss., Yale University, 1996.

Goehr, Lydia. *The Imaginary Museum of Musical Works: An Essay in the Philosophy of Music*. Oxford: Oxford University Press, 1992.

———. *The Quest for Voice: On Music, Politics, and the Limits of Philosophy*. Berkeley: University of California Press, 1998.

———. *Elective Affinities: Musical Essays on the History of Aesthetic Theory*. Columbia Themes in Philosophy, Social Criticism, and the Arts. New York: Columbia University Press, 2008.

Gossett, Philip. "Carl Dahlhaus and the 'Ideal Type.'" *19th-Century Music* 13/1 (1989): 49–56.

Gramit, David. *Cultivating Music: The Aspirations, Interests, and Limits of German Musical Culture, 1770–1848*. Berkeley: University of California Press, 2002.

Halm, August. *Von zwei Kulturen der Musik*. Munich: Georg Müller, 1913.

Hanslick, Eduard. *On the Musically Beautiful: A Contribution towards the Revision of the Aesthetics of Music*. Translated and edited by Geoffrey Payzant, from the 8th edition (1891) of *Vom Musikalisch-Schönen* (orig. publ. 1854). Indianapolis: Hackett, 1986.

Heartz, Daniel. *Haydn, Mozart and the Viennese School 1740–1780*. New York: W. W. Norton, 1995.

———. *Mozart, Haydn and Early Beethoven 1781–1802*. New York: W. W. Norton, 2009.

Hefling, Stephen E., and David S. Tartakoff, "Schubert's Chamber Music." In *Nineteenth-Century Chamber Music*, edited by Stephen E. Hefling. New York: Routledge, 2004.

Hegel, G. W. F. *Phenomenology of Spirit*. 1817. Translated [from the 5th ed., 1952] by A. V. Miller with analysis of the text and foreword by J. N. Findlay. Oxford: Oxford University Press, 1977. (Orig. publ. as *Phänomenologie des Geistes* [1807].)

———. *The Encyclopaedia Logic (with the Zusätze): Part I of the Encyclopaedia of Philosophical Sciences with the Zusätze*. Translated [from the 3rd ed., 1830] by T. F. Geraets, W. A. Suchting, and H. S. Harris. Indianapolis: Hackett, 1991. (Orig. publ. 1817.)

———. *Introductory Lectures on Aesthetics.* Translated by Bernard Bosanquet (1886); edited by Michael Inwood. London: Penguin Books, 1993.

Hepokoski, James. "The Dahlhaus Project and Its Extra-musicological Sources." *19th-Century Music* 14/3 (1991): 221–46.

———. "Sonata Theory and Dialogic Form." In Bergé, *Musical Form, Forms & Formenlehre* (2009), 71–89.

———. "Approaching the First Movement of Beethoven's *Tempest* Sonata through Sonata Theory." In *Beethoven's "Tempest" Sonata: Perspectives of Analysis and Performance*, edited by Pieter Bergé, coedited by Jeroen D'hoe and William E. Caplin, 181–212. Analysis in Context. Leuven Studies in Musicology, vol. 2. Leuven: Peeters, 2009.

Hepokoski, James, and Warren Darcy. "The Medial Caesura and Its Role in the Eighteenth-Century Sonata Exposition." *Music Theory Spectrum* 19/2 (1997): 115–54.

———. *Elements of Sonata Theory: Norms, Types, and Deformations in the Late-Eighteenth-Century Sonata.* New York: Oxford University Press, 2006.

Herder, Johann Gottfried. *Sämmtliche Werke*, 33 vols. Edited by Bernhard Suphan. Berlin: Weidmann, 1877–1913.

Hinton, Stephen. "The Conscience of Musicology: Carl Dahlhaus (1928–89)." *Musical Times* 130 (1989): 737–39.

———. "Adorno's Unfinished *Beethoven*." Review of *Beethoven: Philosophie der Musik*, by Theodor W. Adorno. *Beethoven Forum* 5, edited by Lewis Lockwood (1996): 139–53.

Hoeckner, Berthold. "Schumann and Romantic Distance." *Journal of the American Musicological Society* 50/1 (1997): 55–132.

———. *Programming the Absolute: Nineteenth-Century German Music and the Hermeneutics of the Moment.* Princeton, NJ: Princeton University Press, 2002.

Hoffmann, E. T. A. *Schriften zur Musik: Aufsätze und Rezensionen.* Edited by Friedrich Schnapp. Darmstadt: Wissenschaftliche Buchgesellschaft, 1979.

———. *Musical Writings: "Kreisleriana," "The Poet and the Composer," Music Criticism.* Edited by David Charlton; translated by Martyn Clarke. Cambridge: Cambridge University Press, 1989.

Horton, Julian, and Paul Wingfield. "Norm and Deformation in Mendelssohn's Sonata Forms," In *Mendelssohn Perspectives*, edited by Jacqueline Waeber and Nicole Grimes. Aldershot: Ashgate, forthcoming.

Hoyt, Peter A. "The 'False Recapitulation' and the Conventions of Sonata Form." Ph.D. diss., University of Pennsylvania, 1999.

Hunter, Mary. "Haydn's London Piano Trios and His Salomon String Quartets: Private vs. Public?" In *Haydn and His World*, edited by Elaine Sisman, 103–30. Princeton, NJ: Princeton University Press, 1997.

Jander, Owen. "The 'Kreutzer' Sonata as Dialogue." *Early Music* 16 (1988): 34–49.

Jones, Timothy. *Beethoven: The "Moonlight" and other Sonatas, Op. 27 and Op. 31.* Cambridge Music Handbooks. Cambridge: Cambridge University Press, 1999.

Kallberg, Jeffrey. "Chopin's Last Style." *Journal of the American Musicological Society* 38/2 (1985): 264–315.

———. Review of *The Work Sheets to Chopin's Violoncello Sonata: A Facsimile*, with an Introduction by Ferdinand Gajewski. *Notes*, 2nd Ser., 46/3 (1990): 801–3.

———. *Chopin at the Boundaries: Sex, History, and Musical Genre.* Cambridge, MA: Harvard University Press, 1996.

Kant, Immanuel. *Critique of Judgment.* Translated by James Creed Meredith. Oxford: Clarenden, 1952. (Orig. publ. as *Kritik der Urteilskraft* [1790, rev. 1793].)

Kamien, Roger. "Aspects of the Recapitulation in Beethoven Piano Sonatas." *Music Forum* 4, edited by Felix Salzer, 228–35. New York: Columbia University Press, 1976.

Kaminsky, Peter. "Principles of Formal Structure in Schumann's Early Piano Cycles." *Music Theory Spectrum* 11/2 (1989): 207–25.

Katz, Ruth, and Carl Dahlhaus, eds. *Contemplating Music*, vol. 4. Stuyvesant, NY: Pendragon Press, 1993.

Kinderman, William. "Directional Tonality in Chopin." In *Chopin Studies*, edited by Jim Samson, 50–76. Cambridge: Cambridge University Press, 1988.

———. "Integration and Narrative Design in Beethoven's Piano Sonata in A-flat Major, Opus 110." *Beethoven Forum* 1, edited by Christopher Reynolds (1992): 110–45.

———. *Beethoven*. Berkeley: University of California Press, 1995.

———. "Schubert's Piano Music." In *The Cambridge Companion to Schubert*, edited by Christopher H. Gibbs, 155–73. Cambridge: Cambridge University Press, 1997.

Koch, Heinrich Christoph. *Versuch einer Anleitung zur Composition*, 3 vols. Leipzig: A. F. Böhme, 1782–93. Reprint, Hildesheim: Olms, 1969.

———. *Kurzgefasstes Handwörterbuch der Musik*. Leipzig: J. F. Hartknoch, 1807. Reprint, Hildesheim: Olms, 1981.

Kopp, David. *Chromatic Transformations in Nineteenth-Century Music*. Cambridge: Cambridge University Press, 2002.

Kramer, Lawrence. *Music and Poetry: The Nineteenth Century and After*. Berkeley: University of California Press, 1984.

———. "The Schubert Lied: Romantic Form and Romantic Consciousness." In *Schubert: Critical and Analytical Studies*, edited by Walter Frisch, 200–36. Lincoln: University of Nebraska Press, 1986.

———. *After the Lovedeath: Sexual Violence and the Making of Culture*. Berkeley: University of California Press, 1997.

———. *Franz Schubert: Sexuality, Subjectivity, Song*. Cambridge: Cambridge University Press, 1998.

———. "Primitive Encounters: Beethoven's 'Tempest' Sonata, Musical Meaning, and Enlightenment Anthropology," edited by Lewis Lockwood. *Beethoven Forum* 6, edited by Glenn Stanley (1998): 31–65.

———. *Musical Meaning: Toward a Critical History*. Berkeley: University of California Press, 2002.

Kramer, Richard. *Unfinished Music*. Oxford: Oxford University Press, 2008.

Krebs, Harald. "Third Relations and Dominant in Late 18th- and 19th-Century Music." Ph.D. diss., Yale University, 1980.

———. "Alternatives to Monotonality in Early Nineteenth-Century Music." *Journal of Music Theory* 25/1 (1981): 1–16.

———. "Tonal and Formal Dualism in Chopin's Scherzo, Op. 31." *Music Theory Spectrum* 13/1 (1991): 48–60.

Laitz, Steven. "The Submediant Complex: Its Musical and Poetic Roles in Schubert's Songs." *Theory and Practice* 21 (1996): 123–65.

le Huray, Peter, and James Day, eds. *Music and Aesthetics in the Eighteenth and Early-Nineteenth Centuries*. Cambridge: Cambridge University Press, 1988.

Leppert, Richard. *The Sight of Sound: Music, Representation, and the History of the Body*. Berkeley: University of California Press, 1993.

Lester, Joel. "Performance and Analysis: Interaction and Interpretation." In *The Practice of Performance: Studies in Musical Interpretation*, edited by John Rink, 197–216. Cambridge: Cambridge University Press, 1995.

———. "Harmonic Complexity and Form in Chopin's Mazurkas." *Ostinato Rigore: Revue internationale d'études musicales* 15 (2000): 101–20.

Levarie, Siegmund. *Mozart's "Le Nozze di Figaro": A Critical Analysis.* New York: Da Capo Press, 1977.

Levy, Janet M. "Texture as a Sign in Classic and Early Romantic Music." *Journal of the American Musicological Society* 35/3 (1982): 482–531.

———. "Beginning-ending Ambiguity: Consequences of Performance Choices." In *The Practice of Performance: Studies in Musical Interpretation,* edited by John Rink, 150–69. Cambridge: Cambridge University Press, 1995.

Lewin, David. "Behind the Beyond: A Response to Edward T. Cone." *Perspectives of New Music* 7 (1968–69): 59–69.

———. "Music Theory, Phenomenology, and Modes of Perception." *Music Perception* 3/4 (1986): 327–92.

———. "Music Analysis as Stage Direction." In *Music and Text: Critical Inquiries,* edited by Steven Paul Scher, 163–76. Cambridge: Cambridge University Press, 1992.

———. *Studies in Music with Text.* Oxford: Oxford University Press, 2006.

Litzmann, Berthold, ed. *Clara Schumann: Ein Künstlerleben nach Tagebüchern und Briefen,* 7th ed., 3 vols. Leipzig: Breitkopf & Härtel, 1925. (Orig. publ. 1902–8.)

Lockwood, Lewis. "Beethoven before 1800: The Mozart Legacy," edited by Christopher Reynolds. *Beethoven Forum* 3, edited by Glenn Stanley (1994): 39–52.

———. *Beethoven: The Music and the Life.* New York: W. W. Norton, 2003.

Lockwood, Lewis, and the Juilliard String Quartet. *Inside Beethoven's Quartets: History, Interpretation, Performance.* Cambridge, MA: Harvard University Press, 2008.

Lovejoy, Arthur O. *Essays in the History of Ideas.* Baltimore: Johns Hopkins Press, 1948.

Marston, Nicholas. *Schumann: Fantasie, Op. 17.* Cambridge Music Handbooks. Cambridge: Cambridge University Press, 1992.

———. "Schubert's Homecoming." *Journal of the Royal Musical Association* 125/2 (2000): 248–70.

Marx, A[dolph] B[ernhard]. "Als Recension der Sonate, Op. 111 von L. v. Beethoven." *Berliner allgemeine musikalische Zeitung* 1 (1824): 97–98.

———. *Die Lehre von der musikalischen Komposition, praktisch-theoretisch,* 2nd ed., 4 vols. Leipzig: Breitkopf and Härtel, 1841.

———. "Die Form in der Musik." In *Die Wissenschaften im neunzehnten Jahrhundert,* edited by Johannes Andreas Romberg, vol. 2, 21-48. Leipzig: Romberg's Verlag, 1856.

———. *Musical Form in the Age of Beethoven: Selected Writings on Theory and Method.* Edited and translated by Scott Burnham. Cambridge: Cambridge University Press, 1997.

Maus, Fred Everett. "Music as Drama." *Music Theory Spectrum* 10 (1988): 56–73.

McClary, Susan. *Feminine Endings: Music, Gender, and Sexuality.* Minneapolis: University of Minnesota Press, 1991.

———. *Conventional Wisdom: The Content of Musical Form.* Berkeley: University of California Press, 2000.

McCreless, Patrick. "Song Order in the Song Cycle: Schumann's *Liederkreis,* Op. 39." *Music Analysis* 5/1 (1986): 5–28.

Meyer, Leonard B. *Style and Music: Theory, History, and Ideology.* Philadelphia: University of Pennsylvania Press, 1989.

Misch, Ludwig. *Beethoven Studies.* Translated by G. I. C. de Courcy. Norman: University of Oklahoma Press, 1953.

Moyer, Birgitte Plesner V. "Concepts of Musical Form in the Nineteenth Century with Special Reference to A. B. Marx and Sonata Form." Ph.D. diss., Stanford University, 1969.

Muxfeldt, Kristina. "*Frauenliebe und Leben* Now and Then." *19th-Century Music* 25/1 (2001): 27–48.

Narmour, Eugene. "On the Relationship of Analytical Theory to Performance and Interpretation." In *Explorations in Music, the Arts, and Ideas*, edited by Eugene Narmour and Ruth A. Solie, 317–40. Stuyvesant, NY: Pendragon, 1988.

Neubauer, John. *The Emancipation of Music from Language: Departures from Mimesis in Eighteenth-Century Aesthetics*. New Haven, CT: Yale University Press, 1986.

Neumeyer, David, and Susan Tepping. *A Guide to Schenkerian Analysis*. Englewood Cliffs, NJ: Prentice-Hall, 1992.

Newbould, Brian. *Schubert: The Music and the Man*. Berkeley: University of California Press, 1997.

Newcomb, Anthony. "Those Images That Yet Fresh Images Beget." *Journal of Musicology* 2/3 (1983): 227–45.

———. "Once More 'Between Absolute and Programme Music': Schumann's Second Symphony." *19th-Century Music* 7/3 (1984): 233–50.

———. "Schumann and Late Eighteenth-Century Narrative Strategies." *19th-Century Music* 11/2 (1987): 164–74.

———. "Schumann and the Marketplace: From Butterflies to *Hausmusik*." In *Nineteenth-Century Piano Music*, edited by R. Larry Todd, 258–315. New York: Schirmer Books, 1990.

Niecks, Frederick. *Frederic Chopin as a Man and Musician*, 2nd ed., vol. 2. London: Novello, 1890.

Notley, Margaret. "Schubert's Social Music: The 'Forgotten Genres.'" In *The Cambridge Companion to Schubert*, edited by Christopher H. Gibbs, 138–54. Cambridge: Cambridge University Press, 1997.

Ostwald, Peter. *Schumann: The Inner Voices of a Musical Genius*. Boston: Northeastern University Press, 1985.

Paddison, Max. "Adorno's *Aesthetic Theory*." *Music Analysis* 6/3 (1987): 355–77.

———. *Adorno's Aesthetics of Music*. Cambridge: Cambridge University Press, 1993.

———. *Adorno, Modernism and Mass Culture: Essays on Critical Theory and Music*. London: Kahn & Averill, 1996.

Panton, Clifford D. *George Augustus Polgreen Bridgetower, Violin Virtuoso and Composer of Color in Late 18th Century Europe*. New York: Edwin Mellen Press, 2005.

Plantinga, Leon. *Schumann as Critic*. New Haven, CT: Yale University Press, 1967.

———. *Clementi: His Life and Music*. London: Oxford University Press, 1977.

———. *Romantic Music: A History of Musical Style in Nineteenth-Century Europe*. New York: W. W. Norton, 1984.

———. *Beethoven's Concertos: History, Style, Performance*. New York: W. W. Norton, 1999.

Ratz, Erwin. *Einführung in die musikalische Formenlehre: Über Formprinzipien in den Inventionen und Fugen J. S. Bachs und ihre Bedeutung für die Kompositionstechnik Beethovens*, 3rd ed., enl. Vienna: Universal, 1973.

Reich, Nancy B. *Clara Schumann: The Artist and the Woman*, rev. ed. Ithaca and London: Cornell University Press, 2001.

Réti, Rudolph. *Thematic Patterns in Sonatas of Beethoven*. Edited by Deryck Cooke. New York: Da Capo Press, 1992. (Orig. publ. New York: Macmillan, 1967).

Rink, John. "The Evolution of Chopin's 'Structural Style' and Its Relation to Improvisation." Ph.D. diss., University of Cambridge, 1989.

———. "Tonal Architecture in the Early Music." In *The Cambridge Companion to Chopin*, edited by Jim Samson, 78–97. Cambridge: Cambridge University Press, 1992.

———. "Schenker and Improvisation." *Journal of Music Theory* 37/1 (1993): 1–54.

———. "Chopin's Ballades and the Dialectic: Analysis in Historical Perspective." *Music Analysis* 13/1 (1994): 99–115.

———. "Authentic Chopin: History, Analysis and Intuition in Performance." In *Chopin Studies* 2, edited by John Rink and Jim Samson, 214–48. Cambridge: Cambridge University Press, 1994.

———. *Chopin: The Piano Concertos*. Cambridge Music Handbooks. Cambridge: Cambridge University Press, 1997.

———. "Analysis and (or?) Performance." In *Musical Performance: A Guide to Understanding*, edited by John Rink, 35–58. Cambridge: Cambridge University Press, 2002.

Rorty, Richard. "The Intellectuals at the End of Socialism." *Yale Review* 80 (1992): 1–16.

Rosen, Charles. "Rehearings: The First Movement of Chopin's Sonata in B-flat Minor, Op. 35." *19th-Century Music* 14/1 (1990): 60–66.

———. *The Romantic Generation*. Cambridge, MA: Harvard University Press, 1995.

———. "Should We Adore Adorno?" *New York Review of Books*, October 24, 2002.

Rosenwald, Lawrence. "Theory, Text-setting, Performance." *Journal of Musicology* 11/1 (1993): 52–65.

Ross, Alex. "The Youngest Master: Mendelssohn at Two Hundred." *New Yorker*, February 23 (2009): 77.

Rostal, Max. *Beethoven, The Sonatas for Piano and Violin: Thoughts on Their Interpretation*. Translated by Horace and Anna Rosenberg. New York: Toccata Press, 1985.

Rothfarb, Lee A. "Beethoven's Formal Dynamics: August Halm's Phenomenological Perspective." *Beethoven Forum* 5, edited by Lewis Lockwood (1996): 65–84.

———. "August Halm on Body and Spirit in Music." *19th-Century Music* 29/2 (2005): 121–41.

———. *August Halm: A Critical and Creative Life in Music*. Eastman Studies in Music. Rochester: University of Rochester Press, 2009.

Rothstein, William. *Phrase Rhythm in Tonal Music*. New York: Schirmer Books, 1989.

———. "Analysis and the Act of Performance." In *The Practice of Performance: Studies in Musical Interpretation*, edited by John Rink, 217–40. Cambridge: Cambridge University Press, 1995.

———. "Chopin and the B-major Complex: A Study in the Psychology of Composition." *Ostinato Rigore: Revue internationale d'études musicales* 15 (2000): 149–72.

Rumph, Stephen. *Beethoven after Napoleon: Political Romanticism in the Late Works*. Berkeley: University of California Press, 2004.

Sacks, Oliver. *Musicophilia: Tales of Music and the Brain*, rev. and exp. ed. New York: Vintage Books, 2007.

Salzer, Felix. *Structural Hearing: Tonal Coherence in Music*, 2 vols. New York: Dover, 1962. (Orig. publ. 1952.)

Samson, Jim. *The Music of Chopin*. New York: Routledge, 1985. Reprint, Oxford: Clarendon Press, 1994.

———. *Chopin*. The Master Musicians, edited by Stanley Sadie. Oxford: Oxford University Press, 1996.

———. "Chopin's Alternatives to Monotonality: A Historical Perspective." In *The Second Practice of Nineteenth-Century Tonality*, edited by William Kinderman and Harald Krebs, 34–44. Lincoln: University of Nebraska Press, 1996.

———. "Analysis in Context." In *Rethinking Music*, edited by Nicholas Cook and Mark Everist, 35–54. Oxford: Oxford University Press, 1999.

Schachter, Carl. "Rhythm and Linear Analysis: Aspects of Meter." *Music Forum* 6/1 (1987): 1–59.

———. "Chopin's Fantasy Op. 49: The Two-Key Scheme." In *Chopin Studies*, edited by Jim Samson, 221–53. Cambridge: Cambridge University Press, 1988.

———. "The Triad as Place and Action." *Music Theory Spectrum* 17/2 (1995): 149–69.

———. *Unfoldings: Essays in Schenkerian Theory and Analysis*. Edited by Joseph N. Straus. New York: Oxford University Press, 1999.

Schelling, Friedrich Wilhelm Joseph von. *The Philosophy of Art*. Edited and translated by Douglas W. Stott. Minneapolis: University of Minnesota Press, 1989. (Orig. publ. as *Die Philosophie der Kunst* [1801–4], 1859.)

Schenker, Heinrich. *Der Tonwille,* ten issues. Vienna: A. Gutmann Verlag. (Reprinted in 3 vols. by Universal Edition.)

———. *Free Composition* (*Der freie Satz*). Translated and edited by Ernst Oster. New York: Longman, 1979.

Scherzinger, Martin. "The Return of the Aesthetic: Musical Formalism and Its Place in Political Critique." In Dell'Antonio, *Beyond Structural Listening?* (2004), 252–77.

Schiller, Friedrich. *Werke und Briefe*, 12 vols. Edited by Klaus Harro Hilzinger et al. Frankfurt/Main: Deutscher Klassiker Verlag, 1988–2004.

Schindler, Anton Felix. *Beethoven as I Knew Him* (1860). Edited by Donald W. MacArdle. Translated by Constance S. Jolly. Chapel Hill: University of North Carolina Press, 1966.

Schlegel, August Wilhelm. *Kritische Ausgabe der Vorlesungen*, vol. 1: *Vorlesungen über Ästhetik I (1798–1803)*. Edited by Ernst Behler. Paderborn: Ferdinand Schöningh, 1989.

Schlegel, Friedrich. *Kritische Friedrich-Schlegel-Ausgabe*, vol. 2: *Charakteristiken und Kritiken I*. Edited by Ernst Behler. Munich, Paderborn, and Vienna: Ferdinand Schöningh, 1967.

———. *Schriften zur Literatur*. Edited by Wolfdietrich Rasch. Munich: Deutscher Taschenbuch, 1972.

Schmalfeldt, Janet. "On the Relation of Analysis to Performance: Beethoven's Bagatelles Op. 126, Nos. 2 and 5." *Journal of Music Theory* 29/1 (1985): 1–31. Reissued in Spanish in *Orpheotron*, published by the State Conservatory Alberto Ginastera, Buenos Aires, Argentina, 2001.

———. "Towards a Reconciliation of Schenkerian Concepts with Traditional and Recent Theories of Form." *Music Analysis* 10/3 (1991): 233–87.

———. "Berg's Path to Atonality: The Piano Sonata, Op. 1." In *Alban Berg: Analytical and Historical Perspectives*, edited by David Gable and Robert P. Morgan, 79–109. Oxford: Clarendon Press, 1991.

———. "Cadential Processes: The Evaded Cadence and the 'One More Time' Technique." *Journal of Musicological Research* 12 (1992): 1–52.

———. "Form as the Process of Becoming: The Beethoven-Hegelian Tradition and the 'Tempest' Sonata." In *Beethoven Forum* 4, edited by Christopher Reynolds (1995): 37–71.

———. "On Performance, Analysis, and Schubert." *Per Musi: Revista Acadêmica de Música* 5–6 (2003): 38–54.

Schmidt-Beste, Thomas. "Mendelssohn's Chamber Music." In *The Cambridge Companion to Mendelssohn*, edited by Peter Mercer-Taylor, 130–48. Cambridge: Cambridge University Press, 2004.

Schoenberg, Arnold. *Fundamentals of Musical Composition*. Edited by Gerald Strang and Leonard Stein. New York: St. Martin's Press, 1967.

———. *Style and Idea: Selected Writings of Arnold Schoenberg*. Edited by Leonard Stein; translated by Leo Black. New York: St. Martin's Press, 1975.

———. *The Musical Idea and the Logic, Technique, and Art of Its Presentation*. Edited and translated with commentary by Patricia Carpenter and Severine Neff. New York: Columbia University Press, 1995.

Schopenhauer, Arthur. *The World as Will and Representation*, 2 vols. Translated by E. F. J. Payne. New York: Dover, 1966. (Orig. publ. as *Die Welt als Wille und Vorstellung* [1819].)

Schumann, Robert. *Jugendbriefe*, 2nd ed., 2 vols. Edited by Clara Schumann. Leipzig: Breitkopf & Härtel, 1886.

———. *On Music and Musicians*. Edited by Konrad Wolff; translated by Paul Rosenfeld. New York: McGraw-Hill, 1946.

Schumann, Robert, and Clara Schumann. *Briefwechsel: Kritische Gesamtausgabe*. Edited by Eva Weissweiler with Susanna Ludwig, 3 vols. (Frankfurt: Stroemfeld/Roter Stern, 1984–2001.

Sisman, Elaine. "'The Spirit of Mozart from Haydn's Hands': Beethoven's Musical Inheritance." In *The Cambridge Companion to Beethoven*, edited by Glenn Stanley, 45–63. Cambridge: Cambridge University Press, 2000.

———. "Memory and Invention at the Threshold of Beethoven's Late Style." In *Beethoven and His World*, edited by Scott Burnham and Michael P. Steinberg, 51–87. Princeton, NJ: Princeton University Press, 2000.

Smith, Charles J. "Musical Form and Fundamental Structure: An Investigation of Schenker's *Formenlehre*." *Music Analysis* 15/2–3 (1996): 191–297.

Smith, Peter H. "Structural Tonic or Apparent Tonic? Parametric Conflict, Temporal Perspective, and a Continuum of Articulative Possibilities." *Journal of Music Theory* 39/2 (1995): 273–74.

———. *Expressive Forms in Brahms's Instrumental Music: Structure and Meaning in His* Werther *Quartet*. Bloomington: Indiana University Press, 2005.

Solomon, Maynard. "Franz Schubert's 'My Dream.'" *American Imago* 38 (1981): 137–54.

———. "Franz Schubert and the Peacocks of Benvenuto Cellini." *19th-Century Music* 12/3 (1989): 193–206.

———. *Mozart: A Life*. New York: HarperCollins, 1995.

———. "Schubert's 'Unfinished' Symphony." *19th-Century Music* 21/2 (1997): 111–33.

———. *Beethoven*, 2nd rev. ed. New York: Schirmer Books, 1998.

Solomon, Robert C. *In the Spirit of Hegel: A Study of G. W. F. Hegel's "Phenomenology of Spirit."* New York: Oxford University Press, 1983.

Spitzer, Michael. *Metaphor and Musical Thought*. Chicago: University of Chicago Press, 2004.

———. *Music as Philosophy: Adorno and Beethoven's Late Style*. Bloomington: Indiana University Press, 2006.

Steinberg, Michael P. "Schumann's Homelessness." In *Schumann and His World*, edited by R. Larry Todd, 46–79. Princeton, NJ: Princeton University Press, 1994.

———. *Listening to Reason: Culture, Subjectivity, and Nineteenth-Century Music*. Princeton, NJ: Princeton University Press, 2004.

Subotnik, Rose Rosengard. "Toward a Deconstruction of Structural Listening: A Critique of Schoenberg, Adorno, and Stravinsky." In *Explorations in Music, the Arts, and Ideas: Essays in Honor of Leonard B. Meyer*, edited by Eugene Narmour and Ruth A. Solie, 87–122. Stuyvesant, NY: Pendragon, 1988.

———. *Developing Variations: Style and Ideology in Western Music*. Minneapolis: University of Minnesota Press, 1991.

———. *Deconstructive Variations: Music and Reason in Western Society*. Minneapolis: University of Minnesota Press, 1996.

———. "Afterword: Toward the Next Paradigm of Musical Scholarship." In Dell'Antonio, *Beyond Structural Listening?* (2004), 279–302.

Sutcliffe, W. Dean. Review of James Webster, *Haydn's "Farewell" Symphony and the Idea of Classical Style: Through-Composition and Cyclic Integration in His Instrumental Music* (Cambridge: Cambridge University Press, 1991). *Music Analysis* 13/1 (1994): 125–31.

———. "Chopin's Counterpoint: The Largo from the Cello Sonata, Opus 65." *Musical Quarterly* 83/1 (1999): 114–33.

Swinden, Kevin. "Toward Analytic Reconciliation of Outer Form, Harmonic Prolongation and Function." *College Music Symposium* 45 (2005): 108–23.

Taruskin, Richard. *The Oxford History of Western Music*, vol. 2: *The Seventeenth and Eighteenth Centuries*. Oxford: Oxford University Press, 2005.

———. *The Oxford History of Western Music*, vol. 3: *The Nineteenth Century*. Oxford: Oxford University Press, 2005.

Taylor, Benedict. "The Problem of the 'Introduction' in Beethoven's Late Quartets." *Ad Parnassum* 3/6 (2005): 45–64.

———. "Musical History and Self-Consciousness in Mendelssohn's Octet, Op. 20." *19th-Century Music* 32/2 (2008): 131–59.

Taylor, Charles. *Hegel*. Cambridge: Cambridge University Press, 1975.

———. *Sources of the Self: The Making of the Modern Identity*. Cambridge, MA: Harvard University Press, 1989.

Telesco, Paula J. "Enharmonicism and the Omnibus Progression in Classical-Era Music." *Music Theory Spectrum* 20/2 (1998): 242–79.

Temperley, David. "Hypermetrical Transitions." *Music Theory Spectrum* 30/2 (2008): 305–25.

Thayer, Alexander. *Thayer's Life of Beethoven*. Revised and edited by Elliot Forbes. Princeton, NJ: Princeton University Press, 1967.

Titus, Barbara. "Conceptualizing Music: Friedrich Theodor Vischer and Hegelian Currents in German Music Criticism, 1848–1887." D.Phil. diss., University of Oxford, 2005.

Todd, R. Larry. *Mendelssohn: "The Hebrides" and Other Overtures*. Cambridge Music Handbooks. Cambridge: Cambridge University Press, 1993.

———. *Mendelssohn: A Life in Music*. Oxford: Oxford University Press, 2003.

———. "The Chamber Music of Mendelssohn." In *Nineteenth-Century Chamber Music*, edited by Stephen E. Hefling, 170-207. New York: Routledge, 2004.

Tolstoy, Leo. *The Kreutzer Sonata and Other Stories*. Translated by David McDuff. Harmondsworth: Penguin Books, 1985.

———. *The Kreutzer Sonata and Other Stories*. Translated by Louise and Aylmer Maude and J. D. Duff. Oxford: Oxford University Press, 1997.

Tovey, Donald Francis. *A Companion to Beethoven's Pianoforte Sonatas*. London: Associated Board of the Royal Schools of Music, 1931.

———. *Essays in Musical Analysis: Chamber Music*. Edited by Hubert J. Foss. London: Oxford University Press, 1944.

Treitler, Leo. "Language and the Interpretation of Music." In *Music and Meaning*, edited by Jenefer Robinson, 23–56. Ithaca, NY: Cornell University Press, 1997.

Tull, James Robert. "B. V. Asaf'ev's 'Musical Form as a Process': Translation and Commentary." Ph.D. diss., Ohio State University, 1977.

Turchin, Barbara. "The Nineteenth-century *Wanderlieder* Cycle." *Journal of Musicology* 5/4 (1987): 498–525.

Tusa, Michael C., ed. Review essays by Hermann Danuser, John Daverio, and James Webster about Dahlhaus's *Ludwig van Beethoven und seine Zeit* and his *Ludwig van Beethoven: Approaches to His Music. Beethoven Forum* 2, edited by Christopher Reynolds (1993): 180–227.

Vitercik, Greg. "Mendelssohn the Progressive." *Journal of Musicological Research* 8 (1989): 333–74.

———. *The Early Works of Felix Mendelssohn: A Study in the Romantic Sonata Style*. Philadelphia: Gordon and Breach, 1992.

———. "Mendelssohn as Progressive." In *The Cambridge Companion to Mendelssohn*, edited by Peter Mercer-Taylor, 71–90. Cambridge: Cambridge University Press, 2004.

Wallace, Robin. *Beethoven's Critics: Aesthetic Dilemmas and Resolutions during the Composer's Lifetime*. Cambridge: Cambridge University Press, 1986.

Webster, James. "The Falling-out Between Haydn and Beethoven." In *Beethoven Essays: Studies in Honor of Elliot Forbes*, edited by Lewis Lockwood and Phyllis Benjamin, 3–45. Cambridge, MA: Harvard University Press, 1984.

———. *Haydn's "Farewell" Symphony and the Idea of Classical Style: Through-Composition and Cyclic Integration in His Instrumental Music*. Cambridge: Cambridge University Press, 1991.

———. "Dahlhaus's *Beethoven* and the Ends of Analysis." *Beethoven Forum* 2, edited by Christopher Reynolds (1993): 205–27.

———. "The Concept of Beethoven's 'Early' Period in the Context of Periodizations in General," edited by Christopher Reynolds. *Beethoven Forum* 3, edited by Glenn Stanley (1994): 1–27.

———. "Haydn's Symphonies between *Sturm und Drang* and 'Classical Style': Art and Entertainment." In *Joseph Haydn Studies*, edited by W. Dean Sutcliffe, 28–45. Cambridge: Cambridge University Press, 1998.

———. "Sonata Form." *New Grove* (rev. ed., 2001), vol. 23, 687–701.

———. "Between Enlightenment and Romanticism in Music History: 'First Viennese Modernism' and the Delayed Nineteenth Century." *19th-Century Music* 25/2–3 (2001–2): 108–26.

———. "The Eighteenth Century as a Music-Historical Period?" *Eighteenth-Century Music* 1/1 (2003): 47–60.

———. "*Formenlehre* in Theory and Practice." In Bergé, *Musical Form, Forms & Formenlehre* (2009), 123–39.

Wegeler, Franz Gerhard, and Ferdinand Ries. *Biographische Notizen über Beethoven*. Coblenz, 1838.

Wheelock, Gretchen. *Haydn's Ingenious Jesting with Art: Contexts of Musical Wit and Humor*. New York: Schirmer Books, 1992.

White, Harry. "'If It's Baroque, Don't Fix It': Reflections on Lydia Goehr's 'Work-Concept' and the Historical Integrity of Musical Composition." *Acta Musicologica* 69/1 (1997): 94–104.

Witkin, Robert W. *Adorno on Music*. London: Routledge, 1998.

Wright, Josephine R. B. "George Polgreen Bridgetower: An African Prodigy in England 1789–99." *Musical Quarterly* 66 (1980); 65–82.

Yellin, Victor Fell. *The Omnibus Idea*. Warren, MI: Harmonie Park Press, 1998.

INDEX

Page numbers of music examples, figures (*f*), and tables (*t*) are shown in bold.

Printed and bound by CPI Group (UK) Ltd, Croydon, CR0 4YY